Organizing, Operating, and Terminating Subchapter S Corporations

TAXATION AND ACCOUNTING

by

D. LARRY CRUMBLEY

and

P. MICHAEL DAVIS

Lawyers and Judges Publishing Company
Tucson, Arizona

REVISED EDITION

1974

SUPPLEMENT

1975

Second printing . . . August, 1975

This publication is designed to provide accurate and authori-
tative information in regard to the subject matter covered. It
is sold with the understanding that the publisher is not engaged
in rendering legal, accounting or other professional service. If
legal advice or other expert assistance is required, the services
of a competent professional person should be sought.
*From a Declaration of Principles jointly adopted by a
Committee of the American Bar Association and a
Committee of Publishers and Associations.*

 Lawyers and Judges Publishing Co.

A Division of Communication Skill Builders. Inc.

Offices: 817 E. Broadway
Mailing address: P.O. Box 6081
Tucson, Arizona 85733

Printed in U.S.A.

ISBN 0-88450-507-3

ii

"The art of taxation consists in so plucking the goose
as to procure the largest quantity of feathers
with the least possible amount of hissing."

An old French maxim sometimes
attributed to Colbert

TO

Donna and Irene

About the Authors

D. Larry Crumbley, Ph.D., C.P.A., is a Professor at Texas A & M University. He was Director of the Master of Business Taxation program and Visiting Associate Professor at the University of Southern California. Professor Crumbley has a background in university teaching, public accounting, and consulting. He has previously taught at the University of Florida, New York University, Pennsylvania State University and Louisiana State University. Professor Crumbley participated in a one-year faculty resident program with Arthur Andersen & Co. and has previously been associated with Laventhol, Krekstein, Horwath & Horwath, and Seidman and Seidman.

Professor Crumbley is an active member of a number of professional and honorary societies, including the American Accounting Association. A graduate of Louisiana State University, he is author or co-author of several books, including *A Practical Guide to Preparing a Federal Gift Tax Return* and *Advanced Accounting.* Dr. Crumbley has co-authored a syndicated tax column, called *The Reluctant Taxpayer*, which appeared in numerous newspapers in the United States. Over fifty of his articles have appeared in numerous accounting, business, and tax periodicals.

P. Michael Davis, Ph.D., J.D., C.P.A., is Professor of Accounting at the University of Kentucky College of Business and Economics and is Lecturer on Law at the University of Kentucky College of Law. He received the B.B.A. degree from the University of Cincinnati, the M.A. degree from the University of Florida, the Ph.D. degree from the University of Illinois, and the J.D. degree from the University of Kentucky. Professor Davis is the author of *A Practical Guide to Preparing a Fiduciary Income Tax Return* (with Frederick W. Whiteside) and has published articles in the *Accounting Review, Tax Executive, Journal of Accountancy, Journal of Taxation, Tax Law Review, Taxes,* and *Memphis State University Law Review.*

Professor Davis serves as an accounting and tax consultant to numerous small businesses and has practiced administratively before the Internal Revenue Service. He is also tax adviser to several practicing attorneys in the central Kentucky area. Dr. Davis is a Certified Public Accountant in the states of Florida and Mississippi and has been admitted to the Kentucky and Tax Court Bars. He is a member of the American Accounting Association, American and Florida Institutes of Certified Public Accountants, Kentucky Society of Certified Public Accountants, the National Tax Association-Tax Institute of America, and the American and Kentucky Bar Associations.

Preface

Prior to the enactment of Subchapter S, all corporations were thrown into a single tax pattern. Presently, a Small Business Corporation is taxed partly as a corporation, partly as a partnership, and partly as neither — but double taxation is avoided. This book explains in crystal-clear language how this special election allows a closely-held corporation to decrease its tax burden drastically. The earnings of this special entity are passed through the corporate veil in a way similar to the "conduit principle" of a partnership, and there is no tax at the corporate level.

The Treasury Department, often with the help of the courts, is consistently attempting to limit this optional election to a few small businesses. To escape termination from the numerous possible disqualifications and technicalities, a taxpayer must be cognizant of many sections of the *Code* and of unrelated case law and interpretations. A continuous tax plan is essential if the full benefits are to be obtained and catastrophic tax consequences are to be avoided.

The thin capitalization and sound business purpose doctrines, the ADR system, stockholder agreements, shareholder reference test, disposition of stock, voting trusts, estate planning, liquidations, Section 269, statement presentation, redemptions, and distribution of earnings are only some of the items that are thoroughly discussed insofar as they relate to this election. The reader is also informed of the best methods of terminating an election if circumstances indicate that the normal corporate form of taxation is advantageous. The complex taxation procedure is simplified by the use of definitions such as undistributed taxable income (UTI) or previously taxed income (PTI). Visual aids as well as examples drawn from actual practice are incorporated throughout the book in order to communicate vividly this "conduit principle." The two-and-one-half-month grace period, the Revenue Act of 1971, Section 311(d), and other recent developments are thoroughly covered. Filled-in sample tax forms and numerous checklists are provided. The time-consuming and technical compliance process is discussed.

Subchapter S is far from perfect, but a judicious knowledge of the tax traps and dangers will allow it to be utilized by many of the million corporations that are closely-held. Despite complexity and defects, this optional method of taxation is essential in order to permit businesses to choose the suitable form of legal organization without tax detriment.

This extensively revised manual is intended to make clear the complex provisions and case law governing the tax and accounting consequences of operating a small business corporation. To furnish a complete picture of the present rules in this area, this book compiles in one place material that otherwise can only be found in numerous laws, regulations, rulings, and articles. It attempts to supply realistic illustrations of the problems and solutions encountered by this hybrid form of organization. The importance of tax and financial planning is stressed throughout the book.

The renaissance of Subchapter S corporations as a result of the "Employee Retirement Income Security Act of 1974" makes this an indispensable book for lawyers, public accountants, and owners of closely-held businesses. Further, the book is written in such a style that a practitioner can give a copy to his Subchapter S client in order to show his personal interest in his client's business affairs.

D. Larry Crumbley
College Station, Texas

P. Michael Davis
Lexington, Kentucky

Contents

Chapter 1
THE SUBCHAPTER S CORPORATION IN THE FEDERAL TAX SYSTEM ... 1

Taxability is a Basic Difference. ... 1

Rationale of the Subchapter S Election. ... 2

The Growth of Subchapter S. ... 3
  Subchapter S Returns in Comparison to Total
    Corporate Returns. ... 5
  Use of Subchapter S Election by Selected
    Industry Groups. ... 5
  Relation Between Net Income and Deficit
    Subchapter S Returns and Total Assets
    Categories. ... 10

Conclusion. ... 10

A Glimpse Forward. ... 12

Chapter 2
THE BACKGROUND OF SUBCHAPTER S. ... 13

Supplement S — Tax of Shareholders of Personal
  Service Corporations. ... 13

Treasury Department Tax Studies. ... 14

President Eisenhower's Recommendations — 1954. ... 15

The Technical Amendments Act of 1958. ... 16

Proposed Regulations Plug "Loophole". ... 18

Discrimination Against Community Property States
  Corrected. ... 19

Pro Rata Share of the Corporation's Loss. ... 19

Disqualification by the Acquisition of a Subsidiary. ... 20

Certain Distributions After Close of Taxable Year. ... 20

Grace Periods. ... 21

Capital Gain Tax and Passive Income. ... 22

Thin Capitalization — 1973. ... 22

Fringe Benefits — 1969. ... 24

Farm Loss Loophole Closed. 24

Summary: Legislative History of Subchapter S. 25

Chapter 3

ELECTION AND OPERATION. 27

Stringent Requirements. 27

How and When to make the Election. 28

Recapture of Investment Credit Agreement. 34

Small Business Corporation Stock. 35

Section 351 Transfer of Property. 39

Duration of the Election. 41

Relationship of WHTC and DISC. 41

Relationship with other Provisions. 44

The ADR System. 48

    Annual Election. 48

    Eligible Assets. 49

    First-Year Conventions. 50

    Salvage Value. 51

    Repair and Maintenance Allowance. 53

    Retirement of Assets. 54

    Change in Method of Depreciation. 56

    Checklist for Use of the ADR System. 56

A Glimpse Forward. 57

Illustration. 58

Annual Checklist. 59

Chapter 4

ELIGIBLE SHAREHOLDERS. 61

Requirements to Maintain a Subchapter S Election. 61

New Shareholders. 62

    Trusts. 63

    Partnership. 65

    Nonresident Alien. 66

    Beneficial Owner. 66

    Uniform Gifts to Minors Act. 66

Failure to Consent. 67

Problems Caused by Death of a Shareholder. 69
    Estate. 69
    Alternatives to a Trust. 73
Buy-Sell Agreements. 75
    Stock Redemption Agreement. 75
    Cross Purchase Plan. 76
    Comparison. 76
Avoidance of Termination by New Shareholders. 77
Valuation. 81
Installment Payments of Estate Taxes. 88
Checklist of Tax and Non-Tax Consequences of Buy
    and Sell Agreements. 90
    Stock Redemption Approach. 90
    Cross-Purchase Plan. 92

Chapter 5
QUALIFICATIONS FOR SUBCHAPTER S ELECTION. 95
    Domestic Corporation. 95
        Necessity of a Business Purpose. 95
        Tax Planning for a Business Purpose. 101
        Professional Corporations. 103
    Member of an Affiliated Group. 104
    One Class of Stock. 109
        Thin Capitalization. 114
        Stockholders' Loans. 117
        Tax Planning for Loans by Owners. 125
        Shareholders Guarantee Outside Loans. 126
        Stockholder Agreements. 128

Chapter 6
CONDUIT NATURE OF THE SUBCHAPTER S CORPORATION 135
    Measurement of Subchapter S Net Income. 136
    Pass-Through of Income to Shareholders. 138
    Pass-Through of Long-Term Capital Gain. 140
    Taxation of Certain Long-Term Capital Gains at the
        Corporate Leve[l] 144

Avoidance of Penalty Tax. 146
Pass-Through of Corporate Net Operating Losses. 146
    Wasted NOL. 151
    Tax Planning Tips. 154
Special Problems Created by the Death of a Shareholder . . . 155
Pass-Through of Investment Tax Credit. 156
Recapture of Depreciation. 160
Pass-Through of Tax Preferences. 161
Pass-Through of Interest Deduction Limitations. 162
Member of a Controlled Group. 162

Chapter 7
CORPORATE DISTRIBUTIONS AND THEIR IMPACT UPON
SHAREHOLDERS' TAXABLE INCOME. 163
Sources of Subchapter S Distribution — An Overview. 163
Distributions of Cash. 167
Timing of Cash Distributions. 172
Distribution of Property Other than Cash. 176
Tax Planning for Subchapter S Distributions. 180
Fiscal-Year Corporations. 184
Adjusted Tax Basis. 186
Disposition of Stock. 187

Chapter 8
PROHIBITED INCOME. 191
Passive Investment Income. 192
    Royalties. 194
    Rents. 195
    Interest and Dividends. 200
    Annuities. 201
    Gains from Stock 201
    Miscellaneous. 202
Foreign Income. 203
Implications for Tax Planning. 205

Chapter 9

TAX RETURNS FOR SUBCHAPTER S CORPORATIONS........... 209
  The Subchapter S Return............................. 209
  Supplemental Schedule of Gains and Losses............. 211
  Capital Gains and Losses............................. 221
  Tax Calculation..................................... 221
  Automatic Extension 222
  Additional Extension................................ 222
  The Amending Process................................ 226
  Additional Information to be Filed.................... 226

Chapter 10

THE TERMINATION PROCESS............................. 231
  Voluntary Revocation................................ 231
  Involuntary Termination.............................. 234
  Involuntary Termination vs. Voluntary Revocation........ 237
  Reelection after Revocation or Termination............. 239

Chapter 11

REDEMPTIONS AND LIQUIDATIONS......................... 243
  Redemptions Under Section 302....................... 243
    Not Essentially Equivalent to Dividends.............. 244
    Substantially Disproportionate..................... 246
    Complete Redemption.............................. 247
    Shareholder Treatment............................ 247
    Corporate Treatment.............................. 250
  Partial Liquidations 253
    Types of Partial Liquidations...................... 253
    Overlapping with Stock Redemptions................ 258
    Mechanics of a Partial Liquidation.................. 259
    New Section 311(d)................................ 260
  Liquidations.. 261
    Section 331 Liquidation............................ 263
    Section 337 Liquidation............................ 265
    Section 333 Liquidation............................ 268
    Section 332 Liquidation............................ 271

Collapsible Electing Corporations. 271
Summary. 276

Chapter 12
A COMPARISON OF ORGANIZATIONAL FORMS. 279

Preview. 279
   Sole Proprietorship. 279
   Partnership. 279
   Corporation. 280
   Subchapter S Corporation. 280

Choice of Operating Entity. 280
   Non-Tax Advantages of Incorporation. 280
   Tax Advantages of Incorporation. 281

Advantages and Disadvantages of Subchapter S. 283
   Advantages. 288
   Infancy Period. 288
   Avoidance of Penalty Taxes. 289

Unsubstantiated Expenses and Unreasonable
   Compensation. 289
   Differing Taxable Years. 292
   Section 337 Liquidations. 293

Employee Relationship. 296
   Income Splitting. 300
   Miscellaneous Advantages. 302

Disadvantages and Hazards. 305

Chapter 13
STATEMENT PREPARATION AND RECORDKEEPING. 311

Is it, or is it not, a Corporation?. 311

Similarities in the Four Types of Businesses. 314

Differences in Owner's Equity. 314
   Equity Accounts of a Corporation. 314
   Equity Accounts of a Subchapter S Corporation. 316

Examples of Current Practice. 318

Miscellaneous Accounting Problems. 322
   Provisions for Income Taxes. 322

Comparative Financial Statements. 323
Pro Forma Statements. 324
Disposition of Deferred Income Tax Accounts. 325
Auditor's Opinion. 325

Recordkeeping. 326
Method of Accounting. 327
The Commissioner May Be Arbitrary. 328
Cohan Rule. 329
Adequate Books and Records. 330
Employee-Stockholder Problems. 332

Statute of Limitations. 334

Record Retention. 335

Changes in Accounting Method. 337
Unincorporated Business Becomes Subchapter S
    Corporation. 340
Existing Corporation Elects Subchapter S 341

Chapter 14
CONCLUSION: SUBCHAPTER S TAX PLANNING. 343
Tax Planning Concepts. 343
The Future of Subchapter S. 348

TABLE OF CASES. 351

REVENUE RULINGS. 365

REVENUE PROCEDURES 369

INDEX. 371

1975 SUPPLEMENT. 385

Chapter 1

The Subchapter S Corporation in the Federal Tax System

The proliferation of complex tax laws during this century has complicated the process of satisfying the tax requirements for close corporations. These small businesses are burdened with double taxation but do not derive much economic or legal advantage from operating as a corporation. The small corporation may become extinct if it does not develop new techniques and concepts to cope with the proliferation of more complex tax laws. Small corporations have always faced a shortage of talent, but the introduction of new techniques and the squeeze on profit margins make tax education a vital factor in the continuance of small businesses. A lack of general tax knowledge probably accounts for the larger share of the federal and local taxes being borne by the small corporation when compared to its larger corporate counterpart. The purpose of this book is to explore one technique that can be used in order to get the earnings of a close corporation into the pockets of the stockholders at a minimum loss of profits through taxes.

Taxability is a Basic Difference

Prior to the enactment of Subchapter S* as part of The Technical Amendments Act of 1958, there were two basic ways of structuring a business enterprise for tax purposes — the partnership method (including the sole proprietorship) and the corporate method. The tax effects of these two forms were, and are, different in several respects.

The most basic difference is whether or not the business organization itself is taxed. Normally, a corporation is considered to be an entity, and any income is first taxed to the corporation. If the owners want to get this after-tax income out of the corporation, they must pay individual income tax on the amount received from the corporation. Hence, the income of a corporation is subjected to two separate taxes before it is in the hands of the owners. On the other

---

*The tax term "Subchapter S Corporation" is referred to in tax literature by many other names, such as Small Business Corporation, Tax-option Corporation, Pseudo Corporation, and so forth.

hand, the partnership's entity is not subject to a tax, but the partners must report the results of the operation of the partnership on their personal tax returns. The partnership entity acts merely as a conduit; the income or loss passes through to the individual owners. That is, income of a partnership is taxed to the partners at individual income tax rates whether or not the income is actually distributed. The partnership income thus avoids double taxation.

Rationale of the Subchapter S Election

A closely held business may elect to incorporate in order to obtain the advantages of the corporate form of business, especially the limited liability and the benefits arising from an employee relationship. Except for the difference in limited liability, a closely held corporation may be substantially the same as a partnership. The major stockholders may act as partners in the day-by-day operation of the business and may receive distributions of income or losses similar to that of partners.

The specific mechanics of the operation of the closely held corporation, its economic nature, and the functional relations between its major owners, may be no different than the same business operated under a partnership agreement. Since all corporations are not identical and some may be no more than "chartered partnerships," it is not reasonable to tax closely held corporations on a basis different from that used in taxing partnerships. To impose a tax structure on similar entities on a different basis would result in taxation that is based on form rather than substance. This taxation of form rather than substance causes owners to assign undue weight to income tax consequences in choosing a form of organization.

The Senate Finance Committee recognized this apparent inequality and felt that owners should be free to choose a form of organization which they found most appropriate, without tax detriment as a result of the choice:

> The major problem with which section 68 is concerned is the fact that the present law does not integrate the individual and corporation income taxes and therefore gives rise to the alleged problem of double taxation. The taxability of dividends, as indicated elsewhere, is surely a matter of major concern in the present tax law.
>
> The point is that if a business is taxed as a corporation it is subjected to the ordinary corporate rate of 52 percent. The individual who receives income from the corporation also pays tax on his personal income including the amount from the corporation.

However, if the corporation can be taxed as a partnership, then the income from the corporation is 'passed through' to the partner and he pays taxes on the earnings only to the extent of his personal income-tax liability and escapes the corporate tax.[1] Thus, a provision was enacted in 1958 to permit a corporation to elect to be taxed as a partnership.[2] However, in actuality the provision did not allow the corporation to be taxed as a partnership. It permitted an entity which qualifies to be taxed partly as a corporation, partly as a partnership, and partly as neither. This hybrid form of taxation offers certain benefits which cannot be overlooked.

Important, however, was the fact that an attempt was made to correct the inequality of double taxation in closely held businesses and allow them to choose a form of organization they might find most appropriate, without tax detriment as a result of the choice.

The Growth of Subchapter S

Since the Subchapter S concept was added to the law in 1958, the number of electing corporations has increased substantially each year. The 233,807 Subchapter S corporations in 1969 were about 17 percent more than in 1967 (Table 1-1).

This increase from only 43,945 returns in 1958 is over 532 percent increase in just eleven years. Using the same years as a yardstick, regular corporate returns increased only 67 percent. Likewise, returns filed by sole proprietorships and partnerships have not manifested similar growth. Thus, many of these unincorporated businesses may be incorporating and electing Subchapter S status.

It is interesting to note that in 1958, the first year of the provision's existence, approximately 43 percent of the total returns were filed by loss corporations. In effect, a larger number of the corporations were making the election in order to pass through losses to the stockholders' individual tax returns. However, gradually more and more profit companies have made the election until, in 1969, 65 percent of the returns were from profitable businesses. The education of the taxpayers to this tax-planning tool has probably accounted for much of the long-term trend of increased Subchapter S elections.

Table 1-2 shows the growth of Subchapter S returns when compared to all other tax returns filed. Along with the substantial increase in Subchapter S returns, the regular corporation returns have

---

[1]*Report of the Committee on Finance,* Senate Report No. 1983, 85th Congress, 2nd Session (Washington: United States Government Printing Office, 1958), pp. 265-66.

[2]Chapter 2 discusses in detail the legislative history of the Subchapter S provisions.

3

TABLE 1-1
SUBCHAPTER S INCOME TAX RETURNS FILED

Year	Total		Subchapter S Returns With Net Income		With No Net Income	
	Number	Percent of Total	Number	Percent of Total	Number	Percent of Total
1958	43,945	100	25,203	57.4	18,742	42.6
1959	71,140	100	46,037	64.7	25,103	35.3
1960	90,221	100	56,123	62.2	34,098	37.8
1961	106,048	100	67,817	64.0	38,231	36.0
1962	123,666	100	78,939	63.8	44,727	36.2
1963	139,112	100	88,084	63.4	51,028	36.6
1964	157,855	100	102,585	65.0	55,270	35.0
1965	173,410	100	115,475	66.6	57,935	33.4
1966	181,851	100	118,374	65.1	63,477	34.9
1967	200,784	100	130,038	64.8	70,746	35.2
1968	217,134	100	142,516	65.6	74,618	34.4
1969	233,807	100	151,439	64.8	82,368	35.2

Source: Statistics of Income for 1958, Corporation Returns, Table 7; Statistics of Income for 1966, Business Returns, Table 9.3; Business Income Tax Returns 1967, 1968, 1969, Table 4.1.

4

increased moderately. However, both the sole proprietorship returns and the partnership returns show a downward trend.

Subchapter S Returns in Comparison to Total Corporate Returns

In 1958, only about 4.3 percent of all corporate returns were Subchapter S returns. In contrast, by 1965, more than 12 percent of all corporate returns were Subchapter S returns. (See Table 1-3.)

A less significant increase in the position of Subchapter S returns is shown by the proportion of total corporate gross and net income reported on Subchapter S returns. (No net income tax figure can be shown since the Subchapter S entity does not pay a tax.) In the initial year less than 1.6 percent of aggregate gross income of corporations and an insignificant .23 percent of their net earnings were accounted for on Subchapter S returns. By 1969 the corresponding ratios had increased moderately to 4.4 percent and 2.7 percent respectively. Thus, although the number of returns have increased significantly, the proportion of total corporate gross and net income has remained moderately small. The Subchapter S election remains a tax planning tool for close corporations with moderate earnings.

Use of Subchapter S Election by Selected Industry Groups

A similar index may be used to measure the importance of Subchapter S returns in selected industry groups. For this purpose, the proportion of any industry's income (gross and net) and the number of returns may be compared in two representative years. The years selected for comparison purposes are 1959, 1965, and 1969. (See Table 1-4.)

In 1959, all of the major industry groups (except the Finance, Insurance and Real Estate group) had from 6 to 9 percent of Subchapter S returns filed. The largest percentage increase in these returns occurred in the Agriculture, Forestry and Fisheries group. The use of this special election by "gentlemen farmers" probably helps to account for the fact that 29 percent of all firms in this industry group made the special election by 1969. Also, in terms of total net income and percentage of net income, the Agriculture group was the leader in 1969, followed closely by Contract Construction. Again, only about 6.6 percent of all returns in the Finance group were Subchapter S returns. The requirement that a Subchapter S corporation cannot have more than 20 percent of gross income from passive income prevents many real estate corporations, personal holding companies, and finance companies from making the election.

TABLE 1-2

COMPARISON OF TYPES OF INCOME TAX RETURNS FILED

Year	Proprietorship	Partnership	Subchapter S Corporation	Corporation
1958	8,799,711	953,840	43,945	990,381
1959	9,142,359	949,396	71,140	1,074,120
1960	9,089,985	940,560	90,221	1,140,574
1961	9,241,755	938,966	106,048	1,190,286
1962	9,182,586	932,181	123,666	1,268,042
1963	9,135,954	924,276	139,112	1,323,184
1964	9,192,746	922,160	157,855	1,373,517
1965	9,078,464	914,215	173,410	1,423,980
1966	9,086,714	922,680	181,851	1,468,725
1967	9,126,082	906,182	200,784	1,534,360
1968	9,211,613	917,500	217,134	1,541,637
1969	9,429,822	920,831	233,747	1,658,744

Source: Statistics of Income for 1958, Corporation Returns, Table 7; Statistics of Income for 1966, Business Returns, Tables 9-1, 9-2, 9-3, 9-4; Business Income Tax Returns 1967, 1968, 1969, Table 1.1

TABLE 1-3

NUMBER OF RETURNS, GROSS AND NET INCOME, REPORTED FOR ALL CORPORATE RETURNS AND FOR SUBCHAPTER S CORPORATIONS

	1958	1959	1960	1961	1962	1963	1964	1965	1966	1967	1968	1969
Returns:												
Corporate Returns	990,381	1,074,122	1,140,574	1,190,286	1,286,042	1,323,187	1,373,517	1,423,980	1,468,725	1,534,360	1,541,670	1,658,820
Subchapter S Returns	43,945	71,140	90,221	106,048	123,666	139,112	157,855	173,410	181,851	200,784	217,184	233,806
Ratio of Subchapter S to All Returns	4.25%	6.2%	7.3%	8.18%	8.77%	9.5%	10.3%	10.8%	11.0%	11.5%	12.4%	12.4%
					(Money Figures in Billions)							
Gross income:												
Corporate Returns	735.3	816.8	849.1	873.2	949.3	1,008.7	1,086.7	1,194.6	1,306.5	1,374.6	1,507.8	1,680.4
Subchapter S Returns	11.6	19.2	23.4	26.2	29.8	35.1	40.1	46.4	50.9	56.7	61.7	73.3
Ratio of Subchapter S to All Returns	1.55%	2.2%	2.68%	2.9%	3.0%	3.36%	3.55%	3.7%	3.89%	4.12%	4.09%	4.36%
Net income:												
Corporate Returns	38.5	46.8	43.5	45.9	49.6	54.3	61.6	73.9	80.5	78.1	85.9	80.2
Subchapter S Returns	.09	.4	.4	.6	.7	.8	1.0	1.4	1.6	1.8	1.9	2.2
Ratio of Subchapter S to All Returns	.23%	.84%	.9%	1.29%	1.39%	1.45%	1.59%	1.85%	1.98%	2.30%	2.21%	2.74%

Source: Statistics of Income for 1965, Business Returns, Tables 9.7 and 9.8; Statistics of Income for 1958, Corporation Returns, Table 1; Statistics of Income for 1969, Corporation Returns, Table 25.

7

TABLE 1-4

RATIO OF SUBCHAPTER S RETURNS, GROSS AND NET INCOME TO ALL CORPORATE RETURNS FOR YEARS 1959, 1965, AND 1969 FOR SELECTED INDUSTRY GROUPS

Industry Group	1959			1965			1969		
	# of Returns	Gross Income	Net Income	# of Returns	Gross Income	Net Income	# of Returns	Gross Income	Net Income
		(Thousand Dollars)	(Thousand Dollars)		(Thousand Dollars)	(Thousand Dollars)		(Thousand Dollars)	(Thousand Dollars)
Agriculture, Forestry and Fisheries									
All Corporate	15,603	3,837,620	105,884	27,530	7,524,274	237,229	31,974	12,127,144	257,199
Subchapter S	1,485	177,211	(4,838)*	6,839	1,119,696	89	9,332	1,425,075	11,272
Ratio	8.69%	4.4%	NA	19.89%	12.95%	.036%	29.2%	11.7%	4.4%
Mining									
All Corporate	12,920	10,354,855	645,874	13,285	12,602,087	1,391,939	14,027	16,233,328	1,553,969
Subchapter S	832	130,206	261	1,912	425,073	32,754	2,184	592,739	31,483
Ratio	6.05%	1.2%	.04%	12.58%	3.26%	2.299%	15.5%	3.6%	2.0%
Contract Construction									
All Corporate	66,260	32,140,410	579,108	113,284	56,694,897	1,257,632	127,666	83,912,537	1,660,343
Subchapter S	6,137	1,859,791	33,777	18,000	5,317,183	176,623	21,356	8,991,497	271,222
Ratio	8.47%	5.46%	5.51%	13.71%	8.57%	12.31%	16.7%	10.7%	16.3%
Manufacturing									
All Corporate	156,297	363,157,167	24,985,884	185,924	514,718,841	40,247,559	202,066	710,084,099	41,256,747
Subchapter S	11,849	4,156,795	107,795	22,534	8,239,182	395,148	25,158	11,082,003	475,465
Ratio	7.046%	1.131%	.4290%	10.81%	1.57%	.972%	12.4%	1.5%	1.1%
Public Utilities (Transportation, Communication, Electric, Gas & Sanitary Services)									
All Corporate	43,195	62,308,546	6,790,796	59,676	88,956,519	10,699,309	66,944	125,261,815	10,053,831
Subchapter S	2,510	416,805	16,538	7,090	1,170,673	56,678	9,160	1,819,101	67,251
Ratio	5.40%	.6640%	.2424%	10.619%	1.298%	.5263%	13.7%	1.4%	.6%

8

TABLE 1-4 (Continued)

Industry Group	1959			1965			1969		
	# of Returns	Gross Income	Net Income	# of Returns	Gross Income	Net Income	# of Returns	Gross Income	Net Income
Wholesale & Retail Trade									
All Corporate	334,717	256,647,744	5,567,128	440,304	365,166,475	7,620,764	524,567	508,264,913	10,766,271
Subchapter S	31,616	11,156,330	154,724	68,219	25,904,288	540,257	92,537	41,196,613	917,668
Ratio	8.63%	4.168%	2.696%	13.415%	6.62%	6.619%	17.6%	8.1%	8.5%
Services									
All Corporate	110,005	22,227,256	968,252	188,177	38,377,034	1,590,097	261,633	60,036,636	1,653,105
Subchapter S	8,652	962,596	28,430	28,902	3,217,500	85,386	45,313	5,876,622	251,779
Ratio	7.291%*	4.107%	2.85%	13.31%	7.735%	5.096%	17.3%	9.8%	15.2%
Finance, Insurance & Real Estate									
All Corporate	318,592	65,911,758	7,152,612	388,428	110,465,502	10,844,377	428,969	164,290,937	13,014,453
Subchapter S	7,480	325,581	58,675	19,336	1,036,488	160,361	28,610	2,231,634	225,624
Ratio	2.293%	.49%	.813%	4.74%	.929%	1.457%	6.6%	1.4%	1.7%

*Deficit exceed net income.
Source: Statistics of Income for 1965, Business Returns; Tables 9.7 and 9.8; Business Returns 1969; Tables 9.3 and 9.4.

Relation Between Net Income and Deficit Subchapter S
Returns and Total Assets Categories

An analysis of the division of Subchapter S returns between net income and deficit (no net income) categories from 1958-1969 reveals that the number of electing corporations with net income increased steadily. (See Table 1-1.)

Electing corporations divided into net income and deficit classes may also be categorized by total assets classes. (See Table 1-5.) Such a classification for the year 1969 demonstrates that the proportion of Subchapter S returns in any total assets category showing net income varied almost directly with the size of that total assets class. Likewise, the proportion of Subchapter S returns in any total assets class incurring a deficit varied almost inversely with the size of the total assets class. That is, the larger the total assets categories, the greater was the percentage of returns with net income and the smaller the percentage of deficit returns. For example, electing corporations in the smallest assets-size bracket (zero assets) had only 30 percent of their number in the net income category and 70 percent in the deficit class. Those in the asset class — 5 million to 10 million — had 76 percent of their total in the net income category and only 24 percent in the deficit group.

Another salient fact emerging from the data in Table 1-5 is that the majority of the returns are filed in the lower assets classes, and fewer are filed in the higher assets categories. Two factors may explain this cluster of elections in the lower assets classes. First, many of the stringent requirements for electing this special status tend to disqualify corporations in large assets classes. Second, higher assets categories have a tendency toward higher earnings which, when passed through to the few stockholders, result in a large tax liability due to the progressive individual tax rates.

Conclusion

This analysis demonstrates that the optional Subchapter S election is being used by closely-held corporations with moderate earnings and asset structures. Since the framers of this tax provision intended this election to be available for closely-held corporations that were, in fact, only chartered partnerships, the evidence indicates that the intent of Congress has been followed. However, probably more than one million corporations fall within the definition of closely-held.

Several reasons can be hypothesized as to why less than 20

TABLE 1-5

ALL SUBCHAPTER S RETURNS, SUBCHAPTER S RETURNS WITH INCOME AND WITH NO NET INCOME CLASSIFIED BY TOTAL ASSET CLASSES, 1969

Total Assets Classes	All Subchapter S		Subchapter S With Net Income		Subchapter S With No Net Income	
	# of Returns	% of Class	# of Returns	% of Class	# of Returns	% of Class
Total	233,806	100	151,438	65	82,368	35
Zero Assets	4,798	100	1,432	30	3,366	70
$1 > 50,000	108,208	100	61,328	57	46,880	43
50,000 > 100,000	44,208	100	61,328	57	46,880	43
100,000 > 250,000	44,932	100	33,961	76	10,971	24
250,000 > 500,000	19,614	100	15,172	77	4,442	23
500,000 > 1,000,000	7,553	100	6,172	82	1,381	18
1,000,000 > 5,000,000	4,352	100	3,473	80	879	20
5,000,000 > 10,000,000	51	100	39	76	12	24
10,000,000 > 25,000,000	26	100	20	77	6	23
25,000,000 > 50,000,000	3	100	3	100	0	0
50,000,000 or more	1	100	1	100	0	0

Source: Statistics of Income for 1969, Corporation Income Tax Returns, Table 22.

11

percent of the potential corporations have elected to be taxed as Subchapter S corporations.

1. Stringent requirements (i.e., no trusts as shareholders or only one class of stock) decrease the number of elections.
2. Lack of knowledge on the part of owners of small businesses of the availability of such an election and its advantages.
3. The hostility of the IRS in administering the technicalities of the election (especially in the areas of second class of stock, consents, making the election, passive income, and disqualifying shareholders).
4. Cash shortages develop since earnings must be distributed before two and one-half months after the close of the tax year to avoid the possibility of "locked-in" previously taxed earnings.

A Glimpse Forward

This chapter has examined statistically the position of Subchapter S in the federal tax system. Although only an infant upon the tax scene, this election that enables a corporation to avoid a tax at the corporate level is being used by more and more closely-held corporations. The recent 300% liberalization in the pension plan deduction should cause many proprietorships, partnerships, and regular corporations to convert to Subchapter S status.

The second chapter contains background information in the form of a legislative synopsis and the third chapter discusses the election process. Chapters 4 and 5 examine the attributes which both corporations and shareholders must possess in order to elect and maintain Subchapter S status. In Chapter 6, the manner in which a Subchapter S corporation measures income and passes it through the corporate entity for taxation at the shareholder level is discussed. The effect of distributions upon the corporation and its shareholders is the topic of Chapter 7. Chapter 8 examines the character of income which a Subchapter S corporation is permitted, by statute, to receive, while Chapter 9 reviews the various forms which the Subchapter S corporation is required to file. Chapters 10 and 11 consider the process of divesting the corporation of its Subchapter S status when the entity wishes to return to regular corporate treatment, as well as when it desires to conclude its affairs through liquidation. Chapter 12 follows with a comparison of the Subchapter S corporation with the other major organizational forms and provides a checklist of advantages and disadvantages. Chapter 13 contains a general discussion of financial statements and reports for Subchapter S corporations. Chapter 14 contains concluding remarks.

Chapter 2

The Background of Subchapter S

Justice Holmes once theorized that "a page of history is worth a volume of logic." An examination of the history of Subchapter S should give valuable insight to this tax planning tool. A trace of this conduit concept goes back as far as the Civil War. No income tax was levied during this period on ordinary industrial and mercantile corporations, but the shareholders were taxed on their share of the earnings of the corporation (whether distributed or not).[1]

The modern Subchapter S concept probably evolved from the numerous proposals to eliminate the harsh effects of double taxation of corporate income. Such an opinion that an inequality was present in the tax system began to filter into the tax literature in the thirties. However, only when this opinion merged with the notion that a closely-held corporation is in reality a partnership, was there any constructive action taken. An early study by the National Tax Association suggested partnership-type treatment for all but a few of the larger corporations in order to provide equity from the double taxation of corporate earnings. "With respect to the area within which it is practicable to apply the partnership method, all of us agree that in the case of all corporations whose capital structure is simple and whose securities are not distributed among many holders, the administrative problem is not serious."[2]

Supplement S — Tax of Shareholders of Personal Service Corporations

The forerunner of Subchapter S was probably the provisions added to the 1939 *Code* dealing with personal service corporations.[3] This act, called "Supplement S — Tax of Shareholders of Personal Service Corporation," became law on October 8, 1940. These provisions generally allowed the undistributed Supplement S net income

---

[1]Richard B. Goode, *The Postwar Corporation Tax Structure,* Hearings Before the House Committee on Ways and Means, 80th Congress, 1st Session, part 2 (1947), p. 1154.

[2]Committee on Federal Taxation of Corporations, *Proceedings of the Thirty-Second Annual Conference on Taxation of the National Tax Association,* Vol. 32 (1939), p. 555.

[3]*United States Code, 1939,* 1946 edition, Vol. 3 (Washington: United States Government Printing Office, 1947), pp. 2665-2666, 2693.

of a corporation that qualified to be taxed only at the shareholder level. Each shareholder had to include in his gross income (as dividends) an amount equal to his share of the undistributed Supplement S net income of the corporation for the tax year. The undistributed Supplement S net income was the net income of the corporation *minus* the amount of the dividends paid during the tax year. Only the shareholders on the last day of each taxable year of the corporation were taxed on the income.

A personal service corporation was defined by the *Code* as a corporation whose income was ascribed primarily to the activities of shareholders who were regularly engaged in the active conduct of the affairs of the corporation and who were owners at all times during the taxable year of at least 70 percent of each class of stock. Furthermore, capital could not be a material income-producing factor, and there could not be any foreign income. Finally, the gross income had to consist of less than 50 percent of gains, profits, or income derived from trading as a principal.

Treasury Department Tax Studies

A proposal for partnership-type taxation of corporations was examined by the Treasury for some time in connection with tax suggestions to aid small businesses. The first study, issued on December 6, 1946, discussed the use of a partnership method for corporations having a few shareholders and a simple capital structure.[4] Instead of a pure partnership approach, however, the study indicated that an approach which did not trace special types of income, deductions, and credits through to the shareholders would be simpler and possibly acceptable to the Treasury. "Even though the partnership approach intends to treat stockholders and the corporation as one for tax purposes, it does not seem feasible or necessary to trace all items of receipts and outlays through the corporate organization."[5]

Another study on the taxation of small businesses released by the Treasury Department in October of 1947 discussed and appraised the probable effectiveness of several proposals intended to stimulate small business.[6] Optional partnership tax treatment for certain corporations was suggested in order to equalize the tax burden on

---

[4]*Supra,* note 1, pp. 1136-1181.

[5]*Ibid.,* p. 1155.

[6]United States Treasury Department, Division of Tax Research, *Taxation of Small Business,* Hearings Before the House Committee on Ways and Means, 80th Congress, 1st Session, part 5 (1947), pp. 3741-3742, 3757-3760.

small incorporated and unincorporated businesses. This study indicated that this conduit form of tax treatment might increase the flow of equity capital into small businesses. Understandably, the Treasury study did not want the provision to be available to all corporations. Instead, the Treasury felt that the proposal should be restricted (for administrative convenience) to corporations that had ten to fifteen shareholders and had a simple capital structure. Without such criteria it would be impossible to allocate income satisfactorily among the owners of the various classes of stock.[7] The Treasury apparently favored a limitation on the number of stockholders rather than on the size of corporate assets.[8]

Subsequently, in 1949, the Special Committee to Study Problems of American Small Business issued a report on the hardships of the small business due to double taxation, but partnership tax treatment for small businesses was not included in the recommendations.[9] Shortly thereafter, the President's Cabinet Committee on Small Business recommended several changes in the tax laws for the benefit of small business, and again the election to tax a corporation as a partnership was absent from the suggestions.

President Eisenhower's Recommendations — 1954

President Eisenhower in his Budget Message to the Eighty-Third Congress proposed an option allowing small business entities to be taxed as partnerships:[10]

Small businesses should be able to operate under whatever form of organization is desirable for their particular circumstances, without incurring unnecessary tax penalties. To secure this result, I recommend that corporations with a small number of active shareholders be given the option to be taxed as partnerships and that certain partnerships be given the option to be taxed as corporations.

Both proposals requested by President Eisenhower were received unfavorably by the House Ways and Means Committee and were excluded from its draft of H.R. 8300, the bill which culminated in the 1954 Code. Not to be outdone, however, the Senate Finance

[7]*Ibid.,* p. 3758.

[8]*Ibid.,* p.3741.

[9]*Report of the Special Committee to Study Problems of American Small Business,* Senate Report No. 48, 81st Congress, 1st Session (Washington: United States Government Printing Office, 1949), pp. 1-23.

[10]"Annual Budget Message to the Congress, January 21, 1954," *Public Papers of the Presidents of the United States — Dwight D. Eisenhower, 1954* (Washington: United States Government Printing Office, 1960), p. 86.

Committee inserted both proposals as an integrated arrangement in H.R. 8300. The Senate Committee voiced the following rebuttal:

> Your committee has adopted new provisions which for the first time will eliminate the effect of the Federal tax laws on the form of organization adopted by certain small businesses. This is accomplished by giving certain corporations the option to be taxed as a partnership and by allowing certain proprietorships and partnerships the option to be taxed as a corporation. These provisions are not in the House Bill.[11]

The requirements for I.R.C. Section 1351 were much the same as in the present Subchapter S provisions, except that the election was to be available only to new corporations, the stockholders had to participate actively in the business, and employee-stockholders could not participate in employee pension and profit sharing plans. The stated purpose of this new provision was to eliminate the influence of Federal income tax in the selection of the form of business organization.[12]

As with all legislation in dispute between the two august governing bodies, the legislation in question was sent to the Conference Committee. Through the art of compromise, the Conference Committee accepted the proposal permitting partnerships to choose to be taxed as a corporation, but mysteriously rejected the most important provisions giving the corporation the right to elect to be taxed as a partnership.[13]

The Technical Amendments Act of 1958

Subchapter S came through the Senate door into the Technical Amendments Act of 1958. This Act had its origin in the proposals made in 1956 to the House Ways and Means Committee by the staff of the Joint Committee on Internal Revenue Taxation and the Treasury Department. The text and a summary of the bill (then designated the Technical Amendments Bill of 1957) was prepared by the Joint Committee and released in October, 1956. Subsequently, recommended additions to the Bill, together with a list of unintended benefits and hardships, were released in November, 1956.

In November, 1956, the Subcommittee on Internal Revenue Taxation of the Ways and Means Committee held hearings on the

---

[11]*Report of the Committee on Finance,* Senate Report No. 1622, 83rd Congress, 2nd Session (Washington: United States Government Printing Office, 1954), p. 118.

[12]*Ibid.,* pp. 452-455.

[13]House Report No. 2543, 83rd Congress, 2nd Session, p. 72.

suggested changes.[14] Since a much narrower version of Subchapter S had been prepared by the Treasury staff at the request of the House Ways and Means Committee, it was the narrow version that reached the Ways and Means Committee. However, this narrowing was to no avail, for as the bill was being reviewed and modified by the Ways and Means Committee, even the narrow version of Subchapter S was deleted from the Technical Amendments Bill. Even worse, due to alleged ambiguity and uncertainty in result incorporated in the provisions of the Subchapter R election passed in 1954 (allowing a partnership to be taxed as a corporation) the Ways and Means Committee also suggested its repeal. The Technical Amendments Bill of 1957 was reported to the House by the Ways and Means Committee in June, 1957,[15] and the final form (renamed the Technical Amendments Act of 1958) passed the House in January, 1958.

Hearings were held by the Senate Finance Committee during February, 1958.[16] The Senate committee disagreed with the House version of the Technical Amendments Act of 1958. The provision for optional tax treatment was reborn when, in the course of the hearings, one of the members of the Senate Finance Committee inquired about the death in 1954 of I.R.C. Section 1351, which allowed some corporations to be taxed as partnerships. The Senate committee decided to reinstate the Subchapter R election and to add a Subchapter S provision.

The Senate committee did not build upon the version that was defeated in 1954 but chose the narrow version presented to the Ways and Means Committee by the Treasury staff. President Eisenhower had made certain recommendations in his Budget Message in January, 1958,[17] which the Senate committee incorporated into the Treasury's draft. President Eisenhower had offered similar recommendations earlier in the form of a letter to the chairman of the Committee on Ways and Means, dated July 15, 1957.[18]

---

[14] *Technical Amendments to Internal Revenue Code,* Hearings Before a Subcommittee of the Committee on Ways and Means, 84th Congress, 2nd Session (Washington: United States Government Printing Office, 1956).

[15] *Report of the Committee on Ways and Means,* House Report No. 775, 85th Congress, 1st Session (Washington: United States Government Printing Office, 1957).

[16] *Report of the Committee on Finance,* Senate Report No. 1983, 85th Congress, 2nd Session (Washington: United States Government Printing Office, 1958), pp. 87-89.

[17] *Economic Report of the President:* Transmitted to the Congress, January 20, 1958 (Washington: United States Government Printing Office, 1958), p. 63.

[18] "A Letter to Jere Cooper, Chairman, House Committee on Ways and Means, Regarding Small Business, July 15, 1967," *Public Papers of the Presidents of the United States — Dwight D. Eisenhower, 1957* (Washington: United States Government Printing Office, 1958), p. 539.

After the Senate approved the Finance Committee's version, the act was forwarded to the Conference Committee. To the amazement of many, the Senate's Subchapter S proposal was accepted by the Conference Committee. The Code was amended by the Technical Amendments Act, which President Eisenhower signed on September 2, 1958. Thus, a hastily-written option was enacted into law to permit a small business to choose the form of organization it might find most appropriate, without tax detriment resulting from the choice. "In this respect, a provision to tax the income of the stockholder, rather than the corporate level, will complement the provision enacted in 1954 permitting proprietorships and partnerships to be taxed like corporations."[19] A bill finally became law that would reduce taxes for qualifying closely-held corporations. (See the Subchapter S legislative history summary at the end of this chapter.)

Proposed Regulations Plug "Loophole"

Shortly after the enactment of Subchapter S, the Treasury Department realized that Congress had written a complex provision without any knowledge of its relevance to other complicated provisions already in the statutes. This optional taxation permitted easy circumvention of the strict qualifying rules for the use of I.R.C. Section 337, which provides relief from double taxation when corporate assets are sold while winding up a business. For example, in many situations where a collapsible corporation could meet the requirements for Subchapter S, the corporation could sell its capital assets and pass through a single capital gain to the shareholders.

Later in proposed regulations, the Treasury tried to stop the bail-out possibilities under Subchapter S with two specific regulations. In Prop. Reg. 1.1372-1, the Treasury stipulated that the Subchapter S election would not be available to a corporation which had adopted a plan or was in the process of complete or partial liquidation in the near future. In Prop. Reg. 1.1375-1(d) the Treasury stated that although the character of an asset (whether capital or ordinary) of a Subchapter S corporation is normally determined at the corporate level, the asset will not be considered a capital item if the corporation is availed of by stockholders owning a substantial portion of the stock for the purpose of selling property which would not be a capital item in the hands of such stockholders. For the purpose of determining the type of asset in the stockholders' hands, the activ-

---

[19]Senate Report No. 1983, *op cit.*, p. 87.

ities of other Subchapter S corporations of the stockholders are considered.

The proposed regulation which denied an election to a corporation in the process of liquidation was absent from the final regulations, for the Treasury recognized that there was no statutory authority in the provisions enacted by Congress or from the committee hearings. Prop. Reg. 1.1375-1(d) became part of the final regulations, but the collapsible loophole still remains partially open. Further, there has been no court case testing the validity of this regulation.

Discrimination Against Community Property States Corrected

Three technical changes were enacted in 1959 by Public Law 86-376.[20] One of these changes tried to correct the discrimination against community property states. Originally, the Subchapter S election provided that an electing corporation could have no more than ten stockholders, and every married stockholder in a community property state was generally considered to be two stockholders (since his spouse by state law owned one-half of his stock). Hence, the new law in 1959 provided that, for purposes of determining the number of stockholders for qualification purposes, a husband and wife are to be considered as a single stockholder where stock is held jointly or as community property.[21]

This law in 1959 did not fully settle the issue, for it was applicable only to years beginning after December 31, 1959, and left in doubt the right of corporations to qualify for 1958 and 1959. However, Section 23 of the 1962 Act resolved this problem by extending the benefits of the 1959 law to cover taxable years beginning after 1957 and before 1960. The inequality was not completely cleared up, for the Committee Reports indicated that the new provisions applied only where a timely election was originally made in the earlier years.

Pro Rata Share of the Corporation's Loss

A second change in 1959 corrected an inequality in the treatment of a stockholder who died while owning stock in a Subchapter S corporation. Suppose a stockholder died during the electing corporation's tax year and his estate filed a consent to continue the optional tax treatment. If the corporation had an operating loss for

---

[20]Public Law Number 86-376, 86th Congress, 1st Session (1959).
[21]I.R.C. Section 1371(c), added by Public Law 86-376.

that year, a flaw in the wording of the original act allowed the estate a deduction only for the portion of such loss that was allocable to the period following the shareholder's death. The new amendment made it clear that, in the event of the death of a shareholder, the decedent would not be denied his pro rata share of the corporation's net operating loss.[22]

It is noteworthy that the amendment applied only to shareholders who died after September 23, 1959. Section 30 of the 1962 law, however, extended the relief back to September 2, 1958, the date the Subchapter S provisions were enacted.

Disqualification by the Acquisition of a Subsidiary

A third change in 1959 closed a loophole in the ownership of a subsidiary. The original law provided that the ownership of 80 percent or more of a subsidiary would disqualify a corporation from electing to be taxed under Subchapter S. However, there was nothing in the original law to prevent a corporation from acquiring a controlled subsidiary after it had made its initial election. This amendment made such a purchase a disqualifying factor which caused the Subchapter S election to automatically terminate.[23]

The disqualification of a corporation which owns 80 percent or more of a subsidiary was weakened somewhat by the Revenue Act of 1964.[24] An amendment permits qualification if the only subsidiaries are corporations that have not begun business and do not have taxable income. For example, if a subsidiary is organized in another state to protect the corporate name, this action would not disqualify a corporation from making a Subchapter S election. Likewise, if it is essential to control 80 percent or more of another corporation's stock, there is no prohibition against having less than 80 percent of such stock held by the electing corporation and the remainder by its shareholders.

Certain Distributions After Close of Taxable Year

Another amendment in 1964 dealt with Section 1231 assets. If a Subchapter S corporation sells capital or Section 1231 assets at a gain, the gain is taxed to the stockholders and may be distributed to them without further tax if the distribution is made during the same tax year of the corporation. If, however, the distribution is made after

---

[22]I.R.C. Section 1374(b), as amended by Public Law 86-376.

[23]I.R.C. Section 1371(a), as modified by Public Law 86-376.

[24]I.R.C. Section 1371(a).

the end of the year, it is taxable to the stockholders unless all current earnings have been distributed.[25]

Under Section 233(b) of the Revenue Act of 1964, a corporation (with the consent of its stockholders) could elect, for purposes of I.R.C. Section 1231 capital assets, to treat a distribution of money made after the end of the taxable year as received by its stockholders on the last day of such taxable year. According to Proposed Regulations, the distribution could be made within the first three and one-half months of the following year if the following conditions were satisfied:

1. Proper election must be made.
2. Each shareholder must consent.
3. The holdings of the shareholders must be the same on the distribution date as at the close of the gain's year.
4. A director's resolution to distribute must be adopted in the year the gain is realized.[26]

This section was repealed by Public Law 89-389¶1(a) effective with respect to distributions made after the close of any taxable year of the corporation beginning after April 14, 1966.

Grace Periods

Three significant changes in the Subchapter S rules were signed into law by President Johnson on April 14, 1966. The first change, I.R.C. Section 1375(f), was added to eliminate the almost impossible task of estimating and distributing all of the income before the end of the fiscal year. Prior to 1966 undistributed taxable income (UTI) had to be distributed to the stockholders by the last day of the fiscal year or it would immediately become previously taxed income. (See Chapter 5 for a more thorough discussion of the limitations of PTI.) In 1966, however, Congress helped Subchapter S corporations by giving them a two-and-one-half month grace period after the close of the fiscal year to determine the actual operating results and to distribute the entire income. Cash distributions made within this grace period are treated as distributions of the preceding year. This treatment is allowed even if the special Subchapter S election has terminated as of the close of the taxable year.

For distributions made prior to April 14, 1966 (assuming the requirements of I.R.C. Section 1375(f) are satisfied), a special election

---

[25]I.R.C. Section 1375(b), as amended by Public Law 8363, Revenue Act of 1964.
[26]Prop. Reg. 19.2-1.

is available which permits similar treatment but with a three-and-one-half month grace period. This special election is irrevocable, and, because of the voluminous data that are required, it should *not* be made unless it results in a material amount of refund of prior year's taxes.[27]

Capital Gain Tax and Passive Income

There is one exception to the avoidance of double taxation which was added to the law in 1966 to prevent the use of the Subchapter S election solely to pass through one sizable capital gain. Before this law was passed, a corporation could elect Subchapter S status, sell a sizable asset, and terminate the election at the end of the year. Thus, the capital gain would flow through to the stockholders and avoid a double tax without the necessity of a complete liquidation.

Now, in certain situations where a Subchapter S corporation has capital gains, a tax is imposed at the corporate level. This corporate tax does not apply to a firm which has elected Subchapter S status for the three preceding taxable years, or to a company which has been in existence for less than four years, provided an election has been in effect for each taxable year since incorporation. In all other situations the applicable capital gains tax is imposed on the net long-term capital gain if:

1. The net LTCG exceeds $25,000, and
2. The taxable income of the enterprise exceeds $25,000.

A third change occurs in the area of passive investment income. Prior to 1966 a corporation receiving so-called passive investment income in excess of 20 percent of its total income would generally automatically terminate its Subchapter S election with dire consequences. The 1966 legislation provided an exception to the passive income test for years ending after April 15, 1966. There is no termination in the first or second year of a corporation's existence if the passive income is less than $3,000. The purpose of this exception is to prevent new corporations from losing their special election at the very beginning of their existence.

Thin Capitalization — 1973

The thin capitalization doctrine has created problems for Subchapter S corporations since the beginning. Although thin capitaliza-

---

[27]See A. Salkin, "Proposed Regs Require Voluminous Data to Elect Retroactive Sub S Distribution," *Journal of Taxation,* Vol. 28 (May, 1968), p. 313.

tion is considered in Chapter 3 of this book, the area has sufficient historical significance to justify a brief discussion at this point.

The typical Subchapter S corporation is a natural candidate for thin capitalization. These corporations are typically small and undercapitalized. Capital requirements are often met through loans by shareholders to the corporation. This is especially true if the shareholders wish to avoid the creation of previously taxed income and accordingly advance loans to the corporation to enable it to pay current dividends.[28]

The original regulations stated that "if an instrument purporting to be a debt obligation is actually stock, it will constitute a second class of stock."[29] Although there appeared to be no statutory authority for this regulation, the IRS applied the thin capitalization doctrine to those situations where significant debt was present in the corporation's capital structure. As is noted in Chapter 5, a Subchapter S corporation may have only one class of stock issued and outstanding. The result is termination of Subchapter S status retroactive to the beginning of the tax year in which the second class of stock was created.

The IRS had some success in the courts with this approach.[30] However, other courts refused to hold that loans constituted a second class of stock.[31] Failure of this IRS position caused the Commissioner to amend Regulation 1.1371-1(g). The revised regulation stated that debt that purports to be equity will still be treated as a second class of stock. However, if that debt is owned solely by shareholders of the corporation in proportion to their stock ownership, it will be treated as a contribution to capital rather than as a second class of stock.[32] Thus, proportionality appeared to be a compromise, and several courts indicated that they would accept this position.[33] However, the proportionality test has not withstood the passage of time. The revised Regulation 1.1371-1(g) has been held invalid by several courts.[34]

---

[28]There are problems with this procedure. See discussion in Chapter 7 relative to *George A. Roesel,* 56 T.C. 14(1971) *appeal dismissed,* (5th Cir., 1971).

[29]Regulation 1.1371-1(g), 1959.

[30]*Catalina Homes, Inc.,* T.C.M. 1964-225; *Henderson* vs. *U.S.,* 16 A.F.T.R. 2d 5512 (M.D. Ala., 1965), *appeal dismissed* (5th Cir., 1966).

[31]*Gamman,* 46 T.C. 1(1966), *appeal dismissed* (9th Cir., 1967); *Lewis Building and Supplies, Inc.,* T.C.M. 1966-159, *appeal dismissed* (5th Cir., 1967).

[32]Regulation 1.1371(g), as amended by T.C. 6904 (1966).

[33]*August F. Nielsen, Inc.,* T.C.M. 1968-11; *Milton T. Raynor,* 50 T.C. 762 (1968).

[34]*Portage Plastics Co., Inc.* vs. *U.S.,* 24 A.F.T.R. 2d 69-5301 (W.D. Wis. 1969); *James L. Stinnet, Jr.,* 54 T.C. 221 (1970).

By mid-1973, the Government had lost so many cases on this issue that it decided not to litigate further until Regulation 1.1371-1(g) could be revised.[35] This area is discussed at length in Chapter 5.

Fringe Benefits

In the Tax Reform Bill of 1969, Congress imposed certain restrictions on deductible contributions to retirement plans on behalf of employees who own either directly or by attribution more than 5 percent of the electing corporation any time during the tax year. Such an employee is now taxed currently on any contributed amounts in excess of the lesser of 10 percent of his compensation or $2,500. This legislation provides similar treatment to Subchapter S shareholders as under the self-employed retirement plans of partners. Note: the application of this provision is effective with taxable years beginning after December 31, 1970. However, this punitive restriction was significantly liberalized by the Employee Retirement Income Security Act of 1974. Now a Subchapter S plan is allowed a more adequate $7,500 or 15 percent of earned income for taxable years beginning after December 31, 1973.

Farm Loss Loopholes Closed

The Revenue Act of 1971 dealt with the individual with high non-farm income who incorporated his farming operations into a Subchapter S corporation in order to avoid any Section 1251 recapture. Now a Subchapter S corporation must add to its own non-farm income the non-farm income of that shareholder having the greatest amount of such income. If the combined non-farm income exceeds $50,000, the Subchapter S corporation must make an addition to its EDA for any net farm loss in excess of $25,000.

This same Act eliminates the possibility of using multiple Subchapter S corporations in order to obtain the $25,000 exemption. Not only is the $25,000 exemption disallowed if any one of its stockholders has a net farm loss, but now the exemption is disallowed if any one of its stockholders is a shareholder in another Subchapter S corporation which has a net farm loss.

---

[35]T.I.R.-1248 (7/73).

Summary: Legislative History of Subchapter S

Summary of the Congressional history of the Technical Amendments Act of 1958 that included the Small Business Corporation provision.

1956	Narrow version of Subchapter S prepared by the Treasury staff at the request of the House Ways and Means Committee and included in the Technical Amendments Bill of 1957.
October, 1956	Text and summary of the then designated Technical Amendments Bill of 1957 prepared and released by the Joint Committee on Internal Revenue Taxation and the Treasury Department.
November, 1956	Recommended additions to the Bill and a list of unintended benefits and hardships released by the Joint Committee.
November, 1956	Subcommittee on Internal Revenue Taxation of the Ways and Means Committee held hearings on the Bill.
June, 1957	Ways and Means Committee reported the Bill to the House. The committee deleted the narrow version of Subchapter S from the Bill and recommended that the Subchapter R election passed in 1954 be repealed.
July 15, 1957	President Eisenhower, in the form of a letter to the Chairman of the Committee on Ways and Means, recommended that the Subchapter S provision be included in the Bill.
January, 1958	President Eisenhower recommended a Subchapter S option in his Budget Message to the Congress.
January, 1958	The Bill, renamed the Technical Amendments Act of 1958, passed the House without a Subchapter S provision.
February, 1958	Hearings were held by the Senate Finance Committee. The committee incorporated President Eisenhower's suggestions into the narrow version of the Subchapter S proposal prepared by the Treasury Department in 1956. The committee also reinstated the Subchapter R election.
August 12, 1958	The Senate approved the Finance Committee's version and forwarded it to the Conference Committee.
August 15, 1958	Subchapter S provision accepted by the Conference Committee.
September 2, 1958	The Technical Amendments Act of 1958 signed by President Eisenhower and the Subchapter S provision became law.

Chapter 3

Election and Operation

Not just any business organization can become a tax-option corporation, for the organization must meet some stringent requirements. There are requirements involving stockholders and prohibited income, as well as requirements the corporation must satisfy. Furthermore, if at any time an electing corporation does not satisfy these exact requirements, the election is automatically terminated.

Stringent Requirements

Five requirements deal with eligible shareholders and prohibited income:

1. The requirement of ten or less shareholders limits the election to closely-held corporations. It should be noted that this restriction does not limit the election *only* to small corporations. Large corporations, in terms of total assets, may make the election if they are closely owned.
2. All shareholders must be either individuals or estates. Trusts,[1] partnerships, or corporations cannot be shareholders.
3. No nonresident aliens may be shareholders.
4. No more than 80 percent of gross receipts may be from sources outside of U.S.
5. No more than 20 percent of gross receipts may be from certain passive types of income. (There is a limited exception.)

The requirements that the corporation itself must meet are as follows:

1. The electing corporation must be a domestic corporation organized for the ultimate realization of a profit.[2]
2. Such corporation must not be a member of an affiliated group.
3. The organization must have only one class of stock issued or outstanding. That is, an electing corporation cannot have a capital structure of different types of common stock or of common stock and preferred stock.

These requirements must be continuously satisfied after the

---

[1]The Court in *A & N Furniture and Appliance Co.,* 271 F. Supp. 40 (D.C. Ohio 1967), overruled Regulations that stated that voting trusts disqualify the corporation from an election.

[2]See, for example, *duPont* vs. *U.S.,* 234 F. Supp. 681 (D.C. Del. 1964); *Demler,* T.C.M. 1966-117.

election is made, or the election will be automatically terminated as of the beginning of the tax year in which any requirement is no longer fulfilled. Each of these formal criteria as well as involuntary termina tions are discussed in depth in Chapters 4, 5, and 8. Voluntary termi-nation of the election is discussed in Chapter 10. An annual checklist is provided at the end of this chapter to help avoid the harsh conse-quences of an unintentional termination of an election.

How and When to Make the Election

An election is made on Form 2443 (see Exhibit 3-1) and signed by an officer authorized[3] to sign the Small Business Corporation tax return (Form 1120S). This form is filed in the same manner and same place as the regular corporate tax return. In order for the election to apply for a taxable year, Form 2553 must be filed during the month preceding or following the beginning of the tax year.[4] The first month of its tax year is the earliest of (1) when the stockholders acquire assets, (2) the business begins, or (3) when it acquires assets. The date of incorporation or the fact that no stock has been issued is immate-rial.

In the case of a new corporation, "month" refers to the period beginning with the first day of the tax year and ending with the day preceding the numerically corresponding day of the succeeding month. For example, individuals subscribe to shares and file articles of incorporation on June 17, 1974. The corporation acquires assets and begins doing business on June 29. Before what date must the cor-poration make its election? July 16, at the close of the day preceding the numerically corresponding date in the succeeding month. June 17 is the beginning of the time limit for the election, since, under state law, the subscribers became stockholders on the day the articles of incorporation were filed.[5]

A Subchapter S election may be made even if the principal pur-pose of the election is tax avoidance (e.g., pass through of losses). In one situation the IRS asserted that an election was invalid since the principal purpose of the taxpayer was to offset his personal losses against the corporation's UTI. The Tax Court disagreed with the IRS and indicated that Section 269 may not be used to prevent a Subchapter S election.[6]

---

[3]*Levy,* 46 T.C. 531 (1966).

[4]I.R.C. Section 1372(c).

[5]Rev. Rul. 72-257, 1972-1 C.B. 270.

[6]*Modern Home Fire and Casualty Insurance Co.,* 54 T.C. 839 (1970), *acq.* 1970-2 C.B. xx.

No extension of time can be obtained for filing this election (Rev. Rul. 60-183, 1960-1 C.B. 625). Such an election may not be filed before the corporation is formed.[7] Likewise, if the election is made outside this two-month period, then the election will not apply in the following year since it was not made in the correct months. Permission need not be received under Section 1372(f) to file an election in a subsequent year.[8] Thus, a firm will have to predict at the beginning of the year that a Subchapter S election will be advantageous in the future. Merely an intention to file or a late filing is not sufficient.[9] Further, it must be postmarked within the statutory time limit.[10] A hand-delivered election is not valid even though an election timely postmarked the day before would not have reached the IRS any faster.[11]

Sending the initial election (Form 2553) by registered or certified mail is helpful. A postmarked receipt is prima facie evidence of delivery; whereas, if ordinary mail is used, no record is made of filing. Compare the outcomes of several court cases. In *Round Table, Inc.,*[12] the taxpayer lost because he had no proof that the documents were ever mailed. In *Samuel Zaretsky,*[13] testimony by the taxpayer, his accountant, and his bookkeeper was accepted by the Tax Court to prove that a Subchapter S election and consent were properly completed and mailed within the statutory time period. However, in *Mora,*[14] a taxpayer signed a letter to the IRS requesting Subchapter S status and left it with his accountant. The corporation filed Form 1120S for six years, but in the sixth year the IRS disallowed the pass-through of corporate losses due to the absence of the Subchapter S election. The taxpayer's testimony was insufficient to establish that the election was made, and the Commissioner was not stopped from terminating the election merely because the prior Forms 1120S were not questioned by the IRS. The IRS may not have audited the re-

---

[7]The corporation's Articles of Incorporation must be formally filed; *Frentz,* 44 T.C. 485 (1965); *aff'd* 375 F, 2d 662 (6th Cir. 1967). See *Bone,* 52 T.C. 913 (1969), for another instance of an election that was not timely (ten days late); also *Rowland* vs. *Commissioner,* 315 F. Supp. 596 (D.C. Ark. 1970) (six days late).

[8]Rev. Rul. 71-549, 1971-2 C.B. 319.

[9]*Pestcoe,* 40 T.C. 195 (1963); *In re Round Table, Inc.,* 17 A.F.T.R. 2d 299 (S.D. N.Y. 1965); *M. H. McDonnell,* T.C.M. 1965-125.

[10]*Feldman,* 47 T.C. 329 (1966); the election was postmarked three hours too late.

[11]*Simons* vs. *U.S.,* 208 F. Supp. 744 (D.C. Conn., 1962).

[12]*Op cit.,* note 9.

[13]T.C.M. 1967-247; See also *Frank E. Poulter,* T.C.M. 1967-220, *aff'd per curiam* 397 F. 2d 415 (4th Cir. 1968).

[14]T.C.M. 1972-123; See also *Lyle,* T.C.M. 1971-324.

turns, and even if they had, the Commissioner is not precluded from correcting mistakes of law on later returns.

Where registered or certified mail is not used, an electing corporation and its advisors may still be able to prove that the election was properly filed. However, a court battle can be quite costly, so the least expensive procedure is to retain a registered or certified receipt.

In *Mitchell Offset Plate Service, Inc.,*[15] the electing corporation's attorney testified that the properly signed Form 2553 and executed consent statement were deposited in a mail box in the vicinity of his client's office. The sole stockholder corroborated the attorney's statement. As part of his practice, the attorney maintained a calendar system which reminded him of the filing dates of the material required to organize and qualify a corporation for Subchapter S status. He had a policy of "double checking" with his clients to see that all required materials were prepared and filed on time. Several years passed before the IRS tried to terminate the election, and during this period the records of the IRS service center had been transferred to a new service center. In an enlightened decision, the Tax Court stipulated that the testimony of the taxpayer indicated "a strong presumption of delivery, which calls for an ultimate finding that the documents were 'filed' as required by regulations." Further, "respondent's evidence — negative, at best — that a search of the various files maintained by the Internal Revenue Service failed to disclose any record of the election and consent forms is not, in our view, sufficient to overcome the presumption of delivery."

All persons who are stockholders on the first day of the first tax year affected by the election or on the day on which the election is made (if made after the first day) must consent in writing to the election. Space is provided on the bottom of Form 2553 (see Exhibit 3-1) for the stockholders to consent to this election. However, if separate consent statements are prepared, they should be filed with Form 2553 at the time of the initial election.

Once the election is made, it does not have to be renewed, but all new stockholders, including estates,[16] must file consents to the election within the thirty-day prescribed period beginning with the day on which such party became a new stockholder (see Exhibit 3-2). If the new stockholder is an estate, the thirty-day period begins when the administrator or executor qualifies under local laws, but in no

---

[15]53 T.C. 235 (1969), *acq.* 1970-1 C.B. xv[i].

[16]*Hagerty Oil Co.,* 30 A.F.T.R. 2d 72-5288 (D.C. Mont. 1972).

EXHIBIT 3-1

Form **2553** (Rev. Oct. 1968) U.S. Treasury Department Internal Revenue Service	**Election by Small Business Corporation** (As to taxable status under subchapter S of the Internal Revenue Code)

NOTE.—This election under section 1372(a) (with the consent of all your stockholders) to be treated as a "small business corporation" for income tax purposes may be made only if the corporation is a domestic corporation which meets all five of the requirements stated in instruction A on the reverse.

Name of corporation	Employer identification number	Principal business activity (see instr. E)
The Pamida Corporation	98-7654321	Manufacturing - widgets

Number and street	Election is to be effective for the taxable year beginning (Mo., day, year)
101 University Avenue	January 1, 1973

City or town, State and ZIP code	Number of shares issued and outstanding
Lexington, Kentucky 40500	3,000

Is the corporation the outgrowth or continuation of any form of predecessor? ☐ Yes ☒ No. If "Yes," state name of predecessor, type of organization, and period during which it was in existence.	Date and place of incorporation Lexington, Kentucky January 1, 1965

If this election is effective for the first taxable year the corporation is in existence, submit the following information:

Date corporation first had shareholders	Date corporation first had assets	Date corporation began doing business	Annual return will be filed for taxable year ending (Month)

Name and address (including ZIP code) of each shareholder	Stock No. of shares	Date(s) acquired (see instr. D)	Social Security Number	Internal Revenue office where individual return is filed
1 P. P. Pamida; 609 Canine Way; Lexington, Kentucky 40500	1800	1965	462-08-0402	Memphis, Tennessee
2 W. Y. Pamida; 609 Canine Way; Lexington, Kentucky 40500	1200	1965	302-80-2040	Memphis, Tennessee
3				
4				
5				
6				
7				
8				
9				
10				

NOTE.—For this election to be valid, the consent of each stockholder must accompany this form or be shown below. See instruction D.

Under penalties of perjury, I declare that this election is duly authorized, and that the statements made are to the best of my knowledge and belief true, correct, and complete statements.

Signature and Title of Officer ▶ *P. P. Pamida* .... President .... Date ..January 2......, 1973.

Shareholders' statement of consent (May be used in lieu of attachments—see instruction D)

We the undersigned shareholders consent to the election of the above corporation to be treated as a small business corporation under section 1372(a) of the Internal Revenue Code.

Signature of shareholders and date

1 *P. P. Pamida* 1/1/73	6
2 *W.Y. Pamida* 1-1-73	7
3	8
4	9
5	10

31

event does the period start later than thirty days following the end of the corporate tax year in which the estate became a stockholder.[17] A copy of the new stockholder's consent should be submitted with the next corporate tax return (Form 1120S).

EXHIBIT 3-2

Consent by a New Shareholder to an Election under Subchapter S

(No Official Form)

The undersigned hereby consents to the election under I.R.C. Section 1372(a) to be treated as a Small Business Corporation, made on Form 2553, filed with the District Director of Internal Revenue, New Orleans, on January 18, 1974. It is understood that the taxable income of an electing corporation, to the extent that it exceeds dividends distributed in money out of earnings and profits of the tax year, will be taxed directly to the shareholder to the extent that it would have constituted a dividend if it had been distributed on the last day of the corporation's tax year.

As stipulated in Regulation 1.1372-3(b), the following information is submitted:

1. Name and Address of Corporation:
   The Crumb Corporation, 72-8246890
   210 Long Avenue
   Baton Rouge, Louisiana 70803

2. Name and Address of New Shareholder:
   Darlene Lamer
   2283 Uniformity Drive
   Pierre Part, Louisiana 70801

3. Number of shares of stock owned by new stockholder, the date acquired and and address from whom acquired:
   25 shares acquired on December 28, 2973, from Wilbur Churchill, 1410 North Fork Drive, Port Allen, Louisiana, 70800

7-17-74   DARLENE LAMER
(Date)   (Signature of new stockholder)

If a husband and wife become new stockholders, both are required to file consents[18] even though they are treated as only one shareholder for purposes of the ten-shareholder requirement. Where stock is held as community property, husbands and wives must both file consents.[19] Where a decedent's stock is subject to the possession of an executor or administrator during administration, the estate is a new stockholder even though the stock passes directly to the heirs

---

[17]Regulation 1.1372-3(b).

[18]Regulation 1.1371-1(d)(i).

[19]*Forrester*, 49 T.C. 499 (1968); *Hulsey*, 13 A.F.T.R. 2d 466 (D.C. Tex. 1963); *Clemens*, T.C.M. 1969-235, *aff'd.* 29 A.F.T.R. 2d 72-390 (9th Cir. 1972).

under local laws (Rev. Rul. 62-116, 1962-2 C.B. 207). By now the reader should be convinced that strict compliance with technicalities is necessary to maintain a valid Subchapter S election. For example, in *Lewis Building and Supplies, Inc., T.C.M. 1966-159, appeal dismissed* (5th Cir. 1967), a taxpayer was a shareholder both in his individual capacity and as an executor. The Tax Court held that two consents must be obtained from him as an individual as well as in his capacity as executor. In another case a buyer entered into an agreement to purchase the stock from a taxpayer over a five-year period during which the stock was held in escrow. Since the buyer did not consent to the election and the seller lost substantial domination and control over the stock, the Subchapter S election was terminated.[20]

Where a minor is a stockholder, the consent may be made by himself or by his legal or natural guardian. Even though the stock is held by a custodian under the Uniform Gifts to Minors Act, the custodian cannot consent to the election unless he is also the natural or legal guardian. In Rev. Rul. 68-227, 1968-1 C.B. 381, the IRS stipulated that where the custodian is also the guardian and the consent is given in his guardian capacity, such consent will be deemed to have been properly filed in his guardianship capacity. Likewise, a minor, whose Subchapter S stock is held by a custodian under the Uniform Gifts to Minors Act, is not required to file a consent as a new stockholder when he reaches his majority.[21]

Beneficial owners must also consent to this special election.[22] In *Kean*, 51 T.C. 35 (1968), the Tax Court held that an election was invalid since a beneficial owner of the corporation had not consented to the election. In this case, a brother was not an owner of record but he was the co-owner of stock standing in the name of his brother. Thus, the shareholders must always beware of secret stockholders lest their ignorance result in catastrophic tax consequences.[23] However, an individual who is a mere record holder of stock and who does not have any beneficial interest in the stock does not have to consent to the election.[24]

No extension of time will be granted for filing the Subchapter S

---

[20]*Pacific Coast Music Jobbers, Inc.*, 55 T.C. 866 (1971), *aff'd*. 29 A.F.T.R. 2d 72-816 (5th Cir. 1972).

[21]Rev. Rul. 71-287, 1971-2 C.B. 317.

[22]Regulation 1.1371-1(d)(1).

[23]See also *Morris Kates*, T.C.M. 1968-264.

[24]Rev. Rul. 70-615, 1970-2 C.B. 169.

election,[25] but under limited situations the IRS will grant an extension of time for filing consents.[26] However, there must be reasonable cause for the failure to file such consents and the taxpayer must show that the "interests of the Government will not be jeopardized by treating such an election as valid."[27] See Exhibit 3-3 for an example of a form for requesting an extension of time.

EXHIBIT 3-3

Extension of Time for Filing a New Shareholder's Consent

(No Official Form)

The undersigned asks for an extension of time to file a consent to the election under I.R.C. Section 1372(a) to be treated as a Small Business Corporation, made on Form 2553, filed with the District Director of Internal Revenue, New Orleans, on January 18, 1971.

As stipulated in Regulation 1.1372-3(c), the following information is submitted:

1. Name and Address of Corporation:
   The Crumb Corporation, 72-8246890
   210 Long Avenue
   Baton Rouge, Louisiana, 70803

2. Reason for Failure to File:
   The stockholder in consideration was captured and held as a hostage for twenty-six days by Communist sympathizers in Chile while serving a two-year term with the Peace Corps. The Government will not be jeapordized by treating such election as valid since the corporate tax savings under Subchapter S is nominal. Attached is a schedule showing the tax computation under both statuses.

3. The stockholders will file a proper consent within such extended period of time as may be granted by the District Director.

Under penalties of perjury, I declare that these statements made herein are to the best of my knowledge and belief true, correct and complete statements.

7-21-74	DON PARKER	32
(Date)	(Signature of Stockholder)	(Number of Shares)

Recapture of Investment Credit Agreement

When a regular corporation becomes a Subchapter S corporation, a recapture of investment credit agreement should be filed. Under Reg. 1.47-4(b) (1), a Subchapter S election automatically

---

[25]Rev. Rul. 60-183, 1960-1 C.B. 625.
[26]Rev. Proc. 61-30, 1961-2 C.B. 568, modified by Rev. Proc. 64-20, 1964-1 C.B. 685.
[27]Regulation 1.1372-3(c).

triggers investment credit recapture on any Section 38 property owned by the corporation on the date of the election. In order to avoid such automatic recapture, an agreement must be signed by the electing corporation and by all stockholders on the date the election is filed or on the first day of the tax year in which the Subchapter S election is effective, whichever is later. If the shareholder is a minor or is otherwise under guardianship, this agreement must be signed by the shareholder's natural or legal guardian.[28]

Since there is no official form, a sample agreement has been included (see Exhibit 3-4). In effect, both the stockholders and the corporation must agree to the two following conditions:

1. To notify the District Director of any disposition or cessation of the I.R.C. Section 38 property during the life of the Subchapter S corporation.
2. To assume, jointly and severally, liability for payment of any tax increase which results from such disposition or cessation.[29] In other words, any stockholder, *or* the corporation itself, can be held liable for the repayment of the full amount. Important, however, is the fact that the stockholders are not liable for the repayment of any tax with respect to property acquired before the Subchapter S election when they later dispose of their interest in the business.[30]

The recapture agreement must be filed with the District Director with whom the corporation filed its 1120 income tax return for its last non-Subchapter S year. Likewise, the due date for filing such an agreement is the due date (including extensions) for submitting the last non-Subchapter S tax return. If good cause can be shown, the District Director will permit the agreement to be filed on a later date. The regulations stipulate that the stockholders who sign the agreement should disclose the district in which they filed their returns for the year that includes the final day of the corporation's last non-Subchapter S tax year.

Small Business Corporation Stock

Taxpayers should consider the advantages of issuing I.R.C.

---

[28]Rev. Rul. 70-458, 1970-2 C.B. 3.

[29]Regulation 1.47-4(b)(2).

[30]This was the effect of proposed Regulations, but when the Regulations were made final, this harsh repayment clause was dropped.

EXHIBIT 3-4

Agreement Re Investment Credit Recapture

(No Official Form)

As stipulated in Regulation 1.47-4(b)(2)(ii), the undersigned agree, that in the event of the disposition of any I.R.C. Section 38 property which was taken into account by the undersigned corporation in calculating qualified investment credit in tax years subsequent to the first tax year that an I.R.C. Section 1372 election was effective, to (a) notify the District Director of such disposition or cessation, and to (b) be jointly and severally liable to the District Director for any increase in tax as provided by I.R.C. Section 47.

The Crumb Corporation, 72-8246890
210 Long Avenue
Baton Rouge, Louisiana 70803

By TONY LAMER   NEW ORLEANS
    President   Internal Revenue District

Name, Address, Internal Revenue District of Stockholders	Number of Shares	Signature
Tony Lamer 506 Wright Avenue Baton Rouge, Louisiana 70803 District: New Orleans	210	Tony Lamer
Darlene Lamer 2283 Uniformity Drive Pierre Part, Louisiana 70801 District: New Orleans	25	Darlene Lamer
John Hill 210 North Avenue Baker, Louisiana 70804 District: New Orleans	100	John Hill
Total	335	

1-12-74
(Date)

Section 1244 stock combined with a Subchapter S election.[31] Losses on securities of a regular corporation held more than six months are normally treated as long-term capital losses and are limited to a $1000 deduction per year and must be reduced by 50 percent. The original owner of I.R.C. Section 1244 stock is allowed to deduct as an ordinary loss all or part of any loss sustained in disposing of such stock. How-

---

[31]See S. C. Ward and C. A. Bradford, "Section 1244 and Subchapter S — Two Allies of the Close Corporation," *University of Florida Law Review,* Vol. 18 (Fall, 1965), pp. 270-303.

ever, if a gain results, sucn gain receives favorable capital gains treatment.

An election under I.R.C. Section 1244 must be made at the time the stock is issued. Certain stringent requirements must be met in order to qualify as I.R.C. Section 1244 stock:

1. Only the shareholders that are individuals may receive an ordinary deduction. That is, corporations, trusts, and estates do not qualify for this special treatment.
2. The stock issued must be either voting or nonvoting common stock, issued for money or other property.
3. The stock must have been issued by a domestic corporation under a written plan adopted after June 30, 1958.
4. At the time of the adoption of the plan, the total of (a) the stock offered under the plan and (b) money and property received by the corporation must not exceed $500,000. Further, the total amount of stock that may be issued under the plan plus the equity capital of the corporation may not exceed one million dollars on the date of the adoption of such a plan. It should be noted that debt obligations which are treated as equity contributions under Reg. 1.1371-1(g) may be treated as captial contributions for purposes of Section 1244(c)(2).
5. At the time the loss is incurred, the five-year period immediately preceding the loss year must satisfy either of two conditions:
   a) Less than 50 percent of gross receipts must be derived from passive types of income, such as rents, royalties, dividends, interest, and gains from sales or exchanges of stock or securities.
   b) The corporation has a net operating loss.
6. No portion of a prior offering of stock may be unissued when the plan is adopted or when the I.R.C. Section 1244 stock is issued.
7. The maximum ordinary loss which a taxpayer may deduct under I.R.C. Section 1244 in any single year is $25,000. If a joint return is filed, the maximum amount of loss each year is $50,000, even though the loss may have been sustained by only one spouse. Any amount of loss which exceeds this limitation is treated as a capital loss. Since an I.R.C. Section 1244 loss is a net operating loss, any loss not deductible in a tax year may be carried back three years and carried forward five years against other income. If the basis of Section 1244 stock is increased by UTI, such an increase is treated as allocable

stock which is not Section 1244 stock in order to determine a shareholder's ordinary loss under Section 1244.[32]

A combination of the I.R.C. Section 1244 election with a Subchapter S election can assure an investor of an ordinary loss deduction on any potential loss on his investment. However, the I.R.C. Section 1244 election must be made at the time the stock is issued. See *Raymond G. Hill,* 51 T.C. 621 (1969). Since the Section 1244 election can benefit but cannot harm an investor, it should be made initially, in order to avoid the Commissioner's contention that later additional stock was issued for purposes other than to invest in the corporation.[33] When it becomes apparent that the business is going to suffer net operating losses, a Subchapter S election can subsequently be made.

Consider the following example: On January 1, 1975, a married taxpayer, Mr. P, forms a corporation and pays $150,000 for all of the corporate shares (which constitute small business stock). The Subchapter S election is also made during January. In 1975 the corporation absorbs a $25,000 net operating loss which could be carried through to the stockholder's other income. On January 1, 1976, the taxpayer sells $100,000 of his stock for $80,000 to Mr. G. Mr. P would then have a $20,000 ordinary loss for his 1976 personal tax return (rather than a capital loss). In November, 1976, Mr. G sells all of his stock for $65,000 to another individual. He would then have a $15,000 capital loss, since he is not the original owner of the small business stock. (There is a $1,000 per year limitation on the deductibility of capital losses.)

A formal procedure must be followed for making an election under Section 1244, even though the IRS provides no special forms. The election is a part of the incorporation process. A formal plan is adopted by the shareholders, and notice of such adoption becomes a part of the minutes of the corporation's organizational meeting. Adoption of a formal plan is important in that the taxpayer must be able to prove that the plan existed at the time of incorporation.[34]

It is interesting to note that, unlike the basic Subchapter S election, the election under Section 1244 is not reported to the government. Special forms for this election are available in corporation outfits which may be purchased from legal supply houses.

---

[32]Regulation 1.1244(d)-2.

[33]*Wesley H. Morgan,* 46 T.C. 878 (1966).

[34]*Gerald Hoffman,* T.C.M. 1970-16.

Section 351 Transfer of Property

Upon formation of a Subchapter S corporation, shareholders may have occasion to transfer property other than money for Subchapter S stock. Further, where a shareholder's basis is not sufficient to allow a net operating loss to flow through, the shareholder may wish to contribute enough property to raise the adjusted basis of his stock (or indebtedness) in order that the stockholder's entire NOL would be deductible.[35] Where a taxpayer acquires stock for money, he must generally recognize a gain or loss on the transaction. Such an exchange is a sale or distribution of the property under Section 1001(c); any difference between the value of the stock received and the adjusted basis of the transferred property is a taxable gain or deductible loss. The major exception to this general rule is found in Section 351.

The purpose of this special provision is to permit the transfer of property to a controlled corporation without the recognition of a gain or a loss to the transferer. In essence, "the taxpayer has not really 'cashed in' on the theoretical gain, or closed out a losing venture."[36] Since the Section 351 provisions are not consistent with the Subchapter S provisions, they are applied with respect to both the electing corporation and its shareholders in the same manner that they would be applied had no election been made.[37]

No gain or loss is recognized to a Subchapter S stockholder when two conditions are met. Further, no gain or loss is recognized to the corporation on the issue of their securities where:

1. Property is transferred to the electing corporation solely in exchange for stock or securities of the corporation, and
2. The transferer-shareholder(s) is in control of the corporation immediately after the exchange. Even if Section 1245 or 1250 property is transferred, there is no recapture.

The term "property" includes cash[38] but does not include services.[39] "Stocks or securities" refer to obligations which have adequate continuing interest characteristics. Short-term notes do not qualify as

---

[35]There must be a business purpose for any property loan other than to merely increase the shareholder's stock basis. See *Leroy Hodge,* T.C.M. 1970-280.

[36]*Portland Oil Co.* vs. *Commissioner,* 109 F. 2d 479 (1st Cir. 1940).

[37]Regulation 1.1372-1(c).

[38]I.R.C. Section 351(a); *George M. Holstein,* 23 T.C. 923 (1955); Rev. Rul. 69-357, 1969-1 C.B. 101.

[39]Regulation 1.351-1(b)(2), ex. 1.

stocks or securities.[40] "Control" refers to the ownership of at least 80 percent of total combined voting power, and at least 80 percent of the total number of shares of all other classes of stock.[41] Keep in mind that there can be more than one transferer-shareholder.

An interesting dilemma may confront a thinly capitalized electing corporation if the proportionality requirement of Reg. 1.1371-1(g) is upheld by the courts. If the "securities" are transferred to the transferer-shareholders in proportion to ownership, the "securities" would be classified as "debt," with no election termination, but the debt would not qualify for Section 351 purposes. On the other hand, if "securities" are not in proportion to ownership, then the instruments may be classified as equity (a fatal second class of stock) and would qualify for Section 351 purposes. In fact, not only may Subchapter S shareholders have to meet the 80 percent control requirement, but Reg. 1.1371-1(g) also imposes a more strict requirement, in that transfers may be limited to those involving all shareholders in order to meet the proportionality criteria.

Where a shareholder receives instruments other than stocks or securities, such "boot" is taxable to the shareholder to the extent of any realized gain. The character of the property transferred determines the character of the gain. A loss is not recognized even if boot is received.[42] Boot other than money is given a basis equal to its fair market value.[44] The basis of the property received by the electing corporation is the old basis plus any gain recognized by the shareholders.[45] Where the Subchapter S corporation assumes a liability of the contributing shareholder, Section 358(d) treats this assumption as "money received" by the stockholder on the exchange. This has the effect of reducing the stockholder's basis in the Subchapter S corporation.

The misfortunes of a taxpayer in a recent case should illustrate these rules.[46] Mr. Wiebusch transferred, under Section 351, business assets with an adjusted basis of $119,000 (but subject to liabilities of $180,000) in exchange for all of the stock of a Subchapter S corporation. Since the liabilities exceeded the adjusted basis of the assets, Mr. Wiebusch had to recognize a $61,000 gain ($180,000 - $119,000).

---

[40]*Pinellas Ice & Cold Storage Co.* vs. *Commissioner,* 287 U.S. 462 (1933).

[41]I.R.C. Section 368(c).

[42]I.R.C. Section 351(b).

[43]I.R.C. Section 358(a)(1).

[44]I.R.C. Section 358(a).

[45]I.R.C. Section 362(a).

[46]*G. W. Wiebusch,* 59 T.C. 777 (1973).

Furthermore, his stock basis was zero ($119,000 — $180,000 liabilities plus $61,000 recognized gain). Thus, this shareholder was unable to carry through net operating losses which the Subchapter S corporation incurred in the next three years because he had a zero basis. Section 1374(c)(2) limits any net operating loss to the adjusted basis of his stock (plus any corporate indebtedness).

Duration of the Election

Once a Subchapter S election is made, it remains in effect until the corporation or the government takes steps to remove this status. A corporation may voluntarily revoke its election with the unanimous consent of all persons who are shareholders on the date the revocation is effective. Voluntary revocation is effective on the final day of the following tax year. Moreover, the corporation may find itself no longer eligible for Subchapter S status. Rules for eligibility are considered in detail in Chapters 4, 5, and 8. Involuntary termination is effective on the first day of the current tax year. Under certain circumstances the corporation may desire to remove itself from Subchapter S status with the change effective for the current tax year. Perhaps this can be accomplished by purposely creating a situation whereby the election is "involuntarily terminated." The termination process is considered in detail in Chapter 10. Also considered are the rules governing re-election after termination or revocation.

Relationship of WHTC and DISC

At first glance there would appear to be little relationship between Subchapter S corporations and a Western Hemisphere Trade Corporation (WHTC) or a Domestic International Sales Corporation (DISC). A WHTC deduction is not available to an electing corporation,[47] and a Subchapter S corporation is an ineligible corporation for purposes of the DISC provisions.[48] However, the 14/48 special WHTC deduction or a DISC may be more valuable than Subchapter S, and tax planners should be aware of their benefits. Also, if an electing corporation should have too much foreign source gross receipts for comfort,[49] a WHTC or DISC may be created (with the Subchapter S owning less than 80 percent in the case of a WHTC and the shareholders owning the remaining shares). A Subchapter S corporation must own less than 80 percent of a WHTC, since an

---

[47]I.R.C. Section 1373(d)(2).

[48]I.R.C. Section 992(d)(7).

[49]I.R.C. Section 1372(e)(4); Must have less than 80 percent of gross receipts.

electing corporation may not be a member of an affiliated group.[50] As for a DISC, a Subchapter S corporation can own all of its stock, since, under Section 1504(b)(7), a DISC or former DISC is not a corporation includible in an affiliated group as defined in Section 1504.

A comparison of a WHTC and a DISC is to be found in Table 3-1. Note the similarities between these two and also the similarities with the requirements of an electing corporation under I.R.C. Sections 1372(a) and 1372(e).

TABLE 3-1

COMPARISON OF WHTC AND DISC

WHTC (Sections 921-22)	DISC (Sections 991-97)
Qualification:	
1. Domestic corporation	1. Domestic corporation
2. Gross Income: 95% o/s U.S. — 3-year period 90% active business period	2. Gross Receipts: 95% export-related
3. Assets: No requirement	3. Assets: 95% export-related
4. Capital: No requirement	4. Capital: One class of stock minimum $2,500
5. Election: None required	5. Election: Must elect
Taxability:	
6. Special Deduction: 14/48 of taxable income before WHT Corporation deduction	6. Special Deduction: None Only half of net income taxed directly to stockholders

Dividends from a WHTC or DISC would be classified as passive income for purposes of the 20 percent test.[51] A DISC has at least 50 percent of its taxable income "deemed distributed" to its parent.[52]

---

[50]I.R.C. Sections 1371(a) and 1504(a).

[51]I.R.C. Section 1372(e)(5).

[52]I.R.C. Section 995(b).

Assuming no actual distributions, basically 50 percent of the DISC's taxable income would be taxed to the shareholders as ordinary income dividends (becoming DISC's previously taxed income within the DISC). Whether distributed or "deemed" distributed, the dividends would be treated as foreign-source income.[53] The DISC itself is not taxed, which can result in permanent tax deferral of up to 50 percent of the DISC's taxable income. But in order to maximize deferral, the DISC must pay no dividends. The DISC's stockholders are taxed on their pro rata share of the DISC's earnings and profits.

Any "deemed distribution" is therefore taxed to the DISC's shareholders, becoming previously taxed income (PTI) within the DISC. If this PTI is later paid to a regular corporation, it would not be taxable.[54] However, if this DISC PTI is distributed to a Subchapter S corporation, it would lose its identity as nontaxable income and would eventually be taxed to the Subchapter S shareholders when distributed. This disadvantage may necessitate the ownership of the DISC corporation directly by the stockholders of the Subchapter S corporation.

Where a DISC is set up as a subsidiary of a Subchapter S corporation, any "deemed distributions" may be deferred up to eleven months by having overlapping taxable years. (Keep in mind another deferral of up to eleven months is available by having the Subchapter S tax year differ from its principal shareholders' tax year.) For example, a 22-month deferral could be obtained by having the stockholders on calendar years, the Subchapter S corporation on a fiscal year ending January 31, and a related DISC on a February 28 fiscal year. The Subchapter S corporation would be treated as having received a distribution taxable as a dividend on the last day of the taxable year of the DISC.[55] The Subchapter S shareholders would include UTI (undistributed taxable income) in their taxable income on the last day of the tax year of the Subchapter S corporation.[56] Since DISC corporations and Subchapter S corporations are taxed in the year of receipt where actual distributions are made, actual distributions reduce the deferral potential of overlapping tax years. *Warning*: The Subchapter S corporation must not receive a prohibited amount of passive income.

Where the extra deferral potential of eleven months is not of

---

[53]I.R.C. Section 995(b)(1).
[54]I.R.C. Section 996(a)(3).
[55]I.R.C. Section 995(b)(1).
[56]I.R.C. Section 1373(b).

paramount importance, the DISC corporation may be owned directly by the stockholders of the Subchapter S corporation. Aside from the general flexibility of brother-sister corporations as opposed to parent-subsidiary relationships, there are a number of advantages to this type of organization:

1. The DISC can be owned by trusts and other entities which are not eligible shareholders of a Subchapter S corporation. Thus, the shareholders would have greater flexibility with respect to the disposition of DISC stock.
2. The Subchapter S corporation would not have to worry about receiving a prohibitive amount of income from the DISC.
3. A brother-sister relationship avoids the problem of PTI (of the DISC) losing its identity at the Subchapter S level and being taxed to the Subchapter S shareholders when actually distributed.
4. The PTI of a Subchapter S corporation is personal; whereas under the DISC rules, a transferee of stock which the seller has reported as income (PTI) can receive actual dividends of PTI tax-free.[57]

Where a Subchapter S corporation is engaged in export activities, a DISC offers an unprecedented opportunity to defer U.S. income taxes. A file cabinet and little more than $2,500 capitalization can defer one-half of a company's earnings on export sales without fear of Section 482. Where an additional eleven months deferral is of importance, a subsidiary DISC can be formed. However, greater flexibility can be obtained by having the DISC owned by the shareholders of the Subchapter S corporation. In fact, each stockholder of the electing corporation could have his own DISC.

Relationship with other Provisions

Although an electing corporation is granted special treatment under the tax laws, it still is, in general, governed by those provisions of the *Code* related to a regular corporation.[58] Thus, unless inconsistent with the law under Subchapter S, Sections 269, 382(a), 482, 1551, and the *Libson Shops* doctrine are applicable to an electing corporation.

Section 269 applies (1) where any person (or persons) acquires,

---

[57]I.R.C. Section 996(a)(1) and (d)(1).
[58]Regulation 1.1372-1(c).

directly or indirectly, control of a corporation,[59] or (2) where any corporation acquires, directly or indirectly, property of another corporation (not controlled immediately before such acquisition) by such acquiring corporation or its shareholders with a carryover basis, and the principal purpose for such acquisition was made to evade or avoid Federal income taxes. Where either of these situations occur, the Commissioner may disallow such deductions, credits, and other allowances.

As to the first situation, the Tax Court has indicated that Section 269 does not apply as a way of preventing the use of the Subchapter S election even though the principal purpose of the election may be to flow through large net operating losses. In *Modern Home Fire & Casualty Insurance Company,*[60] the court indicated that the enjoyment of the flow-through benefit of net operating losses (NOLS) is "consistent with the intent of Congress to allow shareholders of electing small business corporations to 'be taxed directly on the corporation's earnings' and to report 'corporate income (whether or not distributed as their own) for tax purposes.'"

As to the second situation, in which a corporation acquires property of another corporation, Section 269 would have little applicability to NOLs, since an electing corporation is unable to use a NOL carryback or carryforward.[61] Furthermore, if the shareholders are unable to use any or all of the NOL because of a lack of adjusted basis in the electing corporation, it cannot be used by either the stockholders or the corporation in future or prior years. However, Section 269 could be used by the Commissioner to disallow other attributes such as capital loss carryovers, investment credit carryovers, surtax exemptions, etc. The provision could apply to the acquired corporation as well as the acquiring corporation. Further, if the electing corporation had NOL carryovers prior to its election and its stock was sold in order to facilitate the utilization of the NOLs, Section 269 might be used to disallow such carryovers. (See subsequent discussion of Section 1551 also.)

Sections 382(a) and 382(b) refer to mechanical restrictions on NOLs; an electing corporation is automatically unable to use a NOL carryback or carryforward under Reg. 1.1374-1. Section 382(a) applies to the purchase of a corporation and a change in its trade or

---

[59]"Control" refers to the ownership of stock possessing at least 50 percent of the total combined voting power of all classes of stock entitled to vote or at least 50 percent of the total value of shares of all classes of stock of the corporation.

[60]54 T.C. 839 (1970), *acq.* 1970-2 C.B. xx.

[61]I.R.C. Sections 1374(a) and 1373(d)(1); Regulation 1.1374-1.

business, whereas Section 382(b) applies to a change of ownership as a result of a reorganization. Keep in mind that a Subchapter S election is terminated when the electing corporation's stock is acquired by another corporation or the electing corporation becomes a member of an affiliated group. Thus, these restrictions would only be applicable to net operating losses which occurred prior to the Subchapter S election.

The status of the continuity-of-business-enterprise approach of the *Libson Shop* doctrine[62] is unsettled as to the 1954 Code. In general, taxpayers have been successful in avoiding its application to 1954 Code years. The Sixth,[63] Eighth,[64] and Ninth[65] Circuits have refused to apply this doctrine to years covered by the 1954 Code. Bittker and Eustice indicate that the *"Libson's* major role will concern transactions and items not specified by Section 381(a) and (c), respectively, as well as the survival of the acquiring corporation's own attributes."[66] Thus, within the parameters as outlined by Bittker and Eustice, this doctrine may be applicable to the Subchapter S area to prevent a taxpayer from merging premerger attributes of one business with postmerger income of another business.

Still another IRS weapon, Section 482, may be applicable to a Subchapter S corporation. This relatively short provision may have wide effects:

> In any case of two or more organizations, trades, or businesses (whether or not incorporated), whether or not organized in the United States, and whether or not affiliated, owned or controlled directly or indirectly by the same interests, the Secretary or his delegate may distribute, apportion, or allocate gross income, deductions, credits or allowances between or among such organizations, trades, or businesses, if he determines that such distribution, apportionment, or allocation is necessary in order to prevent evasion of taxes or clearly to reflect the income of any of such organizations, trades or businesses.

This provision can be used to reallocate deductions and income among various members, but it cannot be used to disallow deductions. There must be two or more organizations or entities, but the term "control" "includes any kind of de facto control, direct or indirect,

---

[62]*Libson Shops, Inc.* vs. *Koehler,* 353 U.S. 382 (1957).

[63]*Frederick Steel Co.* vs. *Commissioner,* 375 F. 2d 351 (6th Cir. 1967) *cert. den.* 389 U.S. 901 (1967).

[64]*U.S.* vs. *Adkins-Phelps, Inc.,* 400 F. 2d 737 (8th Cir. 1968).

[65]*Maxwell Hardware Co.* vs. *Commissioner,* 343 F. 2d 713 (9th Cir. 1965).

[66]B. I. Bittker and J.S. Eustice, *Federal Income Taxation of Corporations and Shareholders,* Boston: Warren, Gorham & Lamont, 1971, pp. 16-69.

whether legally enforceable, and however exercisable or exercised . . . ."[67]

The Subchapter S law has a provision similar to Section 482 — Section 1375(c). This latter provision gives the Commissioner the power to allocate dividends from an electing corporation among its shareholders who are members of a family "in order to reflect the value of services rendered to the corporation by shareholders."[68] In *Rocco*[69] the Commissioner tried to use Section 1372(c) to reallocate dividends from a dozen children to their parents in a Subchapter S corporation. The Commissioner lost, but he argued that the powers conferred by Section 1375(c) were similar to the powers given by Section 482, and a taxpayer must prove that the Commissioner's allocations are unreasonable, arbitrary, or capricious. The Tax Court refused to answer the question as to what standard of proof is prescribed by Section 1375(c).

In *Britt* vs. *U.S.*[70] a citrus grove partnership was incorporated into three corporations which provided for gifts of stock to a number of children. The court ignored the corporations for tax purposes, and the corporate income was treated as that of the individual transfers. Thus, the Commissioner does have broad power to allocate income and deductions. The more limited weapon, Section 1375(c), can be used to allocate dividends among family members of a Subchapter S corporation. Further, the more powerful Section 482 could be used by the Commissioner to reallocate income, deductions, credits, and allowances among related individuals, especially in a brother-sister relationship.

Although a Subchapter S corporation cannot be a subsidiary of another corporation, its stockholders may own stock in other corporations. Thus, a Subchapter S corporation may be a member of a controlled group of corporations. If there is no Section 1378 tax to the Subchapter S corporation, the electing corporation would be classified as an "excluded corporation."[71] But, in a brother-sister situation, the IRS may use Section 1551 to disallow the declining multiple surtax exemption and the declining $100,000 minimum accumulated earnings credit of a related, nonelecting corporation. This section would apply where the brother-sister corporations are created by the transfer of property from their stockholders, and the

---

[67]Regulation 1.482-1(a)(3).

[68]I.R.C. Section 1375(c).

[69]57 T.C. 826 (1972), *acq* 1972-2 C.B. 1.

[70]22 A.F.T.R. 2d 5571 (D.C. Fla. 1968).

[71]Regulation 1.1563-1(b)(2)(ii)(c).

related group is unable to establish "by the clear preponderance of the evidence that the securing of such exemption or credit was not a major purpose of such transfer."[72] This provision would generally not be applicable to Subchapter S members of the group unless there was a Section 1378 taxable gain. In such a situation, however, Section 1551 might be applied to an electing corporation. There is overlapping between Sections 269 and 1551, with the latter narrower in application. (See previous discussion of Section 269.)

The ADR System

The Asset Depreciation Range (ADR) system was instituted in 1971 through Regulations in order to provide a more rapid capital cost recovery method and to reduce controversies between taxpayers and the IRS over useful asset life, salvage value, and repair and maintenance expenditures. After a turbulent controversy over the constitutionality of the Proposed Regulations, Congress codified these Regulations, with some changes, into the Class Life Depreciation System. The major advantage of the system is that it allows a 20 percent variance from the asset guideline period, rounded to the nearest half year.[73] The present tax savings that can be realized by using the shortened guideline lives can provide ample incentive for taxpayers to elect the new system. Perhaps equally important is the opportunity for electing corporations to have more latitude in their depreciation policies and with a reduction in controversies with the IRS. These advantages are not, however, without an associated cost. This cost is primarily the additional record-keeping required by the ADR system.

Annual Election

One of the unique features of the ADR system is that it may be elected each year at the discretion of the taxpayer. Such an election is made by submitting Form 4832 (Revised) on or before the tax return's due date, including extensions of time. Since the election is annual, assets can be depreciated in one year under the ADR system, and under conventional depreciation procedures the following year. It would be to the electing corporation's advantage to calculate its depreciation deduction under both methods each year before elect-

---

[72]I.R.C. Section 1551(a).

[73]I.R.C. Section 167(m). The Class Life System regulations provide a system for determining the reasonableness of depreciation deductions claimed for years beginning after 1970 but before 1971. The Asset Depreciation Range System covers depreciation deductions claimed with respect to property placed in service after 1970.

ing the ADR system. However, if assets are once placed in a vintage account and depreciated under the system, the useful life chosen cannot be changed in a later year by either the taxpayer or the IRS.

Eligible Assets

Practically all depreciable tangible property qualifies for the ADR election if placed in service before December 30, 1970.[74] Both new and used property qualify under this system. However, any used property would be assigned the same guideline life as new assets in the same industry or use. Since it is likely that used property has a shorter useful life than new equipment of the same type, there would appear to be little advantage in depreciating used assets under the ADR system. An exception provided in the system allows used assets to be depreciated separately even if the ADR election is made. The exception applies if the used property placed in service during the year exceeds 10 percent of the value of all eligible property placed in service during the year.[75] If a shorter useful life can be established than is allowed under the ADR guidelines, the exception could be quite valuable in terms of a larger depreciation deduction.

Anytime a useful life can be established for an asset that is less than the ADR, it would be advantageous to exclude the property from the system. However, if the ADR election is made, all eligible property acquired during the year must be depreciated under the system. The exceptions are the used property mentioned above and the following optional exclusions:[76]

1. Property which qualifies for the old (pre-1969) investment credit, but not the "job development credit."
2. Some Section 1250 property on which the taxpayer can establish a shorter useful life than the class life.
3. Subsidiary assets (jigs, dies, molds, etc.) if their total cost is at least 3 percent of the cost of the related assets placed in service during the year.

There are also mandatory exclusions:[77]

1. Property for which an asset guideline class and period are not in effect for the year of the election.
2. Property for which depreciation is computed under a method

---

[74]Regulation 1.167(a)(11)(b)(2).

[75]Regulation 1.167(a)-11(b)(5)(iii).

[76]Regulation 1.167(a)-11(b)(5)(ii).

[77]Regulation 1.167(a)-11(b)(2).

not based on useful life in terms of years (e.g., machine hours, units of production, etc.).

3. Intangible property.
4. Non-depreciable property.
5. Property placed in service before 1971.

Basically, when the ADR election is made, all depreciable assets must be sorted into three classes:

1. Those that must be included.
2. Those that may be included.
3. Those that must not be included.

After the assets are divided into these classes, those that are to be depreciated under the special system are placed in vintage accounts. The term "vintage account" simply refers to the year of asset acquisition. Thus, all assets purchased in 1974 would be grouped into 1974 vintage accounts. The taxpayer can set up as many vintage accounts for a guideline class as he wants and select a class life for each account within the limits of each guideline class. In general, the segregation rules are as follows:

1. New and used property cannot be combined in a single account.
2. Assets of different guideline classes may not be combined.
3. Property which qualifies for the 10 percent salvage value exclusion under Section 167(f) may not be combined with property which does not qualify.
4. Section 1245 property may not be combined with Section 1250 property.

Obviously, the establishment of many vintage accounts entails a large amount of detailed recordkeeping, and this cost may negate some of the advantages of the ADR election. However, if only a few composite accounts are established, the depreciation policies of the Subchapter S corporation are, to a large extent, locked in. For instance, once an account is established it cannot be broken up or combined with another account. Also, the ADR chosen for a vintage account is the useful life for all the assets in the account, even though the system is not again elected. These trade-offs between composite and item accounts must be considered carefully before the ADR election is made and the vintage accounts set up.

First-year Conventions
Once a Subchapter S corporation elects the ADR system, it must select one arbitrary assumption as to the time all eligible prop-

erty is placed into service during the year. Of course, a different convention can be selected in the next year. The two permissable conventions are the half-year convention or the modified half-year convention.[78]

Under the half-year convention, assets in the vintage accounts are assumed to be placed into service equally throughout the year. That is, all purchases or extraordinary retirements occur in the middle of the year. Thus, an electing corporation is allowed one-half year's depreciation for all qualified assets placed in service during their initial year.[79]

On the other hand, a Subchapter S corporation may elect the modified half-year convention. Under this convention, an entire year of depreciation is allowed on eligible property placed into service at any time during the first half of the tax year, but no depreciation is allowable on any assets placed into service during the second half of the year.[80]

To illustrate, assume the following facts in Table 3-2.

TABLE 3-2

When Placed In Use	Guideline Life	Cost	Guideline Life Adopted	Method	Salvage (No Section 167(f) reduction)
1st 6 mos.	00.22	$ 3,000	3	S/L	$ 500
2nd 6 mos.	00.21	22,000	6	S/L	4,000
1st 6 mos.	15.1	80,000	5	S/L	14,000
2nd 6 mos.	15.1	16,000	5	S/L	4,000
1st 6 mos.	15.2	40,000	12	S/L	8,000
2nd 6 mos.	15.2	120,000	12	S/L	25,000
1974 Vintage account		$281,000			$55,500

The depreciation deduction allowable under the half year convention would be $18,600; whereas, $20,333 would be allowable under the modified half-year convention, as computed in Table 3-3.

Salvage Value

When the ADR election is made and assets are placed in a vintage account, it is necessary to estimate the gross salvage value

---

[78]Regulation 1.167(a)-11(c)(2)(i).

[79]Regulation 1.167(a)-11(c)(2)(iii).

[80]Regulation 1.167(a)-11(c)(2)(ii).

TABLE 3-3

COMPARISON OF FIRST-YEAR CONVENTIONS

Class Life		Cost	More or Less than 6 Mos.	Half-Year	Modified Half-Year
00.22	3	$ 3,000	M	$ 500	$ 1,000
00.21	6	22,000	L	1,833	--
15.1	5	80,000	M	8,000	16,000
15.1	5	16,000	L	1,600	--
15.2	12	40,000	M	1,667	3,333
15.2	12	120,000	L	5,000	--
		$281,000		$18,600	$20,333

for each vintage account. This estimate is reported for each vintage account on Form 4832 when the ADR election is made. This requirement applies even though the 10 percent exclusion under Section 167(f) completely eliminates such gross salvage value. Additionally, the salvage value estimate must be as of the year of expected retirement (not as of the end of the depreciable life selected).

Under the ADR system, salvage value is not taken into account in determining the depreciation deduction. However, no vintage account may be depreciated below its salvage value estimate.[81] Of course, the salvage value may be reduced by the provisions of Section 167(f) for determining the maximum allowable depreciation to be taken on a vintage account.

Besides the 10 percent latitude in salvage value allowed by Section 167(f), the ADR system offers an additional 10 percent latitude before the IRS requires a redetermination of salvage value.[82] Since salvage value is only an estimate, this extra 10 percent leeway was established to reduce controversies between taxpayers and the IRS. This provision does not apply if the taxpayer consistently understates salvage values. Since salvage values must be specified when the ADR election is made, memorandum accounts and supporting records of salvage experience should be kept to support salvage estimates.

Two tax-planning objectives should be considered relating to salvage value:

1. Initially, establish the lowest justifiable salvage value for each vintage account.

---

[81]Regulations 1.167(a)-11(c)(1)(i) and (d)(1)(iv).
[82]Regulations 1.167(a)-11(d)(1)(ii) and (v).

2. Reduce original estimates as assets are removed from the vintage account.

The establishment of the lowest justifiable salvage value should be supported by records of calculations and experience. The later reduction of the salvage value estimate for each vintage account is optional with the taxpayer in either of two cases:

1. When any asset is retired from the vintage account.
2. When an asset is removed from a vintage account because it no longer qualifies as eligible property.

It is to the electing corporation's advantage to lower the salvage estimate as assets are removed from an account. This reduction should be made by some reasonable method, such as reducing the salvage value in the proportion of the removed asset to the vintage account. Another method, of course, would be specific identification of the asset and its related salvage value.

Repair and Maintenance Allowance

The ADR system provides a repair allowance limit for each guideline class. The repair allowance is expressed as a percentage for each guideline class and represents a percentage of the unadjusted basis for each vintage account in the guideline class. If repair and some improvement expenditures during the year for those assets in the vintage account are less than the repair allowance, the expenditures are accepted as expenses by the IRS. Expenditures over the allowance, regardless of their nature, must be capitalized.[83]

The repair allowance provision is an option annual election. A Subchapter S corporation may elect to have the repair allowance apply to one guideline class and not apply to others, and it may make the election in one year and not make it in other years.[84] The flexibility of the election and the chance for reduction of controversies with the IRS should make the repair allowance election worthwhile in many cases. However, these advantages are accompanied by the disadvantages of more extended and detailed records concerning each vintage account. These records are necessary both as support for the deductions and as a basis for the decision of whether or not to elect the repair allowance each year.

---

[83]Regulation 1.167(a)-11(d)(2)(iv)(a).

[84]Regulations 1.167(a)-11(d)(2)(ii), (iii), and (iv); Regulation 1.263(f)-1(a). Format of the election could be as follows: This Subchapter S corporation hereby elects for the current taxable year to apply the asset guideline class repair allowance, as provided in Regulation 1.167(a)-11(d)(2).

Certain substantial expenditures which are clearly capital in nature are excluded from the repair allowance. In general, these excluded expenditures are defined under Reg. 1.167(a)-1(d)(2)(vi). Within these limitations, many expenditures, although capital in nature, may be currently expensed if the repair allowance election is made. Conversely, if the election is made and expenditures which are clearly repair expenses exceed the percentage allowance, these expenditures still must be capitalized. In this case it would clearly be to the corporation's advantage not to make the repair allowance election. If the repair allowance is not elected, repair and maintenance expenditures are handled in the conventional manner, even when the ADR election is in effect.

One of the most important features of the repair election is that the percentage limit in general applies to the guideline class and not to specific assets (except for the limitations already noted). Thus, in effect, expenditures made on one asset can borrow the unused allowance of another asset. Since the election is not made until the end of the year, the relative importance of this feature can be judged before the election is made. However, the ability to make an accurate decision requires detailed records whose cost must be balanced against the expected benefit.

Retirement of Assets

Under the ADR system, the distinction between ordinary and extraordinary retirement of assets is quite important. Gains on ordinary retirements are not recognized until the reserve for depreciation exceeds the basis of the account, and losses are not recognized until the vintage account is closed. Instead, proceeds are added to the depreciation allowance account.[85] On the other hand, gains and losses on extraordinary retirements are recognized at the time of retirement.[86] To follow the basic tax planning principle of immediately recognizing losses and deferring recognition of gains, it is to an electing corporation's advantage to classify retirement gains as ordinary retirements and to classify retirements that result in a loss as extraordinary retirements. Even though the definitions of ordinary and extraordinary retirements somewhat restrict the tax planning latitude in this area, there still exist some planning possibilities.

An extraordinary retirement occurs when:

---

[85]Regulation 1.167(a)-11(d)(3)(iii).
[86]Regulation 1.167(a)-11(d)(3)(iv).

1. Any Section 1250 property is retired.
2. A physical casualty causes retirement of a Section 1245 asset.
3. A cessation of a portion of a business involves at least 20 percent of the unadjusted basis of the taxpayer's Section 1245 assets which use the same depreciation period and which are of the same vintage.

An ordinary retirement is any retirement not classified as extraordinary. On an ordinary retirement the depreciation reserve is credited with the salvage realized. If the reserve account does not exceed the basis of the vintage account, then no gain or loss is recognized.[87] However, on an extraordinary retirement the basis of the asset is removed from the vintage account. Any depreciation applicable to the asset is removed from the depreciation reserve account, and any gain or loss is recognized.[88] Also, any retirement that qualifies under other Code provisions as nontaxable or partially nontaxable is treated the same as an extraordinary retirement. In any event, when the last asset is retired from a vintage account, the account is closed and gain or loss is recognized.

Replacement of assets rather than an outright retirement is the more usual transaction in the normal course of business. If the old asset is traded in on a new asset, the transaction would be likely to qualify under Section 1031 as a nontaxable exchange, thereby causing the transaction under Class Life to be treated in the same way as an extraordinary retirement (except that gain is not recognized). In recording the trade-in transaction, the basis of the old asset is removed from the vintage account, and the accumulated depreciation on the old asset is removed from the depreciation reserve account. The new asset would be set up in a current year vintage account if the acquired asset is to be depreciated under the ADR system.

If the old asset were sold rather than traded in, the salvage would be credited to the depreciation reserve account associated with the old vintage account without any adjustment to the old vintage account. The tax planning possibilities of a sale versus trade-in decision depends primarily on the relative size of the old vintage account and its related depreciation reserve account. If the reserve has grown to nearly the size of the vintage account, a sale could result in restricted depreciation or recognition of a gain. A gain would be recognized if

---

[87]Regulation 1.167(a)-11(d)(3)(iii). Where the proceeds from an ordinary retirement causes the depreciation allowance to exceed its basis, a Section 1245 gain is recognized. Regulation 1.167(a)-11(d)(3)(ix)(a).

[88]Regulation 1.167(a)-11(d)(3)(iv).

crediting the salvage value realized to the depreciation reserve account causes the account to be larger than the associated vintage account.

As pointed out earlier, a loss on asset retirement must arise from an extraordinary retirement before such a loss is recognized currently. Therefore, it is necessary to qualify under the definition given for an extraordinary retirement. A retirement due to physical casualty should be documented and if a substantial amount of assets is being retired at the same time, it might be worthwhile to attempt to qualify under the 20 percent rule if a loss is realized or anticipated.

Change in Method of Depreciation

A Subchapter S corporation is allowed the full range of depreciation methods as a regular corporation. Under the ADR system, new liberal rules are applicable for changing the method of depreciation. An electing corporation is allowed to switch from a declining balance method of depreciation to the sum of years' digits method as long as the asset is not used property.[89] Further, a Subchapter S corporation can switch from either the declining balance method or the sum of the years' digits method to the straight-line method of depreciation.[90] Other changes are not permissible.[91] The electing corporation. however, should be aware that the advantage of using accelerated depreciation is nullified to a large extent by the distribution rules in Section 1377 (see subsequent discussion).

Checklist for Use of the ADR System

The following checklist should provide assistance in performing the work to be done for the ADR system and any tax deductions:

1. Prepare schedules of assets placed in use during the tax year, including cost, useful life, estimated salvage, and date placed in use.
2. Determine the guideline classifications for each asset.
3. Record the guideline factors.
4. Select the useful lives, methods of depreciation, salvage values, and the appropriate year to change from the original depreciation method (if any) for each asset.

---

[89]Regulations 1.167(a)-11(c)(1)(iii)(a), (c), and (d); Regulation 1.167(a)-11(c)(1)(iv)(b).

[90]Regulations 1.167(a)-11(c)(1)(iii)(a), (b), and (d).

[91]Regulation 1.167(a)-11(c)(1)(iii)(a).

5. Set up the vintage accounts.
6. Eliminate from ADR any ineligible property and any property elected to be excluded.
7. Select the first-year convention.
8. Prepare the ADR depreciation schedules.
9. Accumulate data for the repair allowance election.
10. Compute repair allowance election results.
11. Decide if the company should elect the ADR system and the repair allowance system.
12. If ADR system is elected, prepare schedules and elections for inclusion in tax return.

A Glimpse Forward

The taxation procedure is complicated and is discussed in detail in Chapters 6 and 7. However, as a preview, suppose we look superifically at the taxation process. The best way to understand the "conduit" nature of a Subchapter S corporation is through several definitions and a simple illustration.

The definitions of two terms are helpful. First, undistributed taxable income (UTI) is the income that is not distributed to the stockholders, but stockholders must pay tax on the amount undistributed. Shareholders must show on their individual tax return all of the income of the business whether or not it is distributed as dividends (constructive income). The income is simply allocated to the shareholders, and they are required to pay income taxes at their personal income tax rates. Second, previously taxed income (PTI) is income that remains in the corporation, but the income has already been taxed and the shareholders will not have to pay tax on it when it is subsequently distributed as a dividend. But, before a corporation can distribute its PTI, it must first distribute current earnings (e.g., it works on the LIFO — Last In, First Out — principle). Furthermore, only the shareholder that actually included the UTI in his taxable income can withdraw PTI tax-free. Thus, if a person dies, or a shareholder gives, exchanges, or sells his stock, the PTI will be taxed again.

Only until recently UTI had to be distributed as cash dividends before the last day of the fiscal year or it would immediately become PTI. This situation caused a serious problem since it was almost impossible to estimate and distribute all of the income before the end of the fiscal year. In 1966, however, Congress helped Subchapter S corporations by giving them a two-and-one-half month grace period after the close of the fiscal year to determine the actual operating results and to distribute the income.

Illustration

In order to demonstrate the taxing procedure and the advantage of distributing income within the two-and-one-half month grace period, an example is appropriate. Suppose a Subchapter S corporation has retained earnings of $200,000 at the beginning of 1973 and earnings during the year of $100,000. Because of the need for working capital, the Subchapter S corporation does not distribute the earnings before two months and fifteen days after the close of the tax year. The $100,000 of earnings (UTI) is taxed to the stockholders even though not distributed (constructively received). In this example, however, the UTI becomes PTI since the income is not distributed; and before the $100,000 PTI can be distributed tax-free, the $60,000 of current earnings during 1974 must be first distributed.

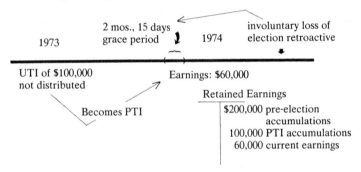

Our example can go a step further. Assume that for some reason the Subchapter S election is involuntarily terminated during 1974. The loss of the election is retroactive to the beginning of 1974, and "locked-in" earnings will result. The $100,000 of PTI will be frozen in the corporation. In order to get these frozen earnings out of the corporation tax-free, all $200,000 of pre-1973 retained earnings, as well as the $60,000 of current earnings, will have to be distributed first.

Two caveats should be stressed. First, if a company keeps its special election, current earnings must first be distributed in order to get tax-free PTI. Second, if the Subchapter S election is involuntarily lost, current earnings as well as retained earnings must first be distributed before the stockholders can obtain tax-free PTI.

Annual Checklist

The checklist below may be placed within an accountant's audit program, a lawyer's review sheet, or a corporation's internal control memorandum. In each case the purpose is to avoid problems that may arise in operating as a Subchapter S corporation.

1. Check to see that Form 2553 and all consent statements have been properly filed when election was made.
   a. Consent statements must also be filed by all new stockholders within the 30-day prescribed time period.
   b. If a shareholder dies, the decedent's estate must also file a timely consent.
   c. Stock owned by a husband and wife as community property, or as tenants by the entirety, joint tenants, or tenants in common requires a consent from each spouse.
2. The corporation must not have more than ten shareholders. Count as one: individual stock held as community property, joint tenants, tenants by the entirety, or tenants in common.
   a. Each shareholder must be an individual or the estate of a deceased individual. Trusts, partnerships, or corporations cannot be stockholders.
   b. None of the stockholders may be nonresident aliens.
3. The corporation must be incorporated within the United States or its territories. Such corporation must be organized for the ultimate realization of a profit.
4. The corporation must have only one class of stock issued and outstanding at all times. Any debt owed to stockholders should be in proportion to stockholdings.
5. The corporation cannot own 80 percent or more of the voting and nonvoting stock of an *active* subsidiary.
6. For an election to be effective, the corporation must have no more than 80 percent of gross receipts from sources outside the United States.
7. No more than 20 percent of gross receipts may be from the following passive types of income: rents, dividends, royalties, interest, annuities, and gains on the sale of stock or securities. However, if the amount of passive income is less than $3,000, this 20 percent requirement does not apply: (1) in the first tax year in which the corporation begins active conduct of a trade or business, or (2) in the next succeeding tax year.
8. The corporation should make arrangements to distribute all earnings to the stockholders each year.

a. Cash distributions should be completed before the end of the two-and-one-half month grace period.
b. Distributions should be made on a pro rata basis in accordance with the number of outstanding shares of stock.
c. Property distributions should be avoided, if at all possible.
9. If the corporation anticipates a taxable loss from operations, each stockholder's basis should be reviewed.
   a. Each stockholder's cost basis in his stock plus his cost basis in any direct debt of the corporation must be at least equal to his share of the anticipated loss or the excess loss can never be deducted by the stockholder.
   b. If his basis is not large enough, the stockholder should contribute the difference to the corporation before year end.
10. The informational return, Form 1120-S, must be filed with the District Director on or before the fifteenth day of the third month following the close of the tax year.
11. The wills of the shareholders should be reviewed to make certain that a deceased stockholder's estate distribution would not result in more than ten stockholders. Likewise, the wills should not contain the typical marital trust clause or other trust arrangements typically used for estate planning purposes.
12. The wills of the stockholders should contain instructions to the executors to file consents to the Subchapter S election.

Chapter 4

Eligible Shareholders

A Subchapter S election is by no means permanent in the sense that it is binding upon the firm for the balance of its corporate life. On the one hand, Subchapter S status may no longer be desirable. Conditions are always subject to change. The shareholders may find that their respective shares of the corporation's undistributed taxable income place them in a prohibitively high tax bracket. In this event, the logical course of action would be to terminate the election and allow the corporate tax to be imposed. Accordingly, the shareholders would be taxed only to the extent of the dividends actually received. This decision must be based upon sound tax planning.

On the other hand, the corporation or its shareholders may create a situation whereby the corporation is no longer eligible for Subchapter S status. In this case, the election is involuntarily terminated and the corporate tax is imposed upon the corporation's taxable income. Moreover, the shareholders are still taxed on the dividends that they actually receive. Thus, an involuntary termination of the Subchapter S election could become quite costly for both the corporation and its shareholders.

As a practical matter, a great deal of tax planning is requisite for merely keeping the election alive. Moreover, the termination of the election should also be based upon a sound tax plan. In Chapter 3, we noted briefly the requirements for Subchapter S eligibility which are specified by the statutes. If the corporation wishes to remain a Subchapter S corporation, it must take numerous steps to insure that no transactions transpire which might jeopardize the election. Along these lines, Chapters 4, 5, and 8 discuss the formal requirements of the Subchapter S election as well as the consequences associated with involuntary terminations.

As stated previously, the corporation may wish to voluntarily abandon its Subchapter S election. Under these circumstances, it can merely revoke its election. However, voluntary revocation may have undesirable effects. These aspects of the problem are discussed in Chapter 10. Therefore, it may be more appropriate to create a situation whereby the election is "involuntarily" terminated.

Requirements to Maintain a Subchapter S Election

At this point, it is appropriate to review the requirements which a corporation must satisfy in order to maintain a valid Subchapter S election:

1. The corporation may have only ten or fewer shareholders.
2. All shareholders must be individuals or estates. Trusts, partnerships, or corporations may not be shareholders.
3. No nonresident aliens may be shareholders.
4. The electing corporation must be a domestic corporation organized for the ultimate realization of a profit.
5. The corporation must not be a member of an affiliated group.
6. The corporation must have only one class of stock issued or outstanding.
7. No more than 80 percent of gross receipts may be from sources outside the United States.
8. No more than 20 percent of gross receipts may be from certain passive types of income.

The first six requirements above must be satisfied when a corporation makes the initial election. This chapter discusses three of these initial qualifications — ten or less shareholders, no nonresident alien shareholders, and all shareholders must be either individuals or estates. Chapter 5 covers the remaining three initial qualifications. The last two requisites must be met after the election has been properly made or the election will involuntarily terminate. These latter two requirements are discussed in Chapter 8.

New Shareholders

The advent of a new shareholder may cause an electing corporation to become ineligible for Subchapter S status. I.R.C. Section 1371(a)(1) states that a Subchapter S corporation may not have more than ten shareholders. Thus, the sale, bequest, or gift of stock to an eleventh shareholder will cause automatic termination of the Subchapter S election. Further, only individuals and estates may be eligible shareholders for a Subchapter S corporation.[1]

Both of these requirements necessitate the determination of who is to be considered a "shareholder." As a general rule, anyone who includes the corporation's taxable income in his gross income is a shareholder. An individual who is a mere record-holder of stock and does not have any beneficial interest in the stock is not a shareholder.[2] Beneficial ownership rather than technical title is significant

---

[1] I.R.C. Section 1371(a)(2).
[2] Rev. Rul. 70-615, 1970-2 C.B. 169.

in that the stock may actually be held by a nominee, agent, guardian, or custodian. However, each person having an interest in the stock is considered to be a stockholder, even though the shareholders are joint tenants, tenants by the entirety, or tenants in common.[3] In 1959, the co-ownership rule was modified for stock owned by husband and wife. Stock held jointly by husband and wife is treated as owned by one shareholder.[4] If both husband and wife own stock in the corporation individually, they are treated as two shareholders. However, if one spouse owns stock individually and both own stock jointly, they are still treated as one stockholder.[5] Note that this rule does not alter the fact that all shareholders must file consents. Moreover, the rule applies only to joint ownership between husband and wife.

State community property laws may present questions relating to the filing of consents. For example, the Texas community property law states that the husband has no interest in the separate property of his wife. Accordingly, one court held that the husband's consent was not necessary when the stock was part of the wife's separate property and allowed the Subchapter S election to stand.[6] However, in *Clemens*, an election was terminated because consents were not filed by all spouses in a community property state.[7]

Courts will probably be reasonable in counting shareholders for purposes of the ten-shareholder rule. For example, one court refused to find a sham transaction in a situation where five shareholders exchanged their stock for debentures.[8]

Trusts

A trust is not a permissible shareholder even though dividends paid to a trust are includible directly in the income of the grantor or some other person.[9] This prohibition greatly restricts the operation of a Subchapter S corporation since such tax-planning tools as short-term or Clifford trusts, *inter vivos* trusts, life insurance trusts, and marital deduction trusts are not available to the stockholders.

A testamentary trust is also not a permissible stockholder. Such

---

[3]Regulation 1.1371-1(d)(1).

[4]I.R.C. Section 1371(d).

[5]Regulation 1.1371-1(d)(2).

[6]*Hulsey* vs. *Campbell*, 13 A.F.T.R. 2d 466 (D.C. Tex. 1963).

[7]*Clemens*, T.C.M. 1969-235, *aff'd.* 29 A.F.T.R. 2d 72-390 (9th Cir. 1972).

[8]*Mazo, et al.*, T.C.M. 1973-125.

[9]I.R.C. Section 1372(a)(2); *Friend's Wine Cellars, Inc.*, T.C.M. 1972-149; *Kean* vs. *Commissioner*, 31 A.F.T.R. 2d 73-344 (9th Cir. 1972), *aff'g.* 51 T.C. 337 (1968).

a trust is often used as a vehicle for generation-skipping. Often a husband will create a trust of his residuary estate for the benefit of his wife and his children. The wife has all the income and certain rights to receive principal from the trust. At her death, any children receive the income for the remainder of their lives, and, upon their death, the final distribution is made to the grandchildren. In *Fulk & Needham, Inc.,*[10] the widow (a life beneficiary) disregarded a testamentary trust as an entity and performed certain actions without regard to the husband's will. But the Fourth Circuit felt that substance and not form governs, and held that the trust could not be disregarded for tax purposes. The Subchapter S election terminated.

Although of questionable validity, the Commissioner will attack a voting trust as a nonpermissible stockholder. Although a voting trust may not necessarily be a trust for tax purposes,[11] Reg. 1.1371-1(d)(1) stipulates that a voting trust is not a permissible stockholder.

Catalina Homes, Inc. was the first case to mention this problem. The Tax Court did not rule directly on the voting trust issue since a shareholder loan to the corporation was held to be a second class of stock. However, the court made the following comment about the government's position on voting trusts:

> However, we do deem it appropriate to note our reservation as to whether these arguments represent a reasonable interpretation of the applicable statutory provisions and the intent of Congress in enacting Subchapter S.[12]

However, in *A & N Furniture and Appliance Co.,* 271 F. Supp. 40 (D.C. Ohio 1967), the shareholders entered into a voting trust agreement in order to insure continuity and stability of policy and management. The wife (and two children) gave the husband an irrevocable right to vote all shares of stock of each stockholder for a period of ten years. Using Reg. 1.1371-1(e), the Commissioner asserted that a voting trust is incapable of being considered a qualifying stockholder. However, the District Court could not conceive of any reason "why, either technically or by implication, a voting trust could be considered a shareholder. . ." "This Court is not excluding the possibility that a voting trust may be considered a 'shareholder' for some purpose other than the Subchapter S election, but it seems clear that Congress did not intend that it be so considered, in reference to Section 1371(a), because the creation of the voting trust did not, and could not, in-

---

[10]*Fulk & Needham, Inc.,* 288 F. Supp. 39 (D.C. N.C. 1968), *aff'd.* 411 F. 2d 1403 (4th Cir. 1969).

[11]See *National Bellas Hess, Inc.* vs. *Commissioner,* 220 F. 2d 415 (8th Cir. 1955).

[12]*Catalina Homes, Inc.,* T.C.M. 1964-225.

crease the size of the electing corporation, nor did it create accounting complications."

Since *A & N* is the first case to involve a direct decision on the voting trust issue, stockholders should move slowly in this area. In a typical voting trust situation, the shareholders transfer legal title of their stock to a trustee who acts as the principal owner (and not an agent).[13] In return for this legal title, the original stockholders are given trust certificates as evidence of benefical ownership. In both Subchapter S situations and other areas of taxation, the incident of taxation depends upon who are the real owners of the stock.[14] Thus, a further argument appears to be that the voting trust is not the beneficial owner and the election should not be terminated. Tax practitioners should watch for further decisions involving the voting trust issue.

There are other alternative control agreements. For example, the legal owner of Subchapter S stock may give another person the authority to vote the shares. Such an agreement may be in the form of an irrevocable or revocable proxy, and, in either case, the only right or incident of ownership affected by the proxy is the power to vote. The shares of stock may be deposited with an escrow or proxy holder in order to stop transfers to persons not familiar with the agreement. Since Rev. Rul. 63-226, 1963-2 C.B. 341 clearly states that an irrevocable proxy is a second class of stock,[15] the safest course may be to have a revocable proxy.

If an estate is held open too long, the Commissioner may apply Reg. 1.641(b)-3 and classify the "prolonged estate" as a trust. Such a situation has been upheld by the Tax Court and affirmed by the Fourth Circuit.[16]

Partnership

A partnership, not its partners, is considered to be the shareholder under Reg. 1.1371-1(d)(1) where a partnership owns stock in a Subchapter S corporation. In one case, the Commissioner attempted to attribute stock ownership to a partnership that had preceded a

---

[13]*Barney* vs. *First National Bank,* 90 F. 2d 584 (Cal. App. 1939).

[14]*Morris Kates,* T.C.M. 1968-264; See also *Ray Guzowski,* T.C.M. 1967-145 and *H.C. Kean,* 51 T.C. 337 (1968), *aff'd.* 31 A.F.T.R. 2d 73-344 (9th Cir. 1972).

[15]Compare the two following cases as to the validity of Rev. Rul. 63-226, 1963-2 C.B. 341: *Samuel Pollack,* 47 T.C. 92 (1966) *aff'd.* 392 F. 2d 409 (5th Cir. 1968) and *A & N Furniture and Appliance Co.* vs. *U.S.,* 271 F. Supp. 40 (D.C. Ohio 1967).

[16]*Old Virginia Brick Co.,* 44 T.C. 724 (1965), *aff'd.* 367 F. 2d 276 (4th Cir. 1966).

corporation. In the process of going from a partnership to a corporation, the shares of stock had been issued in the name of the partnership. The shares should have been divided and reissued in the names of the former partners. Unfortunately, this was never done so the stock was still owned by the partnership. Because partnerships are ineligible shareholders, the Commissioner sought to terminate the election. However, the Tax Court held that the partnership was no longer in existence and that the shares were owned by individuals. Thus, the Subchapter S election was allowed to stand.[17] Nevertheless, it is clear that the original certificates should have been cancelled and reissued, and that an error of this nature should be avoided.

Nonresident Alien

A nonresident alien is not permitted to own stock in a Subchapter S corporation.[18] However, a resident alien may be a shareholder.

Beneficial Owner

As stated earlier, beneficial ownership of the stock is significant in that the law will look through ownership of record and attribute the income or losses directly to the beneficial owners. In one case, the Tax Court terminated a Subchapter S election when the owner of record had filed the appropriate consent but the beneficial owner had failed to do this.[19] Such a catastrophe may be avoided by placing appropriate language in the shareholders' agreement. First, each stockholder should state in the agreement that he (the record holder) is the true holder. Second, the shareholders should agree not to pledge the stock on loans without informing the remaining stockholders. Third, the stockholders should agree to repay any damages resulting from a loss of election from a secret stockholder.

Uniform Gifts to Minors Act

Along these same lines, stock ownership by a minor under the Uniform Gifts to Minors Act may present a source of difficulty in preserving the Subchapter S election. Who should execute the consent form? The Treasury has held that the custodian of the securities under the Uniform Gifts to Minors Act or the Model Gifts of Securities to Minors Act may not file a consent under Subchapter S in his

---

[17]*Ray Guzowski,* T.C.M. 1967-145.

[18]I.R.C. Section 1371(a)(3).

[19]*H. C. Kean,* 51 T.C. 337 (1968), *aff'd.* 31 A.F.T.R. 2d 73-344 (9th Cir. 1972); See also *Kates,* T.C.M. 1968-264; *Ray Guzowski,* T.C.M. 1967-145; and *Pacific Coast Music Jobbers* vs. *Commissioner,* 29 A.F.T.R. 2d 816 (5th Cir. 1972).

capacity as guardian. This consent should be made by the minor's legal guardian or his natural guardian if no legal guardian has been appointed. However, if the custodian happens also to be the minor's legal guardian, the consent can be executed in that latter capacity.[20] In a later ruling, the Treasury held this rule to apply in all cases where a guardian of minor children might be involved.[21] Thus, the legal or natural guardian must file the appropriate Subchapter S consents whenever minor children are involved.

Moreover, the fact that Subchapter S stock is used as collateral to secure a loan has been held not to effect the ownership of the stock for Subchapter S purposes. It was the debtor's responsibility to file the consent, as he remained the beneficial owner.[22]

Failure to Consent

The maintenance of Subchapter S status requires the consent of all new stockholders. In order to avoid termination, a new stockholder must file a statement of consent within thirty days beginning with the day on which he acquires his shares.[23] The statement of consent must show the name and address of the corporation and the shareholder, the number of shares owned by him, date acquired, and the name and address of the previous shareholder or shareholders. (See Exhibit 3-2 for an example of a consent.) The consent should be filed with the appropriate District Director. The corporation should receive a copy of the consent and file the copy with its tax return for the tax year to which the consent applies.[24] An extension of time for filing a consent can be obtained if the election would not have been terminated except for the failure of the shareholder to file a consent within the time limit. The taxpayer must show reasonable cause for the failure to file the consent and must also show that the interest of the government will not be jeopardized if an extension is allowed. The delinquent shareholder, as well as all other shareholders of the electing corporation during the tax year, must file a consent within the extended period granted by the District Director.[25]

---

[20]Rev. Rul. 66-116, 1966-1 C.B. 198; for a more complete discussion, see Crumbley, "Adjusting Gift Programs and Tax Plans in View of the New Gift Tax Climate," *Taxation for Accountants,* Vol. 8 (February, 1972), pp. 96-101.

[21]Rev. Rul. 68-227, 1968-1 C.B. 381.

[22]*Alfred N. Hoffman,* 47 T.C. 218 (1966), *aff'd.* 391 F. 2d 930 (5th Cir. 1968).

[23]Regulation 1.1372-3(b).

[24]*Ibid.*

[25]Regulation 1.1372-3(c).

The Commissioner may refuse to allow an extension of time for filing an extension. However, at least one court has held that discretion was abused when a District Director refused to allow shareholders an extension of time in a situation where the election had been invalidated by the Tax Court. The Ninth Circuit found reasonable cause and ordered that the extension be granted.[26]

Transfers between shareholders do not require a consent. If one shareholder sells or gives some stock to another shareholder in the same electing corporation, a new statement is not required from the stockholder receiving the stock.[27]

In *Richardson Foundation vs. Commissioner,*[28] an estate was composed of a large amount of Subchapter S stock. The decedent's estate filed a consent, and the corporation's tax year ended on July 30, with no cash dividend distributions. The executor had to include as income $650,000 of UTI, which went immediately into distributable net income. The estate could not pay out the UTI since there was no cash available. Subchapter S stock should be removed from an estate as soon as possible, at least before the last day of the corporate year. The estate does not succeed to the decedent's PTI since the estate is a new taxpayer. Obviously, PTI should be taken out of the Subchapter S corporation before a shareholder dies. It should be noted that if the UTI gets into the distributable net income and the will provides that the executor must pay out all income currently, the beneficiaries will be taxed on such income whether distributed or not. A question is raised as to whether UTI goes into fiduciary income. Although this question is unanswered by the Code and Regulations, it would appear to go into corpus. In *Richardson,* the estate transferred the Subchapter S stock to a qualified charity and claimed a charitable deduction. However, the Fifth Circuit denied the deduction on the grounds that to get such a deduction it must be paid from gross income. UTI does not qualify.

If a stockholder does not consent within the time prescribed, the corporation must notify the District Director with whom the election was filed.[29] The Regulations do not stipulate when the notifi-

---

[26]*Kean* vs. *Commissioner,* 31 A.F.T.R. 2d 73-344 (9th Cir. 1972), *aff'g.* 51 T.C. 337 (1968).

[27]I.R.S. telegram to taxpayer, 11/20/61, *Journal of Taxation,* Vol. 16 (May, 1962), p. 319.

[28]306 F. Supp. 775 (D.C. Tex. 1969); *aff'd.* 430 F. 2d 710 (5th Cir. 1970); *cert. denied* 4/5/71.

[29]Regulation 1.1372-4(b)(3).

cation should be sent to the Director, nor do the Regulations provide what action will be taken if the Director is not notified.

A Subchapter S election is not destroyed if stock is redeemed by the corporation.[30] However, it is unclear whether a corporation itself must consent to an election if shares are redeemed by the corporation and held as treasury stock. Stock acquired by a corporation either by purchase or gift is called treasury stock and lies dormant until it has been issued again. It is illogical to require a consent since treasury stock cannot be voted by the corporation, nor is it subject to the payment of dividends in an ordinary corporation. Furthermore, courts have consistently held that preemptive rights do not apply to treasury stock. To be certain of the preservation of the election, however, the electing corporation should file a consent following a reacquisition.

Problems Caused by the Death of a Shareholder

The death of a shareholder can create serious problems which may affect the corporation's status under Subchapter S. However, the appropriate time to consider these problems is in advance of their occurrence. Thus, all stockholders should be made aware of various estate-planning concepts which are necessitated by the Subchapter S rules and regulations.

Estate

Earlier in this chapter, we noted that shareholders must be either individuals or estates. However, the term "estate" in this context refers only to a decedent's estate and excludes estates of bankrupts, incompetents, and minors. Nevertheless, the estates of bankrupts, incompetents, and minors are not prohibited from becoming shareholders as the beneficial ownership rule will cause this type of estate to be ignored for Subchapter S purposes.[31]

Before the shareholder dies, he should make plans for the disposal of his estate in order to insure that this will be done in accordance with his wishes. A trust is not an eligible shareholder, and the corporation's status under Subchapter S is involuntarily terminated if a deceased shareholder's interest in the corporation is distributed to a trust in accordance with his will. This prohibition against a trust creates a lack of flexibility in planning the estate of a Subchapter S shareholder. A commonly used tax-planning tool for a moderate-to-

---

[30]Regulation 1.1371-1(g).

[31]Rev. Rul. 66-266, 1966-2 C.B. 356.

large estate is to leave the decedent's property in a trust providing income for life to his widow. Upon her death, either the remainder is distributed to the children or the trust continues for a specified period of time for the benefit of the children. Since a trust cannot be a shareholder of a Subchapter S corporation, an alternative method must be found. Various devices are available to accomplish the wishes of the deceased. However, sound estate planning dictates that the advantages and limitations of each device be anticipated so that the plan is not destroyed after it is too late to correct its defects. These alternatives are discussed later in this section.

As an estate is an eligible shareholder, there is no problem created by the fact that the estate becomes the shareholder. An estate must file an appropriate consent.[32] Revenue Ruling 62-116 states than an estate must file a consent if the personal representative has any form of administration over the property. Thus, if the state law stipulates that all property passes through the estate because it is subject to the decedent's debts, or because shares in the names of the deceased may be voted only by the personal representative, or because all property is subject to the representative's possession, then a consent must be filed by the estate. The Ruling apparently indicates that under certain state laws it is not necessary for the estate to consent to the election since the legatee is already the new shareholder.[33] To be safe, the estate should file a consent to the election.

This point is made clear in *Lewis Building and Supplies,*[34] wherein one of the major stockholders died, leaving his entire estate to his wife and naming her executrix. She failed to file a proper consent for the estate within the required thirty days, probably because she had consented to the election as a stockholder. Nevertheless, the Tax Court held that since an estate is a stockholder and must file a consent under Section 1371(a)(2), the election was terminated. Also, the Court reaffirmed the idea that the estate is a separate entity for tax purposes and should be treated accordingly.

When a new stockholder is an estate, the thirty-day period begins on the date the executor or administrator qualifies under local law, but in no event shall the period begin later than thirty days following the close of the corporation's tax year in which the estate became a stockholder.[35]

---

[32]I.R.C. Section 1372(e)(1).

[33]Rev. Rul. 62-116, 1962-2 C.B. 207.

[34]T.C.M. 1966-159, appeal dismissed (5th Cir. 1967).

[35]Regulation 1.1372-3(b).

In the confusion surrounding death, the consent requirement is often forgotten. This, unfortunately, works to the detriment of all shareholders as well as the estate and beneficiaries of the estate. Attempts to correct an error of this nature will be futile. For example, in *Hagerty Oil Co.,*[36] the taxpayer argued that the shares in question had been cancelled before the death of the shareholder. The Court refused to allow this line of reasoning which, evidently, could not be substantiated with facts. If the shares had been cancelled, the estate was never a shareholder and no consent is necessary.

A possible solution to this problem may be found in joint ownership of the stock with a right of survivorship. If the stock is owned by husband and wife as joint tenants or tenants by the entirety,[37] ownership of the stock will pass automatically to the surviving shareholder upon the death of the co-tenant. This procedure avoids the need for the estate to file a consent, because the estate will not become a shareholder. Moreover, the surviving spouse has already consented to the election as a co-tenant so there is no danger that the election will be lost for failure to consent. Although the tenancy by the entireties form is available to husband and wife only, the joint tenancy is available to anyone. If the co-tenants are husband and wife, they are treated as one shareholder for purposes of the ten-shareholder limitation.[38] Joint ownership, however, should be avoided if it is contrary to the shareholder's overall estate plan. Additional problems created by the death of a shareholder are considered in Chapter 6.

As a practical matter, it may not be reasonable to expect an estate to file the appropriate consent to maintain the corporation's status under Subchapter S. The executor or administrator of the estate is charged with numerous duties. One very significant duty is the conservation of estate assets. On one hand, the Subchapter S election will increase the taxable income which accrues to the estate. It will be noted in Chapter 6 that income is allocated among shareholders at the end of the tax year. Accordingly, the estate will have a greater liability for federal income taxes if it agrees to continue the Subchapter S election. The additional tax liability may create a real liquidity problem for the estate. This would be especially true if the corporation had not made appropriate dividend distributions. The estate may become insolvent as a result of the increased tax

---

[36]*Hagerty Oil Co.* vs. *U.S.,* 30 A.F.T.R. 2d 75-5288, 72-2 U.S.T.C. ¶9602 (D.C. Mont. 1972).

[37]This form of ownership has been disallowed by statute in some jurisdictions.

[38]I.R.C. Section 1371(c).

liability under Subchapter S in the absence of sufficient dividend distributions to cover this item.

On the other hand, the executor or administrator may materially damage the position of the estate and the heirs in that loss of the election will cause the corporate tax to be imposed. The payment of the corporate tax would reduce the book value per share and accordingly would diminish the worth of the stock for everyone.

On balance, it appears to be in the best interest of all concerned that the election be maintained. If the estate might have difficulty meeting its tax liability, the corporation would be well advised to assist by making the appropriate distributions of dividends to the estate. As a practical matter, the corporation should distribute its earnings on a current basis so the problem of estate liquidity should not arise.

Having accepted the fact that the estate ought to continue the Subchapter S election, how can we assure that the election will actually be maintained? The parties can agree to put clauses in their wills which expressly direct the executor to file the appropriate consent. This suggestion is fraught with difficulties. For example, the shareholder may agree to place this in his will but may not follow through on his agreement. Although the courts have been known to grant specific performance on contracts to make wills,[39] it would be difficult to force the election to be made in time to avoid loss of the election. Moreover, even though the estate files the appropriate consent, there are still problems to be overcome. Eventually the estate will have to be distributed, and steps must be taken to insure that the legatees file the appropriate consent. Failure to secure the appropriate consents will cause the election to be terminated. Also, if the shares go into the estate and are distributed to several legatees, the number of shareholders may be increased to greater than ten. Under these circumstances, the election would be lost.

As a practical matter, an estate is but a temporary vehicle to aid in the settlement of the affairs of the deceased. Once these affairs have been settled, the estate ceases to exist. In *Old Virginia Brick Co., Inc.,*[40] an estate was held to have become a trust because it was kept open for an unreasonably long period of time. Needless to say, the consents filed by the executors were not valid, because a trust is not an eligible shareholder.

Along these same lines, the presence of a trust in the estate plan

---

[39]*Davis* vs. *Jacoby,* 1 Cal. 2d 370, 34 P. 2d 1026 (1934).

[40]367 F. 2d 276 (4th Cir. 1966), *aff'g.* 44 T.C. 724 (1965).

cannot be ignored for Subchapter S purposes even though it may be ignored for operating purposes. In *Fulk & Needham, Inc.,*[41] the Court held that a trust was present in accordance with the deceased's will, even though the beneficiaries ignored the trust as an entity and reported their share of the corporation's net income on their personal tax returns. None of the provisions of the trust were enforced by any beneficiary. Although the results of this case may seem harsh, the whole problem could have been avoided by keeping the Subchapter S shares out of the trust. There can be stockholder agreements whereby the surviving shareholders or corporation could force the estate to sell the stock whenever a transfer to a trust is contemplated. At a minimum, the transfer to a trust can be delayed until the completion of the administration of the estate (but the delay may not be indefinite).

It is most unfortunate that a trust is not permitted to own shares in a Subchapter S corporation. On the surface, this would appear to limit the usefulness of a trust as an estate-planning device. However, the trust can still play an important role in the overall estate plans, even though other plans must be made for the disposition of the Subchapter S stock. Several alternatives are available to estate planners.

Alternatives to a Trust

Stock may be disposed of by specific bequest. This alternative should be especially attractive when the legatee has been active in the business and it is the desire of the testator to have this individual follow in his footsteps. As a practical matter, it is not unfair to bequeth the Subchapter S stock to those relatives who have contributed to the business and bequeth other property to relatives who have no interest in the business. From a tax point of view, this plan will keep the stock out of trust and can help to insure that the number of shareholders does not exceed ten. There are also non-tax advantages to this plan, in that the active participants in the business will not be subject to the excessive demands of sideline shareholders. If the proposed legatees have been active in the business, the direct bequest route probably holds the greatest merit for all concerned. However, if the stock in the Subchapter S corporation would be held by the successors for investment purposes only, the active shareholders would be well advised to consider a buy-sell agreement which would elimi-

---

[41]288 F. Supp. 39 (D.C. N.C. 1968), *aff'd.* 411 F. 2d 1403 (4th Cir. 1969).

nate the estate of the deceased from the picture. We shall consider buy-sell agreements later in this chapter.

Joint ownership of the Subchapter S stock with a survivorship clause provides a way to avoid trust problems in that the ownership of the stock passes to the surviving co-owner at death. If the co-owner has an interest in the business, joint ownership provides an ideal way to dispose of the stock, if this is in accordance with the wishes of the original owner.

As a substitute for a trust, the testator can create a life estate whereby an individual (logically the wife of the testator) owns the Subchapter S stock for life, but at death the stock automatically passes to certain specified remaindermen (perhaps the testator's children). In a life estate, the life tenant is deemed to be the shareholder in an individual capacity so there is no problem with respect to an ineligible shareholder. However, the powers of the life tenant should be restricted in order to insure that he is not held to be a trustee and cause the Subchapter S election to be terminated. One court has held that where wills create life estates and grant broad powers to life tenants as far as the use and dispostion of the property for their needs, a fiduciary relationship is created in that the life tenant also has certain duties to the remaindermen. Accordingly, a trust may be held to exist.[42] This was subsequently declared to be Treasury policy.[43] At best, the life estate is a poor substitute for a trust. Nevertheless, it does allow the testator to control the disposition of the stock through at least one generation.

The usufruct under the Louisiana Civil Code is similar to the life estate which is found in other jurisdictions. The Louisiana Usufructuary has been held an eligible shareholder for Subchapter S purposes.[44] The husband's share of the community property was bequethed to his children with an usufruct for life to his wife. Under Louisiana's law, the wife is eligible for all of the income of the property, although the children actually own the property. The IRS held that the wife, as an usufructuary, is a stockholder for Subchapter S purposes, and she is entitled to all of the usufruct's income, including the dividends paid with respect to the stock. This same reasoning should apply to a legal life estate.

None of these devices provides absolute security for the Subchapter S election. In each case, there is the need for the new share-

---

[42]*de Bonchamps,* 278 F. 2d 127 (9th Cir. 1960).

[43]Rev. Rul. 61-120, 1961-1 C.B. 245.

[44]Rev. Rul. 64-249, 1964-2 C.B. 332.

holder to consent to the corporation's status under Subchapter S. Also, there is an ever-present danger that a shareholder will commit other forbidden acts such as transferring stock to an ineligible or nonconsenting party. For these reasons, the active shareholders should consider buy-sell agreements which eliminate the estate from the picture. Agreements of this nature should be based on sound legal advice. We shall now consider buy-sell agreements as well as general agreements which are effected between shareholders prior to incorporation.

Buy-Sell Agreements

A properly conceived buy-sell agreement should be included in the plans of a Subchapter S corporation. The two most common arrangements for the transfer of stock at death are the stock redemption agreement and the cross purchase agreement. Agreements of this nature offer various advantages to Subchapter S corporations. In the first place, they provide for an orderly settlement with the heirs of the deceased. Second, as a result of the settlement, the estate is eliminated from the picture and control is retained by the remaining shareholders. Moreover, the process creates a basis for placing a value on the stock which was owned by the deceased (Reg. 1.169(a)-2(b), Ex. 4).

Stock Redemption Agreement

The corporation may effect a stock redemption agreement whereby the ownership interest of the deceased is purchased by the corporation. Of course, sufficient cash must be available to the corporation to enable it to purchase the stock. As a practical matter, no corporation could effectively plan to generate this cash internally. Therefore life insurance usually provides the funding for the plan.

Under the stock redemption agreement, the corporation insures the lives of its stockholders naming itself the beneficiary. The corporation pays the premiums on the policies and receives all death benefits under them. Thus, upon the death of a shareholder, the corporation has sufficient cash to purchase the shares owned by the deceased. Although the insurance premiums are certainly "ordinary and necessary" to the operation of the stock redemption agreement, the *Code* expressly prohibits their deduction.[45]

Before an agreement of this type can be considered, the shareholders should determine that the repurchase of stock neither violates

---

[45]I.R.C. Section 264(a)(1).

the corporate charter or is contrary to applicable state law. Usually the law restricts stock purchases to excesses over legal capital. As a practical matter, this is required to insure that the interests of creditors will not be jeopardized by the stock redemption.

Cross Purchase Plan

An alternative to a stock redemption plan is a cross purchase plan. This approach establishes a procedure whereby the shares of the deceased are purchased by the surviving shareholders. Such an arrangement requires the surviving shareholders to have sufficient cash in order to purchase the stock when the need arises. In order to assure that the funds are available when needed, the cross purchase plan is often funded with life insurance. If insurance is used, each shareholder insures the lives of all other shareholders. When a death occurs, the proceeds of the life insurance are used to purchase the stock from the estate of the deceased. Thus, the shareholders are both owners and beneficiaries of the policies. As in the case of the stock redemption plan, the premiums paid on this insurance by shareholders are not deductible for federal income tax purposes.[46]

If a corporation pays the premiums on the policies of the individual stockholders, the insurance proceeds from the policies may be taxed as dividends to the surviving stockholders. In *Ducros vs. Commissioner,* 272 F.2d 49 (6th Cir. 1959), the recipients of the insurance proceeds were not taxed because the proceeds were received from an insurance company instead of the corporation. However, the IRS has stated in Rev. Rul. 61-134, 1961-2 C.B. 250 that it will not follow the *Ducros* case and will classify the insurance proceeds as dividends. Furthermore, if the stock is acquired by a surviving shareholder but paid for by the corporation, a constructive dividend will be imputed to the remaining stockholders under Rev. Rul. 59-286, 1959-2 C.B. 103.

Comparison

It is difficult to assert that one plan is clearly superior to the other in all situations. In fact, it may well be that a combination of a stock redemption plan and a cross purchase plan will provide the best security for all parties. Each plan has its own unique advantages.

Several advantages can be cited in favor of the stock redemption

---

[46]For a thorough discussion of both types of agreements, see Reynolds B. Thomas, Jr., "Buy Outs and Reorganizations," *Trusts and Estates,* Vol. 108 (May, 1969), pp. 447-452, 527-533; Allan E. Abrams, "Tax Planning for Agreements Disposing of a Shareholder's Closely Held Stock at Death," *Georgetown Law Review,* Vol. 57 (June, 1969), pp. 1211-1237.

plan. The number of insurance policies required under it is less than for the cross purchase plan. The cost of a few large policies is less than the cost of a greater number of smaller policies. The plan is much less complicated than the cross purchase plan and will probably not need to be revised after the death of each shareholder. Since the corporation is actually paying the premiums, the plan avoids the situation whereby the smaller shareholders are forced to carry the bulk of the insurance. Also, because the company pays the premiums, the probability that the insurance would be allowed to lapse is materially lessened. Since the corporation is the beneficiary under this plan, the chances that the proceeds would be used for a purpose other than stock redemption are greatly reduced.

Nevertheless, advantages can also be cited in support of cross purchase plans. The insurance policies are owned by the shareholders and are therefore not subject to corporate creditors. The proceeds of the policies are in the hands of the remaining shareholders. Because they actually purchase the stock of the deceased, they receive an increased basis for their stock. Also, the proceeds are tax-free to the shareholders even though they may not be needed to purchase stock. Moreover, the fact that the premiums are paid by individuals will avoid corporate earnings and profits in excess of taxable income.

The evidence does not seem to support an assertion that one plan is clearly superior to the other in all circumstances. The cross purchase plan becomes extremely complicated as the number of shareholders increases. Moreover, a large cross purchase plan may be difficult to control, in that the insurance may be allowed to lapse. However, with only two or three shareholders, the cross purchase plan should be quite effective, especially in a father-and-son relationship. Where there are nine or ten stockholders, they should seriously consider the advantages of stock redemption agreement. In either situation, however, a well constructed buy and sell agreement can best be obtained through the coordinated efforts of the electing corporation's accountant, attorney, and insurance advisor. The reader may wish to review the checklist of the tax and nontax consequences of the two major types of agreement at the end of this chapter.

Avoidance of Termination by New Shareholders

Throughout the book, we have stressed the adverse tax consequences of accidentally losing the Subchapter S election. Regular corporate rates will be applied to the year of termination and dividends during that year will be taxed as ordinary dividends. Thus, it becomes readily apparent that steps ought to be taken to insure that the election is not lost through the improper conduct of a new shareholder. One way to accomplish this is to prohibit by contract the sale of stock to anyone who does not consent to the Subchapter S election. However, it must be determined that such restrictions are the appropriate subject matter for a contract. The common law with respect to restraints on alienation is clearly applicable.

By tradition as well as the common law, one of the privileges associated with ownership of assets is the right to dispose of them as the owner wishes. Corporate stock is certainly no exception. One court held any contract to be void that causes significant rights of ownership to be lost by owners of corporate stock.[47] However, the courts are more reasonable when a clear-cut business purpose for the restrictions can be shown. The preservation of the Subchapter S election is clearly a sound business purpose, and agreements of this nature may be the only way that it can be accomplished with reasonable certainty.

The Subchapter S election may be protected by restrictions placed on the face of the stock certificate, by provisions in the corporate charter, articles of incorporation, or corporate by-laws, or by contracts among the shareholders.

A pre-incorporation agreement between the shareholders can be a useful device in preserving the Subchapter S election. The agreement is intended to set the stage for the formation of the corporation and accordingly considers such matters as the name of the corporation, who will own the stock, the directors, and the by-laws. Moreover, it affirms the intent of the parties to elect and maintain the appropriate status as a Subchapter S corporation.

It is appropriate to examine the aspects of the agreement which are relevant to Subchapter S status. The following agreement is taken from Rabkin and Johnson's *Current Legal Forms with Tax Analysis.*[48]

Agreement to form a Small Business Corporation

7. *Election for tax purposes.* The parties acknowledge their intention that the Corporation shall elect to be taxed as a 'small business corporation' under Subchapter S of the Internal Revenue Code, or such other provisions of law now or hereafter applicable to such election. At the closing, the parties will cause the Corpo-

---

[47]*White* vs. *Ryan,* 15 Pa. County Ct. 170 (1894).

[48]Rabkin and Johnson, *Current Legal Forms with Tax Analysis,* Vol. 6 (New York: Matthew Bender, 1969), pp. 103-105; See also M. J. Jacobowitz, "Shareholders Agreement Must Consider Consequences of Subchapter S Election," *Journal of Taxation,* Vol. 35 (November, 1971), pp. 266-271.

ration to execute the necessary form for exercising such election, each will execute the necessary stockholder's consent, and all will authorize the filing of such election and such consents with the appropriate district director. Such other action shall be taken as may be deemed necessary or advisable by counsel to the Corporation to exercise such election. The parties further acknowledge their intention to continue such election unless they unanimously agree otherwise. None of the parties, without the consent of the others, shall take any action, or make any transfer or other disposition of his shares of stock in the Corporation, which will result in the termination or revocation of such election, and each shall take such action as may be required to continue such election from year to year.

8. *Restrictions on sale of stock.* None of the parties to this Agreement shall sell or otherwise dispose of any of the stock in the Corporation, nor or hereafter acquired by him, except under the following terms and conditions:

(a) The party desiring to sell or otherwise dispose of his stock must first obtain the written consent of the other parties to this Agreement.

(b) In the absence of such written consent, the party desiring to sell or otherwise dispose of his stock must give 60 days' written notice by registered mail to the other parties of his intention to so sell or otherwise dispose thereof. The other parties shall thereupon have the option within said 60 days to purchase all such stock. The election to exercise the option shall be mailed in writing to the party desiring to sell or otherwise dispose of his stock at his address as set forth on the books of the Corporation. The purchase price shall be the book value of such stock as of the end of the month in which such notice is given, such value to be determined by the certified public accountant in charge of the books of the Corporation. His determination as to book value shall be made according to accepted accounting practices and shall be binding upon the parties. The purchase price shall be payable as follows: one-half in cash upon the transfer of the stock and one-half by a promissory note payable one year thereafter bearing interest at 6% per annum. Unless the parties agree otherwise, each party may purchase only that proportion of such stock as the number of shares in the Corporation owned by him bears to the number of shares in the Corporation owned by all stockholders (excluding for the purpose of this proportion the number of shares owned by the party desiring to sell or otherwise dispose of this stock). In the event that all of such stock is not purchased by the other parties, then the restriction imposed by this paragraph upon the sale or other disposition of stock shall forthwith terminate, except to the extent, however, that no sale or other disposition shall be made to any person unless such person is a citizen or resident individual and unless such person submits a consent to the Corporation which will serve to continue the election referred to in paragraph 7.

9. *Option on death.* Upon the death of any one of the parties to this Agreement, the Corporation shall have the option to purchase all the shares of stock of the Corporation owned by the decedent by serving written notice of the exercise of such option on the administrator or executor of the decedent within 90 days after such administrator or executor qualifies. In such event the purchase price shall be the book value of such stock as of the end of the month in which such death occurs, such value to be determined by the certified public accountant in charge of the books of the Corporation. His determination as to book value shall be made according to accepted accounting practices and shall be binding upon the parties, their heirs, executors, and administrators. The purchase price shall be payable in cash against the transfer of the stock by such administrator or executor. In the event this option is not exercised, the administrator or executor of the decedent may sell or otherwise dispose of such stock as he may determine, except to the extent, however, that no sale or other disposition shall be made to any person unless such person is a citizen or resident individual and unless such person submits a consent to the Corporation which will serve to continue the election referred to in paragraph 7.

Paragraph 7 makes clear that it is the intent of the parties that a Subchapter S election be made and furthermore that it be protected. In order to protect the election, the shareholders agree not to transfer the stock to anyone who is unable or unwilling to consent to the Subchapter S election.

The shareholder is provided an orderly method by which he can dispose of his stock in paragraph 8 of the agreement. Earlier, we stated that an absolute restraint on alienation, which has the effect of making it highly difficult for the shareholder to dispose of his stock, would not be upheld by the courts. Under paragraph 8 of the agreement, the shareholder can sell his stock to anyone as long as the other parties to the agreement consent. If the parties do not consent to the sale of the stock, they have a sixty-day option to purchase the stock themselves. If they fail to exercise the option, the stock may be sold to anyone the seller chooses, as long as the sale does not in any way jeopardize the Subchapter S election. Thus, it is clear that the shareholder who wishes to dispose of his stock is provided various alternatives. It is reasonable that the other shareholders be given the right of first purchase when a closely-held corporation is involved. These provisions are designed to insure that the new purchaser will consent to the Subchapter S election.

Similar provisions are provided in paragraph 9 for the disposal of stock upon the death of a shareholder. The corporation is accorded the right of first purchase and the price paid is the book value of the shares, which is to be established by the certified public accountant who advises the corporation. If the corporation fails to exercise its option to purchase the stock, it may be sold to anyone who agrees to maintain the Subchapter S election. An alternative to this approach would be to tie the death option to the sale restriction provisions in that the surviving shareholders might also be accorded a right of first purchase.

One should have no difficulty accepting the premise that a sound business purpose can be found in protecting the Subchapter S election. Moreover, any agreement which provides numerous avenues for the disposal of stock would not be considered an unreasonable restraint on alienation.

Along these lines, it is necessary to insure that all subsequent shareholders are aware of the restrictions placed on the transfer of the stock. In view of this, notice of the restrictions should be placed on the stock certificates. Such notice should contain reference to the agreement and a statement to the effect that the agreement may be viewed at the corporation's principal place of business.

The use of an escrow agent provides additional protection for the Subchapter S election. Under this plan, the stock certificates are all held by a designated individual. It would be his duty to see that the new shareholder is willing and able to effect a Subchapter S agreement before he releases the stock certificates for transfer. The Tax Court has held that the escrow agent is not a shareholder for Subchapter S purposes.[49]

Valuation

The valuation of the stock of a closely-held corporation always presents difficulties, and this is also the case in a Subchapter S context. On one hand, equity dictates that the estate of the deceased be paid a fair and reasonable price for the stock. This price should reflect the contributions which the deceased has made to the enterprise. On the other hand, the loss of a key officer may alter the earnings potential of the firm. For this reason, the surviving shareholders will not wish to pay an excessive price for the stock. Therefore, it is necessary that the agreements provide a basis for valuation of the stock which can be used in settling with the estate. Further, the predetermined price should be reasonable so that the IRS will accept the

---

[49]*Hoffman, supra* note 22.

valuation in the estate tax return, thereby reducing the estate's exposure to a valuation problem.[50]

For estate tax purposes, Subchapter S stock must be included in the decedent's gross estate at either its fair market value on the date of death or six months after the date of death.[51] But when a stockholder dies shortly before the close of the electing corporation's tax year, the undistributed taxable income is included in the decedent's estate if a timely consent is filed by the estate, but the estate is not allowed a deduction under I.R.C. Section 691(c).[52] I.R.C. Section 2031(b) states that the value of closely-held securities "shall be determined by taking into consideration, in addition to other factors, the value of the stock or securities of corporations engaged in the same or a similar line of business which are listed on an exchange." However, in most cases it is almost impossible to find a company comparable to a particular Subchapter S corporation.

Rev. Rul. 59-60, 1959-1 C.B. 237 does list and discuss the eight following factors to be considered in the valuation process:[53]

1. The nature of the enterprise and the history of the business from its inception.
2. The economic outlook in general and the condition and outlook of the specific industry in particular.
3. The book value of the stock and the financial condition of the business.
4. The earnings capacity of the company.
5. The dividend-paying capacity.
6. Whether or not the enterprise has goodwill or other intangible value.
7. Sales of the stock and the size of the block of stock to be valued.
8. The market price of stocks of corporations engaged in the same or in similar lines of business having their stock actively traded in a free and open market, either on an exchange or over-the-counter.

The same ruling indicates that three requirements must be met before a buy-sell agreement will set an estate tax value. First, each

---

[50]Agreements requiring a stockholder to sell stock at a fixed price are normally not effective for gift tax purposes.

[51]Regulation 20.2031-1(b).

[52]Rev. Rul. 64-308, 1964-2 C.B. 176.

[53]This ruling was modified slightly by Rev. Rul. 65-192, 1965-2 C.B. 259 and Rev. Rul. 65-193, 1965-2 C.B. 370; See also Regulation 20.2031-4.01.

party to the agreement must have the first option to purchase the other's shares of stock during their life.[54] Second, there must be a binding agreement upon the administrator to sell the decedent's shares after his death.[55] Third, adequate consideration must be given for the option.[56]

In the sample stockholders' agreement previously discussed, book value was used to determine the value of Subchapter S securities. However, book value is often not a good means of valuing assets for tax purposes, especially where earnings and dividends are involved. (See *Sam F. McIntosh,* T.C.M. 1967-230.)

The use of book value as the formula in a buy-sell agreement may be quite unfair to the parties who die first since the securities must be sold for an unrealistic, low price. Under current accounting practices, the balance sheet shows the assets at their original cost, not at their fair market value. There are several other methods that may be used to establish a value for closely-held securities:

1. A specific amount may be selected and then revised periodically.
2. Some form of appraisal value or a value determined by arbitration may be used.
3. The earnings may be capitalized according to a specific formula.

One popular and simple method of determining the formula in a buy-sell agreement is to establish a specific amount and revise it periodically. Such a method will fix the value of closely-held stock for Federal estate tax purpose if the predetermined price is reasonable.[57] Still another approach is to have the value determined by an appraiser or accept a value set by an arbitrator. However, even one appraisal can be quite costly. Where there are several stockholders, the cumulative appraisal fees after their deaths can become expensive.

If a Subchapter S corporation is to continue after the death of a shareholder, then his estate or survivors should participate in the

---

[54]Regulation 20.2031-2(h).

[55]*Land* vs. *Commissioner,* 303 F. 2d 170 (5th Cir. 1962); *Estate of Littick,* 31 T.C. 181 (1958).

[56]*Hoffman,* 2 T.C. 1160 (1943).

[57]See Leo Schloss, "Valuation of Closed Corporation Stock for Federal Estate Tax," *New York Certified Public Accountant,* Vol. 39 (June, 1969), p. 425.

[58]Raymond Drymalski, Jr., "Valuation of Stock of a Subchapter S Corporation," *Illinois Bar Journal,* Vol. 56 (April, 1968), pp. 672-689.

earnings of the electing corporation for a period after his death. One manner of accomplishing this equitable objective is to capitalize the earnings of the Subchapter S corporation. One commentator suggests that there are basically three ways to capitalize the earnings.[58] First, the electing corporation may be viewed as a partnership and the average of the last five years of earnings may be capitalized at two or three times net profits. Second, the electing corporation may be treated as a regular corporation. Since the before-tax earnings are inflated, the earnings must be restated downward in order to reflect the corporate income tax. The average of the adjusted earnings over a five-year period may then be capitalized at four to ten times earnings.[59] Third, under the present value theory, securities may be valued by discounting to the present value the summation of all dividends expected to be received from the electing corporation.[60] Because of the difficulties involved in the estimation of future dividends, the first and second methods may be more useful for capitalizing the earnings of a Subchapter S corporation.

Redemption of Subchapter S Stock

Dividend payments should be clearly differentiated from payments for the redemption of Subchapter S stock. Such redemptions must be properly timed, or the remaining shareholders may find themselves taxed upon income that was actually shared with the shareholder whose stock has been redeemed.

Regulation 1.1373-1(g)(5) provides an example of this problem:

> An electing small business corporation has taxable income and current earnings and profits of $100,000 for the taxable year. There are no accumulated earnings and profits as of the beginning of the taxable year. During the taxable year the corporation distributes $50,000 in a redemption that qualifies under Section 302(a). The undistributed taxable income of the corporation is $100,000. Since the current earnings and profits of $100,000 are first allocated to the constructive distribution of $100,000, that amount is includible in the gross income of the persons who were shareholders on the last day of the corporation's taxable year.

The Tax Court had an opportunity to apply this concept in *Gordon A. Erickson.*[61] The taxpayer and his Subchapter S corporation entered into a written agreement whereby the corporation would

---

[59]*Ibid.,* p. 688.

[60]Paul F. Wendt, "Current Growth Stock Valuation Methods," *Financial Analysts Journal,* Vol. 21 (March-April, 1965), pp. 91-123.

[61]56 T.C. 1112 (1971), appeal dismissed (8th Cir. 1972).

render his stock at a value which would take certain work in progress into consideration. As the corporation was distributing part of the current year's profit to Erickson, it sought to reduce its taxable income by that amount The Treasury took exception to such treatment, and the Court accepted the Treasury position. The amount paid to Erickson was in redemption of his stock, and the shareholders of the corporation at the end of the tax year had to include the full amount of the corporation's undistributed taxable income in their personal income. The problem could have been avoided if the corporation had distributed its current taxable income by means of a cash dividend before it proceeded to redeem the stock. As discussed previously, a return of capital can occur only if the corporation has distributed its current taxable income in full.

However, a contrary result was obtained in *Henry H. Renard.*[62] As in *Erickson,* the corporation had failed to consider the fact that amounts paid in redemption of stock will not reduce undistributed taxable income even though this was contemplated when the price was established. However, the Judge felt the intent that the payment be a distribution of profits should govern and that substance should prevail over form.

Taxpayers should not rely too heavily on the *Renard* case. As a practical matter, considerable grief may be avoided by proper planning and drafting.

It should be noted that the treatment authorized by Regulation 1.1373-1(g)(5) and followed in *Erickson* represents a windfall to the selling taxpayer. He receives capital gain treatment on amounts in excess of the basis for his stock. Moreover, he obtains no ordinary income as he did not own any stock on the last day of the corporation's tax year.

Redemption Under Section 303

The owners of Subchapter S corporations should not overlook an I.R.C. Section 303 redemption, which provides an opportunity to take assets out of the corporation at little or no tax cost.[63] Under this unique section an estate or the heirs of the stockholders of a Subchapter S corporation may withdraw cash or property from the corporation without paying a dividend tax on an amount equal to the sum of federal and estate death taxes and funeral and administrative expenses. There will be little or no gain or loss on such a redemption

---

[62]T.C.M. 1972-224.

[63]See generally James Nathanson, "The Use of Subchapter S Election as an Estate Planning Technique," *Third Annual Institute on Estate Planning,* Vol. 3 (1969), 69-308.

since the stock will have received a stepped-up basis at the decedent's death.

An option could be created giving the administrator for the decedent's estate the option to require the corporation to redeem from the estate an amount of stock to provide the necessary liquid assets to pay death taxes and funeral and administrative expenses under Section 303. Such an option can be placed in a written agreement between the shareholder and the Subchapter S corporation and should be so designed as to meet the requirements of Section 303.

An estate planner must be sure four basic requirements are met before a redemption can be treated as a distribution to pay death taxes:

1. Any redeemed stock must be included in determining the gross estate of the deceased stockholder.
2. The value for federal tax purposes of all of the stock of the corporation which is included in determining the value of the decedent's gross estate must be either more than 35 percent of the value of the gross estate, or 50 percent of the decedent's taxable estate. The marital deduction generally makes the 50 percent test easier to meet.
3. The amount that can be distributed without dividend treatment is limited to the sum of the death taxes (estate, inheritance, legacy, and succession taxes and any interest thereon) and funeral and administration expenses allowable as a deduction to the estate under I.R.C. Sections 2053 and 2106.
4. The redemption must take place within 90 days after the expiration of the period of limitations for assessment of estate tax provided in I.R.C. Section 6501(a). In Rev. Rul. 69-47, 1969-1 C.B. 94, stock was redeemed more than three years and ninety days after the date the federal estate tax return was filed, but still within three years and ninety days from the date the tax return was required to be filed. Despite the earlier filing of the return, the Service ruled that the redemption still qualifies for tax-free treatment under I.R.C. Section 303, and any qualified cash or property withdrawn is not taxed as a dividend. Therefore, the maximum period for a death tax redemption is four years and six months after the death of the decedent if there is no Tax Court dispute. Where a bona fide Tax Court petition is filed, the stock may be redeemed at any time up to sixty days after the Tax Court decision is finalized.

Even the four-and-one-half year limitation may be circumvented by having the Subchapter S corporation issue notes to redeem the stock. If such notes are not payable during the stipulated time limitation, I.R.C. Section 303 treatment may still not be lost if: (1) the ability to pay for the stock existed at the time the stock was redeemed by the electing corporation, (2) the notes have a fair market value at the time of issuance equal to their face value, (3) they bear at least 4 percent interest, (4) the notes do not represent equity, and (5) all payments are paid on time. (Refer to Rev. Ruls. 65-289 and 67-425 for more discussion.) Thus, a Subchapter S corporation may conserve working capital by extending its pay-out beyond the time limitation. From the point of view of the stockholder, where the price of the redeemed stock rises above its valuation for estate tax purposes, he should try to spread out his gain by using the installment tax method.

Although it is not necessary that the redemption proceeds be in the form of cash, noncash redemptions may not be desirable since funds are most often needed to pay federal and state death taxes and administration costs. However, any property distributions do not actually have to be used to pay death costs. Further, the estate should not be kept open too long. In *Old Virginia Brick Co.,* 44 T.C. 724 (1965), the Tax Court stipulated that an estate eventually becomes a trust and the Subchapter S election terminates.

Since Section 303 applies regardless of the estate's liquidity, qualifying stock can be redeemed at capital gain rates up to the full amount of taxes and other expenses. Furthermore, the Code does not require that amounts received in redemption be used to pay such taxes and expenses, and stockholders may redeem stock that is included in the decedent's estate even though they have no obligation to pay any of the death taxes and expenses. In fact, it is theoretically possible that each redeeming stockholder whose stock passes through the estate could receive capital gains treatment up to the full amount of the taxes and expenses.[64] However, Reg. 1.303-2(g) limits the total amount of the redemptions entitled to capital gains treatment to the total amount of taxes and expenses.

Reg. 1.303-2(f) indicates that executors or administrators of the estate are the most logical parties to this special treatment. This same regulation does allow capital gain benefit to a beneficiary to whom the administrator has distributed the stock, and to any person who acquires the stock under Sections 2031-44, including specific legatees of stock, donees of gifts in contemplation of death, and

---

[64]*U.S.* vs. *Lake,* 406 F. 2d 941 (5th Cir. 1969).

trustees of *inter vivos* trusts, whether or not any of them are respon-sible for the taxes or expenses. This regulation excludes from Section 303 coverage donees or purchasers from a person to whom the stock passed from the decedent and persons receiving stock from the executor in satisfaction of a specific monetary bequest. The Fifth Circuit has invalidated the portion of Regulation 1.303-2(f) that denies 303 treatment to redeeming parties who acquired their stock by purchase where the purchasers do in fact use such proceeds to pay death taxes and other expenses.[65]

Installment Payments of Estate Taxes

A companion to I.R.C. Section 303 is the relief provision of I.R.C. Section 6166 which permits an executor to elect to pay the estate tax in yearly installments over a period as long as ten years. In order to qualify for installment payments, two tests must be met:

1. The value of the interest in the Subchapter S corporation must equal at least 35 percent of the gross value of the estate or at least 50 percent of the taxable estate of the stockholder.
2. The corporation has ten or less shareholders or 20 percent or more of the value of the voting stock of the corporation is included in the decedent's estate.

This second test is automatically met if the corporation is a valid Subchapter S corporation.

If these requirements are satisfied, the executor may elect to pay the estate tax over a ten-year period, in annual installments of two to ten years. This relief election must be made at the time the estate tax return is filed, accompanied by the first installment payment. Interest on the postponed tax is paid at the rate of 4 percent per year.[66] Since an executor is unlikely to distribute all assets while there is still an outstanding debt, this election requires the estate to remain open for ten years. Thus, the Commissioner may try to use the previously-mentioned *Old Virginia Brick Co., Inc.* doctrine to change the estate into a nonqualifying "trust."

Even if the IRS does not attack the open estate, an immediate acceleration of the entire estate tax occurs if any of the following transpires:

1. There is a disposition of 50 percent of the interest in the Sub-chapter S corporation (e.g., excessive redemption of stock).[67]

---

[65]*Ibid.*

[66]I.R.C. Section 6601(b).

[67]Rev. Rul. 72-188, 1972-1 C.B. 383.

2. The installments are not paid when due.
3. Aggregate withdrawals of money or property from the electing corporation equal 50 percent of its value.
4. The undistributed net income remaining in the estate after the fourth installment is not applied in total for payment of the outstanding tax.

There is another relief provision available to the stockholders of a Subchapter S corporation. Under I.R.C. Section 6161, if an executor can show proof that payment of the full estate tax, any installment payment, or estate income tax would result in undue hardship to the estate, the District Director will extend payment of the estate tax at 4 percent interest per year. The primary justification for such an extension is the occurance of substantial financial loss resulting from a forced sale of estate assets at a time when no market exists (see Reg. 1.6161-1(b)).

Finally, under Section 6152, an executor may elect to pay any estate income tax liability in four equal installments. The first installment is due when the whole amount is normally due, and the other three payments are due equally spaced over the following nine months.[68]

Concurrent use of both the provisions of Sections 303 and 6166 requires planning to qualify under both sections. In Rev. Rul. 72-188, 1972-1 C.B. 383, the decedent had owned 100 shares of the corporation's 150 outstanding shares of stock. The stock was included in his gross estate at a value of $500,000. The gross estate amounted to $800,000 and the estate tax was $200,000. Of the $200,000 estate tax, $125,000 was attributed to the corporation stock. The executor and the corporation agreed that the corporation would redeem 10 shares of the stock the first of each November for $50,000 cash during each of the years 1967 through 1976. On December 1, 1967, the estate tax return was filed along with a payment of $87,500. Of this amount, $75,000 was the tax attributable to the estate exclusive of the stock and $12,500 represented the first installment on the remaining tax attributable to the stock. Advice was requested from the IRS whether Sections 303 and 6166 would both apply to the series of stock redemptions and installment payments of the estate tax.

In ruling on this situation, the IRS demonstrated the limitations under both Sections 303 and 6166. It was held that Section 303 would apply to the series of redemptions which fell within the time limita-

---

[68]See generally, J. J. Freeland and S. W. Phillips, "Planning for the Large Single-Asset Estate: A Guide for Practitioners," *Journal of Taxation,* Vol. 36 (April, 1972), pp. 218-225.

tion and the limitation that the redemptions not exceed the amount of the estate tax. In this particular case, the fourth annual redemption would be the last to qualify under Section 303. Since no petition for redetermination had been filed, the time limitation would have been reached before the fifth redemption.

The provisions of Section 6166 applied to this case are somewhat more complex. The primary limitation is that Section 6166 will not apply if 50 percent or more of the interest in the closely-held corporation is distributed, sold, exchanged, or otherwise disposed of. However, Section 6166(h)(1)(B) modifies this limitation in the case of redemptions under Section 303. Under this provision the 50 percent limitation does not come into effect until after the redemptions exceed the amount of estate tax actually paid. In this case, Section 6166(h)(1)(B) applied to the redemptions in 1967 and 1968, since at this time the total redemptions ($100,000) did not exceed the estate tax paid ($100,000); however, subsequent redemptions would exceed the estate tax paid, since each annual redemption was $50,000 and each annual tax payment was only $12,500. At the time that Section 6166(h)(1)(B) ceases to apply, then the interest in the business is valued for purposes of the 50 percent limitation under Section 6166(h)(1)(A). In this case the 50 percent would be $200,000 (.5 x ($500,000 - $100,000) = $200,000). The $200,000 limitation would then be reached after four more redemptions, and the balance of the estate tax would then be due since Section 6166 would no longer apply.

Checklist of Tax and Non-Tax Consequences of Buy and Sell Agreements[69]

The comparison below of the cross-purchase plan with the stock redemption plan assumes that the agreements are funded with in-insurance. To facilitate comparison, each of the fourteen points of the cross-purchase plan corresponds with the same number of the stock redemption approach. Many of these factors are unique to the Small Business Corporation.

Stock Redemption Approach
1. Life insurance premiums paid by the corporation are not deductible.[70]

---

[69]This checklist is adopted from Crumbley, "Buy and Sell Agreements for Subchapter S Corporations," *Trusts and Estates,* Vol. 109 (January, 1969), pp. 17-21, with permission from the publisher.

[70]I.R.C. Section 264(a)(1).

2. Any earnings used for premium payments increase the UTI, which is, of course, taxable to the shareholders according to their proportionate stock ownership (resulting in a corresponding increase in stock basis).

3. Consequently, each stockholder's share of PTI is increased (PTI may or may not be distributed tax-free at a later date, for it will become "frozen-in" at the insured stockholder's death).

4. At the death of the stockholder, any proceeds from the insurance received by a Subchapter S corporation are tax-free as long as they are retained by the corporation.[71]

5. The electing corporation's earnings and profits account is increased by any excess of the death proceeds over the premium cost.

6. Any difference in part 5 above is eligible for capital gain treatment if such proceeds are used for a stock redemption. (See I.R.C. Section 302(b)(3) and Section 303.)

7. The number of insurance policies are minimized with a stock redemption agreement. A few large policies cost less than smaller policies totalling the same face value.

8. A stock redemption is simpler and cleaner. A redemption agreement continues to be adequate even after the death of a stockholder.

9. Stock redemption plans avoid the "transfer for value" problems at the death of shareholders since I.R.C. Section 101(a)(2)(B) provides an important exception to the "transfer for value" rule. This "transfer for value" rule does not apply where there is a transfer to a corporation in which the insured is a stockholder or officer. This exception is a significant advantage of the stock redemption plan.

10. Both the death proceeds and cash values of the life insurance are subject to the claims of the Subchapter S creditors. But the business does own the policies, and they may be used to meet the business needs of the electing corporation.

11. A stock redemption plan avoids having the cost of insurance borne by the stockholders in inverse proportion to stockholdings.

12. Since the electing corporation is the purchaser of the stock, the surviving shareholders do not receive a "stepped-up" cost basis

---

[71]I.R.C. Section 101(a)(1).

even though the value of the survivors' stock may be increased. Thus, a lifetime sale of the stock may result in a much higher taxable gain. However, this disadvantage can be overcome if the survivors hold their stock until death (thereby obtaining a stepped-up basis).

13 Deferred payment terms are often included in an agreement with shareholders, and no interest rate is provided. Any such agreements entered into after June 29, 1963, may be vulnerable to the imputed interest provision (I.R.C. Section 483). The result is that interest income is imputed to the decedent's estate (coupled with a capital loss). This capital loss occurs since, for estate tax purposes, any property has been valued in accordance with the price established in the agreement and its basis is this value.[72]

14. Since the Subchapter S corporation pays the premiums, there is less chance of them not being paid.

Cross-Purchase Plan

1. The shareholders under a cross-purchase plan cannot deduct premium payments.[73]

2. Since the corporate tax is eliminated by the Subchapter S election, premiums paid by the shareholders are not paid with after-tax dollars (which is the situation with a normal corporation).

3. A cross-purchase plan avoids having the premiums that are paid at the corporate level (which become PTI) being "frozen-in" at the death of the stockholder.

4. Any death proceeds are free from federal income tax by the surviving shareholders.[74]

5. and 6. A cross-purchase plan avoids having insurance proceeds that are not used for the stock redemption taxed as dividends to the stockholders when later distributed.

7. Administration and funding of cross-purchase plans become increasingly burdensome as the number of shareholders increases. For example, if there are four stockholders, twelve insurance policies are needed to fund a cross-purchase plan; whereas, only four are needed under a stock redemption plan.

---

[72]I.R.C. Section 1014(a).

[73]I.R.C. Sections 262 and 265(1).

[74]I.R.C. Section 101(a).

8. Rewriting of the agreement is probably necessary with a cross-purchase plan.

9. At the death of a stockholder, his estate will have to sell or transfer the policies to the insureds or to the Subchapter S corporation to avoid unfavorable tax results. If the survivors acquire the insurance policy from the deceased shareholder (in order to continue to fund the agreement) any proceeds of this policy will be taxable over and above (1) the price paid by the transferee, and (2) net premiums paid by the transferee after the transfer.[75] In essence, the surviving stockholders are prevented from purchasing policies owned by the decedent's estate on the life of the surviving stockholders.

10. Corporate creditors do not have a claim against the policies owned by the shareholders. However, the Subchapter S corporation does not have ownership of the insurance policies which may be used to meet the operating needs of the business.

11. Where there is a disparity among shareholders in age or in ownership of stock, the cost will be borne by the shareholders in inverse proportion to stockholdings. For example, suppose Shareholder A owns 90 percent of a Subchapter S corporation and Shareholder B owns 10 percent. Under a cross-purchase plan, the 90 percent shareholder will pay only enough premiums to purchase 10 percent of the stock; whereas the 10 percent shareholder must pay enough premiums to purchase 90 percent of the stock.

12. A surviving shareholder receives a "stepped-up" cost basis for the purchased stock. This increased basis is one of the major advantages of the cross-purchase approach.

13. Just as with the stock redemption plan, the IRS may use I.R.C. Section 483 to impute interest to any deferred payments.

14. Control problems may be encountered with a cross-purchase plan. It is difficult to assure that each shareholder will continue to pay insurance premiums.

---

[75]I.R.C. Section 101(a)(2).

Chapter 5

Qualifications for Subchapter S Election

Chapter 4 discussed three of the initial requirements for a Subchapter S election. In this chapter, the discussion deals with the three remaining initial factors that a corporation must satisfy in order to qualify for this optional tax treatment. A corporation must be a domestic corporation, must not be a member of an affiliated group, and must have only one class of stock issued and outstanding or risk an involuntary termination of its election. The termination is naturally retroactive to the beginning of the taxable year in which the disqualifying act takes place. The corporation will have to pay the normal income tax for the year of termination. Any distributions during that year will be taxed to the recipient as a dividend — a double tax.

Domestic Corporation

A Small Business corporation must be a domestic corporation. A domestic corporation includes associations, joint-stock companies, and insurance companies created or organized in the United States or under the laws of the United States or of any state or territory. It is any group or entity treated as a corporation for income tax purposes even though not organized as a corporation under local laws.

Necessity of a Business Purpose

The above brief paragraph exhausts the information furnished by the *Code* and the Regulations, and some tax practitioners fail to recognize the significance of this characteristic of the Subchapter S corporation. A business purpose may be required in many tax areas: reorganizations, thin capitalization, accumulated earnings tax, transfers to avoid taxes, distributions equivalent to dividends, purchases to avoid taxes, partnerships, transactions entered upon for profit, arm's length transactions, and consolidated tax returns. The Commissioner has not overlooked the opportunity to disqualify and terminate electing corporations by requiring a Subchapter S corporation to have a sound business purpose.

A Subchapter S election cannot be made if the prospective enterprise was not formed for a business purpose. "Though, of course, it is well recognized that a corporate entity will ordinarily be respected, it is equally settled that this is not true under certain circumstances, and that upon examination of all the circumstances it becomes clear that a true business function was not served by the corporate entity, it should not be respected."[1] "Conditions must exist which warrant the conclusion that a particular organization served no actual business purpose."[2]

Even if an enterprise had a business purpose at the time of the Subchapter S election, such election would involuntarily terminate if later the company could not prove that it was operating with a business purpose. The validity of the purpose will probably have to be proven at a later date from the actual creation of the business. Furthermore, the taxpayer "has the burden of proving that there was a business purpose in addition to or other than tax reduction . . ."[3] "The decisive question is whether the corporations were treated to, or did in fact, serve a recognizable business purpose. If so, the same tax consequences would flow from the petitioner's dealings with them as if they were not owned and controlled by him; if not, the Commissioner was not bound to ignore their economic identity with their owner."[4] The election may be automatically terminated if the IRS can show that a Small Business corporation is functioning in order to create a series of losses to be used by the owners on their individual tax returns.

In tax years before 1970, this approach may be used by the IRS to attack so-called "gentlemen farmers" who incorporated, elected Subchapter S status, and deducted heavy losses. In years after 1969, the Commissioner has some new weapons to deal with so-called "hobby" corporations (as discussed further in this chapter). Under the old hobby loss provision,[5] only losses in excess of $50,000 were disallowed even if the corporation had NOLs in excess of $50,000 for five consecutive years. So, in order to supplement this ineffective old hobby loss rule, the IRS may try to use the lack of a sound business purpose to terminate a Subchapter S election.

William DuPont, Jr.,[6] illustrates the necessity of maintaining as a business purpose the "dominant hope and intent of realizing a profit." The electing corporation raised and sold beef cattle. The major shareholder was a wealthy man with a business background, but he did not reside at the cattle ranch.

---

[1] *Thomas K. Glenn,* 3 T.C. 328 (1944).

[2] *Herbert* vs. *Riddell,* 103 F. Supp. 369 (D.C. Cal. 1952).

[3] *David's Specialty Shops, Inc.* vs. *Johnson,* 131 F. Supp. 458 (D.C. N.Y. 1955).

[4] *O'Neill* vs. *Commissioner,* 170 F. 2d 596 (2d Cir. 1948).

[5] I.R.C. Section 270.

[6] 234 F. Supp. 681 (D.C. Del. 1964).

His cattle enterprise incurred large losses annually from 1945 through 1960. The Commissioner maintained that the taxpayer operated the company as a "hobby" rather than as a profit-making organization. The Government asserted that because the taxpayer did not keep records which accurately reflected its profits and losses, this hiatus was indicative of the taxpayer's indifference as to whether the "business" was profitable. As further evidence of the taxpayer's indifference, the Commissioner presented the argument that the taxpayer had never employed a cost accountant or an expert in cattle operations, that no analysis had been made of the ranch's various costs, and that it had never adopted a bonus or incentive plan for the manager's benefit. Understandably, the Government was displeased with the fox hunting and races which took place on the property which the taxpayer leased.

The judge recognized the fact that the taxpayer made most of the important business decisions and the manager of the ranch followed the instructions of the stockholder.

The judge asserted that a series of annual heavy losses incurred during 1945-1960 did not alone make the operation a hobby or indicate that a profit was not the objective of the ranch. The company's records had been inaccurate in certain respects, but the judge did not think that the taxpayer was indifferent as to whether the operations were profitable. Also, the judge was impressed with the many and various efforts employed to improve the operations in order to establish the cattle ranch on a profitable basis. Such efforts as reduction in the labor force to decrease expenses and experiments with new feeds to improve the cattle were introduced to show that a profit motive was present.

Significantly, the judge felt that there must be a *bona fide* interest in making the electing corporation a profitable business. However, the judge did not attach much weight to the Commissioner's argument that the taxpayer's haphazard bookkeeping was indicative of his indifference to profit or that a cost accountant is necessary for a profitable business. Furthermore, the lack of an incentive plan for key personnel evidently does not prove that a profit motive is not a principal purpose of the business. The judge upheld the Subchapter S election. (This case and the two following cases occurred before the new weapons were added by the Tax Reform Bill of 1969.)

In *Seven Sixty Ranch Co.* vs. *Kennedy,*[7] a judge allowed a rancher to carry back a net operating loss of a Subchapter S corporation

---

[7] 66-1 U.S.T.C. ¶9293, 17 A.F.T.R. 2d 587 (D.C. Wyo. 1966).

against the rancher's individual income. The taxpayer asserted that the NOL was due to an unusually severe winter, wet spring, and a summer drought (which he could not have anticipated). Also, since the market price of beef cattle had declined, the court felt that the taxpayer had a "dominant hope and intent to realize a profit." The NOL was allowed.

In another case, *Norman Demler,*[8] the taxpayer formed a corporation in order to design a car to be used exclusively in the Indianapolis 500. Between 1957 and 1965 the electing corporation incurred losses in each year except 1965, even though the car won prize money in varying amounts.

The Tax Court ruled that whether an activity is a "trade or business" depends upon the facts in each situation, but this determination becomes more difficult where the "more sportive segment of the citizenry and their characteristic exploits are involved." However, merely because the activity of racing had been a previous hobby of the taxpayer does not prove that the corporation is not now engaged in a trade or business. One "big win" could turn a loss activity into a very profitable enterprise. The Court ruled that the Subchapter S election was not terminated. This electing corporation had a profit motive which was sufficient to convince the court that it was operating a legitimate trade or business.

Beginning in tax years after 1969, any deductions of a Subchapter S corporation from "activities not engaged in for a profit" are deductible only to the extent of hobby income. However, certain expenses (i.e., interest, taxes, casualty losses) are deductible even if the activity is a hobby, but such expenses do not reduce the hobby income which could otherwise be offset against hobby expenses.

I.R.C. Section 183(d) does establish a presumption that an electing corporation has a profit motive if a profit occurs in two out of five consecutive years. If the Subchapter S corporation breeds, trains, shows, or races horses, a profit has to be shown only in two out of seven consecutive years. The IRS initially applied a literal interpretation of these rules and would not allow a Subchapter S corporation to take advantage of the presumption if it had not shown a profit year after starting the activity. Only taxable years beginning after December 31, 1969, count in identifying the tax year in which the electing corporation first engaged in the activity. Under the Revenue Act of 1971, a Subchapter S corporation may elect to delay a determination as to whether the Section 183(d) presumption applies until

---

[8]*Norman Demler,* T.C.M. 1966-117; See also *Joseph W. Curran,* T.C.M. 1970-160.

the end of the fourth tax year after the tax year in which the electing corporation first engages in the activity (the sixth year in the case of horse breeding, training, showing, or racing). An electing corporation must execute a waiver of the statute of limitations in order to make this new election which is available for tax years beginning after December 31, 1969.

Even though a Subchapter S corporation satisfies the two-year profit rule, the IRS can still classify the NOLs as hobby losses, but the Commissioner will have to prove that the activity was not for a profit. Further, where the electing corporation does not satisfy the two-year profit rule, it has the burden of proving a profit motive.

For tax years beginning after 1969, the IRS has several other weapons to combat the "gentlemen farmers."

One weapon is the "excess deduction account" (EDA). The EDA accumulates the electing corporation's current farm losses that exceed $25,000 in any year after 1969 where non-farm adjusted gross income exceeds $50,000. Non-farm adjusted gross income means taxable income computed without regard to income or deductions attributable to the business of farming. The electing corporation must add to its own non-farm income the non-farm income of whichever of its stockholders has the greatest amount of such income. If the combined non-farm income exceeds $50,000, the electing corporation must make an addition to its EDA for any net farm loss in excess of $25,000. Further, the electing corporation is not allowed the $25,000 exemption if any one of its stockholders also has a net farm loss or if any one of its stockholders is a stockholder in another Subchapter S corporation which has a net farm loss. This latter rule, which is effective for tax years ending after December 10, 1971, eliminates the possibility of using multiple Subchapter S corporations in order to obtain the $25,000 exemption.[9]

Although these losses are deductible as incurred, any amount in the EDA not reduced by future net farm income is recaptured as ordinary income when any related depreciable realty or farm land is sold at a gain. When such assets are sold and there is an amount in the EDA, any gain is ordinary income to the extent of the lesser of (1) the realized gain, or (2) the amount in the EDA. The mechanics of this new section may be illustrated by the following:

Dlar, Inc., a Subchapter S corporation, has three stockholders whose non-farm adjusted gross incomes are as follows:

[9]I.R.C. Section 1251(b)(2)(B).

	Stockholder A	Stockholder B	Stockholder C
1970	$22,000	$19,000	$16,000
1971	22,000	14,000	17,000
1972	19,000	18,000	23,000
1973	20,000	18,000	22,000
1974	17,000	19,000	20,000

The electing corporation incurs the following transactions:

	Farm income or (loss)	Non-farm AGI
1970	($40,000)	$42,000
1971	(40,000)	28,000
1972	(22,000)	60,000
1973	10,000	42,000
1974	(40,000)	47,000

If none of the stockholders has a personal net farm loss and none is a shareholder in another Subchapter S corporation, the amount in the EDA at the end of 1974 would be $20,000. If the electing corporation sells some farm assets for a realized gain of $15,000, the entire amount would be ordinary income, with $5,000 remaining in the EDA. However, if the electing corporation sells the farm assets for $25,000, the electing corporation would have $20,000 of ordinary income and $5,000 capital gain, with zero remaining in the EDA.

Three comments are appropriate as to the effectiveness of Section 1251. First, this new recapture provision does not consider the time value of money. Any farm losses may be used as incurred in order to save taxes, and, where such tax savings are invested, substantial earnings may still occur over time. Second, death tends to erase any EDA at the individual level since beneficiaries receive a stepped-up basis in farm assets equal to the fair market value of the farm assets.[10] But death does not eliminate the EDA at the Subchapter S level, so, in this respect, it may not be advantageous to have a Subchapter S corporation accumulate net farm losses. Third, in the case of a gift, the donor is not subject to recapture, but the donee acquires the donor's EDA if the potential gain on all gifts made within a one-year period is more than 25 percent of the potential gain on all farm recapture assets owned by the donor immediately prior to the first gift.[11]

Section 1250 property is excluded from the definition of farm recapture assets, and each recapture provision operates indepen-

---

[10]I.R.C. Sections 1251(d)(1) and (2).
[11]I.R.C. Section 1251(b)(5)(B).

dently of the other.[12] Thus, any income recognized under Section 1250 enters into the computation of farm net income or loss and reduces the EDA of the electing corporation. Most farm recapture assets are also Section 1245 property, and the priority of Section 1245 or 1251 is unclear from the *Code* and Committee Reports. Since only farm net income or gains from the sale or exchange of farm recapture assets taxed as ordinary income solely by reasons of Section 1251 reduces the electing corporation's EDA,[13] a Subchapter S corporation will wish to apply Section 1251 first in order to reduce both the EDA and the amount subject to Section 1245 recapture. Obviously, the IRS may attempt to apply Section 1245 first since the EDA would not be reduced.

Another weapon the IRS can use to combat "gentlemen farmers" for tax years after 1969 is the provision that the exchange of livestock of different sexes may no longer receive tax-free exchange treatment.[14]

The IRS has still another weapon at its disposal. Even if a taxpayer has no amount in his EDA, any gain on the disposition of farm land is taxed as ordinary income to the extent of a declining percentage of post-1969 deductible soil and water conservation expenditures (Section 175 expenses) and expenditures for clearing of land (Section 182 expenses):[15]

If Land Held	Recapture this % of Deductible Expenditures
5 years or less	100%
6 years	80%
7 years	60%
8 years	40%
9 years	20%
10 years	none

To the extent that Section 1251 applies, it will have precedence over Section 1252.[16]

Tax Planning for a Business Purpose

Thus, under both the old and new hobby loss rules, there is a need for an electing corporation to have a sound business purpose.

---

[12] I.R.C. Section 1251(e)(1)(A).
[13] I.R.C. Section 1251(b)(3).
[14] I.R.C. Section 1031(e).
[15] I.R.C. Section 1252(a).
[16] I.R.C. Section 1252(a)(1).

What actions and precautions can be taken by shareholders of a Subchapter S corporation to assure that the election is not terminated and NOLs are not disallowed? Whether an electing corporation is treated as a valid tax entity usually depends upon the purpose for the formation of the corporation.

The doctrine of corporate entity fills a useful purpose in business life. Whether the purpose be to gain an advantage under the law of the state of incorporation or to avoid or to comply with the demands of creditors or to serve the creditor's personal or undisclosed convenience so long as that purpose is the equivalent of business activity or is followed by the carrying on of business by the corporation, the corporation remains a separate taxable entity.[17]

The *L.B. Whitfield Estate* case can serve as a guideline for a valid business purpose:

If the . . . Co. had no purpose other than to hold bare title, and did not engage in business, as petitioners assert, the case would fall within a recognized exception to the general rule. . . Here, there were other purposes, and the formation of the corporation was followed by activities sufficient to constitute a business separate from the individual.[18]

A sound business purpose for the operation of a company should be present when the parties elect to be taxed as a Subchapter S corporation. It must be proven by the taxpayers that the purpose existed at the date of election. "The controlling intention of the taxpayer is that which is manifested at the time . . . not subsequently declared intentions which are merely the products of afterthought."[19] Beware, however, the validity of the purpose may have to be established at a later date.[20]

Where a corporation is formed for a legitimate business purpose, such purpose should be pursued. Contemporary evidence should be retained. ("Nowhere in the record can we find any convincing indicia of business motive, good faith, intent, or anything else that might erase the surface impression of a tax dodge."[21]) Efforts should be made to eliminate as many errors as possible from the bookkeeping

---

[17]*Moline Properties, Inc.* vs. *Commissioner,* 319 U.S. 436 (1943).

[18]*L. B. Whitfield Estate,* 14 T.C. 776 (1950).

[19]*The Smoot Sand and Gravel Corp.* vs. *Commissioner,* 241 F. 2d 197 (4th Cir. 1957).

[20]See Robert S. Holzman, *Sound Business Purpose* (New York: The Ronald Press Company, 1958), pp. 105-109, for a list of business purposes which have been upheld by courts.

[21]*Roughan* vs. *Commissioner,* 198 F. 2d 253 (4th Cir. 1952).

system. If the accounting system follows generally accepted accounting principles and is audited regularly, such an atmosphere should help to prove that the electing corporation has a "dominant hope and intent of realizing a profit."

To satisfy the Commissioner, a cost accountant could be consulted periodically. Also, some form of incentive plan for key personnel may appease the revenue agents who audit the company's books. If the business of cattle raising, which is frequently thought of as one of the gentleman farmer's hobbies, can avoid the clutches of the Commissioner in the *duPont* decision, then some tax planning beforehand should avoid any future trouble for Subchapter S corporations in the area of an adequate business purpose.

If a Subchapter S corporation is faced with the problem of proving the existence of a valid business purpose, a jury trial may be more desirable than the Tax Court or the Court of Claims. The petitioner should try to place as many businessmen as possible on the jury. A more sympathetic decision in favor of the taxpayer may be obtained from fellow businessmen than from a case-hardened judge. To a businessman-juror, the desire to avoid tax may not have the bad connotation that it would have to a professional judge who has had years of experience with tax administration and courtroom technology.[22]

Professional Corporations

A related situation occurs where a professional corporation elects to be a Subchapter S corporation. The Commissioner has conceded that the so-called Kintner Regulations outlawing professional corporations are invalid, but only after about twelve straight losses in the courts (T.I.R.1019, 8/8/69). Of course, the major reason for a professional corporation is to obtain tax deductions for various fringe benefits even though the professional person is an owner-employee. Qualified corporate pension or profit-sharing plans offer more benefits than the Keogh plans for partners.

A recent case illustrates that the Commissioner may merely shift to new battlegrounds in this highly sensitive area. In *Jerome J. Roubik*,[23] four unrelated and geographically separated radiologists organized a professional corporation, set up a pension plan, and elected Subchapter S treatment. However, they made the mistake of operating

---

[22]Holzman, *op. cit.*, p. 177; for a more complete discussion, see Crumbley, "When Does a Pleasurable Hobby Turn into an Investment for Tax Purpose," *Taxation for Accountants,* Vol. 10 (January, 1973), pp. 18-24.

[23]53 T.C. 365 (1969).

exactly as before (i.e., under their own names, separate equipment and supplies, separate employees) except that their fees and expenses were run through a corporate checking account. Each stockholder-doctor was credited with the fees he earned and charged for his related expenses and his salary. The net amount for each doctor was shown as his share of the taxable income of the electing corporation.

The Tax Court felt that the organization did not operate like a corporation since the doctors retained control over the performance of their services. "In the case of a corporation which provides personal services for a fee, income is 'earned' by the corporation or by the person who actually performs the services, whoever has the 'ultimate direction and control over the earning of the compensation.'" Further, the court was critical of the lack of factors showing that there was a business separate from the individuals. "We know of no case which has decided that two or more professionals engaged separately in their own practices can become, in respect of the income from those practices, 'employees' of a corporation through the purely formal device of incorporating a set of bookkeeping sheets."

In the years 1971-1973 the deductible contributions for 5 percent shareholder-employees of Subchapter S corporations were limited to the lower of 10 percent of salary or $25,000 – the same limitation imposed on partners under the Keogh plan. Even though other Keogh limitations did not apply, this limitation decreased this one advantage of incorporating and electing Subchapter S status. Since many professional corporations do elect Subchapter S treatment, such a limitation on this status decreased the attractiveness of professional corporations. However, for taxable years beginning after December 31, 1973, this parsimonious restriction was increased to $7,500 or 15 percent of earned income. This higher limitation should be quite adequate for most closely-held businesses.

Member of an Affiliated Group

The Subchapter S provisions originally provided that a corporation could not be a member of an affiliated group as defined in I.R.C. Section 1504. This section asserted that an electing corporation was not an includible corporation within the meaning of the definition of an affiliated group. In other words, a corporation already a member of an affiliated group was ineligible to make an election. However, once the election was made, the corporation could take on any number of additional subsidiaries.

A 1959 amendment closed this loophole by changing the law to provide that a corporation upon becoming a member of an affiliated group, as defined in I.R.C. Section 1504, loses its eligibility to be a Subchapter S corporation. The consequence of the amendment was to terminate the electing corporation upon the creation of a relationship between the electing corporation and another which would permit the filing of consolidated returns, and to maintain the right to file such returns for the related corporations. The avoidance of complex allocation of income problems and complicated capital structures were the probable reasons for this limitation.

To a certain extent there is still a loophole, since the Subchapter S language adopts the definition of an affiliated group in Section 1504. Thus, a Subchapter S corporation can own 80 percent or more of the seven nonincludible corporations in Section 1504(b), such as a DISC, a foreign corporation, a regulated investment company, a real estate investment trust, or others.

The Revenue Act of 1964 weakened the disqualification of a corporation with an 80 percent or more subsidiary. Effective with respect to taxable years of corporations beginning after December 31, 1962, a Subchapter S corporation can own inactive subsidiaries without thereby forfeiting its election. According to the *Code,* an inactive subsidiary is one which (1) has not begun business at any time on or after the date of its incorporation and before the close of the electing corporation's taxable year, and (2) does not have any taxable income for the period within such taxable year. For example, assume a calendar-year parent corporation owned all the stock of a subsidiary which was on a June 30 fiscal year basis. The parent company would not be disqualified for making an election in 1970 if the subsidiary did not begin business before January 1, 1970, through June 30, 1970, or July 1, 1970, through December 31, 1970.[24]

In clarifying the provision, the Senate Finance Committee noted the handicap that the old rule against owning any kind of subsidiary had imposed on a small business which anticipates future expansion. The Committee asserted that it is common practice for a corporation to preserve its corporate name in states where it plans to do business in the future by creating in these states inactive subsidiaries with names that are the same as, or similar to its own.[25] If it is necessary to control 80 percent or more of another corporation's stock, there is no statutory provision against having less than 80 percent of such stock held by the electing corporation and the remainder by its

---

[24]Report of the Committee on Finance, Senate Report No. 830, 88th Congress, 2d Session (Washington: United States Government Printing Office, 1964), p. 264.

[25]Senate Report No. 830, *op. cit.,* p. 146.

stockholders. Also, there is no prohibition against brother-sister corporations.

In *Coca-Cola Bottling Company*,[26] a Subchapter S corporation created a new subsidiary in order to operate a new territorial franchise. The stated purposes for the new subsidiary were (1) to hold a franchise to bottle various soft drinks, (2) to obtain more advertising money from the national bottling company, (3) to separate geographically the two companies, and (4) to carry out the desires of the national bottling company. However, the Tenth Circuit agreed with the Commissioner's arguments that the subsidiary was engaged in a business as a separate corporation and had taxable income during the period under question. The parent's Subchapter S election was terminated retroactively to the beginning of the tax year. The Court felt that this subsidiary did not meet the previously mentioned definition of an inactive subsidiary.[27]

Where the stock of an electing corporation is acquired by another corporation, the electing corporation may become a member of an affiliated group that files consolidated returns. If a consolidated return is filed, the income of the Subchapter S corporation up to the date of the acquisition is included in the consolidated tax return.[28] A question often arises as to whether the acquisition of an electing corporation during the year of a Subchapter S election terminates the election as it applies to the portion of income applicable before the acquisition. For example, suppose a Subchapter S corporation is acquired by another corporation on June 30, 1970. If the electing corporation incurred a $50,000 loss up to the date of the acquisition, should the loss be shown on the stockholders' personal tax returns or included in the consolidated tax return?

Revenue Ruling 64-94, 1964-1 C.B. 317, states that the election does not terminate with respect to income for the period ending with the sale of the corporation's stock via an "A" reorganization, provided a consolidated return is filed by the affiliated group of which it becomes a member. The period ending with the acquisition is a separate tax year. The rationale of the IRS is that where the event that causes the corporation to be disqualified from the election also terminates its tax year, the election continues throughout the entire tax year so terminated. The IRS viewed this short year as ending the day before acquisition of the stock. Further, in Rev. Rul. 69-566, 1969-2

---

[26]69-2 U.S.T.C. ¶9465 (D.C. N.M. 1969), *aff'd.* 443 F. 2d 1253 (10th Cir. 1971).
[27]See also *Barnes Motor & Parts Co.* vs. *U.S.,* 309 F. Supp. 298 (D.C. N.C. 1970).
[28]Regulation 1.1502-76(b)(2).

C.B. 165, the Commissioner ruled that the election as well as the taxable year of a Subchapter S corporation are not terminated where such Subchapter S corporation acquires a non-electing corporation in a tax-free statutory merger under I.R.C. Section 368(a)(1)(A). The non-electing corporation was, of course, dissolved.

In Rev. Rul. 70-232, 1970-1 C.B. 177, two electing corporations were consolidated under Section 268(a)(1)(A). The final tax years of the two electing corporations ended on the day of the consolidation under Section 381(b)(1). The IRS ruled that no termination of their election occurred under Section 1372(a) and the five-year waiting period on reelection outlined in Section 1372(f) was not applicable.

The IRS has informally advised that a Subchapter S corporation is disqualified for the short period preceding its joining an affiliated group via a "B" reorganization, since the acquiring corporation is a stockholder on the last day of the short period.[29]

Under Rev. Rul. 72-201, 1972-1 C.B. 271, if an electing corporation is acquired through a "B" reorganization, the Subchapter S status is terminated at the beginning of the taxable year. For example, S, a Subchapter S corporation on a fiscal year ending August 31 was acquired October 16, 1969, by P through a "B" reorganization. P filed a consolidated return with S for P's year ending December 31, 1969. The IRS held that, since P became a shareholder of S on October 16, S's election to be treated as a Subchapter S corporation is terminated for the entire year beginning September 1, 1969. S must also file a separate corporation return for the portion of the taxable year beginning September 1 and ending October 16, 1969, which is not includable in the P-S consolidated return for P's 1969 taxable year. Originally, an electing corporation was listed in Section 1504(b) as an excluded corporation, but this exclusion has been repealed because an affiliation will terminate the Subchapter S election.

Taxpayers should be aware of the apparent position of the Commissioner in a stock-for-stock transaction. Thus, a Subchapter S corporation should distribute undistributed taxable income before the end of the 2½-month grace period of the year prior to the tax year in which the "B" reorganization occurs.

A "C" type of acquisition (a nontaxable reorganization) can be accomplished through the issuance of a part of one corporation's voting stock for substantially all of the assets of another corporation (stock for assets)[30] The newly acquired subsidiary would immediately

---

[29]"Affiliated Group Acquisition May Disqualify Subchapter S Election," *New York Certified Public Accountant,* Vol. 39 (September, 1969), pp. 708-709.

[30]I.R.C. Section 368(a)(1)(c).

liquidate, but the momentary holding of the assets of another corporation could terminate the election under the member of an affiliated group rule. For example, P corporation (a Subchapter S corporation) issues part of its common stock for the assets of B corporation. Subsidiary B would be immediately liquidated, but the parent would be a member of an affiliated group for an instant.

The IRS has ruled that Subchapter S status is not affected by such a "C" type reorganization.[31] The electing corporation in the ruling agreed to transfer its assets in a transaction that qualified as a "C" reorganization. Within two and one-half months after its tax year ended, the Subchapter S corporation made distributions of its previous year's UTI. All remaining estimated income for this short year terminating upon consummation of the reorganization were paid on the closing date. Since this event is not one of the specified events stated in Section 1372(e), the "C" reorganization did not terminate the Subchapter S election. The distributions constitute payments of UTI and the earnings and profits of the corporation's final tax year.

A momentary holding of a corporation's stock occurs in a spin-off, which again brings up the problem of an election termination. This question was considered in Rev. Rul. 72-320 and it was held that:

". . . since X never contemplated more than momentary control of Y, the affiliation will not be considered as terminating the small business corporation election. . ."[32]

It appears that the intentions of the parties involved controlled the consequences of this situation. This factor, however, could create a problem if the intentions were not well documented and the holding period of the stock was prolonged for any reason.

As a guide, here briefly is the situation presented in Rev. Rul. 72-320. X corporation, a Subchapter S corporation, was a manufacturer of heavy construction equipment and had been in business in California since 1965. All the stock was owned by four brothers — A, B, C, and D — in equal amounts. In 1970 the corporation opened a division in New York which was operated by brothers C and D. Later some basic differences arose between the brothers A and B in the California division and brothers C and D in the New York division over the business objectives of the corporation. To reconcile this conflict a plan of reorganization was agreed to whereby X corporation created Y corporation and transferred all the assets of the New York division, subject to all the liabilities, to Y corporation in ex-

---

[31]Rev. Rul. 71-266, 1971-1 C.B. 262.

[32]Regulation 1.1502-13(g); Rev. Rul. 72-320, 1972-1 C.B. 270.

change for all the stock of Y corporation. Immediately thereafter C and D exchanged all their stock in X for all the stock of Y corporation. All transactions qualified under the relevant *Code* sections as tax-free, and, under the ruling, X corporation retained its Subchapter S election.

Also, under Reg. 1.1502-13(f), an election can be made to treat a subsidiary which has been a member of the affiliated group for less than thirty-one days as not having been a member of the group during the tax year. To illustrate, a Subchapter S corporation forms a new subsidiary corporation. The subsidiary is created at the end of the tax year of the parent corporation, and the assets are placed in the subsidiary at the close of the last business day. If the subsidiary is spun off on the same day, the inactive exception enacted in 1964 should prevent the election from being lost. But if the assets are placed into the subsidiary before the close of the parent's tax year, this relief provision (I.R.C. Section 1371(d)) may not apply, and the Subchapter S election will terminate automatically.[33]

Finally, the Commissioner has ruled that an "F" reorganization (i.e., change in the state of incorporation) does not terminate a Subchapter S election.[34]

One Class of Stock

One of the most stringent requirements of an electing corporation is that there can be only one class of stock issued and outstanding.[35] Preceding the enactment of the Subchapter S provisions, the Treasury Department issued a research study that stated that this criteria would help confine this option to corporations similar in many essential respects to genuine partnerships and would greatly simplify administration:

> The reason for the requirement as to capital structure is largely administrative. It would be almost impossible to allocate corporate income satisfactorily among owners of various classes

---

[33]Crumbley, "Avoid Unintentional Disqualifications of Subchapter S Corporations," *Taxes — The Tax Magazine,* Vol. 44 (June, 1966), p. 376.

[34]Rev. Rul. 64-250, 1964-2 C.B. 333.

[35]Crumbley, *op. cit.,* pp. 374-382; M. J. Matheson, "Shareholder Advances to Thin Subchapter S Corporations," *Stanford Law Review,* Vol. 19 (February, 1967), pp. 628-635; J. D. McGaffey, "The Requirement That a Subchapter S Corporation May Have Only One Class of Stock," *Marquette Law Review,* Vol. 50 (February, 1967), pp. 365-390; "Application of the Thin Incorporation Doctrine to Subchapter S One-Class-of-Stock Requirement," *Duke Law Review,* Vol. 1967 (December, 1967), pp. 1202-1214; "Federal Income Taxation — Subchapter S Election — One Class of Stock Requirement," *Iowa Law Review,* Vol. 52 (August, 1966), pp. 128-133.

of stock. In many cases the claims of owners of different classes of stock to earnings do not become definitive until long after profits are earned. For example, common stockholders, as residual owners, would presumably be allocated any profits retained in any year after satisfaction of prior claims of preferred stockholders. In later years, however, these earnings might be distributed as preferred dividends.[36]

Later, in acting upon H.R. 8300 in 1954, the Senate added to it the defunct I.R.C. Section 1351. To qualify for this tax option election, a corporation had to have only "one class of stock outstanding." "No class of stock may be preferred over another as to either dividends, distributions, or voting rights."[37] The only explanation given for the "one class" requirement was that if "this requirement were not made, undistributed current earnings could not be taxed to the shareholders without great complication."[38] Elaboration was set forth even more clearly elsewhere in the report, where the Finance Committee said: ". . . in order to avoid possible complications in the taxation of preferred stock not earned in the year distributed, only corporations having one class of stock outstanding may qualify."[39]

Without any explanation, the one-class-of-stock requirement was included in the 1958 Subchapter S provision that later became law. However, even though the Committee's Report gave no indication of the reason for this one class requirement or what was meant thereby, it seems rational to infer that the one class requirement was intended to facilitate a simple and uncomplicated allocation of income and loss among stockholders.

A corporation must continue at all times to meet the initial one-class-of-stock requirement or the election will be terminated involuntarily. In determining whether a business has more than one class of stock outstanding, only stock which is issued and outstanding should be considered. Thus, authorized but unissued stock of another class and treasury stock of another class which has previously been issued and redeemed will not terminate the election. For example, a corporation has common stock outstanding and authorized but unissued preferred stock on hand. The unissued preferred stock does not constitute another class of stock. However, if the unissued preferred

---

[36]United States Treasury Department, Division of Tax Research, *Taxation of Small Business,* Hearings Before the House Committee on Ways and Means, 80th Congress, 1st Session, part 5 (1947), p. 3758.

[37]Senate Report No. 1622, *op. cit.,* p. 453.

[38]*Ibid.*

[39]*Ibid.,* p. 119; See also Senate Report No. 830, *op. cit.,* p. 146.

stock is sold, then the corporation would lose its special tax treatment. Also, if any treasury stock of another class is sold, the election will terminate.[40]

The Commissioner has made mild concessions with respect to the one-class-of-stock limitation. The Federal Housing Administration requires private corporations holding property covered by mortgages insured by the F.H.A. to issue shares of special stock to them, usually preferred stock. The IRS has ruled that this special stock will not be considered as a class of stock for disqualification or termination.[41] Also, unexercised stock options, warrants, and convertible debentures do not constitute a fatal second class of stock if they have none of the typical characteristics of immediate stock ownership (e.g., right to receive dividends or the right to vote).[42] A corporation does not qualify for Subchapter S where a state administrator creates unequal voting, dividend, and liquidation preferences among the shareholders.[43]

This concession with respect to warrants can provide considerable flexibility in controlling an electing corporation with a nominal amount of investment. For example, suppose one stockholder has an invention but lacks the necessary capital to start a business. Another stockholder could provide the necessary capital by buying all the stock while the inventor buys options to purchase stock at the initial price. Both individuals can enjoy the growth of the business even though only one of the shareholders owns most of the stocks. Further, by careful use of options, warrants, or convertible debentures, more than ten individuals can have ownership interest similar to a stockholder's interest. A voluntary or involuntary termination of the election can then be consummated before these vehicles are exercised. Tax practitioners should not overlook these devices as tax-planning tools.

These are mild concessions when considered in light of the special problems existing where a corporation is heavily capitalized with debt to equity (i.e., the stockholders loan money to the corporation or the shareholders guarantee outside loans). The Regulations originally said that "if an instrument purporting to be a debt obligation is actually stock, it will constitute a second class of stock."[44]

---

[40]Regulation 1.1371-1(g).

[41]Rev. Rul. 64-309, 1964-2 C.B. 333.

[42]Rev. Rul. 67-269, 1967-2 C.B. 298; See Crumbley and Boyles, "Registered Warrants as a Compensatory Tool," *The Tax Executive,* Vol. 25 (October, 1972), pp. '2-24.

[43]Rev. Rul. 71-552, 1971-2 C.B. 316.

[44]Regulation 1.1371-1(g).

By applying this doctrine to the Subchapter S single class of stock rule, the Commissioner has been able to retroactively disqualify several Subchapter S elections.[45]

The year 1966 manifested a change in judicial thought on this matter, for the taxpayer was finally allowed to prevail. The Treasury's position as suggested by Regulation 1.1371-1(g) had begun to crumble. In *W. C. Gamman*,[46] the shareholders had advanced funds to their Subchapter S corporation in excess of their investment in the corporation's stock. The transactions were evidenced by demand notes that specified interest at 6 percent. Each shareholder held the notes pro rata to his investment in stock. The shareholders argued that the notes represented debt capital. The Tax Court, however, held that the notes "had the characteristics of equity capital" in that they were "placed at the risk of business." Nevertheless, the Court refused to find a second class of stock and thus to terminate the corporation's Subchapter S status. Accordingly, the Court held Regulation 1.1371-1 (g) to be invalid to the extent that it automatically treated notes by shareholders as a second class of stock.

This position was followed in subsequent cases. In *Lewis Building and Supplies, Inc.*,[47] the Tax Court used the *Gamman* decision as authority for the proposition that the advances were merely additional capital contributions that did not constitute a second class of stock. It should be noted that appeals in both cases were dismissed. About this time, a District Court found that a genuine debt existed because it believed that the taxpayer had not intended "to take the risk incident to a capital investment when he made the . . . loans."[48]

The Treasury's position was shifted through a revision of Regulation 1.1371-1(g) by Treasury Decision 6904.[49] The Regulation now states that debt obligations that are, in reality, equity contributions will still constitute a second class of stock. However, if the debt is held solely by shareholders in proportion to their stock ownership, such advances will be treated as non-stock capital contributions. Thus the non-stock equity concept was created. Cases after the 1966

---

[45]*Catalina Homes, Inc.*, T.C.M. 1964-225; *Henderson vs. U.S.*, 245 F. Supp. 782 (D.C. Ala. 1965), *appeal dismissed*, (5th Cir. 1966).

[46]46 T.C. 1 (1966), appeal dismissed per stipulation (9th Cir. 1967).

[47]*Lewis Building and Supplies, Inc.* vs. *Commissioner*, T.C.M. 1966-159 (1966), appeal dismissed (5th Cir. 1967).

[48]*Seven Sixty Ranch Co.* vs. *Kennedy*, 17 A.F.T.R. 2d 587, 66-1 U.S.T.C. ¶9293 (D.C. Wyo. 1966).

[49]1967-1 C.B. 219.

amendment to Regulation 1.1371-1(g) are discussed later in this chapter.

There is no justification for the Treasury to classify debt as equity-type obligations in order to terminate an election. This is a worse penalty than the normal disallowance of interest deductions. The benefits of a high debt-to-equity ratio to a Subchapter S corporation are not as great as under the normal corporate form. The foregoing legislative history of the one-class requirement indicates that the restriction was intended to facilitate a simple and uncomplicated allocation of income and loss among shareholders and not to frustrate the overriding purpose of Congress in enacting its 1958 legislation.[50]

The typical "thin corporation" is a corporation with a financial structure composed of a maximum amount of debt financing and a minimum of equity financing. Until the Tax Reform Bill of 1969 there was no definition of a "thin corporation" in either the *Code* or the Regulations. However, Congress recently instructed the Treasury to issue Regulations prescribing factors to be taken into account in determining if a debtor-creditor relationship exists.

Such factors are to include, among others, the following:

"(1) whether there is a written unconditional promise to pay on demand or on a specified date a sum certain in money in return for an adequate consideration in money or money's worth, and to pay a fixed rate of interest,
"(2) whether there is subordination to or preference over any indebtedness of the corporation,
"(3) the ratio of debt to equity of the corporation,
"(4) whether there is convertibility into the stock of the corporation, and
"(5) the relationship between holdings of stock in the corporation and holdings of the interest in question."[51]

Practitioners should watch for these Regulations.

This tax concept has been introduced by the IRS many times, and the courts have decided a great number of non-Subchapter S cases and some Subchapter S cases in favor of the Government. The courts have not issued an all-embracing definition applicable in every case but have often limited each opinion to the specific facts that were presented by the parties.

---

[50]See *A & N Furniture and Appliance Co.*, 271 F. Supp. 40 (D.C., Ohio, 1967), for such an opinion.

[51]I.R.C. Section 385(a).

However, even though at least two courts have indicated that the traditional debt-equity tests do not apply to Subchapter S situations,[52] it is still beneficial to look at some factors generally used by courts when confronted with the debt-equity question. Besides, these same two courts indicated that the traditional debt to equity tests may be applicable where the Subchapter S corporation has accumulated earnings and profits from a period prior to the election.

However, a Subchapter S corporation has apparently two diametrically opposed routes it may take. First, the corporation may establish many of the traditional "favorable" debt-equity factors (except that the debt should be in proportion to the equity holdings).[53] This route follows the desire of the IRS. Second, the electing corporation can establish many of the traditional "unfavorable" factors and rely on the *Gamman* and related court decisions. The debt should be in proportion to equity holdings. Ironically, the Subchapter S corporations that fall within the center of these two extremes may be in trouble (in the unsafe zone in Exhibit 5-1 below). Although both Safety Zones 1 and 2 are preferable to the middle-of-the-road, we prefer Safety Zone 1 instead of Safety Zone 2. The remainder of this chapter assumes that the electing corporation is attempting to remain in Safety Zone 1.

EXHIBIT 5-1

Safety Zone 1	UNSAFE ZONE	Safety Zone 2
Many favorable debt-equity factors (except debt should be in proportion to equity)		Many unfavorable debt-equity factors (including debt in proportion to equity)

Suppose we now look at some of the most common types of "thin corporations."

Thin Capitalization

The most commonly-known pattern is the thinly capitalized corporation. A new corporation issues to its stockholders a minimum

---

[52]*Portage Plastics Co., Inc.,* 24 A.F.T.R. 69-5301 (W.D. Wisc. 1969); *W. C. Gamman,* 46 T.C. 1 (1966); See following discussion of stockholder's loans.

[53]Professor Holzman, in "The Interest-Dividend Guidelines," *Taxes — The Tax Magazine,* Vol. 47 (January, 1969), pp. 4-11, lists 38 such factors; See also A. J. Dixon, "The Interest-Dividend Syndrome: What Are the Criteria?" *New York University Tax Institute,* Vol. 24 (1966), pp. 1267-1290.

amount of stock and a maximum amount of debt instruments (usually proportionate to their stockholdings). Some of the purposes of this pattern for non-Subchapter S corporations may be summarized as follows:[54]

1. To obtain an interest deduction for the corporation instead of a nondeductible dividend payment.
2. To obtain additional protection from the accumulated earnings tax as a result of retaining funds to retire the debt.
3. To obtain additional protection from the personal holding holding company tax.
4. To obtain a possible fully deductible bad debt rather than a capital loss.
5. To obtain a tax-free repayment of the debt rather than a possible taxable dividend on the repayment of an equity interest.

The very nature of this special election allows an electing corporation to avoid the corporate tax, so there is no advantage in labeling a payment "interest" rather than "dividend." Further, no accumulated earnings tax or personal holding company tax can be imposed on an electing corporation. The ordinary versus capital loss problem normally is not applicable to Subchapter S corporations, since net operating losses may be deducted pro rata by the stockholders. Finally, an electing corporation may obtain the fifth advantage (i.e., avoidance of a taxable dividend on repayment of equity) only if it has accumulated earnings and profits from non-Subchapter S years and the loans were made *prior* to the Subchapter S election. Or if earnings and profits are in excess of taxable income (i.e., tax-free interest) during an electing year, debt may be used to avoid the dividend tax on such excess amount.

There are, however, several advantages to thin capitalization which are unique to electing corporations:[55]

1. Since a stockholder may deduct a corporate net operating loss only to the extent of his stock and debt obligations,[56] additional loans to the electing corporation allow a shareholder to preserve his deduction.

---

[54]For a complete list of advantages, see William H. Hoffman, "Coping with the Thin Corporation Problem" *Tulane Tax Institute,* Vol. 17 (1968), pp. 50-54.

[55]For a discussion of these and other advantages, see Lorence Bravenec, "The One Class of Stock Requirement of Subchapter S — A Round Peg in a Pentagonal Hole," *Houston Law Review,* Vol. 6 (October, 1968), pp. 215-289.

[56]I.R.C. Section 1374(c)(2).

2. Where the stockholders are all in the same family, it is advantageous for the shareholders in high tax brackets to capitalize the business with debt instruments. Thus, most of the UTI will be taxed to the family members in the low tax brackets. The reverse is, of course, true. If the electing corporation is expected to operate at a loss, the family members in the highest tax brackets should hold the stock.

3. As has been pointed out in previous chapters, it is wise for a Subchapter S corporation to distribute all current earnings before the close of the 2½-month grace period. But such a policy of distributing all earnings results in an anemic cash position. One practical solution to this problem is for the stockholders to immediately loan the dividends back to the corporation.

4. Another advantage of thin capitalization is that it allows an electing corporation to distribute property "dividends" as a repayment of debt obligations. Such a repayment is treated in a manner similar to the distribution of PTI. As you will recall, a normal property dividend does not reduce each stockholder's UTI[57] — resulting in a tax liability greater than actual earnings.

5. Debt instruments may be used instead of equity in order to circumvent some of the stringent requirements of Subchapter S status (i.e., ten stockholders, trust).

Since there is still present the incentive for the stockholders to attempt to thinly capitalize an electing corporation, mention should be made of some tax-planning aids designed to avoid application of the thin capitalization doctrine. It should be remembered, as with all patterns of thin corporations, no one or two factors will necessarily insulate the debt from ultimately being classified as capital. However, many factors when considered together will help to defend a corporation from attacks by IRS agents.

Generally, the debt-to-stock ratio should not be greater than about four to one, but these ratio tests have been refined by some courts in order to reflect the amount of debt normally needed by different types of businesses.[58] There is a strong presumption that "debt" is actually equity capital if the debt-equity ratio is so "dispro-

---

[57]See I.R.C. Section 1.1375-4(b) and Regulation 1.1375-4(b).
[58]See *P. M. Finance Corporation,* 302 F. 2d 786 (3d Cir. 1962).

portionately high" that it indicates a "suspicious circumstance."[59] However, other favorable factors may overcome even a high debt-equity ratio.[60] There should be a formal authorization for the debt,[61] and the corporation should actually pay interest.[62]

For Subchapter S corporations the debt should be in the same proportion as to the stockholdings per Reg. 1.1371-1(g).[63] In one case, the Tax Court was impressed because the taxpayer's accountant had "found" some debt which was not proportionate and the debt was brought into line immediately.[64] However, several courts have stated that the debt need not be proportionate to equity as stipulated in Reg. 1.1371-1(g).[65] Taxpayers would be well advised to keep debt in proportion to equity holding if at all possible.

It is quite helpful if a sinking fund is established.[66] If the electing corporation fails to make payments when due, the default provision should be invoked by the stockholders.[67] The electing corporation should continue to pay cash dividends that are normal for its particular industry. Generally, many of the above factors are examined by the courts to determine whether a transaction is debt or equity.[68] However, since there are differences in opinion among the courts, an electing corporation should examine the "thin capitalization" cases in its own circuit in order to determine the emphasis given to the various tests.

Stockholders' Loans

A second pattern of thin corporations results from the inherent nature of the taxation aspect of a Subchapter S corporation. The stockholders of an electing corporation must list on their individual tax return all of the income of the corporation for that year whether or not the earnings are distributed to the shareholders. This income

---

[59] *Gloucester Ice and Cold Storage Co.*, 298 F. 2d 183 (1st Cir. 1962).

[60] *Creston Corp.*, 40 T.C. 937 (1963); *Milton T. Raynor*, 50 T.C. 762 (1968), *Sam Novell*, T.C.M. 1969-255.

[61] *W. T. Ray* vs. *U.S.*, 409 F. 2d 1322 (6th Cir. 1969); *Sam Novell, supra,* note 60.

[62] *Donald J. Peterson*, T.C.M. 1965-151.

[63] *W. C. Gamman, supra,* note 52; *Lewis Bldg. & Supplies, Inc., supra,* note 47; *Milton Raynor, supra,* note 60; *Sam Novell, supra,* note 60.

[64] *Sam Novell, supra,* note 60.

[65] *August F. Nielsen*, T.C.M. 1968-11; *Portage Plastics Co., Inc., supra,* note 52.

[66] *Fellinger*, 363 F. 2d 826 (6th Cir. 1966); *Alfred N. Hoffman*, 47 T.C. 218 (1966).

[67] *Gooding Amusement Co., Inc.* vs. *Commissioner*, 236 F. 2d 159 (6th Cir. 1956), *cert. denied* 352 U.S. 1031 (1957); *W. C. Gamman, supra,* note 52.

[68] *McSorley's Inc.*, 323 F. 2d 900 (10th Cir. 1963); See *Sam Novell, supra,* note 60 and *Portage Plastics Co., Inc., supra,* note 52, for a review of many of these factors.

that is taxable (but not distributed before the close of the 2½-month grace period) becomes previously taxed income. PTI may be available to the shareholders, but it has already been taxed, and the shareholders who included it in their income may receive it tax-free. However, the corporation must first distribute current earnings before PTI can be distributed. If the Subchapter S election is lost involuntarily, the lost election goes back to the beginning of the year, and the earnings will be "locked-in." In other words, the earnings will be frozen in the corporation until it distributes all of the retained earnings and current earnings.

Another reason to distribute income of the corporation currently is that the right to withdraw PTI tax-free accrues only to those shareholders who have actually included it as income on their tax return. Hence, if a stockholder's shares are transferred (whether by gift, sale, or death), his share of PTI cannot be withdrawn tax-free by the new shareholder. The right to get PTI is personal and this right cannot be assigned or transferred.[69]

These two tax hazards necessitate the distribution of all the income (including capital gains) as cash dividends before the end of the 2½-month period after the close of the tax year. Special problems are often created due to the inability to distribute all of the current earnings, because these same funds are needed for day-by-day operations. If all the income is distributed, a shortage of cash may occur.

This second pattern of thin corporations may originate by an entirely different process. Suppose a new electing corporation starts its business life with an amount of stock which is insufficient for future business needs. The shareholders may intentionally invest an inadequate amount of capital in the corporation. Subsequently, the owners make loans to the company in order to meet the working capital needs. The obvious effect is that the capital structure is "thinned" as the company's loans increase.[70]

A logical way of dealing with possible cash shortages (if it were capable of accomplishment) is to distribute currently all corporate income and then loan it back to the corporation when funds are needed. These loans to the corporation convert UTI into a debt obligation that can be repaid at some future time and can be freely transferred. However, the Commissioner may attack such loans as a second class of stock and the courts have acted in favor of the Gov-

---

[69]Rev. Rul. 66-172, 1966-2 C.B. 198, Regulation 1.1375-4(e).

[70]For an example of this, see *Henderson,* 245 F. Supp. 782 (D.C. Ala. 1965).

ernment in some instances.[71] However, the courts have been more favorable to the taxpayer since the *Gamman*[72] decision.

Since the 1966 amendment to Regulation 1.1371-1(g), there have been several major court cases related to these types of advances. In *August F. Nielsen Co., Inc.,*[73] the Tax Court held that advances by the stockholders to the electing corporation were, in fact, equity capital, but since these "loans" were in proportion to the shareholders' previous equity, the owners did not receive any additional rights or interests. Thus, the "loans" were not a second class of stock. In a slightly related case, *Alfred N. Hoffman,*[74] an owner prior to Hoffman placed the corporation's stock in escrow as security for the payment of the company's obligation to her on a note. The Tax Court held (without explanation) that she was not considered a shareholder and her advances to the corporation were not a second class of stock. Similarly, in *Brennan* vs. *O'Donnell,*[75] advances by stockholders were not equity contributions.

In *Milton T. Raynor,*[76] several individuals operated a number of bowling alleys as separate corporations, and the Commissioner tried to terminate the Subchapter S elections for the loss corporations. Each corporation was debt-financed by a variety of arrangements — advances, guaranteed outside loans, etc. Although the stockholders made nonproportionate advances, they agreed that the amounts owed by each corporation were to be considered owed to the shareholders in proportion to their stockholdings, without regard as to who in fact advanced the funds on open accounts. Although the court felt that such an "informal partnership agreement" resulted in a "confused" set of books, the advances did not represent a second class of stock since the "shareholders intended that their advances were to be made in proportion to their stockholdings."

Later, in *Sam Novell,*[77] a Subchapter S corporation had many of the factors which normally indicate a "thin corporation." However, the Tax Court was lenient in this case since some of the advances were initially not in proportion to the stockholdings. "And we do not believe that the shareholders intended by these advances to

---

[71]See cases cited in note 45.

[72]See cases cited in notes 46 and 47.

[73]T.C.M. 1968-11.

[74]47 T.C. 218 (1966), *aff'd.* 21 A.F.T.R. 2d 957 (5th Cir. 1968).

[75]21 A.F.T.R. 2d 1028 (N.D. Ala. 1968).

[76]50 T.C. 762 (1968).

[77]*Supra,* note 54.

create any preference in regards to income, liquidation, etc., that were disproportionate to their stockholdings."

The proportionality requirement of Regulation 1.1371-1(g), as amended in 1966, was to become the subject for considerable litigation after 1968. The Government appealed *Brennan* vs. *O'Donnell*[78] on the theory that the 1968 decision had failed to take the amended regulation into consideration. The Fifth Circuit remanded the case for consideration of this issue.[79] However, the Government was not to prevail, because the proportionality requirement had been held invalid by the time that the District Court could reconsider its decision.[80] The following cases indicate the extent to which this issue has been litigated.[81]

Perhaps the first case to test the proportionality requirement was *James L. Stinnett*,[82] in which a partnership was converted into a corporation by issuing stock to the existing partners.[83] Partnership capital accounts were transferred to the corporation as debt capital. The facts illustrate an extreme case of a thinly capitalized chartered partnership in that the stock is purely nominal and the corporation's true capital is provided by loans to the corporation. Accordingly, it would be difficult to agree that the notes did not represent an equity investment. As these amounts were not in proportion to stock ownership, the Commissioner held that a second class of stock existed.

The Tax Court held the proportionality requirement of Regulation 1.1371-1(g) to be invalid. In framing its opinion, the Court drew heavily upon the legislative history and purposes of various sections of the statute. The Court noted that Section 1376(b)(2) contemplated that loans would be made to the corporation by its shareholders and that such debt is to be treated as part of the shareholder's equity interest. Moreover, two concurring judges offered additional reasons why the taxpayer's position should be upheld. Judge Tannenwald argued that the notes could not be a second class of stock if they are not treated as stock by state corporate law.[84] Judge Featherstone

---

[78]*Supra,* note 75.

[79]25 A.F.T.R. 2d 70-1250 (5th Cir. 1970).

[80]A.F.T.R. 2d 71-1560 (N.D. Ala. 1971).

[81]For additional discussion of these cases, see Galant, *Proportionality and the Single Class of Stock Requirement Under Subchapter S,* 51 Taxes 300 (1973).

[82]54 T.C. 221 (1970), *appeal dismissed without opinion* (9th Cir. 1973).

[83]For purposes not made clear in the report, the stock was not issued equally to all partners.

[84]54 T.C. 221 at 234.

noted that the purpose of the one-class-of-stock requirement is to provide a "simple corporate structure" and that such purpose is not frustrated by the presence of loans in the capital structure of the corporation.[85] In fact, the role of shareholder loans is expressly acknowledged by Section 1374(c)(2), which allows net operating losses to be deducted by the shareholder to the extent of the adjusted basis for his stock plus the adjusted basis of any indebtedness of the corporation to the shareholder.[86] The *Stinnett* case is currently on appeal to the Ninth Circuit.

The reasoning in the *Stinnett* case was followed in *H. R. Spinner Corporation,*[87] where the Tax Court stated that "ordinary debt instruments, held disproportionately by the shareholders of a thinly capitalized corporation, did not constitute a second class of stock within the meaning of Section 1371(a)." The Court saw no reason to distinguish *Stinnett* and noted, at least on the facts presented, that it made no difference whether the advance "be regarded as debt or equity."

Stinnett was also followed in *Estate of William M. Allison.*[88] The opinion was written by Judge Tannenwald, who had prepared a concurring opinion in *Stinnett.* The position that he had enunciated in that concurring opinion became the basis for decisions in this case to the effect that Section 1371(a)(4) was applicable only if state law would require the notes to be treated as stock. Thin capitalization, by itself, would not violate the single-class-of-stock rule. Moreover, the purpose of that rule, which is to simplify the process of allocating profits and losses to shareholders, was also a basis for this decision. The Government appealed this decision to the Seventh Circuit, but the appeal was dismissed in 1973.

The *Portage Plastics* group of cases add an interesting chapter to the judicial development of the one-class-of-stock rule. The controversy arose because two individuals (in 1957) each advanced the corporation $12,500 and, in return, received notes from the corporation. Interest on these notes was stated to be 5 percent of the net profits of the company before taxes. Balance sheets for this period indicated that the corporation was thinly capitalized. With thin capitalization and payment for the use of funds that had characteristics more of dividends than of interest, it is not difficult to under-

---

[85]54 T.C. 221 at 235.

[86]See discussion in Chapter 6.

[87]T.C.M. 1970-99, *appeal dismissed* (9th Cir. 1973).

[88]57 T.C. 174 (1971), *appeal dismissed per stipulation* (9th Cir. 1973).

stand why the Commissioner would challenge the corporation's status under Subchapter S.

The Government argued that the two $12,500 notes constituted a second class of stock in violation of Section 1371(a)(4). The Court noted that the debt equity issue is a question of fact and if the notes were held to be a class of stock, they would constitute a second class of stock. It also considered "most persuasive" the fact that interest was computed as a function of profits. The taxpayer argued that the notes were, in fact, loans to the corporation and that there was nothing wrong with paying interest as a function of profits.

The Court concluded that the notes did not constitute a second class of stock within the meaning of Section 1371(a)(4).[89] It noted that the legislative purpose of that section would not be served by so holding. Moreover, it stated that the traditional debt equity tests are not relevant to the general purpose of Subchapter S. However, the Court did hold that the loans were, in fact, a contribution of capital.

The Government, armed with the non-stock equity concept, then decided to litigate the issue of whether holders of notes should consent to Subchapter S status as is required for other owners of equity interests.[90] As a diversionary tactic (and not particularly critical to the current discussion), the Government could accomplish the same short-range purpose by a victory on this issue. However, such victory was not to be forthcoming. The Government argued that the notes constituted a "second class of stock." The Court stated that the creditors in question were not shareholders within the meaning of Section 1372(a) and that no consent was required. An appeal to the Fifth Circuit was made by the Government on both issues.

At long last, the Government was able to convince a Court that its arguments had merit.[91] Up to a point, the Fifth Circuit accepted the reasoning of the lower Court. However, it was unwilling to accept the non-stock equity concept and held that the capital, as evidenced by the notes, did constitute a second class of stock in violation of Section 1371(a)(4). Moreover, the Court concluded that Regulation 1.1371-1(g) is a "reasonable and consistent interpretation of Section 1371(a)(4) when used properly." Significant to the Court's decision were the facts that interest was a function of net profits and the notes were subordinated to other creditors. It refused to expressly reject the thin capitalization doctrine but held that many factors of this

---

[89]24 A.F.T.R. 2d 69-5301 (W.D. Wisc. 1969).

[90]27 A.F.T.R. 2d 71-1038 (W.D. Wisc. 1971).

[91]30 A.F.T.R. 2d 72-5229 (7th Cir. 1972).

type should be allowed to govern, such as the true nature of the debt. Proportionality was never an issue because the owners of the notes did not own stock in the company. This enabled the Court to distinguish the *Portage* case from *Stinnett* and *Allison,* because in the latter cases the notes were held by shareholders. Judge Cummings dissented from the majority opinion. He refused to find an application for the thin capitalization doctrine in a Subchapter S context unless it could be shown that tax avoidance has resulted. He also noted that the outcome required by the majority represents a severe penalty for the corporation.

The *Portage Plastics* story does not end here. In the interim, another series of cases had evolved through the Fifth Circuit with a contrary result. The Sixth Circuit was asked to reconsider its holding in *Portage.* Before considering the results of that reconsideration, it is appropriate to review the two Fifth Circuit cases.

In *Amory Cotton Oil Co.* vs. *U.S.,*[92] shareholders had loaned the corporation funds and had received promissory notes as evidence of the loans. This had taken place over fifteen years, and no effort had been made to repay the notes. The corporation was thinly capitalized, and the loans by shareholders were subordinated to those of non-shareholders. The District Court concluded that the advances were capital but did not constitute a disqualifying second class of stock. This conclusion was supported by the reasoning of *Gamman, Stinnett,* and the District Court opinion in *Portage.* The Government appealed this decision to the Fifth Circuit.[93] However, the taxpayer's position was allowed to prevail. The Court stated that the debt-equity issue is relevant in a Subchapter S context and the Commissioner is not required to accept a "debt" label merely because the taxpayer claims that debt is created. Section 385(a)[94] of the *Code* allows the Commissioner to prescribe regulations to determine whether an interest in a corporation is debt or equity. However, the Court said that this is only one element for finding a second class of stock and other factors must be considered. One such factor is the purpose and legislative history of Subchapter S. The Court then stated that Section 1376(b)(2) makes it clear that "the statute contemplates that the stockholders of a Subchapter S corporation would make advances or lend money to the corporation." From the application of this reasoning, the Court concluded that the District Court had decided the case

---

[92]27 A.F.T.R. 2d 71-567 (N.D. Miss. 1970).

[93]30 A.F.T.R. 2d 72-5665 (5th Cir. 1972).

[94]Section 385(a) was added by Section 415 of the Tax Reform Act of 1969.

properly. The opinion concluded with the statement that Regulation 1.1371-1(g) "is invalid both facially and as applied in this case."

A similar case had also developed in the Fifth Circuit. In *Shores Realty Co., Inc.,* vs. *U.S.,*[95] a District Court was asked to find that loans to the corporation constituted a disqualifying second class of stock. Citing *Stinnett* and *Spinner* as authority for its decision, the Court was unwilling to treat advances by shareholders as a second class of stock because this would "defeat the interest of Congress regarding the tax liabilities of small business corporations." The Government appealed this adverse decision to the Fifth Circuit. On the same day that it decided *Amory,* another panel of judges of the Fifth Circuit found for the taxpayer in *Shores.*[96] It held that the debt-equity analysis was not relevant to a Subchapter S case. Moreover, the Court rejected the proportionality request of Regulation 1.1371-1(g).

At this time the taxpayer found considerable uncertainty. The Government had a victory in the Seventh Circuit (*Portage*) and defeats in the Fifth Circuit (*Amory* and *Shores*). With apparent conflict among the judicial circuits, the time was right for the Supreme Court to decide the issue. Unfortunately, this was not to happen, as the Seventh Circuit agreed to reconsider its decision for the Government in *Portage.* Upon reconsideration, the Court changed its mind and affirmed the judgment of the District Court.[97] The opinion was written by Judge Cummings, who had dissented in the earlier case. Noting a similar outcome in *Amory* and *Shores,* the Court concluded that "the traditional thin capitalization doctrine tests for determining whether a purported loan should be treated as an equity contribution in order to prevent improper tax avoidance in other contexts are not suitable for determining whether a purported loan constitutes a second class of stock within the meaning of Section 1371(a)(4)." The purpose of the single-class-of-stock requirement was stated to be the simplification of the process of allocating profits and losses among shareholders. The opinion also affirms the invalidity of Regulation 1.1371-1(g).

This area now appears to be fairly well settled, for the Government's arsenal seems to be depleted, at least for a while. The Government has generally been unable to sustain the validity of Regulation

[95]27 A.F.T.R. 2d 71-681 (S.D. Fla. 1971).
[96]30 A.F.T.R. 2d 72-5672 (5th Cir. 1972).
[97]31 A.F.T.R. 2d 73-864 (7th Cir. 1973).

1.1371-1(g). The reconsideration in *Portage* plus the dismissal without opinion in *Stinnett* has convinced the Government to reconsider its position in the second-class-of-stock issue. In July, 1973, T.I.R.-1248 was issued to the effect that the IRS will no longer litigate this issue and that it will revise Regulation 1.1371-1(g). Thus, at the time of this writing,[98] the issues appear to be resolved. Unfortunately, this temporary accord between IRS and taxpayers may last only until new regulations are developed. Taxpayers should still remain alert to problems and developments in this area.

Tax Planning for Loans by Owners

It is clearly established that a shareholder may be a lender as well as an owner. However, the purported debt held by the stockholders must meet the requirement of a formal debt instrument, and the shareholders must have an intention to enforce the debt. Whether stockholder "loans" are debt or equity-type contributions depends upon the intent of the parties to the transaction. Adequate tax planning necessitates the creation of supporting records which show the intent of the parties to create a *bona fide* loan and to show that repayment of the loan is expected.[99] Furthermore, the advance must represent realistic debt which conforms with "arms-length" standards and "substantial economic reality."[100]

Most of the tax-planning factors discussed under the thinly capitalized pattern apply here also. Since *Gooding Amusement Co.,*[101] the courts have placed less emphasis on the debt-to-stock ratios. In *Gooding,* the Tax Court held that notes from the stockholders were equity capital even though the ratio (based upon the use of a reasonable value of goodwill) was approximately one to one.

A combination of a number of factors should materially strengthen the position of an electing corporation in the event of trouble in this area. If at all possible, advances to Subchapter S corporations by stockholders should be in direct proportion to the equity investment of the owners in order to meet the requirement of Regulation 1.1371-1(g). Naturally, the accounting and tax records of both the creditors and the debtors should clearly indicate that the advances are loans and not equity.[102] The promissory note should contain a

---

[98]April, 1974.

[99]*August F. Nielsen, supra,* note 65; *Wood Preserving Corp.* vs. *U.S.,* 347 F. 2d 111 (4th Cir. 1965).

[100]*Nassau Lens Co.* vs. *Commissioner,* 308 F. 2d 39 (2d Cir. 1962).

[101]*Supra,* note 67.

[102]*Ortmayer* vs. *Commissioner,* 265 F. 2d 848 (7th Cir. 1959).

reasonable rate of interest[103] with a fixed maturity.[104] Any supporting documentation should show that the loan is for a temporary shortage of working capital rather than to obtain long-term working capital.[105] When the obligation matures, the stockholder should demand to be repaid. If he does not receive the repayment, the electing corporation should execute a new promissory note at a new face value which contains all unpaid interest.

Shareholders Guarantee Outside Loans

The problems resulting from advances by the owners to an electing corporation may be avoided by securing the required funds from an outside lending institution, but quite often the shareholders will have to personally guarantee the loans. The loan continues status as debt and is repayable to the outside lender without dividend consequences to the stockholders. But this advantage is of little importance if the electing corporation is newly formed with little or no accumulated earnings. These guarantees are advantageous only after the election has terminated and the capital is returned to the stockholders without dividend consequences. The major disadvantage of outside loans is that the stockholder does not increase his basis for the purpose of the limitation on the net operating loss deduction in I.R.C. Section 1374(c)(2).[106] In other words, a stockholder's loss deduction is limited to his stock basis and advances to the company.[107]

A loan from an outside lender guaranteed by the stockholders may be a substantial improvement over other methods of acquiring additional working capital where an electing corporation does not anticipate initial losses. However, guaranteed loans may not be a perfect remedy as some writers profess, for this method may also be

---

[103]*Donald J. Peterson, supra,* note 62, but see *Lewis Bldg. & Supplies, Inc., supra,* note 47.

[104]But see *Lewis Bldg. & Supplies, Inc., supra,* note 47; *Milton Raynor, supra,* note 60; *Alfred N. Hoffman, supra,* note 66.

[105]*Jennings* vs. *U.S.,* 272 F. 2d 842 (7th Cir. 1959); *Albert W. Peterson,* T.C.M. 1965-145; but see *August F. Nielsen,* T.C.M. 1968-11; *Milton Raynor, supra,* note 60.

[106]*Neal* vs. *U.S.,* 25 A.F.T.R. 2d 896 (D.C. Calif. 1971); *P.E. Blum,* 59 T.C. 436 (1973); See also *Wheat* vs. *U.S.,* 31 A.F.T.R. 2d 73-808 (S.D. Tex. 1973).

[107]*William H. Perry,* 47 T.C. 159 (1966), *aff'd.* 392 F. 2d 458 (8th Cir. 1968); *Joe E. Borg,* 50 T.C. 257 (1968); *Milton T. Raynor,* 50 T.C. 762 (1968). Also, an electing corporation's forgiveness of a stockholder's debt is a property distribution which reduces his stock basis. In *Jack Haber,* 52 T.C. 255 (1969), such a forgiveness reduced a stockholder's basis to zero and a corporate loss was not allowed to be passed through to the shareholder.

vulnerable.[108] The frequency with which this suggested loan procedure is followed by Subchapter S corporations has not been overlooked by the Commissioner. In *Putnam* vs. *Commissioner,* 352 U.S. 82 (1959), the Supreme Court reviewed the status of a shareholder-guarantor and indicated by dictum that the guarantee was essentially a direct loan by the stockholder to his corporation. However, in one Subchapter S case, *Milton T. Raynor,* 50 T.C. 762 (1968), a partnership type agreement by the shareholders satisfied the Tax Court that guaranteed loans and advances were proportionate to equity holdings. Thus, there was no second class of stock.

To summarize — if the electing corporation can show that the particular guaranteed loans are at a reasonable rate of interest, are reasonable in amount compared to the equity capital, and are proportionate to equity, the courts may not recast the form of the transaction. However, where the loans are from unrelated parties with a high debt-to-equity ratio, the unrelated parties have been considered equity owners in non-Subchapter S cases.[109] Conversely, where the business arrangement is bona fide, fair, and reasonable, the transaction has not been recast.[110] Borrowing from nonshareholder sources on the corporation's own credit is, of course, the safest policy to follow.

Although the courts appear to be decreasing the Commissioner's power to disqualify thinly capitalized electing corporations through the one-class-of-stock requirement, it is questionable whether the IRS should have any such power at all. The House Ways and Means Committee studied an amendment in 1969 which would have provided that debt would not be regarded as a separate class of stock. This amendment would have applied to any interest not designated as stock which has neither voting rights nor distribution rights beyond a fixed annual interest rate and a fixed amount upon redemption or payment. Regrettably, this amendment was not included in the 1969 Tax Reform Bill, but taxpayers can hope that it will be eventually passed. The thin capitalization doctrine can be useful to the Commissioner to prevent electing corporations from abusing the tax advantages available through a thin capital structure.[111] But the

---

[108]See *Merlo Builders. Inc..* 1964-34; *Easson* vs. *U.S.,* 294 F. 2d 653 (9th Cir. 1961), *rev'g.* 33 T.C. 963 (1960); *Kobacker,* 37 T.C. 882 (1962), *acq.,* 1964-2 C.B. 6; *Murphy Logging Co.* vs. *U.S.,* 339 F. Supp. 794 (D.C. Ore. 1965), *rev'd.,* 378 F. 2d 222 (9th Cir. 1967).

[109]*Marsan Realty Corp.,* T.C.M. 1963-297.

[110]*Truschel,* 29 T.C. 433 (1957); *Howes,* 30 T.C. 909 (1958).

[111]See "Shareholder Lending and Tax Avoidance in the Subchapter S Corporation," *Columbia Law Review,* Vol. 67 (March, 1967), pp. 500-501.

Commissioner should not be allowed to disqualify a Subchapter S election by using this doctrine to enforce the single-class-of-stock requirement.

Stockholder Agreements

Still another problem exists in determining what constitutes a class of stock. Under the Rulings and Regulations, a standard business arrangement which is used to provide for the management of a corporation may create a second class of stock. The restrictive Regulation provides that:

> If the outstanding shares of stock of the corporation are not identical with respect to the rights and interest which they convey in the control, profits, and assets of the corporation, then the corporation is considered to have more than one class of stock. Thus a difference as to voting rights, dividend rights, or liquidation preferences of outstanding stock will disqualify a corporation.[112]

The Treasury's position is that most shareholder control agreements will create a fatal second class of stock. Revenue Ruling 63-226, 1963-2 C.B. 341, discusses the incorporation of a partnership consisting of eight active partners and two limited partners. One class of stock (a voting common stock) was authorized and issued to the ten partners in accordance with their pro rata interest in the partnership. After incorporation, the shareholders entered into an agreement whereby any stockholder who was not actively engaged in the business would grant an irrevocable proxy to vote his stock to one or more of the active stockholders. Two former limited partners (now inactive stockholders) granted irrevocable proxies to the active stockholders. The IRS ruled that this agreement created a second class of stock which disqualifies a corporation from obtaining special tax treatment. Since the rights and interest of the inactive stockholders in the control of the corporation were not identical with the rights and interest of the active stockholders, the Commissioner held that there were two classes of stock.[113]

Further, the Commissioner deviates from the facts outlined in the Revenue Ruling and prohibits the use of most stockholder control agreements:

> Furthermore, in the event that the outstanding stock of a corporation is subject to any other type of voting control device or arrangement, such as a pooling or voting agreement or a

---

[112]Regulation 1.1371-1(g).

[113]Rev. Rul. 63-226, 1963-2 C.B. 341.

charter provision granting certain shares a veto power or the like, which has the effect of modifying the voting rights of part of the stock so that particular shares possess disproportionate voting power as compared to the dividend rights or liquidation rights of those shares and as compared to the voting, dividend and liquidation rights of the other shares of stock of the corporation outstanding, the corporations will be deemed to have more than one class of stock.[114]

Although of questionable validity, the IRS clearly states that differences in voting rights may arise not only by the creation of nonvoting stock in the corporate charter but also as a result of agreements between the stockholders.

There is no justification for the Treasury to classify stockholder agreements as a second class of stock in order to disqualify or terminate an election. It has been discussed elsewhere in this chapter that the one-class-of-stock requirement was intended to facilitate a simple and uncomplicated allocation of income and loss among shareholders and not just to deny many small corporations the opportunity of this tax treatment. The Senate Finance Committee in 1954, while elaborating on the defunct I.R.C. Section 1351, did state that no class of stock could be preferred over another as to "either dividends, distributions or voting rights."[115] Voting control has no relevance in allocating income to shareholders. Furthermore, no mention was made about voting control when the Subchapter S provision was enacted in 1958.

A requirement of the Supplement S provision in 1940 provides some basis for the Treasury's contention that disproportionate voting rights should terminate electing corporations. The Supplement S election for personal service corporations required that the shareholders would be regularly engaged in the active conduct of the affairs of the corporation.[116] This same requirement was included in the Senate Bill dealing with I.R.C. Section 1351 in 1954. An electing corporation had to be "actively engaged in the conduct of the business of the corporation (i.e., such shareholders must all occupy managerial positions)."[117] Thus, the condition that all stocks have equal voting rights may have been intended to implement the requirement that every shareholder be an active participant in the business.

The I.R.C. Section 1351 election was eliminated by the Confer-

---

[114]*Ibid.*

[115]Senate Report No. 1922, *op. cit.,* p. 453.

[116]United States *Code,* 1936, *op. cit.,* p. 2693.

[117]Senate Report No. 1622, *op. cit.,* p. 453.

ence Committee and did not become a part of the 1954 Code. In 1958, neither the Senate Bill nor the Subchapter S provisions ultimately enacted contained the condition that each stockholder be actively engaged in the business.

Since the 1958 Act and the 1954 proposal were similar and the one-class requirement appeared in each, as well as in the Supplement S provision in 1940, it is reasonable for the IRS to use the 1940 and the 1954 legislative history for guidance in interpreting the purpose of Congress in 1958. If the 1954 Committee statement as to voting rights was intended to fulfill a test that all shareholders be active participants, there is no justification for the IRS to require any condition as to equality of voting rights. "Moreover, even if Congress had mistakenly assumed that the existence of differences in voting rights would create problems in allocating income, a recognition by the Treasury that no such problems in fact exist would provide it with justification for interpreting the statute in a manner which did not give effect to the mistaken impression of Congress."[118]

Logically, disqualification as a result of a difference in voting rights is statutory only if difficulties exist in allocating income to the shareholders. There are no complexities in imputing income to the stockholders when the only differences between the shares of stock are merely differences in voting rights. It certainly is not unfair to tax a shareholder on income even though he may not have a voice in whether the income is to be distributed to him. The stockholder must file a written consent to the Subchapter S election and he, in effect, chooses to accept his share of any income. Further, a shareholder can easily terminate the election by transferring a share of stock to a trust or to a nonconsenting person. If the Congressional reason underlying the one-class condition is the avoidance of complexity in allocating income, the Treasury's position that voting and nonvoting stock creates a second class of stock is of debatable validity.

In *Barnes Motor & Parts Co.* vs. *U.S.,*[119] a corporation was unable to prove that a certain class of stock was voting stock because all corporate decisions had been unanimous. Even though all the shares in question had been treated as voting shares for at least twenty years, all of the "nonvoting" shares had not been cancelled

---

[118]Marvin W. Weinstein, "Stockholder Agreements and Subchapter S Corporation," *Tax Law Review,* Vol. 19 (March, 1964), p. 396; See also Note, "Invalid Election and Involuntary Termination of Subchapter S Status," 29 *Wash. & Lee L. Rev.* 407 (1972); W. W. Wilson, "Subchapter S and Voting Trusts," *Baylor Law Review,* Vol. 25 (Winter, 1973), p. 92.

[119]25 A.F.T.R. 2d 70-1241 (D.C. N.C. 1970).

on the corporate books. A disqualifying second class of stock did exist when the election was made.

One District Court has held that Rev. Rul. 63-226 is invalid. In *A. & N. Furniture & Appliance Co.*,[120] shareholders entered into a voting trust agreement whereby a trustee was given the irrevocable right to vote all the shares of stock over a ten-year period. The purpose of the agreement was to insure continuity and stability of policy and management. The Commissioner asserted that the voting trust created a second class of stock, citing Regulation 1.1371-1(g) and Revenue Ruling 63-226.

Noting that the Tax Court had previously questioned the Commissioner's logic,[121] the District Court declared that the ruling was invalid and Regulation 1.1371-1(g) did not apply to voting trusts. The creation of the voting trust gave the trustee no interest in the securities except the power to vote them. "The grant of full power to the trustee to vote the stock is inconsistent with a power to destroy the beneficial ownership of the stock, by sale or otherwise."[122]

This court stressed the fact that the voting trust arrangement was not used to circumvent the ten-shareholder limitation and did not create accounting complications for the Commissioner in allocating profits or losses among the stockholders. "The creation of the voting trust did not, and could not, increase the size of the electing corporation, nor did it create accounting complications."[123] One court has criticized the *A & N* reasoning. In *Fulk & Needham, Inc.*,[124] the court felt that size was not the only consideration in formulating the trust restriction. "The existence of another corporation, a trust, or a partnership as a shareholder in the electing corporation complicates the structure by adding another entity through which earnings must be passed."

Thus, the voting trust issue is probably far from settled, and practitioners should watch for further court decisions regarding this sensitive issue.

The Tax Court in a split decision has indicated that Regulation 1.1371-1(g) and Rev. Rul. 63-226 are too broad in light of their intent. The *Parker Oil Co.*[125] case concerns a lawsuit over stock ownership.

---

[120]*A & N Furniture & Appliance Co.*, 271 F. Supp. 40 (D.C. Ohio 1967).

[121]*Catalina Homes, Inc.*, T.C.M. 1964-225.

[122]*A & N, supra*, note 120.

[123]*Ibid.*

[124]*Fulk & Needham, Inc.*, 288 F. Supp. 47 (D.C. N.C. 1968).

[125]*Parker Oil Co.*, 58 T.C. 985 (1972).

Some of the stock belonging to an electing stockholder contained an irrevocable proxy designated to a third party. A notation of this proxy appeared on the face of the applicable stock certificates. The Commissioner said that this difference in voting rights caused a fatal second class of stock. However, five concurring judges disagreed. They felt that the proxy could not conceivably alter the reporting of profits, and that there are many business problems in electing corporations that can be solved by such agreements. Although the Tax Court did not reject the Regulation, five judges felt that the proxy was not a second class of stock (whether or not the proxy was irrevocable) because all stock had the same rights. Instead, the proxy merely specified who would exercise the rights. (Three dissenting judges would have upheld the Commissioner.)

Non-tax business problems do exist in closely-held operations. The shareholders of close corporations often attempt to operate their business as partnerships or proprietorships. In fact, the Senate Finance Committee asserted that close corporations are "essentially partnerships."[126] Shareholder agreements are often used to solve the non-tax business problems and help the business operate as a partnership or proprietorship. Such agreements may provide that each stockholder will vote for the other as a director, or that some shares will have disproportionate voting power to enable them to elect directors, or that each stockholder will have veto power as to the election of directors, or that two or more stockholders will pool their shares and vote together. However, if the Commissioner's position in Rev. Rul. 63-226 and Regulation 1.1371-1(g) is accepted by the courts, a small businessman will not "have the freedom to choose the type of business organization he desires without considering tax consequences. . ."[127]

Regulation 1.1371-1(g) does allow a corporation to provide artificial classes for the purpose of electing directors "in a number proportionate to the number of shares in each group" without incurring a second class of stock. One electing corporation learned the hard way that four classes of stock with unequal voting power without proportionality results in a terminated election. In *Samuel Pollack* vs. *Commissioner*,[128] four individuals organized a corporation in order to acquire a hotel. Each stockholder contributed an

[126]Senate Report No. 1622, *op. cit.*, p. 119.

[127]*A & N, supra,* note 120.

[128]392 F. 2d 409 (5th Cir. 1968), *aff'g.* 47 T.C. 92 (1966).

equal amount of capital, but the two shareholders who were actively to manage the hotel each received one-third of the stock, and the two remaining owners each received one-sixth of the total stock. The corporate charter divided the 100 shares of stock into four classes; each class of stock had the right to elect one director. The Tax Court upheld (with the Fifth Circuit affirming) the Commissioner's contention that a mere difference in voting power to elect directors results in more than one class of stock since proportionality was missing.

Chapter 6

Conduit Nature of the Subchapter S Corporation

In 1819, Chief Justice John Marshall described a corporation as ". . . an artificial being, invisible, intangible, and existing only in contemplation of the law."[1] This concept of the corporation has, over the years, become generally accepted. The tax laws adopted the so-called entity concept for regular corporations in levying a corporate income tax. Under this entity theory a firm is considered to be a separate unit operating for the benefit of the stockholders. However, the proprietary theory is used in determining the basis used in not allowing an expense deduction for dividends paid by the corporation. Under this proprietary approach, the proprietor or owner is the focus of attention. The various forms of organization are compared in Chapter 12.

In 1958 the tax law adopted the proprietary concept in limited situations. This proprietary theory is adhered to in not levying a corporate income tax on certain small business corporations. The corporation which elects Subchapter S treatment is, in many respects, a corporation (see Chapter 13 for an expanded discussion). Accordingly, those characteristics which are attributed to nonelecting corporations also apply to electing corporations. In the area of taxation, the Subchapter S corporation is subject to the rules of corporate taxation in all cases except where I.R.C. Sections 1371-1379 and the related regulations have modified this treatment. Taxable income is measured in a similar fashion by both the electing and nonelecting corporation. Corporations differ from partnerships in that the corporation is a tax-paying entity as well as a reporting entity; whereas the partnership serves as a reporting entity only. A partnership, as was suggested earlier, is a "conduit" in that income is measured at the partnership level and allocated among the partners for purposes of taxation. The actual tax, then, is levied on each partner's taxable income. Moreover, the character of the income and deductions is not lost at the partnership level. Long-term capital gains, additional first-year depreciation and the charitable contributions deduction all retain their respective characteristics in the hands of the partners.

Income from Subchapter S corporations is taxed in a manner

---

[1]*Dartmouth College* vs. *Woodward,* 17 U.S. (4 Wheat.) 581, 5 L. ed. 629 (1819).

which is similar to the treatment accorded partnership income. Except in the case of certain capital gains, no tax is levied on Subchapter S net income at the corporate level. Most income is passed through to the corporation's shareholders in accordance with the rules to be developed in this chapter.

But it is a gross oversimplification to describe a Subchapter S corporation as a corporation which has elected to be taxed as a partnership.[2] As a practical matter, the Subchapter S corporation is taxed as a hybrid in that the taxing process involves certain partnership and corporate concepts as well as many tax concepts which were developed specifically for electing corporations. Moreover, because the Subchapter S corporation is not normally subject to a tax at the corporate level, it is probably incorrect to describe the subject as the taxation of Subchapter S corporations, when one is referring to the manner in which the income of a Subchapter S corporation is taxed. The purpose of this chapter, then, is to consider in detail the taxation of income attributable to a Subchapter S corporation.

Measurement of Subchapter S Net Income

I.R.C. Section 446 provides the general rule that taxable income is to be computed using the same methods that the taxpayer uses for bookkeeping and income measurement purposes. Except as modified by other sections of the *Code,* taxable income is to be computed in accordance with generally accepted accounting principles as applied to the taxpayer's particular circumstances and conditions.[3] However, the differences between book income and taxable income are many and have contributed to the confusion which is ever present in our federal income tax law. In spite of this confusion, the *Code* has provided a concept of income for tax purposes which is applicable to corporations as well as to individuals.

Taxable income for a Subchapter S corporation is, for the most part, computed in the same manner as the taxable income for a non-electing corporation. However, I.R.C. Section 1371(d) provides exceptions to this rule, in that the net operating loss deduction (I.R.C. Section 172) is not considered. Also, the special deductions allowed corporations by Part VIII of Subchapter B are not allowed. Among these are the deduction for partially tax-exempt interest

---

[2]*Wilhelm* vs. *Commissioner,* 257 F. Supp. 16 (D.C. Wyo. 1966); *Byrne* vs. *Commissioner,* 361 F. 2d 939 (7th Cir. 1966), *aff'g.* 45 T.C. 151 (1965).

[3]See generally *Paul H. Travis,* 47 T.C. 502 (1967); *E. Morris Cox,* 43 T.C. 448 (1965); *W. H. Leonhart,* T.C.M. 1968-98, *aff'd. per curiam,* 414 F. 2d 749 (4th Cir. 1969).

(I.R.C. Section 242) as well as the deductions for certain types of dividends received and paid by corporations (I.R.C. Sections 243-247). Only the deduction for organization costs (I.R.C. Section 248) is considered in computing the taxable income of a Subchapter S corporation. Chapter 13 discusses the various methods of accounting which are available to a Subchapter S corporation.

Moreover, the Subchapter S corporation faces many of the same problems in measuring its income as does the nonelecting corporation. The IRS may object to the corporation's measure of income. In one case, the Commissioner objected to the corporation's use of the cash basis on grounds that it did not clearly reflect income as is required by I.R.C. Section 446(b). The use of the accrual method caused the corporation's taxable income to be increased.[4] The Commissioner may also disallow certain deductions which were used in measuring Subchapter S taxable income. In another case, the Commissioner disallowed deductions for travel and entertainment expenses.[5] Similarly, the IRS has indicated that where a bonus is accrued in one year but not paid until the next year, the bonus deduction is disallowed under Section 267 and does not reduce earnings and profits. However, the disallowed bonus payment is includable in the shareholder's gross income.[6]

Thus, the computation of taxable income presents no extraordinary problems for the Subchapter S corporation. However, the taxation of that income is indeed another matter. As a tax-paying entity, the nonelecting corporation is subject to a normal tax of 22 percent of its total taxable income and a surtax of 26 percent on all but the first $25,000 of its taxable income. Thus, the nonelecting corporate enterprise faces a 48 percent tax rate, which, obviously, reduces the amount which is available for distribution to the corporation's shareholders.

At the shareholder level, corporate distributions are a part of taxable income and are therefore taxed at various rates, depending upon the income circumstances of the recipient of the dividend. Because the personal income tax is progressive, it is difficult to generalize the impact of this tax on corporate earnings and to arrive at an effective rate of taxation. Nevertheless, the combined corporate and personal tax rates are sufficiently high to make the corporation an unattractive form of organization for many small enterprises. An

---

[4] *Paul H. Travis,* 47 T.C. 502 (1967).

[5] *Theodore T. Benson,* T.C.M. 1967-74.

[6] Rev. Rul. 70-306, 1970-1 C.B. 179.

election to be taxed as a Subchapter S corporation eliminates most of the adverse effects of this double taxation. Further, the Subchapter S election can be coupled with income averaging at the shareholder level in order to spread the corporate earnings over a greater time period.[7]

Pass-Through of Income to Shareholders

The Subchapter S corporation is an information reporting entity as opposed to a tax-paying entity. Taxable income is computed at the corporate level and is allocated among the shareholders of the corporation to be included in their respective taxable incomes. Form 1120S (which is reproduced in Chapter 9) provides for the computation of Subchapter S taxable income as well as for its allocation among the shareholders.

The *Code* is specific as to how the income is to be allocated among the shareholders. I.R.C. Section 1373(b) states that the undistributed taxable income shall be distributed on a pro rata basis to the shareholders on the last day of the corporation's tax year. Changes of ownership during the tax year are ignored for purposes of this allocation, as the ownership at the end of the tax year is used as the allocation basis. For example, if a shareholder dies before the end of the electing corporation's tax year, the UTI is included in his estate if a timely election is made by his estate, but no deduction is allowable under I.R.C. Section 691(c).[8]

While the use of the last day of the tax year may appear to be arbitrary, it is no more so than the use of a date of record for purposes of paying corporate dividends. Just as the stockholders as of the date of record are entitled to corporate dividends regardless of how long the stock has been owned, the Subchapter S shareholder at the close of the tax year is taxed on his pro rata share of the corporation's taxable income. This aspect of the Subchapter S corporation should present no difficulty as long as it is understood by all concerned parties. In fact, a bona fide shift of ownership at the close of the tax year can be a highly effective tax-planning device in that income can be shifted to individuals in lower tax brackets.[9] (Refer to Chapter 12 for a discussion of income splitting.)

---

[7]See I.R.C. Section 1301; Herman Schneider, "Many Problems Under Income Averaging Unresolved," *Journal of Taxation,* Vol. 22 (January, 1965), pp. 44-49.

[8]Rev. Rul. 64-308, 1964-2 C.B. 176.

[9]See Jerry J. McCoy, "Assignment of Income: Possibilities Under Subchapter S," *Tax Law Review,* Vol. 23 (January, 1968), pp. 213-226.

The application of these rules can be illustrated by the following:

The Pamida Corporation began operations and made a valid Subchapter S election early in January, 1974. Pamida had 300 shares of stock outstanding which were owned equally by X, Y, and Z (100 shares each). Taxable income for the corporation in 1974 was $600,000. Late in 1974 X, Y, and Z each sold 25 shares to W. Each shareholder will include $150,000 in his gross income even though W had only owned his stock for a short period of time.

Here are some other examples of this procedure:[10]

An electing small business corporation has taxable income and current earnings and profits of $100,000 for its taxable year. During that year, it distributed $8,000 to each of its ten equal shareholders. This amount is considered to be a dividend from current earnings and profits, and, accordingly, should be included in the taxpayer's gross income for the year of receipt. At this point, the corporation has $20,000 of undistributed taxable income which must also be included in the taxpayer's gross income for the year of receipt. Thus, $2,000 is allocated to each shareholder as a constructive dividend even though the amount was not actually distributed.

Suppose that the corporation had only $75,000 of taxable income. The difference between taxable income and current earnings and profits may be because certain deductions taken to arrive at taxable income do not reduce current earnings and profits. The $80,000 is still included in the shareholders' gross income as indicated above, even though this amount exceeds taxable income. However, the corporation has no undistributed taxable income, and therefore for tax purposes each shareholder includes only $8,000 in his gross income.

The above examples illustrate the pass-through of earnings concept which is central to the Subchapter S corporation. For purposes of taxation, the corporate entity appears to have been ignored as the taxable income was merely allocated among the shareholders. The reader, however, is cautioned against drawing too many conclusions from these highly simplified illustrations. Nevertheless, they do serve as a basis upon which to consider the more complicated features of the election.

The taxable income of an electing corporation that is included in the gross income of a stockholder is considered a "dividend" and not "income derived from a trade or business" for purposes of computing a stockholder's net operating loss under I.R.C. Section 172(c).

---

[10]Regulation 1.1373-1(g).

For purposes of computing the NOL, deductions which are not attributable to a taxpayer's trade or business are allowable only to the extent of his gross income not derived from a trade or business. However, any salary paid to the stockholders by the electing corporation is business income from a trade or business.[11]

Pass-Through of Long-Term Capital Gain

As most items are passed through a Subchapter S corporation, they forego their right to special tax treatment. This is in sharp contrast to a partnership, which allows the special characteristics of most income and expense items to be considered at the partner level. However, the long-term capital gain is passed on to the shareholder of a Subchapter S corporation. I.R.C. Section 1375(a)(1) states that the excess of an electing corporation's net long-term capital gain over its net short-term capital loss is entitled to long-term capital gain treatment at the shareholder level.

The rules of the *Code* with respect to the nature, holding period, and computation of long-term capital gains apply to electing as well as nonelecting corporations. In other words, it is the *net* long-term capital gain that is entitled to special consideration. As a general rule, the various components of the capital gain are not individually passed through to the shareholders. For example, I.R.C. Section 1231 accords capital gain treatment to the sale or exchange of assets used in a trade or business. If the net result of all sales or exchanges of Section 1231 assets results in a gain, the gain is accorded long-term capital gain treatment. However, if the sum of these transactions results in a loss, the loss is treated as an ordinary loss. At the shareholder level, it is not necessary to consider Subchapter S Section 1231 gains to determine the taxpayer's status with respect to Section 1231. In other words, if the net of all Section 1231 transactions results in a gain, the amount is passed through to shareholders as a part of the corporation's net long-term capital gain. However, if these transactions result in a loss, the amount is passed through to shareholders as a part of ordinary income or loss.[12]

In order to determine if the gain on the sale of an asset is entitled to capital gains treatment in the hands of the shareholders, it may be necessary to consider the activities in which the shareholders themselves are involved. Regulations state that "if an electing corporation is availed of by any shareholders or group of shareholders owning a

---

[11] Rev. Rul. 66-327, 1966-2 C.B. 357.
[12] Rev. Rul. 65-292, 1965-2 C.B. 319.

substantial portion of the stock of such corporation for the purpose of selling property which in the hands of such shareholder or shareholders would not have been an asset, gain from the sale of which would be capital gain, then the gain on the sale of such property by the corporation shall not be treated as a capital gain."[13] Thus, a Subchapter S corporation may not be used to create a capital gain situation for the sale of assets. A good illustration of the application would be the fact that a real estate agent could not convert ordinary income into capital gain by selling real estate through a Subchapter S corporation.

It is questionable that this shareholder reference test is valid, and it should be invalidated by the courts. In effect, the IRS has pierced the corporate veil of the Subchapter S corporation even though in Chapter 13 it is shown clearly that a Subchapter S corporation is a corporation and not a partnership. Possibly because of unwillingness on the part of IRS, the courts have yet to determine the validity of this regulation. However, in *Howell,* the Tax Court approached such a determination.[14]

In *Howell,* several men formed a Subchapter S corporation in order to purchase and hold one piece of property. For four years there were operating losses at the Subchapter S level which were passed through and deducted on the stockholders' personal tax returns. When the electing corporation sold the property for a gain, the stockholders showed the profit as capital gain on their tax returns.

The IRS presented a three-part position on the subject. First, the Commissioner said that the real property was not a capital asset since the property was held primarily for sale to customers in the ordinary course of corporate trade or business. Since the real estate was unimproved, not advertised for sale, and held for a significant period of time, the Tax Court held that the Subchapter S corporation "was engaged in investment activities in acquiring and selling the real estate." Therefore, the gain was capital gain at the corporate level.

Second, the Commissioner asserted that if the corporation was holding the real estate for investment purposes, then it could not be a Subchapter S corporation, since it had no active trade or business. The Tax Court said that the corporation was "attempting to make a profit and thereby was a business corporation . . . and the gain realized on the sale of the property is passed through to the shareholders."

The third issue concerned the character of the gain at the stock-

---

[13]Regulation 1.1375-1(d).
[14]*Howell,* 57 T.C. 546 (1972).

holder level where a substantial portion of the stock is held by a real estate agent. The court refused to pass on the validity of Regulation 1.1375-1(d):

> Specifically without passing on the validity of this regulation we note that, though one of the shareholders was a real estate broker, this does not necessitate a determination that he was in the business of buying and selling property. Therefore, assuming arguendo that the regulation is valid, we find on the facts presented that the real estate would have been a capital asset in the hands of the shareholders thereby requiring the gain . . . on the sale of the property to be taxed as capital gain at the shareholder level.

One can hope that the next court will hold that Regulation 1.1375-1(d) is invalid.[15] The IRS will not allow a taxpayer to pierce the corporate veil when it is to the favor of the taxpayer.[16]

A Subchapter S corporation may not pass through a capital loss. These losses are carried forward and used to offset capital gains which may be realized in future years. If a Subchapter S corporation has a net capital loss, it may be carried forward for up to five years and used to offset any net capital gains occurring in those years.[17]

The amount of this long-term capital gain pass-through is limited to the corporation's taxable income for the year.[18] Thus, a corporation may not sustain losses from operations and still pass through a long-term capital gain for special treatment.

At least one court refused to allow the Commissioner to treat a capital gain distribution as compensation income.[19] A Subchapter S corporation sold a portion of its business at a considerable profit which was entitled to capital gains treatment. Distributions of the proceeds were made to the shareholders and this was inadvertently treated as compensation in the accounting system. The court concluded that the facts of the case required treatment as a capital gains distribution because the corporation had never paid a salary to the taxpayer.

Regulation 1.1375-1(b) provides four steps to determine each stockholder's share of a long-term capital gain.

1. Compute the excess of the corporation's net long-term capital

---

[15]But compare *International Trading Co.* vs. *Commissioner,* 32 A.F.T.R. 2d 73-5500 (7th Cir. 1973), *rev'g.* 57 T.C. 455 (1972).

[16]*Richardson Foundation* vs. *U.S.,* 26 A.F.T.R. 2d 5144 (5th Cir. 1970).

[17]I.R.C. Section 1212.

[18]I.R.C. Section 1375(a)(1); *Byrne* vs. *Commissioner,* 361 F. 2d 939 (7th Cir. 1966).

[19]*John G. Carzis,* T.C.M. 1971-73.

gain over its net short-term capital loss for the tax year. This amount will also be reduced by any capital gains tax imposed on the corporation by I.R.C. Section 1378.

2. Compute the corporation's taxable income for the year in accordance with I.R.C. Section 1373(d).

3. Determine the amount of dividends from earnings and profits of the current taxable year included in each shareholder's gross income in accordance with paragraphs (d) and (e) of Regulation 1.1373-1.

4. Determine the amount of dividends from earnings and profits of the current taxable year included in the gross income of all shareholders of the corporation during the tax year.

The pro rata share is the amount which bears the same ratio to the lesser of the amounts determined in 1 and 2 above as the amount determined in 3 above bears to the amount determined in 4 above.

Examples in the pass-through of long-term capital gains are provided in Regulation 1.1375-1(e):

A Subchapter S corporation which has three equal shareholders has a net long-term capital gain of $9,000 for the taxable year 1969. In that year it has taxable income and current earnings and profits in excess of $9,000, but makes no distributions. Each shareholder will include $3,000 in his gross income as a long-term capital gain.

Another electing corporation has taxable income and current earnings and profits of $80,000 for the taxable year. This corporation has four equal shareholders and a net long-term capital gain of $100,000. It distributes $100,000 in money during the year, $25,000 to each shareholder, all of which is treated as a dividend. However, since the amount which will be treated as long-term capital gain by the shareholder cannot exceed the corporation's taxable income for the year, the amount which can be treated as long-term capital gain by each shareholder is $20,000 (¼ of $80,000).

An electing small business corporation on the calendar year has two equal shareholders on fiscal years ending June 30. For the taxable year 1969, the corporation has taxable income and current earnings and profits of $200,000 (including a long-term capital gain of $80,000). The corporation distributes cash dividends of $75,000 to each of its shareholders on March 15, 1969. Each shareholder's pro rata share of the corporation's capital gain is $40,000 (½ of $80,000). Of this share of the capital gain, $30,000 ($75,000/100,000 of $40,000) is includable by each shareholder in his taxable year ending June 30, 1969, and $10,000 thereof in his taxable year ending June 30, 1970.

Keep in mind that a short-term capital gain does not pass through but is added to other income items in arriving at undistributed taxable income. A Section 1231 gain does not pass through as such but is treated as a long-term capital gain in accordance with the rules under Section 1375(a).

Taxation of Certain Long-Term Capital Gains at the Corporate Level

Earlier we stated that the Subchapter S corporation was a tax reporting rather than a tax-paying entity. The exception to this status is the taxation of certain long-term capital gains under I.R.C. Section 1378. This provision entered the *Code* as a result of a 1966 tax law.[20]

This change in the treatment of long-term capital gains allows a tax to be levied on them at the corporate level. It may be appropriate to describe this action as an attempt to plug a tax loophole. The Subchapter S concept, as it was initially approved, created certain problems that the fiscal planners had not bargained for. A standard corporation cannot pass capital gains through to shareholders. The preferential treatment given to long-term capital gains benefited corporate shareholders only in that reduced tax payments left a greater amount available for dividends.

However, a standard corporation could, prior to 1966, time its transactions in such a way as to cause considerable capital gains to be accrued to a particular tax year. Then it could make a valid election and pass the gains through to shareholders, untaxed at the corporate level. Having accomplished its purpose, the election could be terminated and the corporation would return to its former mode of taxation. The tax advantage of this tactic is clear. Accordingly, it was only a matter of time until an attempt was made to eliminate this advantage of Subchapter S.

A Subchapter S corporation is now taxed on its capital gain if it meets the following requirements. First, the taxable income of the corporation must exceed $25,000. Second, the excess of the net long-term capital gain over the net short-term capital loss must exceed $25,000. Third, this amount must exceed 50 percent of the corporation's taxable income for the year.[21]

However, the corporation may fall within the above requirements and still avoid the penalty tax at the corporate level because of certain exceptions to these rules. For example, the tax will not

---

[20]Public Law 89-389; 80 Stat. 111 (1966).

[21]I.R.C. Section 1378(a).

apply to those corporations which have had valid elections in effect for the three previous tax years. Moreover, a new corporation can avoid the tax if it has operated under Subchapter S since it was founded.[22]

Thus, the effect of Section 1378 has been to hinder the use of Subchapter S on a "one shot" basis in order to avoid the tax on corporate capital gains. However, the corporation which has elected Subchapter S for sound business reasons will find its pattern of taxation unaffected by the realization of capital gains.

The alternative corporate capital gains rate is applied only to those gains that exceed $25,000. The total tax will be no more than the amount which would result from applying the standard corporate rates to the total taxable income (22 percent of the first $25,000; 48 percent of any amount over $25,000).[23] Any tax applied at the corporate level reduces the amount of the long-term capital gain to be passed through to shareholders.[24]

The effect of this tax is illustrated by the following:

A Subchapter S corporation which has four equal shareholders has taxable income and current earnings and profits of $100,000 for the taxable year. It also has a $100,000 net long-term capital gain which is taxable under Section 1378 of the *Code*. Assume that the capital gain tax at the corporate level is $22,500 which is 30 percent of $75,000. The first $25,000 of net long-term capital gain is exempt from this tax. Since the amount which will be treated as long-term capital gain by shareholders is reduced by any tax paid at corporate level, the amount which can be treated as long-term capital gain by each shareholder is $19,387.50. This amount is computed by subtracting the tax ($22,500) from $100,000 and dividing the amount into four equal parts. Thus, each shareholder would include $19,387.50 in his personal long-term capital gains and the capital gains tax would be based upon this combined amount.[25]

I.R.C. Section 1378 attempts to prevent one abuse of the Subchapter S corporation, in that a standard corporation may not avoid the capital gains tax at the corporate level by making a temporary Subchapter S election. However, where capital gains are taxed at the corporate level, the overall tax may be less under Subchapter S than

---

[22]I.R.C. Section 1378(c).

[23]I.R.C. Section 1378(b).

[24]I.R.C. Section 1375(a)(3).

[25]Regulation 1.1375-1(e)(2)(ii). This illustration has been adapted to reflect change of the alternative capital gain tax from 25 percent to 30 percent.

it would be for the nonelecting corporation. Further, it may be possible to avoid this penalty tax imposed by I.R.C. Section 1378.

If an electing corporation is subject to the Section 1378 tax, it may also be subject to a 10 percent minimum tax (see subsequent discussion). Further, if any of its shareholders own stock in other corporations, the electing corporation may be a member of a controlled group of corporations. A controlled group of corporations is limited to one $25,000 surtax exemption which may be split among the various corporations. Until 1975, however, these corporations may elect a declining multiple surtax exemption with the payment of an extra 6 percent penalty tax on the exempted income, other than one $25,000 surtax exemption (I.R.C. Section 1562(b); I.R.C. Section 1564). If a Subchapter S corporation is a member of an electing controlled group of corporations, it would be classified as an "excluded member" if there is no Section 1378 tax (Regulation 1.1563-1(b)(2) (ii)(c)). However, if the Subchapter S corporation has a Section 1378 tax and the group has elected multiple surtax exemptions, the Subchapter S corporation would be subject to the 6 percent penalty tax.

Avoidance of Penalty Tax

A Subchapter S corporation may use the installment tax method under I.R.C. Section 453(b) and avoid this penalty tax on capital gains.[26] For example, if an electing corporation anticipates a capital gain in excess of the $25,000 limitation in I.R.C. Section 1378, the corporation may elect to spread the gain over a number of years or at least beyond the third electing year. I.R.C. Section 453(b) is, of course, limited to the casual sales of non-inventory personal property for an amount in excess of $1,000 and of real property. The payments must not exceed 30 percent of the selling price in the year of the sale.

This manner of circumventing the I.R.C. Section 1378 penalty tax can be most fruitful where Sections 1245 and 1250 assets are involved. Under both Regulation 1.1245-6(d) and Regulation 1.1250-1 (c)(6), all ordinary income is recognized first; thus, the electing corporation can recognize the ordinary income first and save the I.R.C. Section 1231 gains for years after the third electing year.

Pass-Through of Corporate Net Operating Losses

One of the more interesting aspects of the Subchapter S legislation has been those provisions which allow a net operating loss

---

[26]See Irving M. Grant et al., "The Relative Tax Advantages of Partnership and Subchapter S Corporations," *Twenty-First Tax Institute of University of Southern California,* Vol. 21 (1969), p. 455; See Rev. Rul. 65-292, 1965-2 C.B. 319.

(NOL) to be passed through to the corporation's shareholders. The shareholders of a standard corporation have difficulty in obtaining tax benefit from net operating losses since in order to accomplish this they must actually divest themselves of their stock. If a Subchapter S corporation sustains a net operating loss for a certain tax year, such a loss is deductible by the shareholders for the year in which the corporation's tax year ends.[27] Obviously, the corporation is not entitled to the net operating loss, and such a loss has no effect on the computation of earnings and profits.[28]

In the hands of a shareholder, a Subchapter S net operating loss is a "trade or business loss." Under I.R.C. Section 1374(d), the loss is deducted from gross income in arriving at adjusted gross income. Thus, the shareholder may receive a tax benefit from the net operating loss and still elect the standard deduction. Moreover, the shareholder's allowable share of the net operating loss is subject to the carryback and carryforward provisions of the *Code* where the stockholder does not have sufficient income to absorb the NOL.

Since a NOL is a "trade or business loss," any deduction is subject to the hobby loss limitation. Under I.R.C. Section 183, any deductions which result from activities not engaged in for a profit are deductible in taxable years after 1969 only to the extent of any hobby income. Certain expenses (which would be allowable without regard to whether the activity is a hobby) are still deductible, but these expenses (i.e., interest, taxes, casualty losses) reduce the hobby income which could otherwise be offset against hobby expenses.

A Subchapter S corporation is presumed to have a profit motive if a profit occurs in two out of five consecutive years. In the case of an electing corporation involved in breeding, training, or racing horses, a profit only has to be shown in two out of seven consecutive years. If the electing corporation meets the two-year profit rule, the Commissioner can still attack the losses as hobby losses, but the IRS will have to prove that the activity is not engaged in for a profit. Similarly, if the electing corporation does not satisfy the two-year profit rule, it has the burden of proving a profit motive. Thus, Congress has given the Treasury a powerful weapon to combat the so-called "gentlemen farmers."

Moreover, the Tax Reform Act of 1969 contains provisions which place limitations upon unlimited farm loss deductions. The losses are not disallowed, but are merely accumulated in an excess

[27]I.R.C. Section 1374.

[28]I.R.C. Section 1377(c).

deduction account which can be used to offset gains from farming when they arise. The rules apply only to farmers whose non-farm adjusted gross income exceeds $50,000. Also, the first $25,000 of the loss is not affected by these provisions. These rules apply to Subchapter S corporations. For example, if none of the shareholders have, in their individual capacity, a net loss from farming, the above provisions apply. That is, the corporation's non-farm taxable income must exceed $50,000 and its farm loss must exceed $25,000. However, if any individual shareholder has a farm loss, the dollar limitations are not applied. Thus, if any one shareholder has a net farm loss in any amount, the regular corporate rules apply (i.e., no $25,000 and $50,000 safety valves).[29]

The net operating loss for a Subchapter S corporation is computed in the same manner as it is computed for a nonelecting corporation except that the special deductions provided by I.R.C. Sections 241-247 are not allowed.[30] These exceptions relate to the dividends received deduction as well as to the deduction for partially tax exempt interest. These rules are consistent with the rules for computing the net income of a Subchapter S corporation, as discussed earlier in the chapter.

Net operating losses are not allocated among shareholders in the same manner as is income. In the case of income, the basis for allocation is stock ownership on the last day of the corporation's tax year. Conversely, net operating losses are allocated on a daily basis to all shareholders who owned stock during the tax year.[31] Apparently, the purpose of the daily basis allocation is to prevent taxpayers from purchasing losses near the end of the tax year.

There is a three-step plan for computing the amount of the net operating loss that each shareholder is entitled to deduct:[32]

1. Determine the net operating loss per day by dividing the corporation's net operating loss by the number of days in the tax year.
2. Determine each shareholder's ratio of stock ownership for each day. This step seems like a complicated procedure but, in most cases, the stock ownership will change very few times during the year. Once determined, the ratio applies to all subsequent days until the ownership changes again.

---

[29]I.R.C. Section 1251.
[30]I.R.C. Section 1374(c)(1).
[31]*Ibid.*
[32]Regulation 1.1374-1(b)(3).

3. Multiply the daily loss by the ownership ratio and then multiply this amount by the number of days that the ownership remained unchanged. For purposes of this rule, all stock is considered to be held by the transferee rather than the transferor on the date of the transfer.
4. To compute each shareholder's deduction, merely combine the amounts as computed in the preceding section. If the calculations have been correct, the sum of the amounts allocated to all shareholders should be equal to the net operating loss.

If the stock ownership remains unchanged throughout the entire tax year, the ownership ratio for the year becomes the basis for allocating the net operating loss among shareholders. Regulation 1.1374-4 provides an example of the allocation of a net operating loss under these circumstances:

A Subchapter S corporation has a net operating loss of $10,000 for the tax year ended December 30, 1974. The stock of this corporation was at all times during the tax year owned by the same ten shareholders, each of whom owned 10 percent of this stock. Each shareholder is entitled to deduct $1,000 from his gross income for his tax year in which the corporation's tax year ends.

The more complicated procedure of allocating the net operating loss where both the number of shares outstanding and the ownership of the shares has changed during the tax year is illustrated by the following:

The Pamida Corporation, which has made a valid election under Subchapter S, sustains a net operating loss of $73,000 for the year ending December 31, 1974. On January 1 of that year, the stock consisted of 100 shares and was owned by three shareholders. A owned 50 shares; B and C owned 25 shares each. On March 15, A sold 25 shares to D. On July 15, the corporation sold 100 additional shares of stock, with A, B, C, D, and E each buying 20 shares. On September 1, B sells his 45 shares to E. The following steps are necessary to allocate the $73,000 net operating loss among Pamida's shareholders:

1. It is necessary to compute the net operating loss per day. This is accomplished by dividing $73,000 by 365. The net operating loss per day is $200.
2. The ownership periods are computed. Note that the new ownership period begins on the date of the transfer. The Pamida Corporation had four ownership periods during the tax year 1974.
3. Allocate the net operating loss to each ownership period

149

by multiplying the number of days in the period by $200, the daily net operating loss.

4. Compute each shareholder's share of the net operating loss for each ownership period. Take the ratio of each shareholder's stock to the total stock and multiply this by the net operating loss which has been allocated to the ownership period.

5. Combine the net operating losses which have been allocated to each shareholder for the various ownership periods. This amount represents each shareholder's share of the net operating loss for the tax year 1974, allocated in accordance with Regulation 1.1374-1(b). See Table 6-1.

TABLE 6-1

PAMIDA CORPORATION
DISTRIBUTION OF NET OPERATING LOSS, 1974

| Period | Shareholders | | | | |
	A	B	C	D	E
1. January 1 to March 15	50 Sh.	25 Sh.	25 Sh.		
73 days					
Ratio	½	¼	¼		
Loss 73 x $200 = $14,600	$7,300	$3,650	$3,650		
2. March 15 to July 15	25 Sh.	25 Sh.	25 Sh.	25 Sh.	
122 days					
Ratio	¼	¼	¼	¼	
Loss: 122 x $200 = $24,400	$6,100	$6,100	$6,100	$6,100	
3. July 15 to September 1	45 Sh.	45 Sh.	45 Sh.	45 Sh.	20 Sh.
48 days					
Ratio	45/200	45/200	45/200	45/200	20/200
Loss: 48 x $200 = $9,600	$2,160	$2,160	$2,160	$2,160	$960
4. September 1 to December 31	None	45 Sh.	45 Sh.	45 Sh.	65 Sh.
122 days					
Ratio		45/200	45/200	45/200	65/200
Loss: 122 x $200 = $24,400	None	$5,490	$5,490	$5,490	$7,930

Calculation of Daily Loss

$$\frac{73,000 \text{ (loss)}}{365} = \$200 \text{ per day}$$

Recapitulation of Loss

Shareholder	Amount
A	$15,560
B	17,400
C	17,400
D	13,750
E	8,890
Total	$73,000

Wasted NOL

A shareholder may not necessarily receive the benefit from a net operating loss which is allocated to him. I.R.C. Section 1374(c)(2) limits the shareholder's deduction to the "adjusted basis" of his stock *plus* the "adjusted basis" of any indebtedness of the corporation to the shareholder. In both cases, an end-of-tax-year basis is specified. Essentially, "adjusted basis" means cost plus and/or minus the adjustments allowed by I.R.C. Section 1376. Basis of stock is increased by the net income of the corporation which the shareholder has actually included in his gross income under I.R.C. Section 1371(b). Stock basis is reduced (but not below zero) by the stockholder's portion of corporate net operating losses as allowed by I.R.C. Section 1374(c). If a taxpayer is unable to prove his tax basis, any net operating loss can be denied to the shareholder under Section 1374(c)(1).[33] See Chapter 7 for a comprehensive discussion of stock basis.

After the shareholder's adjusted stock basis has been eliminated by a net operating loss, any excess net operating loss is used to reduce the shareholder's basis for any loans made to the corporation (but never below zero). Basis for loans is established by the actual advances made to the corporation and not by indirect loans. For example, a wife who becomes a Subchapter S shareholder through inheritance cannot increase her tax basis by allowing the Subchapter S corporation to borrow from her husband's estate even though she is the sole beneficiary. The estate and not the shareholder is the creditor.[34]

The fact that a shareholder has guaranteed a loan made to the corporation by a third party has no effect upon the shareholder's loan basis unless he has actually made payments as a result of that guaranty. The Tax Court has held that "indebtedness of the corporation to the shareholder" within the meaning of I.R.C. Section 1374 (c)(2)(B) does not exist because a shareholder is primarily liable on indebtedness to a third party. Furthermore, where guaranteed loans exist and the Subchapter S corporation is thinly capitalized, a taxpayer may not use the "substance over form" theory to recharacterize the guaranteed loans as equity capital in order to increase his stock basis.[35] No form of indirect borrowing increases a shareholder's basis

---

[33]*Sauvigne,* T.C.M. 1971-30; *Wise,* T.C.M. 1971-38.
[34]*Prashker,* 59 T.C. 172 (1972).
[35]*P. E. Blum,* 59 T.C. 436 (1973).

unless payments have been made on the obligation.[36] If basis is considered necessary to justify a net operating loss deduction, it is reasonable that indirect borrowing not be allowed to increase that basis.

Thus, the fact that the Subchapter S corporation owes money to a trust of which the shareholder is a beneficiary will not increase the shareholder's debt basis. Clearly, the debt must be to the shareholder.[37]

The IRS has held that when, in a subsequent year, a guarantor-stockholder is required to make payment on a note on which his corporation has defaulted, such a payment creates an indebtedness to him from the corporation which increases his adjusted basis. This increase in basis does not relate back to prior years in which the net operating loss exceeded his adjusted basis.[38] Furthermore, a shareholder cannot exchange his demand notes for his Subchapter S corporation's long-term notes in the same amount in order to create an indebtedness under Section 1374(c)(2)(B). The Tax Court has held that such a transaction amounts to little more than the posting of offsetting book entries since the taxpayer is economically unimpaired.[39] Shareholders' attempts to increase the basis for their stock by giving notes to the corporation in exchange for that stock have also been held a sham. Cost of stock cannot be increased in this manner.[40]

Suppose a stockholder's share of a net operating loss is greater than both his stock basis and the basis of his indebtedness. The excess net operating loss cannot be used by the stockholder, since the basis in both stock and debt is reduced to zero. Furthermore, the excess net operating loss is wasted completely and cannot be used by either the stockholder or the corporation in future or prior years.[41] Tax planning measures to avoid this adverse situation are subsequently discussed.

The statutes governing partnership taxation allow partners more flexibility with respect to net operating losses. Where a net operating

---

[36]*Milton T. Raynor,* 50 T.C. 762 (1968); *William H. Perry,* 47 T.C. 159 (1966), *aff'd.* 392 F. 2d 458 (8th Cir. 1968); *Joe E. Borg,* 50 T.C. 257 (1968); *Neal* vs. *U.S.* 25 A.F.T.R. 2d 70-896 (D.C. Calif. 1970).

[37]*Robertson* vs. *U.S.,* 32 A.F.T.R. 2d 73-5556 (D.C. Nev. 1973).

[38]Rev. Rul. 71-288, 1971-2 C.B. 319; Rev. Rul. 70-50, 1970-1 C.B. 178.

[39]*William H. Perry,* 54 T.C. 1293 (1970), *aff'd.* 27 A.F.T.R. 2d 71-1464 (8th Cir. 1971); *Miles Production Co.,* T.C.M. 1969-274, *aff'd.* 29 A.F.T.R. 2d 72-855 (5th Cir. 1972).

[40]*Silverstein* vs. *U.S.,* 31 A.F.T.R. 2d 73-902 (E.D. La. 1973).

loss exceeds a partner's tax basis, a suspense account is established and the excess loss is carried forward indefinitely until his adjusted basis is sufficient to absorb the excess loss. Congress should amend I.R.C. Section 1374(c)(2) to preserve any portion of a net operating loss which exceeds the tax basis of a Subchapter S shareholder. Shareholders of Subchapter S corporations should have the same carryback and carryforward privilege as a regular corporation.

Once a shareholder has exhausted his basis for loans made to the corporation, he will have income to the extent that the loans are subsequently repaid even if there is subsequent UTI.[42] This anomaly occurs because there is no provision in the statutes to restore the basis of any debt that has been reduced as a result of a stockholder deducting his share of a net operating loss. Some commentators have suggested that this anomaly should be corrected by legislation. Both the American Bar Association and the Treasury Department have recommended that the basis of the debt be restored.[43]

If a shareholder's debt basis is only partially consumed by a net operating loss deduction, loan repayments must be allocated partly to a return of basis in the loan and partly to income. This result is a generally-accepted tax procedure in situations where the amount to be received is predictable with some degree of certainty.[44] Also, additional loans during one year cannot offset repayments of prior year loans; that is, a taxpayer may not report as income only the total decrease in the debt as of the end of each year.[45]

An issue arises as to whether the income should be considered capital gain or ordinary income. The current position is that the form of the transaction governs. If the corporation issued a note as evidence of the debt, repayment constitutes an amount received in exchange for a capital asset, and that which exceeds the shareholder's basis is entitled to capital gain treatment.[46] However, if the loan is

---

[41]See *Byrne* vs. *Commissioner,* 361 F. 2d 939 (7th Cir. 1966), *aff'g.* 45 T.C. 151 (1965); *Richard L. Plowden,* 48 T.C. 666 (1967), *aff'd. per curiam* 398 F. 2d 340 (4th Cir. 1968); *Joe E. Borg, supra,* note 36; *Roberts* vs. *Commissioner,* 398 F. 2d 340 (4th Cir. 1968), *aff'g.* 2d T.C. 666 (1967), *cert. denied,* 393 U.S. 936 (1968); *Perry* vs. *Commissioner,* 392 F. 2d 458 (8th Cir. 1958); *Herbert Levy,* 46 T.C. 531 (1966); *Donald M. Perry,* 49 T.C. 508 (1968).

[42]*Cornelius,* 58 T.C. 421 (1972); see also *Sam Novell,* T.C.M. 1970-31.

[43]1959 A.B.A. Section of Taxation Program and Committee Reports 90; U.S. Treasury Department, *Tax Reform Studies and Proposals* (Part 2) 287, 288 (Comm. Print 1969).

[44]*Darby Investment Corporation* vs. *Commissioner,* 37 T.C. 839 (1962), *aff'd.* 315 F. 2d 551 (6th Cir. 1963).

[45]*Cornelius,* 58 T.C. 421 (1972).

[46]Rev. Rul. 64-162, 1964-1 C.B. 304.

made on open account, the repayment constitutes ordinary income to the extent that it exceeds the shareholder's basis for the loan.[47] Thus, it is clear that a note should be given in order to obtain capital gain treatment for the income which results from its repayment. Care must be taken, however, to insure that the note does not constitute a second class of stock and terminate the Subchapter S election with severe tax consequences for all shareholders. This tax-planning problem is considered in Chapter 5.

One final comment is appropriate. Net operating losses from nonelecting Subchapter S years cannot be utilized at the corporate level, nor can they be passed through to the shareholders. Further, the running of the carryback and carryforward period continues during the Subchapter S period.[48] Thus, it may not be appropriate for a corporation that has unused net operating losses to make this election. Further, if a corporation is expecting losses in the future, an election should be made before the loss years.

Tax Planning Tips

The Subchapter S net operating loss provisions create a need for sound tax planning. If it appears that the corporation is going to sustain a net operating loss, each shareholder's basis situation should be analyzed to determine if it can absorb his share of the loss. If his basis is insufficient to absorb the loss, additional investments are in order. Such investment can be accomplished through increased lending to the corporation, or additional stock can be purchased from the corporation or from other shareholders. This action will insure that appropriate benefit is received from the net operating loss.

Since losses are apportioned according to the length of time the shareholder holds the securities, there may be a tax danger in buying Subchapter S stock in the middle of a year. For example, suppose some securities of a fiscal year Subchapter S corporation are sold to a buyer on October 1. If a large casualty loss occurs after the sale but before the end of the year, the buyer of the stock must share the loss with the seller. The seller, in effect, receives a windfall gain: an ordinary loss deduction with a corresponding increase in his capital gain on the sale. Therefore, buy stock only on the first day of the tax year.

---

[47]Rev. Rul. 68-537, 1968-2 C.B. 372; See *Joe E. Smith,* 48 T.C. 872 (1967), *aff'd.* 424 F. 2d 219 (9th Cir. 1970), for an example of this result; also *Cornelius,* 58 T.C. 421 (1972).

[48]Regulations 1.172-1(g) and 1.1374-1(a).

Special Problems Created by the Death of a Shareholder

Special problems are created by the death of a shareholder. If ownership of the shares passes to the estate, the executor or administrator of the estate must consent to the election of Subchapter S status in an official capacity. This is true even though the executor or administrator owns shares in a personal capacity. Under certain circumstances, the stock may pass directly to a beneficiary. In this case, the beneficiary must consent to the election if this has not already been done. Under all circumstances, the consents must be filed within the thirty-day statutory period. Moreover, problems are created by the fact that the estate may not want to be taxed under Subchapter S. These problems were considered in Chapter 4.

The presence of the estate injects another entity into an already complicated pattern of taxation. Estates and Subchapter S corporations are similar in that both act as conduits. A Subchapter S corporation measures its profit or loss and passes the result through for benefit of the shareholders. The corporation itself is taxed only to the extent of certain capital gains. An estate is permitted a deduction for distributions to beneficiaries, so it is taxed only on that income which it does not distribute.[49] Unlike a Subchapter S corporation, an estate cannot, under normal circumstances, pass a loss through to its beneficiaries.

Consider the problems created by insolvency at both the corporate and estate levels as suggested by the following hypothetical example:

> The Allen Lane Corporation was practically insolvent when its sole shareholder, M. Calico, died. B. M. Grintone was appointed executor under Calico's will. Within the thirty-day statutory period, Grintone, in his official capacity, consented to the continuation of Allen Lane's status as a Subchapter S corporation.

> Allen Lane sustained a loss for the year 1971. This loss is passed through to the estate and is considered a deduction at this level. If the estate has other income, the Subchapter S loss is deducted in computing taxable income. Unfortunately, Calico's estate had no income, so a net operating loss results.

The problems presented in this example are probably beyond the scope of a treatise on Subchapter S corporations. Nevertheless, the tax advisor to the estate may not be aware of these special prob-

---

[49]For a discussion of the income taxation of estates, see Davis and Whiteside, *A Practical Guide to Preparing a Fiduciary Income Tax Return* (Tucson: Lawyers and Judges Publishing Co., 1975).

lems. The duty to plan for such losses and to protect the election may fall to the corporation's tax advisor.

Losses are not routinely passed from the estate to beneficiaries. Section 642(d) allows an estate to benefit from a net operating loss carryover. Thus, a loss in one year will reduce taxable income in a subsequent year. Beneficiaries may benefit from losses indirectly, in that the loss will reduce the taxable portion of the distributions. However, the estate cannot take advantage of the loss unless it has income to be offset. Section 642(h) allows unused loss carryovers to be passed through to certain beneficiaries in the final year when the estate is terminated for tax purposes. The Regulations under Section 642(h) are specific as to how the loss is to be used and who may benefit from it. Regulation 1.642(h)-3(a) states that the loss is made available to "those beneficiaries . . . who bear the burden of any loss for which a carryover is allowed." In a Subchapter S context, it would appear that the beneficiary who received the stock is entitled to benefit of the net operating loss deduction.

Matters of timing are also important. Regulation 1.642(h)-1 prevents the estate from being used to extend the period to which a net operating loss can be applied. Thus, the estate that is unable to use a net operating loss should be terminated within the statutory period so that benefit to beneficiaries is not allowed to expire.

As a practical matter, this problem may be avoided by keeping the Subchapter S stock from passing to the estate. (Possibilities for a form of ownership with survivorship rights were discussed in Chapter 4.) If joint ownership is contrary to the estate plan, an attempt should be made to distribute stock to beneficiaries as soon as possible. In this manner, the magnitude of the carryover can be kept to a minimum.

Pass-Through of Investment Tax Credit

Only three tax credits are allowed on a Subchapter S tax return. Where a Subchapter S corporation has obtained an extension of time and has deposited the required 50 percent of the tentative tax on any capital gains with an authorized commercial depository or Federal Reserve Bank, then the electing corporation is later allowed a credit for the amount deposited when Form 1120S is filed. Further, an electing corporation may claim a credit for federal excise taxes paid on nonhighway gasoline and lubricating oil.[50] Form 4136 must be com-

---

[50]See Rev. Proc. 67-5, 1967-1 C.B. 575 for procedures to file a claim for credit of such excise taxes for an electing corporation having a tax year beginning after June 30, 1965, and ending before December 31, 1966.

pleted and attached to the electing corporation's Form 1120S. A Subchapter S corporation is *not* allowed a foreign tax credit;[51] if foreign taxes are paid, an election should be made to deduct them under I.R.C. Section 164(a).

The investment tax credit was reinstated by the Revenue Act of 1971. Under this provision a direct credit can be taken against a Subchapter S shareholder's tax liability for a certain percentage of qualified investments in equipment after August 15, 1971. In general, the credit is allowed for investment in depreciable property which is:

1. Tangible personal property.
2. Other tangible property (other than buildings and their structural components) used as an integral part of manufacturing, production or extraction, or as an integral part of furnishing transportation, communications, electrical energy, or other public utility services, or of research facilities for these activities, or of storage facilities for the bulk storage of fungible commodities.
3. New elevators and escalators.
4. Livestock (other than horses) used in business. (The credit is limited where the taxpayer sold other similar livestock within six months before or after acquisition of this livestock.)
5. Coin operated washing machines and dryers in apartment buildings.

A full credit of 7 percent of cost or other basis of equipment is allowed for property which the taxpayer expects to use for seven years or more. The credit is 4-2/3 percent if the useful life is five or six years, and 2-1/3 percent if the useful life is three or four years. Although the credit reduces the cost of equipment by the amount of the credit, it does not affect the tax basis of the equipment for depreciation or other purposes. Used property qualifies for the credit only up to $50,000 of cost or other basis of the property ($25,000 on separate returns of married couples if each owns such property). The property must be acquired by an arms-length purchase.

The useful life of the property as determined for depreciation purposes must also be used for credit purposes. A taxpayer is not required to use any particular method (e.g., flow-through method, etc.) for purposes of financial reports.

Any qualified new or used tangible personal property (Section 38 property) is apportioned pro rata among the persons who are stock-

---

[51]Rev. Rul. 68-128, 1968-2 C.B. 17.

holders of the electing corporation on the last day of the tax year.[52] Each stockholder includes his pro rata share with any other qualified property and then computes his investment tax credit. The electing corporation is subject to a $50,000 limitation per year on used Section 38 property,[53] and each stockholder is also subject to the $50,000 limitation on used property.[54] Section 38 property does not lose its character as new or used property as it passes through. Further, the estimated useful life of the property in the hands of the stockholders is deemed to be the estimated useful life of such property in the hands of the electing corporation.[55]

The Subchapter S election itself does not cause a recapture of the investment credit if both the corporation and all shareholders file an agreement with the District Director.[56] Refer to Chapter 3 for an extended discussion and for a sample agreement form. Further, a termination or voluntary revocation of the election does not result in a recapture of the credit.[57] However, where Section 38 property is disposed of before the end of its useful life, each stockholder must recapture some or all of his pro rata share of the investment credit (depending upon the length of time the asset was held).[58] The Fifth Circuit has upheld the recapture provision in Regulation 1.47-4. In *Charbonnet*,[59] the court validated the trigger mechanism even though the Subchapter S election had terminated before the fatal stock disposition.

The following examples should illustrate the above recapture rules. Suppose Mr. Flip owns 1,000 of the 2,000 shares of a new Subchapter S corporation. The company buys $80,000 of new equipment with an estimated useful life of seven years during 1973. Flip's share would be $40,000, on which he would take a $2,800 investment credit (7 percent of $40,000).

Situation 1: In 1974, Flip sells 300 shares. Here there is no recapture since he did not dispose of one-third of his shares.

Situation 2: In 1974, Flip sells 500 shares. Flip will have a $1,400 recapture in 1974.

---

[52]I.R.C. Section 48(c); Regulation 1.48-5(a)(1).

[53]Regulation 1.48-5(a)(2).

[54]Regulation 1.48-5(a)(3).

[55]Regulation 1.48-5(a).

[56]Regulation 1.47-4(b)(1).

[57]Regulation 1.47-4(d).

[58]Regulation 1.47-4(a).

[59]*Charbonnet*, 27 A.F.T.R. 2d 71-751 (D.C. La. 1971), *aff'd.* 29 A.F.T.R. 2d 633 (5th Cir. 1972).

Situation 3: Same as situation 2 except that Flip disposes of 150 more shares during 1975. Since his interest is only down to 35 percent and he has already recaptured the credit on the first one-third disposition, there is no recapture in 1975. That is, there is no further recapture until the stock ownership is further reduced below 33-1/3 percent of what it was at the time of pass-through.

A disposition of shares of stock by stockholders results in recapture determination. Under Regulation 1.47-4(a), a stockholder must recapture the investment credit where, at the end of any tax year, he has disposed of more than 33-1/3 percent of the stock interest of the electing corporation which he held in the year in which he claimed the investment credit. He must recapture the credit to the extent of the disposition of the stock. Further, in any year in which the stockholder has remaining less than 33-1/3 percent of the shares which he held in the tax year in which he claimed a credit from the electing corporation, he must again recapture the credit to the extent of the disposition less any investment credit previously earned or recaptured.[60]

A stockholder's proportionate stock interest in an electing corporation may be reduced by a sale, a gift, a redemption, or by the issuance of additional shares of stock. The IRS has ruled that the exchange of all the stock of a Subchapter S corporation for 75 percent of the stock of a nonelecting corporation is not a disposition. The stockholder's interest is not reduced below 66-2/3 percent since each of the stockholders still owns indirectly 75 percent of his former proportionate interest. However, if the property is disposed of after the reorganization by the former electing corporation before the end of the estimated useful life, the former stockholders will be treated as having made a disposition.[61]

One of the disadvantages of the Subchapter S election occurs where a regular corporation has an investment credit which it cannot use because of a loss year. If the corporation makes a Subchapter S election, this carryover investment credit cannot be passed through to the stockholders and each Subchapter S year counts as a year to which the credit may be carried.[62]

In selecting the estimated useful life (EUL) of a machine, a taxpayer must be careful since the selected lifetime must be used for both depreciation and investment credit purposes. It is not a safe conclusion to pick an EUL which will result in the largest investment

---

[60]Regulation 1.47-4(a).

[61]Rev. Rul. 69-168, 1969-1 C.B. 24.

[62]Regulation 1.46-2(h).

credit. For example, Mr. Brown purchases on January 1 a $100,000 airplane which has as asset depreciation range of five to seven years and no salvage value. At first glance, a current $7,000 investment credit along with depreciation over a seven-year period looks superior to a $4,667 (two-thirds) tax credit and a five-year depreciation write-off period. However, a larger initial cash flow results when the smaller credit and larger depreciation deduction are used. Using a 10 percent discount value, a smaller credit is $2,873 superior to the larger credit (see Exhibit 6-1). Obviously, this result may not always be the same.

EXHIBIT 6-1

Comparison of Useful Lives

Years	Depreciation 5 years[1]	7 years[1]	Present Value at 10% 5 years[2]	7 years[2]
1	$40,000[3]	$28,571[3]	$36,364	$25,974
2	24,000	20,408	19,834	16,865
3	15,750[4]	14,968[4]	11,833	11,245
4	11,251	12,979	7,684	8,865
5	6,749	10,095	4,190	6,268
6	2,250	7,211	1,270	4,071
7	--	4,326	--	2,220
8	--	1,442	--	673
			81,175	76,181
Discounted investment credit			+ 4,243	+ 6,364
			$85,418	$82,545

[1]Assumes a switch to SYD method under Rev. Proc. 67-40 at the beginning of the third year and a 48% tax rate.

[2]The tax benefits from the depreciation deductions and investment credits are assumed to be realized on the last day of the tax year.

[3]The executive elects the modified half-year convention.

[4]Regulation 1.167(a)-11(c)(1)(iii)(c), (d), and (f) require the taxpayer to assume that depreciation was allowed for a half-year during the first year regardless of what first year convention was adopted.

Recapture of Depreciation

I.R.C. Sections 1245 and 1250 provide for the recapture of depreciation on the sale or disposition of certain depreciable property. An election or termination of a Subchapter S corporation does not cause a recapture of depreciation and the resulting recognition of ordinary income.[63] However, where an electing corporation disposes of Sections 1245 and 1250 properties (even if it is pre-election property), any Sections 1245 or 1250 gains are included in ordinary taxable income of the corporation.[64] If the gain is deferred under the installment tax plan, the ordinary income is first recognized before any I.R.C. Section 1231 gain.[65] If Sections 1245 or 1250 properties are disposed of to a stockholder for less than fair market value, any gain is computed on the fair market value rather than the sales price.[66]

Pass-Through Tax Preferences

The Tax Reform Act of 1969 imposes an additional tax of 10 percent on certain items which have received very favorable tax treatment (such as accelerated depreciation, excluded half of capital gain, amortization of pollution control facilities, stock options, depletion, and excess investment interest).[67] The tax is levied against the sum of these preference items minus a $30,000 exemption. The tax liability for the year is also subtracted. The resultant is taxed at 10 percent.

A Subchapter S corporation accumulates the preferences at the corporate level, using Form 4626, and passes them through to the shareholders in the same manner as I.R.C. Section 1372(c)(1) requires losses to be passed through.[68] It will be recalled that losses are passed through to shareholders on a daily basis.

A minimum tax may also be levied at the corporate level. If the Subchapter S corporation is subject to a capital gains tax, the minimum tax also applies. However, such treatment at the corporate level allows the shareholder to reduce his share of the preferences by the amount of the capital gains tax as well as the minimum tax paid by the corporation.

For example, assume an electing corporation has a capital gain of $800,000. The capital gain tax would be 30 percent of $775,000 or $232,500. The tax preference would be 37.5 percent of the $800,000 or $300,000 less the $30,000 exclusion and the capital gain tax of $232,500, to result in $37,500 of tax preferences. The 10 percent tax

---

[63]W. J. McAnallen, "The Recapture Rules — Sections 47, 1245, 1250: How They Work, What They Mean, How To Plan." *Journal of Taxation,* Vol. 21 (November, 1964), pp. 272-280.

[64]I.R.C. Sections 1245(a)(1) and 1250(a)(1).

[65]See I.R.C. Section 453(b); Regulation 1.1245-6(d); Prop. Reg. 1.1250-1(b)(6).

[66]Regulation 1.1245(1)(c) and Prop. Reg. 1.1250-1(a)(4).

[67]I.R.C. Sections 56-58.

[68]I.R.C. Section 58(d)(1).

at the corporate level would be $3,750 (10 percent × $37,500). There would be a pass-through of $563,750 of tax preferences to the shareholders ($800,000 − $232,500 − $3,750 = $563,750).

Pass-Through of Interest Deduction Limitations

The Tax Reform Act of 1969 places limitations on the deduction of interest used to carry investments which provide no taxable income.[69] The first $25,000 of such interest will continue to be deductible. This rule is applicable to tax years after 1971.

The excess interest will be passed through to shareholders just as if it had been incurred by the shareholders. The basis for allocation is I.R.C. Section 1374(c)(1) which specifies the manner in which losses are to be passed through to shareholders.[70] As the limitation is imposed at the shareholder level, the $25,000 exemption appears to apply to each shareholder. As a practical matter, however, this provision should have little effect upon Subchapter S corporations because of the passive investment income rules.[71]

Member of a Controlled Group

If an electing corporation is subject to the Section 1378 tax, it also may be subject to a 10 percent minimum tax. Further, if any of its shareholders own stock in other corporations, the electing corporation may be a member of a controlled group of corporations. A controlled group of corporations is limited to one $25,000 surtax exemption which may be split among the various corporations. Until 1975, however, these corporations may elect a *declining* multiple surtax exemption with the payment of an extra 6 percent penalty tax on the exempted income (other than one $25,000 surtax exemption).[72] If a Subchapter S corporation is a member of such a group of electing controlled group of corporations, it would be classified as an "excluded member" *if there is no Section 1378 tax.*[73] But if the Subchapter S corporation has a Section 1378 tax and the group has elected multiple surtax exemptions, the Subchapter S corporation would be subject to the 6 percent penalty tax.

---

[69]I.R.C. Section 163(d).

[70]I.R.C. Section 163(d)(4)(C).

[71]For a complete discussion, see S. R. Josephs, S. A. Tuller, and M. Greenberg, "The Excess Interest Limitation: How it Works and How to Plan for it," *Journal of Taxation,* Vol. 39 (October, 1973), pp. 214-219.

[72]I.R.C. Section 1562(b); I.R.C. Section 1564; See Crumbley and Marshall, "Tax Alternatives for Controlled Corporate Groups Under the 1969 Tax Reform Act," *Taxes,* Vol. 48 (November, 1970), pp. 676-690.

[73]Regulation 1.1563-1(b)(ii)(c).

Chapter 7

Corporate Distributions and Their Impact Upon Shareholders' Taxable Income

In the normal course of business activity, corporations make distributions to their shareholders. The distribution may or may not be taxable, depending upon the character or source of the distribution. For example, some distributions may constitute a return of capital. A distribution of this character is not taxable to the shareholder. However, the distribution may be from the corporation's current net income. In Chapter 6 we considered the manner in which a Subchapter S corporation's net income is allocated among its shareholders, having escaped taxation at the corporate level. The tax treatment of the distribution in the hands of the shareholder is dependent upon its character. Some distributions are accorded capital gain treatment, while others are taxed as ordinary income.

Moreover, the distribution may be cash or property or perhaps a combination of the two. Each of these situations calls for a special tax treatment. From a tax planning point of view, the timing of the distribution is also significant, as there may be dire consequences if assets are not distributed at the appropriate time. Thus, an understanding of the taxation of distributions at the shareholder level is necessary if maximum tax benefit from the Subchapter S election is to be received by all concerned. The purpose of Chapter 7 is to consider the tax treatment of distributions of Subchapter S corporations.

Sources of Subchapter S Distribution — An Overview

Reference has already been made to the significance of the source and character of the distribution in the determination of its tax treatment. The *Internal Revenue Code* has developed six concepts which provide a general framework for distribution:

1. Taxable income
2. Current earnings and profits
3. Accumulated earnings and profits
4. Undistributed taxable income (UTI)
5. Previously taxed income (PTI)
6. Return of capital

The concept of taxable income for a Subchapter S corporation is considered in Chapter 6. Generally, taxable income results from the matching of revenues generated in the ordinary course of business activity during a period with the ordinary and necessary expenses which are incurred in this process. More specifically the *Code* states that the taxable income of a Subchapter S corporation is computed in the same manner as it is for a nonelecting corporation.[1] However, neither the net operating loss deduction nor the special dividend deductions as provided by I.R.C. Sections 243-247 are allowed. The concept of taxable income offers few problems in a Subchapter S context.

The earnings and profits concept is perhaps more difficult to handle in that neither the *Code* nor the Regulations has provided a satisfactory definition of it. In attempting to understand the concept of earnings and profits, it may be helpful to draw a parallel to the accounting concept of retained earnings. Retained earnings in an accounting context is the balance of net profits, income, gains and losses of a corporation from its beginning *minus* the distributions of those items to shareholders.[2] The Regulations do provide some insight into what is meant by earnings and profits in a tax context. All income enters into the calculation of earnings and profits, whether it be taxable or not. Thus, interest on tax exempt municipal bonds is part of earnings and profits even though it is excluded from taxable income. Earnings and profits are reduced by nondeductible expenses as well as by dividend type distributions.[3] In fact, the presence of earnings and profits in a Subchapter S corporation causes a distribution in excess of net income to be taxed as a dividend to the shareholders. Current earnings and profits are those which relate to a particular tax year, while accumulated earnings and profits, as the term suggests, refers to the cumulative position of the enterprise with respect to this measure.

As a general rule, earnings and profits are computed in the same manner for both electing and nonelecting corporations.[4] For example, earnings and profits are reduced by cash distributions,[5] but any distributions in excess of earnings and profits cannot cause a deficit in the current earnings and profits account.[6] However, there can be a deficit in accumulated earnings and profits account (e.g., in case of

[1]I.R.C. Section 1373(d).

[2]Paul Grady, *Inventory of Generally Accepted Accounting Principles* (New York: American Institute of Certified Public Accountants, 1965), p. 412.

[3]Regulation 1.312-6(b).

[4]Regulation 1.1377-2(b).

[5]I.R.C. Section 312(a)(1).

[6]Regulation 1.1377-2(a)(2), ex. (2).

a capital loss, etc.). Tax exempt interest, accelerated depreciation in excess of straight-line, and percentage depletion in excess of cost all increase current earnings and profits.

The *Code* does provide three special rules that affect the earnings and profits of a Subchapter S corporation. In the first place, net operating losses which are passed through to shareholders under I.R.C. Section 1374 do not reduce either current or accumulated earnings and profits. Second, accumulated earnings and profits are reduced by nondeductible expenses. However, current earnings and profits are not reduced by this type of expenditure. Third, accumulated earnings and profits are reduced to the extent that undistributed taxable income is included in the taxpayer's gross income. Moreover, earnings and profits are not reduced by distributions of previously taxed income to shareholders (including distribution of UTI during the 2½-month grace period).[7]

As its name suggests, undistributed taxable income is the amount of the current year's taxable income which has not been distributed to shareholders on the last day of the tax year. In Chapter 6 it was noted that undistributed taxable income is allocated among the shareholders on the last day of the tax year to be included in gross income. The *Code* describes the components of undistributed taxable income as Subchapter S taxable income *minus* any capital gains tax imposed at the corporate level and money distributed to shareholders to the extent that it comes out of current earnings and profits.[8] The Regulations specify that undistributed taxable income is not reduced by non-cash distributions.[9] Therefore, it appears that undistributed taxable income can be reduced only through the distribution of cash to shareholders.

In Chapter 6, we noted that undistributed taxable income is allocated among the shareholders of record as of the close of the tax year to be included in their taxable incomes. Each individual's share of the undistributed taxable income is the excess of the amount the shareholder included in his gross income over the amount which has been distributed.[10]

As a practical matter, the *Code* and Regulations tend to complicate a relatively simple concept in that the shareholder is taxed on his share of the corporation's taxable income at the close of the tax

---

[7]I.R.C. Section 1377.

[8]I.R.C. Section 1373(c).

[9]Regulation 1.1373-1.

[10]Regulation 1.1375-6(a)(3).

year. This is true whether or not any distributions have been made. Although distributions decrease the individual's share of undistributed taxable income for a year, they increase his Subchapter S dividend income for that year. Thus, the tax is levied against the individual based upon his share of the corporation's taxable income. UTI is not deductible as a charitable bequest, even though Subchapter S stock is owned by an estate and the will provides that all estate income is to go to a specified charity. The UTI has not left the corporation and is not in the control of the executor.[11] Presumably the results would be different if the income were actually distributed to the estate.

The Regulations require the corporation to keep records which reflect each individual's share of the corporation's undistributed taxable income. Moreover, each individual shareholder is required to keep a record of his undistributed taxable income.[12]

If a corporation does not distribute its taxable income for each year, it will have previously taxed income. Previously taxed income is the sum of all amounts included in gross income by shareholders *minus* all net operating losses which have been deducted from gross income by shareholders and amounts of previously taxed income actually distributed to shareholders. Previously taxed income is actually undistributed taxable income which has been previously taxed to shareholders.[13] The corporation is required to keep a record of each shareholder's share of previously taxed income. Also, each shareholder is required to maintain his own records which reflect this information.[14] As will be seen later in the chapter, the avoidance of previously taxed income is a significant goal of Subchapter S tax planning.

The return of capital concept suggests that the shareholder is receiving back a portion of his investment in the corporation. A distribution of this nature is not normally subject to taxation at the shareholder level. However, a return of capital will reduce a shareholder's basis for his stock.

As a general rule, actual cash or property distributions [except stock of the distributing corporation under Section 305(a)] to stockholders are treated as dividends to the extent of any current or

---

[11]*Richardson Foundation* vs. *U.S.*, 26 A.F.T.R. 2d 5144 (5th Cir. 1970).

[12]Regulation 1.1375-6(a)(5).

[13]I.R.C. Section 1375(d).

[14]Regulation 1.1375-4(f).

accumulated earnings and profits.[15] Likewise, any actual dividend distributions are taxable when received by the stockholders.[16]

The balance of this chapter is concerned with the interrelationships of these six concepts as specified by I.R.C. Section 1375 and related Regulations. As was suggested earlier, distributions of property are treated in a different manner than are distributions of cash. Moreover, the timing of the distribution may have significant tax consequences. To a certain extent, this area lends itself to successful tax planning. Therefore, it will be appropriate to consider tax planning for Subchapter S distributions.

Distributions of Cash

Neither the *Code* nor its supporting Regulations provide a listing of the order in which distributions of a Subchapter S corporation are applied to the various income components. However, it is possible to piece together an order of distribution from various sections of the *Code* and Regulations.

1. If the distribution is made during the first 2½-months, it is treated as a distribution of undistributed taxable income of the previous year to the extent that the corporation had such at the close of the previous tax year.

2. Distributions are next allocated to taxable income for the current year, to be treated as ordinary income or capital gain in accordance with the pass-through rules discussed in Chapter 6. Taxable income which remains undistributed at the end of the tax year is allocated among the shareholders on the basis of end-of-year stock ownership. After 2½-months, it becomes previously taxed income.

3. Distributions are next allocated to current earnings and profits to the extent that they exceed taxable income. Distributions out of current earnings and profits in excess of taxable income would not be allocated to shareholders in the absence of distribution. Accordingly, they are taxable as ordinary income.

4. Distributions are next allocated to previously taxed income. Because this income has already been taxed to the shareholder, its distribution does not normally result in taxable income.

---

[15]Regulations 1.1372-1(c)(2) and (7); I.R.C. Sections 301(a) and (c); I.R.C. Section 316(a).

[16]Regulations 1.301-1(b) and 1.1373-1(f).

5. Distributions in excess of previously taxed income are allocated against accumulated earnings and profits from previous years. These distributions are taxed as ordinary income.

6. Distributions which exceed accumulated earnings and profits are considered to be a return of capital. As such, they do not result in taxable income until the shareholder's tax basis for the stock has been fully recovered.

7. Distributions which exceed the shareholder's tax basis for the stock are taxable as capital gains.

TABLE 7-1

ORDER OF CASH DISTRIBUTIONS

Source	Tax Consequences
1. Undistributed taxable income at the close of the previous tax year.	Not taxed to shareholder who included it in his gross income (only if distribution made within two and one-half months after the close of the previous tax year).
2. Taxable income of the current year.	Subchapter S dividend to be taxed as capital gain or ordinary income, depending upon the character of the income.
3. Current earnings and profits.	Taxed as ordinary income (ordinary dividend subject to the $100 dividend exclusion).
4. Previously taxed income.	Not taxed to shareholder who included it in his gross income.
5. Accumulated earnings and profits.	Taxed as ordinary income (ordinary dividend subject to the $100 dividend exclusion).
6. Return of capital.	Not taxed to shareholder.
7. Amount in excess of shareholders' tax basis.	Taxed as capital gain.

The order of distribution and the tax treatment which results therefrom are presented in Table 7-1. In analyzing the order of distribution, one must keep in mind that a particular Subchapter S corporation may lack certain of these sources. For example, a corporation which has always operated under Subchapter S, distributed its income currently, and caused its book income to conform with tax concepts will have neither previously taxed income nor earnings and profits in excess of taxable income. In this case, distributions in excess of taxable income would constitute a return of capital. As a practical matter, most well managed Subchapter S corporations will distribute their earnings on a current basis so that all distributions are out of undistributed taxable income. As will be seen later in the chapter, the firm has two and one-half months to accomplish this. Moreover, a great deal of trouble can be avoided by making it a policy of the corporation to always distribute its earnings on a current basis.

Under certain circumstances, the corporation may wish to deviate from the usual order of distributions which has just been described. A special election is available to the corporation which will allow it to reverse the positions of previously taxed income and accumulated earnings and profits in the order of distribution.[17] This has been done in Table 7-2. All shareholders must agree to this election by signing a simple statement which indicates that they agree to have all distributions in excess of current earnings and profits to be treated as distributions out of accumulated earnings and profits, rather than out of previously taxed income.

No official form has been provided by the IRS for the purpose of making this special election. Exhibit 7-1 provides a sample form which contains the information required for a valid election under Regulation 1.1375-4(c).

The election applies only to the distributions of a particular year which would be distributions of previously taxed income in the absence of the election. A new election can be made for subsequent years if the corporation so desires.

At this point it is sufficient to note that the special election will cause income to be taxable which could have been received tax-free in the absence of the election. As a practical matter, there must be sufficient tax planning reasons to justify the election. We shall consider this aspect of Subchapter S tax planning later in the chapter.

The terms "ordinary dividend" and "Subchapter S dividend" have been used in reference to the taxability of certain distributions. The difference in these terms lies in the application of I.R.C. Section 116, which considers the partial exclusion from gross income of dividends received by individuals. Simply stated, Subchapter S dividends will not qualify for the dividend exclusion, while ordinary dividends

---

[17]Regulation 1.1375-4(c).

TABLE 7-2

ORDER OF CASH DISTRIBUTIONS
SPECIAL ELECTION UNDER REGULATION 1.1375-4(c)

Source	Tax Consequences
1. Undistributed taxable income at the close of the previous tax year.	Not taxed to shareholder who included it in his gross income (only if distribution made within two and one-half months after the close of the previous tax year.
2. Taxable income of the current year.	Subchapter S dividend to be taxed as capital gain or ordinary income, depending upon the character of the income.
3. Current earnings and profits.	Taxed as ordinary income. (Ordinary dividend subject to the $100 dividend exclusion).
4. Accumulated earnings and profits.	Taxed as ordinary income. (Ordinary dividend subject to the $100 dividend exclusion).
5. Previously taxed income.	Not taxed to shareholder who included it in his gross income.
6. Return of capital.	Not taxed to shareholder.
7. Amount in excess of shareholder's tax basis.	Taxed as capital gain.

will qualify.[18] These points are illustrated by the following example adopted from the Regulations:[19]

> ... A Subchapter S corporation has taxable income of $10,000 for the tax year 1974 and accumulated earnings and profits through 1973 of $20,000. During 1974, the corporation pays a $15,000 cash dividend. Of the amount distributed, $10,000 is not excludable under Section 116 since it is paid out of the earnings and profits of the corporation's current tax year. The $5,000 excess which is paid out of accumulated earnings and profits is subject to the partial dividend exclusion under Section 116.
>
> Another Subchapter S corporation is in the same position as the one above with respect to accumulated earnings and profits. However, its taxable income for the year is only $9,000,

---

[18]Regulation 1.1375-2(a); I.R.C. Section 1375(b).

[19]Regulation 1.1375-2(b).

EXHIBIT 7-1

Election by Small Business Corporation to Reverse the Order of Distributions as Provided by Regulation 1.1375-4(c)

(No Official Form)

The Crumb Corporation, 210 Long Avenue, Baton Rouge, Louisiana, 70821, has elected to be taxed under Subchapter S of the Internal Revenue Code. It does hereby elect to reverse the order of its distributions in order to consider all distributions in excess of current earnings and profits which would normally be out of previously taxed income to be distributions of accumulated earnings and profits in accordance with Regulation 1.1375-4(c) for the tax year ended December 31, 1974.

_1-3-74_	__TONY LAMER__	PRESIDENT
(Date)	(Signature of Officer)	(Title)

The undersigned are all shareholders of The Crumb Corporation. We do hereby consent to the above election for the year ended December 31, 1974.

Name of Each Stockholder	Signature
Tony Lamer	Tony Lamer
Darlene Lamer	Darlene Lamer
John Hill	John Hill

_1-3-74_
(Date)

because the corporation received $1,000 of tax exempt interest. Of the $15,000 distributed, only $9,000 would be considered a Subchapter S dividend not subject to Section 116. The $6,000 would be an ordinary dividend.

Earlier, it was suggested that current earnings and profits in excess of current taxable income would not exist if the Subchapter S corporation uses tax concepts in computing income for accounting and reporting purposes. Most timing differences can be avoided by adopting the same methods for both tax and book purposes. However, the existence of tax-exempt interest will create an excess of current earnings and profits over current taxable income, since tax-exempt interest does not increase UTI (Regulation 1.1375-2(b), example 2). Such interest is income in the economic sense, regardless of its tax treatment. To the extent that differences between taxable income and book income exist, a situation is created whereby the corporation may distribute taxable dividends. This point is often overlooked. Moreover, to allow a Subchapter S corporation to receive tax-exempt income is unwise because the income loses its tax-exempt character as it is passed through to the shareholders. In the above example, the $1,000 ends up being taxable to shareholders as ordinary income.

Before going to the topic of timing of cash distributions, we shall consider a highly simplified example which utilizes the concepts developed thus far:

> The Pamida Corporation has been operating under Subchapter S for two years. At the beginning of 1974, it had accumulated earnings and profits of $15,000. During 1974, the corporation had taxable income of $18,000 and a book income of $20,000, the difference having been caused by the use of accelerated depreciation for tax purposes. It had failed to distribute all of its taxable income for the tax year 1973 and therefore had previously taxed income amounting to $3,000. Pamida's one shareholder has a tax basis for his stock of $10,000. In 1974 he receives a $30,000 cash distribution.

First, the distribution is analyzed and the sources of its various components are listed. Then, the various components are considered for their tax consequences. It will be recalled that the distribution may constitute ordinary income, capital gain, or a tax-free distribution. The tax aspects of this distribution are illustrated in Table 7-3. Table 7-4 is based upon the same example, except that the total distribution is $50,000. In either case a part of the current taxable income could be accorded capital gain treatment in accordance with the flow-through procedure developed in Chapter 6. For these illustrations, however, we have chosen to ignore this aspect of the problem.

Timing of Cash Distributions

Chapter 2 refers to the fact that the original Subchapter S legislation stipulated that all income not distributed by the end of a tax year automatically became previously taxed income. In order to avoid the problems associated with previously taxed income, all taxable income must be distributed currently. Yet, by the time that the income was measured, the tax year had come to a close. This requirement led to the practice of anticipating the net income and distributing it before the close of the tax year.

However, it is equally clear that the proper measurement of taxable income takes time and can be done with reasonable accuracy only after the close of a tax year. On the one hand, if the corporation overanticipated its taxable income, dividends would have resulted if there were earnings and profits in excess of current taxable income. On the other hand, however, the corporation might under-

TABLE 7-3

PAMIDA CORPORATION
ORDER OF CASH DISTRIBUTION

Source	Amount
1. Taxable income of the current year	$18,000
2. Current earnings and profits in excess of current taxable income	2,000
3. Previously taxed income	3,000
4. Accumulated earnings and profits	7,000
	$30,000

Tax Treatment of the Distribution

Tax-free distribution:		$3,000
Previously taxed income		
Ordinary income:		
Taxable income of the current year	$18,000	
Current earnings and profits	2,000	
Accumulated earnings and profits	7,000	27,000
Total Distribution		$30,000

anticipate its taxable income, and the result would be previously taxed income. Needless to say, this uncertainty reduced the effectiveness of the Subchapter S corporation in achieving its tax goals.

In 1966, I.R.C. Section 1375(f) was added to the law. This provision specifies that distributions made within two and one-half months after the close of the previous tax year will be treated as a distribution of the corporation's taxable income for that year. Now a corporation has two and one-half months to measure its taxable income, and, if necessary, become sufficiently liquid to distribute it to its shareholders. Previously taxed income can thus be avoided. In the process of avoiding previously taxed income, however, the Subchapter S corporation may create for itself some working capital difficulties. Again, the need for sound planning becomes evident. We shall consider this planning requirement later in the chapter.

No special elections are necessary to make the provisions of I.R.C. Section 1375(f) applicable to a particular Subchapter S corporation. Any distribution made within the two and one-half month period is automatically a distribution of the previous year's taxable income, even if the distributions are made in the two and one-half months during the year in which the election is terminated.[20] The following example illustrates the application of the two and one-half month rule:

The Pamida Corporation was formed on January 1, 1973, and has made a valid election under Subchapter S. In 1973 it has taxable income of $25,000 but makes no distributions during the year, because this fact is not known until February 1, 1974. On March 1, 1974, it distributes the full $25,000 to its shareholders, all of whom owned their stock on December 31, 1973.

Under the old rule, the Pamida Corporation would have previously taxed income of $25,000 at the close of the tax year 1973. The $25,000 distribution would have been considered out of the 1974 taxable income. However, the new rule allows the distribution to be out of 1973 taxable income, and so Pamida and its shareholders would avoid the problems associated with previously taxed income.

An interesting problem is created by the relationship between previously taxed income and the two and one-half month rule. I.R.C. Section 1375(f) makes it quite clear that the two and one-half month rule applies only to distributions of the previous year's taxable income. If a Subchapter S corporation has previously taxed income, the two and one-half month rule will be of no assistance in its distribution to shareholders. If this point is overlooked, the corporation's plan for distribution may result in unplanned consequences. Thus, it is incumbent on all to keep this fact in mind when planning for distributions.

At this point, it may be appropriate to review the order of distribution which was developed earlier in the chapter. During a particular year, all distributions are out of that year's taxable income. To the extent that undistributed taxable income exists at the close of the previous year, distributions during the first two and one-half months are applied against those amounts. In the current year, current taxable income plus current earnings and profits in excess of current taxable income must be distributed before previously taxed income may be distributed. The problem is illustrated by the following example.

The Pamida Corporation has been operating under Subchapter S for several years. For various reasons it has failed to distribute all its taxable income currently and therefore has $30,000 of previously taxed income. In 1974 it was highly success-

[20]Rev. Rul. 71-102, 1971-1 C.B. 263.

TABLE 7-4

PAMIDA CORPORATION
ORDER OF CASH DISTRIBUTION

Source	Amount
1. Taxable income of the current year	$18,000
2. Current earnings and profits in excess of current taxable income	2,000
3. Previously taxed income	3,000
4. Accumulated earnings and profits	15,000
5. Basis of taxpayer's stock	10,000
6. Amount in excess of the basis of taxpayer's stock	2,000
Total Distribution	$50,000

Tax Treatment of the Distribution

Tax-free distribution:		
Previously taxed income	$ 3,000	
Basis of taxpayer's stock	10,000	$13,000
Ordinary income:		
Taxable income of the current year	$18,000	
Current earnings and profits	2,000	
Accumulated earnings and profits	15,000	35,000
Capital gain:		
Amount in excess of the basis of taxpayer's stock		2,000
Total Distribution		$50,000

ful in collecting its receivables and sought to distribute its previously taxed income. In both 1973 and 1974, its taxable income was $30,000.

On February 1, 1974, Pamida distributes $60,000 to its shareholders, hoping to apply this first to 1973 taxable income and then to previously taxed income. The two and one-half month rule applies only to the previous year's taxable income. Therefore, the $60,000 distribution of February 1, 1974, applies first to 1973 taxable income and then to 1974 taxable income. Previously taxed income remains unchanged at $30,000 in spite of the $60,000 distribution.

In the above example, the Pamida Corporation could have accomplished its stated objective by distributing $60,000 on December

15, 1973. The first $30,000 would be applicable to 1973 taxable income and the balance applied to previously taxed earnings. In this situation the corporation must anticipate its current taxable income. As was the case before the two and one-half month rule, overanticipation results in excessive distributions, while underanticipation results in the failure to eliminate previously taxed income. Simply stated, a corporation must be prepared to distribute its taxable income *plus* previously taxed income before the close of the tax year, if it expects previously taxed income ever to be reduced. Sound planning may help a corporation to distribute its previously taxed income. However, the problem is one additional reason why taxable income should be distributed within two and one-half months after the close of a tax year to avoid the problem of previously taxed income.

The distribution of previously taxed income may also be affected by the existence of earnings and profits in excess of current taxable income. Earlier in the chapter, the order of distribution specified that current earnings and profits must be distributed before previously taxed income can be reduced. Thus, the failure to distribute all income currently may create a situation where taxable dividends are received by shareholders. As in all other cases, current distribution appears to be essential.

It should be noted that there is no procedure for obtaining exemption from the two and one-half-month rule. This is true even though the corporation obtains an extension for filing Form 1120S. At least two courts have upheld this practice.[21] Taxpayers and their advisors should keep this in mind as they plan for corporate distributions.

Distribution of Property Other than Cash

The *Code* clearly differentiates between distributions of cash and distributions of property other than cash. Property distributions might appear to be the logical way to distribute undistributed taxable income and previously taxed income at a time when the firm lacks sufficient resources to make cash distributions. However, this approach is prohibited by the *Code* and Regulations. The *Code* states that undistributed taxable income may be reduced only by cash distributions.[22] Moreover, the Regulations specify that distributions

---

[21]*Attebury, et. al.* vs. *U.S.,* 26 A.F.T.R. 2d 70-5317 (5th Cir. 1970), *rev'g.* 23 A.F.T.R. 2d 69-912 (N.D. Tex. 1969); *Randall N. Clark,* 58 T.C. 94 (1972).

[22]I.R.C. Section 1373(c).

of property are never distributions of previously taxed income.[23] As we shall see later, the Regulation in question has been tested in at least one court and has been held valid.

As a practical matter, property distributions often create tax consequences which are not anticipated. In the first place, the fair market value of the property is used as the basis for the distribution.[24] At fair market value, the property is allocated ratably to a constructive distribution of undistributed taxable income and the distribution of property. However, we have already stated that property distributions do not reduce undistributed taxable income. It is appropriate to look to an example contained in the Regulations for an explanation of this apparent inconsistency.[25]

A Subchapter S corporation has taxable income and earning and profits of $10,000 for the current tax year. It has no accumulated earnings and profits at the beginning of the year. During this tax year, the corporation distributes property other than money with a basis of $10,000 and a fair market value of $20,000. The undistributed taxable income remains $10,000 since the property distribution does not reduce taxable income for purposes of that computation. However, the current earnings and profits are allocated ratably to the constructive distribution of undistributed taxable income and the distribution of property, considered at its fair market value. [$10,000 (current earnings and profits) + $20,000 (fair market value of property) =$30,000.] Therefore, $3,333 (10/30 × $10,000) is allocated to the constructive distribution of undistributed taxable income and $6,667 (20/30 of $10,000) is allocated to the distribution of property. Even though UTI is $10,000, only $3,333 would be treated as a dividend on a distribution of undistributed taxable income, and that is the amount that shareholders include in gross income as required by I.R.C. Section 1373(b).

In this example, $13,333 would be treated as a return of capital

The presence of accumulated earnings and profits further complicates the picture as indicated by this modification of the above example:[26]

The corporation has the same fact situation except that it also has $20,000 of accumulated earnings and profits at the beginning of the tax year. This amount is sufficient to cover that portion of the property distribution which is not out of current

---

[23]Regulation 1.1375-4(b).

[24]I.R.C. Section 301(b)(1)(A).

[25]Regulation 1.1373-1(g)(3).

[26]Regulation 1.1373-1(g)(4).

earnings and profits ($13,333) and that portion of the constructive distribution which is not out of current earnings and profits ($6,667). Therefore the property distributions (at fair market value) as well as the corporation's UTI will be fully taxable as dividends ($30,000).

Accumulated earnings and profits represent earnings retained in the business from pre-Subchapter S years and earnings and profits in excess of UTI. In the absence of a Subchapter S election, distributions from this source would be taxed as ordinary dividend income. However, as is noted earlier in Table 7-4, a Subchapter S corporation distributes current taxable income, current earnings and profits in excess of current taxable income, and previously taxed income before it distributes accumulated earnings and profits. If the corporation is making a property distribution, Section 1373(c) and Regulation 1.1375-4(b) preclude the reduction of these items through a property distribution. Thus, to the extent that the corporation has accumulated earnings and profits, an ordinary taxable dividend results from distributions of property to shareholders.

Some unusual results are obtained by applying the provisions of the *Code* and Regulations to the distribution of property. Perhaps the firm ought to avoid the distribution of property. If the purpose of the proposed property distribution is to place the property in the hands of the shareholders, the firm can merely sell the property to the shareholders. A cash dividend may logically accompany such a transaction, and this will appropriately reduce UTI. This plan may provide an acceptable alternative to a property distribution. However, the possibility that the IRS may collapse the time transactions into a direct property distribution should be considered. This problem is discussed later in the chapter.

Property distributions may be appropriate under certain circumstances. One commentator suggests that a property distribution can be a useful tax-planning device when the asset to be distributed contains a large amount of unrealized capital gain in relation to the current earnings and profits for the year in question.[27] If the assets were sold by the corporation as suggested above, the corporation might face a capital gain tax under I.R.C. Section 1375. To the extent that the fair market value of the distributed property exceeds the shareholder's basis, a capital gain results at the shareholder level. However, this is no detriment, because a similar gain would have been present at the corporate level had the assets been sold by the

---

[27]Robert C. Odmark, "A Practitioner's Guide to Subchapter S Planning Opportunities and Pitfalls," *Journal of Taxation,* Vol. 30 (June, 1969), p. 366.

corporation. It must be noted that the shareholder's basis for his stock is reduced by property distributions. The shareholder must have sufficient basis before he can benefit from any pass-through of a net operating loss. Accordingly, the Subchapter S corporation should avoid a property distribution which causes any shareholder's basis to be reduced to a point where it cannot absorb the net operating loss. The Tax Court has upheld this position.[28] Moreover, if the corporation has earnings and profits accumulated prior to electing Subchapter S treatment, a property distribution may cause the taxpayer to have ordinary income.

The issue of property distributions seems fairly well settled. Attempts so far to have Regulation 1.1375-4(b) declared invalid have failed. For example, in *De Treville* vs. *United States*,[29] the taxpayer was able to convince a district judge that the regulations were, in fact, invalid. The taxpayer argued that a double tax resulted when the shareholder was taxed on her share of the corporation's current taxable income, as well as on her share of accumulated earnings distributed in the form of a property distribution, and that this was contrary to the intent of Congress when it established Subchapter S. As a practical matter, the taxpayer is protected from double taxation through adjustments of the basis for shares. When a shareholder is taxed on his share of the corporation's current taxable income, the income becomes capital and the basis for the stock is increased. This previously taxed income may be withdrawn tax-free under appropriate circumstances. Such distributions, however, reduce the shareholder's basis for his stock. The apparent double taxation is caused by the presence of accumulated earnings and profits, rather than because the regulation is contrary to the intent of Congress. Using this reasoning, the Government successfully appealed the *De Treville* case.[30]

The Government used the holding in *De Treville* to find a property distribution where a corporation issued notes and debentures in order to be able to fund a cash dividend paid at about the same time.[31] It argued that the two transactions should be viewed as one transaction, a distribution of notes and debentures, and that the law of property distributions must be applied. The taxpayer asserted that the transactions must be viewed separately and constituted, both in

---

[28]*Jack Haber,* 52 T.C. 255 (1969).

[29]312 F. Supp. 362 (D.S.C. 1970).

[30]445 F. 2d 1306 (4th Cir. 1971).

[31]*George A. Roesel,* 56 T.C. 14 (1971) *appeal dismissed* (5th Cir. 1971).

substance and form, a distribution of cash and a sale of debt obligations. In the past, Subchapter S corporations have been advised to borrow from shareholders in order to pay dividends and avoid the accumulation of previously taxed income. It is possible that the Government will object to transactions of this type in the future on the basis that they lack substance. Under these circumstances the maximum time should be allowed to lapse between transactions of this type.

This same result was also obtained in a situation where the corporation distributes notes to shareholders in an attempt to reduce undistributed taxable income at a time when the corporation lacked funds to pay a cash dividend. The notes were paid in full later in the year. The Tax Court applied *DeTreville* and *Roesel* to this fact situation and held that the notes constituted a property distribution and, as such, could not reduce undistributed taxable income.[32]

The Government appears to be interested in transactions of this nature. It has successfully defended the notion that current taxable income cannot be distributed with checks drawn on the corporation's account at a time when there are insufficient funds to allow them to clear.[33] The shareholders endorsed the checks back to the corporation and thereby attempted to create a loan. The plan failed.

The property distribution area is, by no means, settled at the time of this writing.[34] Advisors of Subchapter S corporations should remain alert for future developments.

Tax Planning for Subchapter S Distributions

In this chapter, we have considered the rules and regulations which govern Subchapter S distributions. However, the distributions should be based upon proper tax planning in order that all concerned may achieve their tax goals as closely as possible. Thus, it is appropriate here to consider certain key areas where sound tax planning for Subchapter S distributions is especially important.

Perhaps the greatest problem lies in the fact that previously taxed income is essentially "locked in" the corporation to the extent that it cannot be distributed until the current earnings and profits for a particular year have been distributed. Consider the following

---

[32]*Randall N. Clark,* 58 T.C. 94 (1972).

[33]*C. D. Fountain, et al.,* 59 T.C. 696 (1973).

[34]For an expanded discussion of the property distribution area, see Davis and Crumbley, "Property Distributions and Subchapter S," *Memphis State University Law Review,* 237 (1972).

case as an example of how the earnings became "locked in," as well as the steps necessary to free them.

The Garrett Corporation was organized on June 1, 1968, and made a valid election to be taxed as a Small Business Corporation. For the short tax year ended December 31, 1968, it had a taxable income of $14,959.47 and a book income of $14,978.96. The $19.49 difference between taxable income and book income was caused by the fact that depreciation for tax purposes was slightly greater than the amount which was used for book purposes. Dividends of $7,083.28 were distributed to shareholders before the close of 1968. Thus, at December 31, 1968, a partial capital section of Garrett's balance sheet would show the following balances:

Undistributed Taxable Income	$14,959.47
Less: Dividend Distributions	7,083.28
	$7,876.19
Additional Current Earnings and Profits	19.49
	$7,895.68

During the first two and one-half months of 1969, the Corporation distributed additional dividends of $4,346.70, which, in accordance with I.R.C. Section 1375(f)(1), are treated as a distribution of 1968 UTI. On March 15, 1969, the above items were changed to appear as follows:

Previously Taxed Income	$3,529.49
Accumulated Earnings and Profits	19.49
	$3,548.98

Thus, the Garrett Corporation has allowed $3,548.98 to become locked in, to the extent that this amount cannot be distributed to shareholders without a great deal of planning. In this particular case, there was no excuse for allowing the earnings to become locked in because throughout this period an unusually high cash balance was carried. The earnings could have been distributed at any time during the two and one-half month period with no adverse effect upon Garrett's cash position.

A possible defense for this action might be the fact that most accounting systems (including Garrett's at the time that the error was made) do not place this information adequately before the Subchapter S shareholders. However, accounts along the lines of those developed in Chapter 13 of this book should provide sufficient information to enable this situation to be avoided.

How does the Garrett Corporation distribute the locked-in earnings? Sound planning for distributions is also appropriate here. In order to free these earnings, the Corporation must first distribute its 1969 income. Then it can distribute PTI. Since the two and one-half month rule applies only to the distribution of UTI, the entire distribution must be made before the close of 1969. As was required before 1966, an estimate of income will form the basis for the distribution. The Corporation can afford to be liberal, as an overdistribution constitutes a return of capital with no adverse tax consequences. However, an underdistribution results only in failure to accomplish the stated purpose, which was to eliminate PTI.

This discussion has been predicated upon the availability of sufficient cash to support the distributions. However, even the most successful small business may face working capital shortages. In this event, the need to distribute earnings currently will place even greater strains upon the firm's working capital. Yet, this fact does not diminish the need for current distribution. The two and one-half month rule allows planning time, as it creates a permanent lag between earnings and distribution. However, if this fails to relieve the situation, the firm may have to borrow in order to raise the required cash.

The decision to borrow ought to be based upon sound planning, for the firm should select the most appropriate source of funds. If the firm has a good credit standing, funds can be obtained from a commercial bank or other external lender. However, a loan from this source may have unsatisfactory strings attached to it. Loans from shareholders provide the firm with greater flexibility. This may, in fact, be the only source available to the firm. This course of action may be highly appropriate, but the loan must be evidenced by a properly drawn note, complete with an adequate rate of interest and date of maturity. Moreover, the interest should be paid and the note renewed at maturity if necessary. Care must be taken, however, to insure that the note does not constitute a second class of stock, which would terminate the firm's Subchapter S election. This problem is discussed in Chapter 5.

The Regulations provide a general rule that previously taxed income is personal and cannot be transferred to another in any manner. Thus, the purchaser of a share of Subchapter S stock does not receive the right to receive any previously taxed income tax-free.[35] The Treasury has amplified this position by holding that previously taxed income is personal to the individual who included it in his

---

[35]Regulation 1.1375-4(e).

gross income and may not be distributed to another individual as previously taxed income. If a stockholder transfers only part of his stock, his net share of PTI is not reduced as a result of the partial transfer. If he transfers all of his stock, any right to this PTI lapses entirely, unless he again becomes a stockholder in the corporation while it is subject to the same Subchapter S election. The harsh consequences of the application of this rule are shown by the following example:

> Husband and wife jointly owned all the shares of a Subchapter S corporation which had $60,000 of previously taxed income on January 1, 1975. During 1975, the husband died. At the close of that year the corporation distributed the $60,000 and the wife sought to treat this as a distribution of previously taxed income. However, it was held that only $30,000 was a distribution of PTI and the husband's shares constituted an ordinary dividend in the hands of the wife. The right to retain PTI is personal and lapses upon the taxpayer's death.[36]

This example provides additional evidence to support the current distribution of taxable income each year. With previously taxed income at zero, the firm and its shareholders can avoid many problems. In addition to the possibility that the benefit of previously taxed income might be lost because of the death of a shareholder, the presence of previously taxed income will cause adverse consequences to result from the sale of the stock. As a practical matter, a shareholder would be quite reluctant to sell a share of stock if he could not also receive value for his share of the previously taxed income. But a purchaser may not be willing to pay full price to the seller since he (the purchaser) cannot receive the PTI tax free. All these problems can be avoided by distributing all taxable income on a current basis.

Another planning area is created by Regulation 1.1375-4(c), which allows the corporation to reverse the order of the taxability of distributions. Under normal circumstances, previously taxed income is received after current earnings and profits are exhausted. However, if all shareholders agree and a special election is filed, accumulated earnings and profits are distributed before previously taxed income. This election does result in taxable dividends. However, the overall tax picture may indicate that it would be to the shareholders' advantage to have taxable income in a particular year. A shareholder may have, in his personal capacity, a deductible loss

---

[36]Rev. Rul. 66-172, 1966-1 C.B. 198.

which could be used to offset the taxable income that results from the election.

This special election must be approved by all shareholders and is binding upon them for one year only. There are probably few situations where the special election would be useful to one shareholder and even fewer where all shareholders would find it beneficial. Nevertheless, its possibility ought to be considered anytime a shareholder has a loss he wishes to offset.

Fiscal-Year Corporations

A Subchapter S corporation may elect a tax year that does not end on December 31. Such elections may represent sound tax planning because they can enable shareholders to defer for a year tax liability on any income from the corporation. The corporation allocates its profit to shareholders on the last day of its tax year in proportion to stock ownership. Thus, calendar-year corporations and shareholders derive no advantage, for the corporation's income for 1973 is included in shareholder's tax calculations for 1973. However, if the corporation moves its tax year forward only one month, a different result will occur. A fiscal-year corporation whose tax year ends on January 31, 1974, will pass through income for the year to shareholders at that date. Shareholders will include this income in their 1974 taxable income. A shift of only one month allows the tax effects to be postponed for a year.

Under normal circumstances, this procedure creates no problems for either the corporation or its shareholders. However, a distribution from the corporation before the close of the shareholder's tax year presents a problem, because at that date it is impossible to determine the character[37] of the distribution. For example:

The Duckhollow Oil Corporation was organized in 1974 for the purpose of leasing oil properties to drilling operators. It made a valid[38] election to be treated as a Subchapter S corpo-

---

[37]Ordinary income, capital gain, or return of capital.

[38]Obviously, this corporation could not be a Subchapter S corporation because the receipt of oil royalties by a nonoperating company would constitute passive investment income. (See Chapter 9.) Duckhollow did earn a profit for the year ended December 31, 1975. Because the corporation was incligible for Subchapter S treatment, it became liable for the corporate income tax. It had relied on its Subchapter S status when it paid all its cash to shareholders in the form of dividends. Accordingly, the corporation was forced to borrow funds from a shareholder to satisfy its tax liability. The whole problem could have been avoided if the corporation's tax adviser had understood the Subchapter S process. Additional problems were created because the shareholders had been assured that operations would result in a loss and they treated the distribution as a return of capital.

ration. In order to shift taxable income from the shareholders' 1974 tax returns, the corporation's advisor, B. M. Grintone, selected a taxable year ending July 31, 1975.

On September 1, 1974, the corporation collected its first royalties and immediately paid a substantial cash dividend to the shareholders. At December 1, 1974, it was impossible to determine the character of this income. If the corporation would be profitable for the year ended July 31, 1975, the distribution would be taxable to shareholders as ordinary income. However, if the corporation has a loss for that tax year, the distribution would constitute a return of capital only.

The problem is created by the fact that distributions affect the shareholder's tax return for the tax year in which they are received. Accordingly, a fiscal-year corporation can avoid this problem for its shareholders by postponing distributions until January of the following year.

Assuming that the corporation proceeds to make the distribution before the end of the calendar year, shareholders can handle the resulting difficulties in one of two ways. First, they can ask the corporation to analyze the situation and estimate whether the distribution will ultimately be ordinary income, capital gain, or a return of capital. When the estimate proves to be incorrect, the taxpayer should file an amended return in order to correct the situation. However, the possibilities that the filing of an amended return will cause the taxpayer's return to be audited should be given appropriate consideration. Second, the taxpayer can avail himself of the extension procedure. A two-month automatic extension may be obtained by filing Form 4868 and paying at least 90 percent of the tax due. At this point, the taxpayer can obtain an extension for a period of no more than four months. This extension is obtained by filing Form 2688. The form suggests the usual period of extension is two months, but then states that "a longer period of time will not be granted unless sufficient need for such extended period is clearly shown." It would appear that the need to identify the character of a Subchapter S distribution will establish "sufficient need." Accordingly, the taxpayer should merely file Form 2688 before the close of his filing period and state the reason for the request to be the need to identify a Subchapter S distribution. If the taxpayer needs to pay additional tax to meet the 90 percent requirement, Forms 4868 and 2688 can be filed simultaneously. It should be noted that the extension period may not exceed six months, which will be October 15 for a calendar-year taxpayer.

The only satisfactory solution to the problem lies in proper planning for distributions at the corporate level.

Adjusted Tax Basis

Now that Chapters 6 and 7 have provided a detailed look at the procedural aspects of the taxation of an electing corporation, it is appropriate to consider how to determine the adjusted tax basis of the shares of stock in the hands of Subchapter S stockholders.

The initial tax basis of stock in an electing corporation is determined in a similar fashion as stock in a regular corporation. If a stockholder is an initial organizer of the corporation, his tax basis is normally the summation of the amount of cash contributed to the enterprise and the basis of contributed property.[39] Where the shares of stock are purchased, the stockholder's initial basis is cost.[40] If the stockholder inherits the shares, his tax basis is the fair market value at the date of death or six months later.[41] In the case of a gift, the basis of the stock depends upon the date of the gift and whether the basis is being used to determine a gain or to determine a loss on the disposition of the stock.[42] I.R.C. Section 1374(c)(2) does not indicate which basis should be used. The basis of stock is not its fair market value at the time the corporation elects Subchapter S status.[43] The amount in the retained earnings account will differ from the stockholder's adjusted basis.

Once the initial tax basis is determined, various transactions during the life of the electing corporation affect the shareholder's stock basis. His proportionate share of undistributed taxable income increases his stock basis.[44] The *Code* defines undistributed taxable income as taxable income less (1) any capital gains tax at the corporate level and (2) cash dividend distributions.[45] A property distribution may also reduce the shareholder's basis.

Property dividends may reduce basis faster than cash dividends, because property dividends never reduce undistributed taxable in-

---

[39]See I.R.C. Sections 351 and 358.

[40]I.R.C. Section 1212; *Byrne* vs. *Commissioner,* 361 F. 2d 939 (7th Cir. 1966); *Richard L. Plowden,* 48 T.C. 666 (1967), *aff'd. per curiam* 398 F. 2d 340 (4th Cir. 1968); *Jack Ziegelheim,* T.C.M. 1967-87.

[41]I.R.C. Section 1014(a); See *Sam F. McIntosh,* T.C.M. 1967-230.

[42]See I.R.C. Section 1015.

[43]*Byrne* vs. *Commissioner, supra,* note 40; *Richard L. Plowden, supra,* note 40.

[44]I.R.C. Section 1376(a); *Byrne, supra,* note 40; *Jack Ziegelheim, supra,* note 40

[45]I.R.C. Section 1373(c); See *Jack Haber,* 52 T.C. 255 (1969).

come.[46] The increase in basis relates only to the shares of stock held by the shareholder at the end of the tax year. It will be recalled that income is allocated to shareholders on the last day of the tax year.[47] Earnings and profits which are accumulated before the corporation elects to be taxed as a Subchapter S corporation are not capital contributions by the stockholder and do not increase his tax basis. This appears reasonable in view of the fact that distributions out of accumulated earnings and profits prior to election would be taxable to the recipient as ordinary dividends.

A distribution of previously taxed income under I.R.C. Section 1375(d) reduces the stockholder's basis.[48] Further, distributions that exceed current as well as accumulated earnings and profits also reduce the stock basis since such distributions are considered to be return of capital.[49] The stock basis cannot be reduced below zero, so distributions greater than stock basis are treated as capital gains.[50]

A stockholder's portion of the electing corporation's net operating loss reduces his stock basis (but not below zero).[51] If the NOL exceeds the shareholder's stock basis, such excess reduces the basis of any indebtedness due the stockholder (again, not below zero).[52] Any NOL in excess of both the stock basis and debt basis is lost forever.[53] Of course, his stock basis can be increased by additional capital contribution. Likewise, his indebtedness basis may also be increased by additional lending to the corporation. Both of these actions can avoid wasting a NOL.

Disposition of Stock

Whenever a stockholder sells his stock to an individual or his stock is redeemed by his electing corporation, caution is important for several reasons. Only the stockholders at the end of the electing corporation's tax year include any UTI in their taxable income.[54] If a

---

[46]Odmark, *op. cit.,* p. 366.

[47]Regulation 1.1376-1.

[48]Regulation 1.1375-4(a); I.R.C. Section 301(c)(2); *Sam Novell,* T.C.M. 1969-255.

[49]I.R.C. Section 301(c)(2).

[50]Regulation 1.1375-4(a); I.R.C. Section 301(c)(3).

[51]I.R.C. Section 1376(b)(1).

[52]I.R.C. Section 1374(c)(2); *Sam Novell,* T.C.M. 1969-255.

[53]*Byrne, supra,* note 40; *Plowden, supra,* note 40; *Perry* vs. *Commissioner,* 392 F. 2d 458 (8th Cir. 1968); *Herbert Levy,* 46 T.C. 531 (1966); *Roberts* vs. *Commissioner,* 398 F. 2d 340 (4th Cir. 1968), *aff'g.* 48 T.C. 666 (1967); *Donald M. Perry,* 49 T.C. 508 (1968).

[54]I.R.C. Section 1373(b). Conversely, net operating losses are allocated on a daily basis to all stockholders who own stock during the tax year. I.R.C. Section 1374(c)(1).

stockholder sells his stock or his stock is redeemed *during the tax year,* a windfall gain can result to the selling stockholder if the selling price of the stock includes his share of UTI up to the point of the sale or redemption. The selling (or redeemed) shareholder receives capital gain treatment, but the remaining shareholders are taxed on any UTI at the end of the tax year.[55] Several steps can be taken to avoid this unfair treatment. First, the buying stockholders should bargain for a lower sale price since they must pay taxes on the UTI. Second, cash dividends can be declared before the sale or redemption. Or third, the sale or redemption can be arranged to be consumated at the beginning of the tax year.

Where PTI has accumulated in a Subchapter S corporation, a stockholder should take steps to remove such PTI before transferring his stock or before death. PTI is a personal right and cannot be transferred. The PTI can be paid out in cash before a stockholder sells his stock or otherwise transfers his stock. But, since current UTI must be distributed first, most electing corporations do not have a cash flow position which allows such a payout. A more feasible alternative is to pay a cash dividend only to the one shareholder whose stock is to be transferred. This technique works best in a year when there is little UTI.

For example, assume a Subchapter S corporation has two unrelated stockholders, A and B. There is PTI of $20,000 accumulated in the corporation, and B would like to sell his stock. But the $10,000 of PTI which belongs to B is personal and would not carry over to any transferee (including B's estate). During a year in which there is taxable income and earnings and profits of $5,000, a cash distribution of $15,000 is made to A and B, but A agrees to wait until next year for his money. B must include $5,000 of gross income (the dividend out of current income),[56] but the $10,000 remainder would be a nontaxable distribution of PTI.[57]

Note that the above example of a non-pro rata distribution of dividends deals with unrelated stockholders. Regulation 1.1375-3(d) indicates that if a non-pro rata distribution is made to members of a family group, the member of the family who receives less than his pro rata share is deemed to have waived his right to dividends, and the "amount distributed to members of the family group shall be reallocated among all the members of the group in accordance with the

---

[55]See for example *Erickson,* 56 T.C. 1112 (1971).

[56]I.R.C. Section 316(a).

[57]I.R.C. Section 1375(d).

number of shares owned by each member." This reallocation is inappropriate if the stockholder can prove that the distribution was made disproportionate without his consent. The IRS *may* apply this reallocation to nonrelated shareholders where the disproportionate taxation results in an overall tax advantage.

Payments made to qualified pension and profit-sharing plans may reduce PTI even in a loss year. The IRS has ruled that where an electing corporation incurs a net operating loss during the year which does not exceed accumulated previously taxed income, such contributions may decrease accumulated and previously taxed income.[58] Keep in mind, however, that the deductible contributions for a 5 percent or greater shareholder-employee of an electing corporation is limited to the smaller of 15 percent of salary *or* $7,500.[59]

---

[58]Rev. Rul. 71-257, 1971-1 C.B. 131.

[59]I.R.C. Section 1379(b).

Chapter 8

Prohibited Income

Two requisites must be met after an election has been properly filed or the election will be involutarily terminated. No more than 20 percent of the corporation's gross receipts can be passive investment income, and no more than 80 percent of the corporation's gross receipts can come from foreign sources. These requirements must be satisfied on a continuous basis after the election, or the corporation will forfeit its status under Subchapter S. The purpose of this chapter is to consider the problems associated with prohibited income with a view toward maintaining the corporation's right to be taxed as a Subchapter S corporation.

A distinction must be made between gross receipts and gross income. "Gross receipts" is the total gross amount received or accrued under the corporation's accounting method, except that gross receipts from the sale or exchange of stock are taken into account only to the extent of gains. No reductions in the receipts are made for returns and allowances, costs, or deductions.[1] In other words, gross receipts includes the total amount received from the sale or exchange of property (except for limitation to gains from stocks or securities), from investments, and for services rendered. Amounts resulting from a sale or exchange made by a corporation in a twelve-month liquidation that does not produce a taxable gain or loss are included in gross receipts. Amounts received as a contribution of capital, as a loan, as a repayment of a loan, or on the issuance of its own stock are not part of the gross receipts.[2]

The Regulations illustrate the determination of the gross receipts:[3]

1. A corporation on the accrual method sells property (other than stocks and securities) and receives part cash and the remainder as a notes payable. The gross receipts are the cash plus the face amount of the note.

2. A corporation reports a long-term contract on the percentage-of-completion method. The gross receipts are the portion of

---

[1]Regulation 1.1372-4(b)(5)(iv)(a).

[2]*Ibid.*

[3]Regulation 1.1372-4(b)(5)(iv)(b).

the gross contract price equal to the percentage of the entire contract completed during the year.

3. A corporation which regularly sells personal property on the installment plan has gross receipts equal to the installment payments actually received during the year.

As a practical matter, it is probably to the advantage of the Subchapter S corporation that this gross receipts test is used rather than a gross income test. In any given year, gross receipts will probably be larger than gross income. Therefore, the gross receipts test will allow a greater amount of prohibited income to be received before the election is terminated.

Passive Investment Income

The *Code* states that the election is terminated if, during any taxable year, the corporation has passive investment income which is greater than 20 percent of its gross receipts for that year.[4] Passive investment income is defined by the *Code* as "gross receipts derived from royalties, rents, dividends, interest, annuities, and sales or exchanges of stock or securities." However, for purposes of this definition, only the gain on the sale of the stocks or securities is considered, rather than the gross sales price.[5] The apparent reason for this provision is to deny Subchapter S treatment to personal holding companies.

The personal holding company rules of I.R.C. Sections 541-547 represent an attempt by Congress to limit, under certain circumstances, the use of the corporate form as a tax-planning device. A corporation is considered a personal holding company if (1) during the tax year at least 60 percent of its adjusted gross ordinary income consists of dividends, rents, mineral, oil, and gas royalties, copyright royalties, produced film rents, and personal service contracts, and (2) more than 50 percent of the value of the outstanding stock is owned directly or indirectly by five or less individuals at any time during the last half of the tax year.[6] In absence of the onerous personal holding company provisions, a high-bracket taxpayer could incorporate his investment activities and cause any income tax to be limited to cor-

---

[4]I.R.C. Section 1372(e)(5)(A); there is a limited exception to the 20 percent rule which is discussed later.

[5]I.R.C. Section 1372(e)(5)(C).

[6]I.R.C. Sections 542(a)(1) and (2); For an excellent discussion, see N. H. Lipoff, "Personal Holding Companies: A Walking Tiger," *Florida Law Review,* Vol. 18 (Fall, 1965), pp. 304-329.

porate rates. Although dividends would be taxable to shareholders when received, the close corporation could so time these distributions to achieve the lowest possible personal tax rates. Since activities of this sort are ordinarly carried on by individuals, the personal holding company is often referred to as an "incorporated pocketbook." However, the personal holding company rules discourage the use of this device by applying a penalty tax of 70 percent of the undistributed personal holding company income in addition to imposing the ordinary corporate rates to the corporation's income before distributions.

Although the Subchapter S income limitations appear at first glance to be similar to the personal holding company rules, their purposes are somewhat different. For example, a Subchapter S corporation will be wholly ineffective as an income timing device, as its income is taxed to shareholders at the end of the tax year even though it is not distributed as dividends.

The general test for disqualification under Subchapter S is different from the test relating to personal holding companies where the personal holding company penalty tax is applied to corporations whose gross income is 60 percent or more of passive income. For example, the personal holding company status is determined by a gross income test and not a gross receipts test. Income from commodity transactions or personal service contracts is not within I.R.C. Section 1372(e)(5), even though it comes within I.R.C. Section 543. Conversely, rental income which is 50 percent or more of a corporation's gross income is within I.R.C. Section 1372(e)(5) but does not fall within I.R.C. Section 543. Therefore, the typical real estate corporation is disqualified under Subchapter S. Also, only 20 percent or more prohibitive income is enough to terminate an election, while at least 60 percent is needed to cause a personal holding company penalty tax. Hence, certain businesses with interest income are exempt under the personal holding company provisions, but are disqualified under the Subchapter S election.

In 1966 Congress provided a limited amount of relief from the passive investment income provisions.[7] Before that date, the passive income rule created real problems for newly formed corporations. In many cases, a new corporation will not be active during the first few years after it is organized. This time is often spent selling stock, acquiring assets, and making plans for production. What about the funds that the corporation has acquired from the sale of its stock

---

[7] Public Law 89-389, 80 Stat. 111 (1966).

and the assets that it has purchased with these funds? Prudent financial management dictates that these funds be invested in interest-bearing time deposits or in readily marketable securities until they are needed. Moreover, buildings and other assets of production might be rented until the newly formed corporation begins its own productive processes. However, the receipt of any returns on these assets would cause the corporation's Subchapter S election to be terminated. Thus, the corporation had to allow these assets to remain idle.

Section 1372(e)(5)(B) waives the application of the 20 percent rule for the first tax year in which the corporation actively conducts business, as well as for the next succeeding tax year. However, the amount of passive investment income received must be less than $3,000.

A taxpayer has already sought benefits of Section 1372(e)(5)(B) for years prior to 1966. In *Weldon F. Osborne,*[8] the taxpayer argued that this 1966 amendment proves that Congress never intended to penalize a corporation for premature passive income. The Tax Court rejected this argument.

This provision applies only to newly formed corporations; the standard corporation which later elects Subchapter S status cannot avail itself of this relief. As a practical matter, this should not be a problem for established corporations. Fortunately, the newly formed corporation is no longer forced to allow its assets to remain idle in order to protect its election.

The *Code* stipulates that the prohibited personal holding company income includes royalties, rents, interest, dividends, annuities, and sales or exchanges of stocks or securities.[9]

Royalties

The Regulations state that "royalties" encompasses all royalties. Royalties include mineral, oil, and gas royalties (whether or not the aggregate amount of such royalties constitutes 50 percent or more of the gross income of the corporation for the tax year). Amounts received for the privilege of using patents, copyrights, secret processes and formulas, goodwill, trademarks, trade brands, franchises, and other like property are classified as royalty income. Amounts from timber or coal or from patent rights are excluded from royalty income. The gross amount of royalties is not reduced by the cost of the

---

[8]55 T.C. 329 (1970).

[9]I.R.C. Section 1372(e)(5).

right under which they are received or by any amount allowable as a deduction in computing taxable income.[10]

The Regulations state that mineral, oil, and gas royalties are defined in the Regulations for personal holding company income.[11] They state that "the term 'mineral, oil or gas royalties' means all royalties, including production payments and overriding royalties, received from any interest in mineral, oil, or gas properties."[12] However, one court held that reserved oil payments do not constitute royalties and thus declared this Regulation invalid.[13] Still another court has held that oil and gas bonuses are neither royalties nor rents and do not constitute passive income. The court noted such bonuses are paid for by the execution of a lease and are not dependent upon production. Bonuses result from considerable bargaining, and this bargaining represents an active part of land management. The court concluded that bonuses and royalties are two different items and that the receipt of such bonuses will not terminate a Subchapter S election.[14]

Rents

"Rents" under this provision means amounts received for the use of the corporation's real or personal property, whether or not such amounts constitute 50 percent or more of the gross income of the corporation for the tax year. Despite the lodging element, income derived from such operations as hotels, motels, boarding houses, apartment hotels, and tourist homes is not rent if significant services are also rendered primarily for the tenants' convenience. The Regulations state that services are considered to be rendered to the occupant of such establishments if they are primarily for his convenience, and are other than the kinds of services customarily rendered in connection with the rental of rooms or space only. Thus, a business should furnish maid service, catering service, and so forth so that the rent will not terminate an election. Supplying heat and light, cleaning public entrances, exits or lobbies, and the collection of trash are not classified as rendering services. Payments for living quarters in duplex or multiple housing units, for offices in an office building, and for the use or occupancy of entire private residences are rents. Payments for

---

[10]Regulation 1.1372-4(b)(5)(v).

[11]*Ibid.*

[12]Regulation 1.1543-1(b)(11)(ii).

[13]*525 Company* vs. *Commissioner,* 342 F. 2d 759 (5th Cir. 1965).

[14]*Swank and Sons, Inc.* vs. *U.S.,* 32 A.F.T.R. 2d 73-5781 (D.C. Mont. 1973).

the parking of cars generally do not constitute rent. If significant services are rendered in connection with the payments for the warehousing of goods or for the use of personal property, these payments are not treated as rent.[15]

Thus, the Regulations provide a general view toward the manner in which the IRS will treat the concept of rent in a Subchapter S context. To supplement this Regulation, however, it is appropriate to consider the various court cases and rulings which have interpreted and modified the effects of rental income. Of importance here is the notion of what significant services are necessary to remove the income from the rent classification for Subchapter S purposes.

For example, the Tax Court has held that merely providing recreational facilities is not sufficient to cause rental income to be removed from its classification as prohibited. In one case, the taxpayer operated a summer resort. He based his case on the fact that he provided recreational facilities and organized several recreational events. On this basis, the taxpayer lost his case as well as his Subchapter S election.[16]

Rents do not include a landowner's income from sharefarming if he materially participates in the farm production through physical work, management, or management decisions.[17] Moreover, amounts received by a corporation from leasing silverware, glassware, tables, chairs, and electronic equipment are not rents if the business performs delivery and pick-up functions with respect to the items, and washes, polishes, repairs, and stores them prior to the lease to the customer.[18]

The Treasury has ruled that rental income from leasing motor vehicles on a short-term basis does not constitute rent for Subchapter S purposes. Its rationale is that the leasing company must furnish maintenance services such as "gas and oil, tire repair and changing, cleaning and polishing, oil changing and lubrication, and engine and body repair." These services were held to be "significant services" within Regulation 1.1372-4(b)(5). The fact that some of these services were performed by nonemployees on a contract basis was not significant.[19]

---

[15]Regulation 1.1372-4(b)(5)(vi).
[16]*Max Feingold,* 49 T.C. 461 (1968).
[17]Rev. Rul. 61-112, 1961-1 C.B. 399.
[18]Rev. Rul. 64-232, 1964-1 C.B. 34.
[19]Rev. Rul. 65-40, 1965-1 C.B. 429.

Along these same lines, the Treasury has issued two separate rulings which provide a number of examples of rental income which is not considered rent for Subchapter S purposes:[20]

1. R Corporation derives all of its income from leasing barricades for use around areas of construction and danger areas and for traffic control purposes. Each barricade consists of a steel frame, a sign board and a flashing light. R delivers the barricades to the job site, services them twice weekly (replacing batteries, bulbs, and lenses as well as parts stolen or broken), and picks up the barricades upon completion of the project.

2. S Corporation leases golf carts at various golf courses in its area at a charge which is based on the number of rounds of golf for which they are used. The payment received is divided with the owner of the course involved, whose employees handle the actual rental of the carts to the golfers. The costs of maintaining and servicing the carts (including the wages of a full-time mechanic) are paid by S.

3. The income of T Corporation is derived from charges made for the use of its crane. The charges are usually made on an hourly, daily, weekly, or monthly basis, although, occasionally, an agreed-upon amount is paid for a particular job. The operator is furnished and paid by T.

4. U Corporation is a men's clothing store. In addition to selling clothes, it rents dress suits to individuals. No charges are made for alterations, and each suit is cleaned and pressed before it is used by a customer.

I.R.C. Section 1372(e)(5) provides that a Subchapter S election shall terminate if, for any taxable year of the corporation for which the election is in effect, more than 20 percent of the gross receipts of the corporation is derived from rents and certain other types of income. Regulation 1.1372-4(b)(5)(iv) excludes from the term "rents," as used in I.R.C. Section 1372(e)(5), payments for the use of personal property where significant services are rendered in connection with such payments. Accordingly, it is held that the payments received by the corporations for the use of personal property in each of the above situations do not constitute rents within the meaning of I.R.C. Section 1372(e)(5) since, in each instance, significant services are performed by the corporation in connection with such payments.

5. M Corporation owns two buildings and related equipment used for the storage of grain. Separate fees are charged for receiving the grain and for taking the grain out of storage and loading it on carriers for shipment. While in storage, services

[20]Rev. Rul. 65-83, 1965-1 C.B. 430; Rev. Rul. 65-91, 1965-1 C.B. 431; Rev. Rul. 70-206, 1970-1 C.B. 177.

must be performed to prevent spoilage and infestation of the grain. These services include periodic inspection and turning of the grain. If the grain were to be improperly handled during storage, the corporation would be liable (without the possibility of insurance protection) for the full value of the spoiled grain.

Under these circumstances, it is held that fees received for the storage of grain are not rents within the meaning of I.R.C. Section 1372(e)(5) because of the significant services performed in connection with the storage.

6. O Corporation operates a cotton warehouse. Because the cotton available for storage in the area where O's warehouse is located has declined in recent years, the corporation has endeavored to store other commodities in its warehouse. At the present time, three of the eight rooms in the warehouse are used for the storage of manufactured goods under a specific contract between O and a manufacturer of cotton cloth. Under the contract (termed a lease) the manufacturer has the right to use for a term of one year specific rooms in the warehouse for storage. The manufacturer is also responsible for the locks and fastenings on the doors of the rented compartments.

Since, under the terms of the contract, the owner of the stored goods is entitled to specific space for a fixed term and provides for its own storing, loading, unloading, and other handling and protecting services required for its goods, the payments received under the contract are rents within the meaning of I.R.C. Section 1372(e)(5).

7. The gross receipts of P Corporation are derived from payments received for the handling and storage of goods in its refrigerated warehouse. Most owners of goods pay on a perpound or per-container basis. These charges include refrigeration service, maintenance of proper humidities, housekeeping, handling in and out of the warehouse, and record-keeping in connection with the preservation of and accounting for the commodities in storage. An arrangement is occasionally made whereby a customer has exclusive use for a fixed term of specified space. Charges for this type of arrangement are usually on a square-foot or flat-rate basis and vary depending upon whether P or the customer supplies the necessary labor for moving the goods in and out of the warehouse and for providing housekeeping services. In any event, P supplies the refrigeration and other necessary services, and is responsible for maintenance.

Under these circumstances, it is held that none of the payments received by P corporation are rents within the meaning of I.R.C.

Section 1372(e)(5).

8. Q Corporation owns and operates an automobile parking lot. The cars are left with an attendant at the entrance to the lot who parks them in any available space.

The payments received by Q from the customers under these circumstances are not rents within the meaning of I.R.C. Section 1372(e)(5).

9. A Corporation makes television sets available to patients of a hospital. The company services the sets which includes locking and unlocking, and adjusting and repairing the sets. Amounts received for this service are not "rent" within the meaning of Section 1372(e)(5) of the *Code.*

In each case it is important to note that the rendering of significant services provides the rationale for the decision.

Two recent cases divided on the issue that significant services were not provided in connection with the rental activity. In *Bramlette Building Corp., Inc.,* the Tax Court held that services such as building maintenance, maid services, elevator services, and security services were those "usually or customarily rendered to office building occupants and . . . that the services were not significant.[21] In *City Markets, Inc.,* the issue was again significant services. Petitioners owned and rented a shopping center. They provided such services as cleaning and sweeping five public rest rooms, the sidewalks and alleys around the buildings and some parts of the interior of the buildings, repairing the parking area pavements, spraying garbage cans with insecticides to keep down flies, unblocking stopped-up sewer lines, repairing electrical equipment and heating and air conditioning equipment, making roof repairs, and replacing broken windows. The petitioners sought to convince the Tax Court that these services were significant and, accordingly, that the income was not rent for Subchapter S purposes. The Court, however, cited *Feingold* and *Bramlette* as authority and held that the services rendered were not significant.[22]

The effect of these rules and decisions is to deny Subchapter S benefits to corporations engaged in the rental of real property on a long-term basis. Although this line of thinking is a carryover from the "incorporated pocketbook" aspects of the personal holding company provisions, there is no justification for its application to Subchapter S corporations. To the extent that the rental corporation is excluded

---

[21]52 T.C. 200 (1969), *aff'd.* 25 A.F.T.R. 2d 70-1061 (5th Cir. 1974).

[22]T.C.M. 1969-202, *aff'd.* 26 A.F.T.R. 2d 70-5760 (6th Cir. 1970).

from Subchapter S benefits, its decision process with respect to organizational form is distorted. There are many *bona fide* business reasons why a rental company might desire corporate status, yet the tax consequences may make the cost of this choice prohibitive. One can only hope that this requirement will be purged from the rules as soon as possible.

Interest and Dividends

The term "interest" includes any amounts received for the use of money even if it is tax-exempted or specifically exempted from the personal holding company provision (i.e., banks and licensed personal finance companies).[23]

Most cases dealing with interest in a Subchapter S context are concerned with swelling gross receipts so that interest income will be less than 20 percent of that income. It should be noted that the 20 percent rule virtually excludes financial institutions from Subchapter S treatment. In *Valley Loan Assn.* vs. *U.S.*,[24] the Court noted that Section 1372(e)(5) operates to exclude finance and loan companies from the benefits of Subchapter S. The Court found "nothing in Subchapter S which specifically excludes from gross receipts the amount received from repayment (principal) of . . . loans." Regulation 1.1372-4 was held invalid as applied to the facts of this case, and the company was allowed to obtain the benefits of Subchapter S. However, the Tax Court has held that Congress did not intend to exempt interest, no matter what the source, from prohibition under Subchapter S.[25] Moreover, the Tax Court refused to allow a cash-basis taxpayer to treat the entire sales price of houses as gross receipts when the amounts were to be received in future installments.[26]

Clearly, taxpayers have not fared well in the interest area. The position of the statute is difficult to defend, for there is certainly nothing passive about the operation of a small loan company. Not withstanding this reasoning, the Tax Court has stated that interest income is passive even though the corporation is in the loan business.[27] Nevertheless, this represents the state of the law, and taxpayers had best plan accordingly.

---

[23]Regulation 1.1372-4(b)(5)(viii).

[24]18 A.F.T.R. 2d 5793 (S.D. Colo. 1966).

[25]*Joseph L. House, Jr.,* T.C.M. 1970-125, *rev'd.* on other grounds; 29 A.F.T.R. 2d 72-360 (4th Cir. 1972).

[26]*Alfred M. Sieh,* 56 T.C. 1386 (1971), *aff'd.* 31 A.F.T.R. 2d 73-419 (8th Cir. 1973).

[27]*I. J. Marshall,* 60 T.C. 242 (1973).

"Dividends" include any corporate distributions or redemptions that are taxed as dividends and includes foreign personal holding company income taxed to the United States stockholders plus any consent dividends.[28] The dividend area has not created any litigation.

Annuities

The Regulations stipulate that the term "annuities" encompasses the entire amount received as an annuity under an annuity, endowment, or life insurance contract, regardless of whether only part of such amount would be includable in gross income under I.R.C. Section 1372.[29]

Gains from Stock

The 20 percent limitation on gross receipts also applies to gains from the sale or exchange of stock. In *Temple N. Joyce*,[30] the corporation under consideration had elected Subchapter S treatment since substantial losses were anticipated in the development of a patent. The electing corporation had total income of $2,100, consisting almost entirely of net long-term capital gains on the sale of certain securities. The corporation also had operating losses of $211,000, which would have produced a tax saving of $46,000 on the stockholder's personal income tax return.

Unfortunately, losses are not used to reduce gains in determining the personal holding company income under Subchapter S.[31] Therefore, the personal holding company income (gain on the sale of the securities) was more than 20 percent of the corporation's gross receipts, and the election terminated.

The gross receipts from the sale of stock is not the sale price or the amount received, but it is the excess of the amount realized over the adjusted basis of the stock. Gross receipts from the sale or exchange of stocks and securities include gains received from such sales or exchanges even though the corporation is a regular dealer in stocks and securities.[32]

Suppose the corporation was organized to engage actively in the business of purchasing and selling securities. Regulation 1.1372-4(b)(5)(x) expressly states that "gross receipts from the sale or ex-

---

[28]Regulation 1.1372-4(b)(5)(vii).
[29]Regulation 1.1372-4(b)(5)(ix).
[30]42 T.C. 628 (1964).
[31]Regulation 1.1372-4(b)(5)(x).
[32]*Ibid.*

change of stocks and securities include gains received from such sales or exchanges by a corporation even though such corporation is a regular dealer in stocks and securities." In *Zychinski,*[33] the taxpayer sought to avail himself of the active interest-passive interest dichotomy which the Fifth Circuit has developed in *House* vs. *Commissioner.*[34] In this case, the taxpayer was able to convince the Court of Appeals that Section 1372(e)(5) did not intend to consider the earned interest income of a lending and finance company to be passive income. However, the Tax Court stated that it would not follow the reasoning of the Fifth Circuit and held that interest is, by definition, passive.[35] The Tax Court found nothing inconsistent with the language of Regulation 1.1372-4(b)(5)(x) which applies Section 1372(e)(5) to regular dealers in stocks and securities. Thus, at the time of this writing,[36] prospects for the success of this theory of passive income do not appear to be favorable. Nevertheless, sufficient conflict to justify litigation seems to be developing. Taxpayers should remain alert to potential problems in this area.

The Tax Court has held that a gain realized on a liquidation distribution from a corporation constituted a gain from the exchange of stock and was therefore subject to the 20 percent limitation on gross receipts.[37] The case suggests that when liquidating or selling a less than 80 percent subsidiary, the distribution should extend over a number of years or the transaction should be planned as a tax-free reorganization.

Miscellaneous

The Tax Court held that promissory notes are securities within the meaning of Section 1372(e)(5). A mortgage company bought some notes and sold them to insurance companies at a discount. The income from these transactions was greater than 20 percent of the company's gross receipts, and its Subchapter S election was terminated.[38] However, the Treasury has ruled that amounts received by a railroad transportation company for allowing its stock to stand

---

[33]*Zychinski,* 60 T.C. No. 100 (1973).

[34]29 A.F.T.R. 2d 72-360 (5th Cir. 1972).

[35]*I. J. Marshall,* 60 T.C. 242 (1973).

[36]May, 1974.

[37]*Lansing Broadcasting Co.* vs. *Commissioner,* 52 T.C. 299 (1969), *aff'd.* 25 A.F.T.R. 2d 70-1398 (6th Cir. 1970).

[38]*Buhler Mortgage Company, Inc.* vs. *Commissioner,* 51 T.C. 971 (1969), *aff'd. per curiam,* 28 A.F.T.R. 2d 71-5252 (6th Cir. 1971).

idle at the shipper's dock (demurrage) is not passive investment income.[39] Moreover, income received by a sports franchise from television and radio networks for the right to broadcast football games is also not passive income for Subchapter S purposes.[40] Profit from trading in commodity futures is not considered passive.[41]

The meaning of the term "gross receipts" can also be a source of trouble. In *Branch* vs. *U.S.,*[42] a taxpayer was allowed to increase his gross receipts for payments received on option contracts. By increasing gross receipts, a greater amount of prohibited income is allowed before the Subchapter S election is terminated. The taxpayer cited Regulation 1.1372-4 which states that gross receipts means "the total amount received or accrued under the method of accounting used by the corporation in computing its taxable income." The Court realized that it may have created a loophole whereby gross receipts could be increased in order to bring the prohibited income within the 20 percent rule. However, it stated that it could not change its interpretation of statutory language in order to plug the loophole. Citing *Hanover Bank* vs. *Commissioner,*[43] the Court remarked that a loophole created should be closed by Congress, if necessary. Also, along these same lines, the Treasury has stated that the gross receipts from the sale of insurance policies by insurance agencies will be considered gross receipts for Subchapter S purposes rather than merely the commissions received.[44] Thus, an insurance agency is allowed to earn more prohibited income before its Subchapter S election is jeopardized. Moreover, in computing a Subchapter S corporation's share of gross receipts from a joint venture, the distributive share of the venture's gross receipts is considered, rather than the distributive share of its profit or loss.[45] The effect of this is to increase gross receipts and, therefore, increase the amount of passive investment income which may be earned.

Foreign Income

A Subchapter S election terminates if, for any taxable year, the corporation derives more than 80 percent of its gross receipts from

---

[39]Rev. Rul. 70-110, 1970-1 C.B. 176.

[40]Rev. Rul. 71-407, 1971-2 C.B. 318.

[41]Rev. Rul. 72-457, 1972-2 C.B. 510.

[42]20 A.F.T.R. 2d 5302, 67-2 U.S.T.C. ¶9396 (D.C. Ga. 1967).

[43]369 U.S. 672, 82 S. Ct. 1080, 9 A.F.T.R. 2d 1492 (1962).

[44]Rev. Rul. 69-192, 1969-1 C.B. 207.

[45]Rev. Rul. 71-455, 1971-2 C.B. 318.

sources outside the United States. The election terminates retroactively to the beginning of the year in which the prohibitive income is received. Even worse, the termination is effective for all succeeding years of the corporation. The principles of I.R.C. Section 861 and the succeeding provisions of the *Code* apply in determining the sources of income.[46]

The rationale for this provision is not clear. Perhaps Congress wanted to avoid the problems associated with foreign income. The international allocation of business income is not unlike the problems encountered in allocating the income of multistate enterprises among the several states for state corporate income tax purposes. However, this theory tends to be discredited by virtue of the fact that a corporation can derive 80 percent of its income from foreign sources and not jeopardize its election.

The Regulations do provide an example as to how foreign income is to be computed:[47]

A corporation has gross receipts from the sale of personal property produced (in whole or in part) by the corporation within the United States and sold within a foreign country. An independent factory or production price has not been established.[48] One-half of the gross receipts from the sale of the property should be apportioned in accordance with the value of the corporation's property within the United States and within the foreign country. The portion attributable to sources within the United States is determined by multiplying one-half of the gross receipts by a fraction. (The numerator of this fraction consists of the value of the corporation's property within the United States, and the denominator consists of the total of the corporation's property within the United States and within the foreign country.) The remaining one-half of the gross receipts should be apportioned in accordance with the gross sales of the corporation within the United States and within the foreign country. The portion attributable to sources within the United States is determined by multiplying the one-half by a fraction; the numerator of which consists of the corporation's gross sales for the taxable year within the United States, and the denominator consists of the corporation's gross sales for the taxable year both within the United States and within the foreign country.

---

[46]Regulation 1.1372-4(b)(4)(i).

[47]Regulation 1.1372-4(b)(4)(ii).

[48]Regulation 1.863-3(b)(2) provides for the establishment of an arms-length factory price to be used as the selling price for federal income tax purposes. This selling price can be matched with expenses to arrive at a taxable income. Under this procedure, there is no need for an allocation formula.

The foreign income area has not created significant problems for Subchapter S corporations. No rulings and only one case can be found on a foreign income question. However, in *Helis* vs. *Usry*,[49] the taxpayer owned shares in a Subchapter S corporation that had significant foreign operations. The issue here was over the definition of gross receipts. The company had exchanged certain inventory items for similar items owned by other companies. The corporation had assumed that these transactions would constitute tax-free exchanges under Section 1031(a) of the *Code*, and that an exchange could not produce gross receipts. However, the government's position was that the transactions were sales and that gross receipts had been produced. As the company had no other income, all of its income would be from foreign sources in violation of the 80 percent foreign income limitation. The Court held that the transactions did not generate gross receipts and, accordingly, the corporation's election was not terminated.

The typical Subchapter S corporation is not involved in foreign activity. However, if the corporation has foreign income, it should take steps to insure that it is maintained below the 80 percent level. In *Helis,* the taxpayer had taken steps to insure that the materials in question were exchanged rather than sold. The transaction was structured to achieve the desired result. The 80 percent level is high, and it is unlikely that a corporation would violate this provision by accident.

A Subchapter S corporation may not act as a conduit for purposes of passing credit for foreign taxes paid through to stockholders. Accordingly, benefit for such payments may be obtained only through a deduction at the corporate level.[50]

Implications for Tax Planning

Tax planning aspects of operating a Subchapter S corporation are stressed throughout this book. The prohibited income area lends itself to fruitful planning in order to avoid possible adverse tax consequences. Failure to consider these aspects places the Subchapter S election in constant danger of being involuntarily terminated.

In the first place, a Subchapter S corporation should not receive prohibited income. Of all the types of passive investment income discussed earlier in the chapter, rental income is the only logical one

---

[49]30 A.F.T.R. 2d 72-5107 (5th Cir. 1972), *aff'g.* 27 A.F.T.R. 2d 71-1266 (E.D. La. 1971).

[50]Rev. Rul. 68-128, 1968-1 C.B. 381.

which would be of interest to a Subchapter S corporation. Clearly, a Subchapter S corporation can function neither as a personal holding company nor a real estate investment corporation. What possible advantage could accrue to ten or fewer shareholders to own an undivided interest in bonds, stocks, or annuities? We noted that dividends and interest lose their character as they are passed through to shareholders. For this reason, interest on municipal securities becomes taxable as it passes through the Subchapter S conduit. Thus, it becomes readily apparent that investments which produce interest and dividends should be held by the shareholders in their individual capacities, and the Subchapter S corporation should be left completely out of the picture.

Rental income is the one exception to this line of reasoning. Just as the corporate form holds advantages for rental companies, it logically follows that their shareholders would desire to avail themselves of Subchapter S benefits. We noted earlier that the presence of significant services would remove the income from its classification as rent. Thus, a motel or auto rental agency presents no problem. However, it is a present-day fact of life that corporations engaged in the rental of either apartments or office space should not consider Subchapter S. If the shareholders wish to take part in this sort of activity, they should form a separate corporation.

Hopefully, the law will be revised so that rental income from whatever source can be earned by a Subchapter S corporation. Fairness dictates that the rental area receive prime consideration when the Subchapter S rules come up for a significant revision.

If absolutely necessary, there is no reason why the Subchapter S corporation could not own the rental corporation as a subsidiary. However, care must be taken to insure that the Subchapter S corporation does not own more than 79 percent of the voting stock.

Note that we still do not completely escape the 20 percent limitation upon prohibited income. However, the dividend policy of the subsidiary can be controlled to the extent that dividends are paid in such a way that they do not violate the 20 percent rule. Thus, if it is absolutely necessary, the Subchapter S corporation can effectively own rental property. As stated earlier, however, the Subchapter S corporation will avoid many problems by steering clear of the passive income pitfall.

Nevertheless, the Subchapter S corporation may find that its income from nonpassive sources has dropped and that it may conclude the tax year with an excess of 20 percent from prohibited sources. Of course, if this is allowed to happen, the election will be terminated retroactively to the first of the tax year. If passive income greatly exceeds the 20 percent limit, there is probably nothing that can be done to save the election. However, if the outcome is likely to be close, the corporation can engage in certain transactions which are designed to expand its gross receipts and cause the passive income to fall back within the 20 percent limitation. Sales of fixed assets will have the desired effect on gross receipts, and maintaining the Subchapter S election makes any adverse consequences which result from these transactions seem worthwhile. Earlier in the chapter, we noted that proceeds from an option to sell fixed assets would increase gross receipts.

Chapter 9

Tax Returns for
Subchapter S Corporations

Although a Subchapter S corporation does not normally have a tax liability, it still must comply with certain reporting requirements. The purpose of this chapter is to consider the various tax forms which the Subchapter S corporation must file and also to view some of the more troublesome compliance problems.

The Subchapter S Return

A Subchapter S corporation is required to file Form 1120-S within two and one-half months of the close of its tax year. Unlike the requirement upon individuals, this informational return is filed regardless of any profit or loss. In general, the return measures any profit or loss and indicates how it is to be divided among the shareholders of record on the last day of the Subchapter S tax year.

The appropriate place to begin the discussion is with a set of hypothetical financial statements. In actual practice, data to complete the return may come from a formal accounting system, or it may have to be reconstructed by means of a worksheet prepared especially to facilitate preparation of the return. Exhibits 9-1 and 9-2 present financial data of the Pamida Corporation at December 31, 1973, as well as operating results for the year then ended.

A completed Form 1120-S is presented in Exhibit 9-3. This return is based upon the information contained in Exhibits 9-1 and 9-2. The reader will note that the form of this return is quite similar to the one filed by a regular corporation (Form 1120) or a partnership (Form 1065). Page 1 of each of these returns enables the entity to compute its taxable income, and page 2 provides certain supporting data, such as compensation of officers, analysis of bad debts activity, and a depreciation schedule. Page 3 of the partnership and Subchapter S returns enable the entity to allocate profits and losses among the owners of the entity. Page 4 provides balance sheets, reconciliation of book income to taxable income, and an analysis of changes in capital.

Taxable income is computed on page 4 of the return. In the example, taxable income differs from book income because the corporation has received tax-exempt interest. Schedule M-1 provides a reconciliation of book income to taxable income. Both nontaxable income and nondeductible expenses are omitted from page 1 of the return. Gains and losses become a part of taxable income as a result of their inclusion on page 1. These items are discussed later in the chapter.

Undistributed taxable income is computed in Schedule K on page 3 of the return. Schedule K-1 was added to the package for the 1972 tax year. The purpose of this schedule is to allocate various items to shareholders. Schedule K-1 supports the information contained in Schedule K. A Schedule K-1 is prepared for each shareholder. Copy A is submitted to the IRS with the return. Copy B is given to each shareholder to enable him to prepare his personal tax return. Copy C is retained by the corporation. Exhibit 9-4 provides the Schedules K-1 for the two shareholders of the Pamida Corporation.

A calendar-year situation is relatively simple. Undistributed taxable income is merely taxable income minus cash dividends out of current earnings and profits less any tax on capital gains. It should be noted that Schedule K-1 does not report dividends actually received by the shareholder and, accordingly, a shareholder who bases his return solely on that schedule may be filing an incomplete return. Actual dividend distributions computed on lines 4, 5, 6, and 7 of Schedule K should be reported to shareholders on Form 1099-DIV. (See Exhibit 9-5.) Thus, both Schedule K-1 and Form 1099-DIV will be needed to enable the shareholder to file a complete tax return.

A fiscal-year corporation presents additional problems, however. Dividends become income to shareholders in the year of distribution. For example, if the Pamida Corporation had been a fiscal-year corporation with a tax year ending June 30, 1973, the results would be different. This difference is especially true if the dividends (line 1, Schedule K; page 3, Form 1120-S) had been paid before December 31, 1972. They would have been taxed to shareholders on their 1972 tax returns, even though the actual character of these dividends could not be known until June 30, 1973. Under this circumstance, an allocation is required so that the dividends will reflect their proportional share of capital gain as well as ordinary income. This calculation is not difficult once the appropriate data is identified. First, the ratio of capital gains to total taxable income is determined. Then, the ratio of ordinary income to taxable income is computed. Capital gain information is found on Schedule D. (See Exhibit 9-8 and the discussion later in this chapter.) Ordinary income is taxable income minus capital gain. Thus, the Pamida Corporation's taxable income on a fiscal-year basis can be accounted for as follows:

Dividend allocation to capital gains (1972)	$ 3,872.36
Dividend allocation to ordinary income (1972)	16,127.64
Undistributed taxable income allocation to capital gains (1973)	7,027.63
Undistributed taxable income allocation to ordinary income (1973)	29,268.76
Total taxable income	$56,296.39

The shareholders of the Pamida Corporation will report the dividend allocation on their tax returns for 1972 and the undistributed taxable income allocations on their 1973 returns. Supporting calculations are provided in Exhibit 9-6. Note that the corporation may be taxed on its capital gains; this possible tax is discussed later in the chapter. If the corporation is taxed in this manner, the allocation is the ratio of ordinary income to taxable income, *minus* the tax, and the ratio of capital gains *minus* the tax to taxable income *minus* the tax. In effect, the tax paid represents a direct allocation of profits to the government. These profits are not available for shareholders and must be excluded from the calculation.

Schedule L (page 4 of Form 1120-S) requires balance sheets both at the beginning and the end of the tax year. Although the official instructions are not clear, these balance sheets appear to require the use of financial accounting (book) concepts, rather than tax concepts. Thus, this information is obtained from the accounting records. Book income and taxable income are reconciled in Schedule M-1. The beginning and ending balance sheets are related to each other through Schedule M-2, which reconciles the retained earnings figures at these two times. Through this procedure, it is possible to prove the mathematical and conceptual accuracy of the measurement process.

Supplemental Schedule of Gains and Losses

Since 1961, certain gains on the sale of business assets have been denied capital gain treatment. The calculations are made on Form 4797. (See Exhibit 9-8.) Part III of Form 4797 is used to compute the gain on sale of these assets and allocate that gain between capital gain and ordinary income treatment. Capital gain income is transferred to

EXHIBIT 9-1

The Pamida Corporation
Comparative Balance Sheets
December 31, 1972 and December 31, 1973

	Balance Sheet December 31, 1972		Balance Sheet December 31, 1973	
Assets				
Cash		$ 69,342.81		$149,376.20
Accounts Receivable	$ 71,982.12		$ 75,072.98	
Allowance for Bad Debts	7,198.21	64,783.91	7,507.29	65,565.69
Inventory		81,149.13		93,672.44
Federal Bonds		35,000.00		35,000.00
State Bonds		30,000.00		30,000.00
Other Assets		5,000.00		5,000.00
Buildings	$290,400.00		$240,300.00	
Accumulated Depreciation	145,283.00	145,117.00	130,142.01	110,157.99
Land		40,000.00		35,000.00
Total Assets		$470,392.85		$523,772.32
Liabilities				
Accounts Payable		$ 62,941.00		$ 70,014.77
Other Current Liabilities		7,392.10		9,166.14
Bonds Payable		20,745.00		15,731.19
Other Liabilities		500.00		4,473.92
Total Liabilities		$ 91,578.10		$ 99,386.02
Capital				
Capital Stock	$300,000.00		$300,000.00	
Retained Earnings – Appropriated	7,721.93		15,497.13	
Retained Earnings – Unappropriated	71,092.82		72,592.78	
Undistributed Taxable Income			36,296.39	
Total Capital		378,814.75		424,386.30
Total Liabilities & Capital		$470,392.85		$523,772.32

EXHIBIT 9-2

The Pamida Corporation
Income Statement for Year Ended
December 31, 1973

Operating Income		
Sales	$755,838.31	
Less: Sales Returns	20,193.50	
Net Sales		$735,644.81
Cost of Goods Sold:		
Beginning Inventory	$ 81,149.13	
Merchandise Purchased	374,823.00	
Wages	109,472.80	
Manufacturing Overhead	15,679.93	
Total	$581,124.86	
Less Ending Inventory	93,672.44	
Cost of Goods Sold		487,452.42
Gross Profit		$248,192.39
Operating Expenses		
Officer's Salaries	$ 50,000.00	
Employee's Salaries	91,458.31	
Repairs	9,901.40	
Bad Debts Expense	6,439.81	
Taxes	19,349.37	
Interest	1,408.10	
Contributions	1,000.00	
Depreciation	9,765.00	
Advertising	4,503.82	
Miscellaneous	18,871.60	
Total Operating Expenses		212,697.41
Net Profit from Operations		$ 35,494.98
Non-Operating Income		
Interest on State Bonds	$ 1,500.00	
Corporate Dividends	250.00	
Interest on Federal Bonds	1,750.00	
Rent (Net)	6,000.00	
Gain on Sale of Stock	500.00	
Gain on Sale of Truck	1,900.00	
Gain on Sale of Warehouse	10,400.00	
Miscellaneous	1.41	
Total Non-Operating Income		22,301.41
Net Income		$ 57,796.39

EXHIBIT 9-3

Form **1120S**	**U.S. Small Business Corporation** **Income Tax Return** for the calendar year 1973 or	**1973**
Department of the Treasury Internal Revenue Service	other taxable year beginning ...., 1973, ending ...., 19......	

A Date of election as small business corporation 1 - 1 - 73	Name The Pamida Corporation	C Employer Identification No. 98-7654321
B Business Code No. (see page 7 of instructions) 4321	Number and street 101 University Avenue City or town, State, and ZIP code Lexington, Kentucky 40500	D County in which located Fayette E Enter total assets from line 14, column D, Schedule L 523,772.32

IMPORTANT—All applicable lines and schedules must be filled in. If the lines on the schedules are not sufficient, see instruction N.

GROSS INCOME			
1 Gross receipts or gross sales 755,838.31 Less: returns and allowances 20,193.50	1	735,644.81
2 Less: cost of goods sold (Schedule A) and/or operations (attach schedule)	2	487,452.42
3 Gross profit.	3	248,192.39
4 (a) Domestic dividends.	4(a)	250.00
(b) Foreign dividends.	4(b)	
5 Interest on obligations of the U.S. and U.S. instrumentalities	5	1,750.00
6 Other interest	6	
7 Gross rents	7	6,000.00
8 Gross royalties	8	
9 Gains and losses (separate Schedule D, Form 1120S and/or Form 4797):		
(a) Net short-term capital gain reduced by any net long-term capital loss . . .	9(a)	
(b) Net long-term capital gain reduced by any net short-term capital loss (if more than $25,000, see instructions).	9(b)	10,900.00
(c) Ordinary gain or (loss) from Part II, Form 4797 (attach Form 4797)	9(c)	1,900.00
10 Other income (see instructions—attach schedule)	10	1.41
11 Total income, lines 3 through 10	11	268,993.80

DEDUCTIONS			
12 Compensation of officers (Schedule E)	12	50,000.00
13 Salaries and wages (not deducted elsewhere)	13	91,458.31
14 Repairs (see instructions)	14	9,901.40
15 Bad debts (Schedule F if reserve method is used)	15	6,439.81
16 Rents	16	
17 Taxes (attach schedule)	17	19,349.37
18 Interest	18	1,408.10
19 Contributions (not over 5% of line 28 adjusted per instructions—attach schedule) . .	19	1,000.00
20 Amortization (attach schedule)	20	
21 Depreciation (Schedule G)	21	9,765.00
22 Depletion (attach schedule)	22	
23 Advertising	23	4,503.82
24 Pension, profit-sharing, etc. plans (see instructions)	24	
25 Employee benefit programs (see instructions)	25	
26 Other deductions (attach schedule)	26	18,871.60
27 Total deductions, lines 12 through 26	27	212,697.41
28 Taxable income, line 11 less line 27	28	56,296.39

TAX			
29 Income tax on capital gains (Schedule J)	29	-0-
30 Minimum tax (see instructions.) Check here ☐ if Form 4626 is attached	30	-0-
31 Total tax (add lines 29 and 30)	31	
32 Credits: (a) Tax deposited with Form 7004 (attach copy) . . . 32(a)		
(b) Tax deposited with Form 7005 (attach copy) . . . 32(b)		
(c) Credit for U.S. tax on special fuels, nonhighway gas, and lubricating oil (see instructions—attach Form 4136) . . 32(c)		
33 TAX DUE (line 31 less line 32). See instruction G for depositary method of payment →	33	-0-
34 OVERPAYMENT (line 32 less line 31) . . . . →	34	-0-

Under penalties of perjury, I declare that I have examined this return, including accompanying schedules and statements, and to the best of my knowledge and belief it is true, correct, and complete. Declaration of preparer (other than taxpayer) is based on all information of which he has any knowledge.

The Internal Revenue Service does not require a seal on this form, but if one is used, please place it here.	3-15-74 Date	*P. P. Pamida* Signature of officer	President Title
	3-15-74 Date	*P. Michael Davis CPA* Signature of individual or firm preparing the return	881 Windmill Dr. 542-88-5632 Preparer's address Emp. Ident. or Soc. Sec. No. Lexington, Ky. 40502

EXHIBIT 9-3 (Continued)

Schedule A — COST OF GOODS SOLD (See Instruction 2)

Method of inventory valuation (specify) ▶ ....
Lower of cost or market

Was there any substantial change in the manner of determining quantities, costs, or valuations between opening and closing inventory? . . ☐ Yes ☒ No. If "Yes," attach explanation.

1 Inventory at beginning of year	81,149.13	5 Total of lines 1 through 4		581,124.86
2 Merchandise bought for manufacture or sale . .	374,823.00	6 Less inventory at end of year		93,672.44
3 Salaries and wages	109,472.80	7 Cost of goods sold (enter here and on line 2, page 1)		487,452.42
4 Other costs (attach schedule)	15,679.93			

Schedule E — COMPENSATION OF OFFICERS (See instruction 12)

1. Name of officer	2. Social security number	3. Title	4. Time devoted to business	5. Percentage of corporation stock owned	6. Amount of compensation	7. Expense account allowances
P. P. Pamida	462-08-0402	Pres.	All	60%	30,000	
W. Y. Pamida	302-80-2040	V. Pres.	All	40%	20,000	
Total compensation of officers (enter here and on line 12, page 1)					50,000.00	

Schedule F — BAD DEBTS—RESERVE METHOD (See instruction 15)

1. Year	2. Trade notes and accounts receivable outstanding at end of year	3. Sales on account	4. Current year's provision	5. Recoveries	6. Amount charged against reserve	7. Reserve for bad debts at end of year
1968	50,344.88	378,923.91	4,034.48	700.00	4,500.00	5,034.48
1969	55,416.21	391,401.75	4,541.62	800.00	4,834.48	5,541.62
1970	60,142.30	426,530.98	5,014.23	1,000.00	5,541.62	6,014.23
1971	63,288.14	475,623.31	5,328.81	900.00	5,914.23	6,328.81
1972	71,982.12	509,843.18	6,198.21	700.00	6,028.81	7,198.21
1973	75,072.98	592,141.70	6,439.81	800.00	6,930.73	7,507.29

Schedule G — DEPRECIATION (See instruction 21)
Note: If depreciation is computed by using the Class Life (ADR) System for assets placed in service after 1970, or the Guideline Class Life System for assets placed in service before 1971, you must file Form 4832 (Class Life (ADR) System) or Form 5006 (Guideline Class Life System) with your return. Except as otherwise expressly provided in regulations section 1.167(a)–11(b)(5)(vi) and regulations section 1.167(a)–12, the provisions of Revenue Procedures 62–21 and 65–13 are not applicable for taxable years ending after 1970.

Check box(es) if you made an election this taxable year to use ☐ Class Life (ADR) System and/or ☐ Guideline Class Life System. See Publication 534.

1. Group and guideline class or description of property	2. Date acquired	3. Cost or other basis	4. Depreciation allowed or allowable in prior years	5. Method of computing depreciation	6. Life or rate	7. Depreciation for this year
1 Total additional first-year depreciation (do not include in items below)						
2 Depreciation from Form 4832						
3 Depreciation from Form 5006						
4 Other depreciation:						
Buildings	1-1-65	150,000.00	30,000.00	St. line	40 yr	3,750.00
Furniture and fixtures . . .	1-1-73	10,000.00	-0-	St. line	5 yr	2,000.00
Transportation equipment . .						
Machinery and other equipment . .	1-1-71	80,300.00	8,030.00	St. line	5%	4,015.00
Other (specify)						
5 Totals		240,300.00				9,765.00
6 Less amount of depreciation claimed in Schedule A						-0-
7 Balance—enter here and on line 21, page 1						9,765.00

Schedule H — SUMMARY OF DEPRECIATION (other than additional first-year depreciation)

	Straight line	Declining balance	Sum of the years-digits	Units of production	Other (specify)	Total
1 Depreciation from Form 4832 .						
2 Depreciation from Form 5006 .						
3 Other	9,765.00					9,765.00

Schedule J — TAX COMPUTATION (See instructions)

1 Taxable income (line 28, page 1)		
2 (a) Enter 48% of line 1 (members of controlled groups, see instructions)	6,500.00	
(b) Subtract $6,500 and enter difference		
3 Net long-term capital gain reduced by net short-term capital loss (from line 9(b), page 1)		25,000.00
4 Subtract $25,000. (Statutory minimum.)		
5 Balance (line 3 less line 4) (see instructions)		
6 Enter 30% of line 5 (see instructions)		
7 Income tax (line 2 or line 6, whichever is lesser). Enter here and on line 29, page 1.		

EXHIBIT 9-3 (Continued)

Form 1120S (1973)   Page **3**

Schedule K COMPUTATION OF UNDISTRIBUTED TAXABLE INCOME AND SUMMARY OF DISTRIBUTIONS

Computation of Corporation's Undistributed Taxable Income

1 Taxable income (line 28, page 1)		56,296.39
2 Less: (a) Money distributed as dividends out of earnings and profits of the taxable year	20,000	
(b) Tax imposed on certain capital gains (line 31, page 1)		
3 Corporation's undistributed taxable income		36,296.39

SUMMARY OF DISTRIBUTIONS AND OTHER ITEMS (attach additional sheets if necessary)

1. Name and address of each shareholder	2. Social security number	3. Stock ownership			4. Compensation	5. Percentage of time devoted to business
		Number of shares	Period held From	To		
A P. P. Pamida	462-08-0402	1800	1/1 1965	12/31 1973	30,000	All
B W. Y. Pamida	302-80-2040	1200	1/1 1965	12/31 1973	20,000	All
C						
D						

4 Actual dividend distributions taxable as ordinary income (Do not include amounts shown on line 6)	20,000.00
5 Actual dividend distributions taxable as long-term capital gains (after tax)*	
6 Actual dividend distributions taxable as ordinary income and qualifying for dividend exclusion	
7 Nondividend distributions	
8 Undistributed taxable income—taxable as ordinary income or (loss)	25,396.39
9 Undistributed taxable income—taxable as long-term capital gain (after tax)*	10,900.00

*Each shareholder must be notified as to what amount of his pro rata share of long-term capital gains may qualify as subsection (d) gains. See section 1201(d).

10 INTEREST ON INVESTMENT INDEBTEDNESS:		(2) Railroad rolling stock . . .	
(a) Investment interest expense . . .		(3) On-the-job training facilities .	
(b) Net investment income or (loss) . .		(4) Child care facilities	
(c) Excess expenses over rental income attributable to net lease property .		(c) Reserves for losses on bad debts of financial institutions	
(d) Excess of net long-term capital gains over net short-term capital losses attributable to investment property .		(d) Excess percentage depletion . .	
11 ITEMS OF TAX PREFERENCE:		(e) Net long-term capital gain (after tax) .	10,900.00
(a) Accelerated depreciation of:		12 INVESTMENT CREDIT PROPERTY:	
(1) Low-income rental housing . .		Basis of new Investment property (a) 3 or more but less than 5 years .	
(2) Other real property		(b) 5 or more but less than 7 years .	
(3) Personal property subject to a net lease.		(c) 7 or more years	
(b) Amortization of:		Cost of used Investment property (d) 3 or more but less than 5 years .	
		(e) 5 or more but less than 7 years .	
(1) Certified pollution control facilities .		(f) 7 or more years	

Schedule K-1 COMPLETE A SEPARATE SCHEDULE K-1 FOR EACH SHAREHOLDER—File Copy A with Form 1120S, give Copy B to each shareholder, and keep Copy C for your records.

F Date incorporated ......1965......

G Did the corporation at the end of the taxable year own, directly or indirectly, 50% or more of the voting stock of a domestic corporation? ☐ Yes ☒ No. (For rules of attribution, see section 267(c).) If the answer is "Yes," attach a schedule showing:
(a) name, address, and employer identification number; and
(b) percentage owned.

H Did the corporation during the taxable year have any contracts or subcontracts subject to the Renegotiation Act of 1951? ☐ Yes ☒ No If "Yes," enter the aggregate gross dollar amount billed during the year . . . .

I Amount of taxable income or (loss) for: 1970 ...31,698.50...; 1971 ...35,110.90...; 1972 ...40,358.01...

J Refer to page 7 of instructions and state the principal;
Business activity ...Manufacturing...
Product or service ...Widgets...

K Were you a member of a controlled group subject to the provisions of sections 1561 or 1562? . . . . ☐ Yes ☒ No

L Did you claim a deduction for expenses connected with any:
(1) Entertainment facility (boat, resort, ranch, etc.)? . . ☐ Yes ☒ No
(2) Living accommodations (except employees on business)? . . . . ☐ Yes ☒ No
(3) Employees' families at conventions or meetings? ☐ Yes ☒ No
(4) Employee or family vacations not reported on Form W-2? . . . . ☐ Yes ☒ No

M Did you file all required Forms 1099, 1096 and 1087? ☒ Yes ☐ No

N Did the corporation, at any time during the taxable year, have any interest in or signature or other authority over a bank, securities, or other financial account in a foreign country? . . . . ☐ Yes ☒ No If "Yes," attach Form 4683. (For definitions, see Form 4683.)

O Answer only if (1) this is the first 1120S return filed since your election to be treated as a small business corporation and (2) the corporation was in existence for the taxable year prior to the election and had investment credit property:
Was an agreement filed under section 1.47-4(b) of the Regulations? . . . . ☐ Yes ☐ No

EXHIBIT 9-3 (Continued)

Schedule L — BALANCE SHEETS (See Instructions)

ASSETS	Beginning of taxable year (A) Amount	(B) Total	End of taxable year (C) Amount	(D) Total
1 Cash		69,342.81		149,376.20
2 Trade notes and accounts receivable	71,982.12		75,072.98	
(a) Less allowance for bad debts	7,198.21	64,783.91	7,507.29	65,565.69
3 Inventories		81,149.13		93,672.44
4 Gov't obligations: (a) U.S. and instrumentalities .		35,000.00		35,000.00
(b) State, subdivisions thereof, etc.		30,000.00		30,000.00
5 Other current assets (attach schedule)				
6 Loans to shareholders.				
7 Mortgage and real estate loans				
8 Other investments (attach schedule)		5,000.00		5,000.00
9 Buildings and other fixed depreciable assets . . .	290,400.00		240,300.00	
(a) Less accumulated depreciation	145,283.00	145,117.00	130,142.01	110,157.99
10 Depletable assets				
(a) Less accumulated depletion				
11 Land (net of any amortization)		40,000.00		35,000.00
12 Intangible assets (amortizable only)				
(a) Less accumulated amortization				
13 Other assets (attach schedule)				
14 Total assets		470,392.85		523,772.32
LIABILITIES AND SHAREHOLDERS' EQUITY				
15 Accounts payable		62,941.00		70,014.77
16 Mtgs., notes, bonds payable in less than 1 year . .				
17 Other current liabilities (attach schedule)		7,392.10		9,166.14
18 Loans from shareholders				
19 Mtgs., notes, bonds payable in 1 year or more . .		20,745.00		15,731.19
20 Other liabilities (attach schedule)		500.00		4,473.92
21 Capital stock		300,000.00		300,000.00
22 Paid-in or capital surplus (attach reconciliation) . .				
23 Retained earnings—appropriated (attach schedule) .		7,721.93		15,497.13
24 Retained earnings—unappropriated		71,092.82		72,592.78
25 Shareholders' undistributed taxable income previously taxed				36,296.39
26 Less cost of treasury stock		( )		( )
27 Total liabilities and shareholders' equity . .		470,392.85		523,772.32

Schedule M-1 — RECONCILIATION OF INCOME PER BOOKS WITH INCOME PER RETURN

1 Net income per books	57,796.39	7 Income recorded on books this year not included in this return (itemize)	
2 Federal income tax		(a) Tax-exempt interest $....................	
3 Excess of capital losses over capital gains . .			
4 Taxable income not recorded on books this year (Itemize)			1,500.00
....		8 Deductions in this tax return not charged against book income this year (itemize)	
5 Expenses recorded on books this year not deducted in this return (itemize)			
....		9 Total of lines 7 and 8	
6 Total of lines 1 through 5	57,796.39	10 Income (line 28, page 1)—line 6 less line 9 .	56,296.39

Schedule M-2 — ANALYSIS OF UNAPPROPRIATED RETAINED EARNINGS PER BOOKS (line 24 above)

1 Balance at beginning of year	71,092.82	5 Distributions out of current or accumulated earnings and profits: (a) Cash	20,000.00
2 Net income per books	57,796.35	(b) Stock	
3 Other increases (itemize)		(c) Property	
....		6 Current year's undistributed taxable income or net operating loss (total of lines 8 and 9, Schedule K)	36,296.39
....		7 Other decreases (itemize)	
....		8 Total of lines 5, 6, and 7	
4 Total of lines 1, 2, and 3	128,889.17	9 Balance at end of year (line 4 less line 8) .	72,592.78

☆ U.S. GOVERNMENT PRINTING OFFICE : 1973—O-500-115   25-1118272

EXHIBIT 9-4

SCHEDULE K-1 (Form 1120S) Department of the Treasury Internal Revenue Service	**Shareholder's Share of Undistributed Taxable Income, etc.—1973** For the calendar year 1973, or other taxable year beginning _ _ _ _ _ _ _ _ _ _ _, 1973, ending _ _ _ _ _ _ _ _ _ _ _ _, 19_ _ _ (Complete a separate Schedule K-1 for each shareholder—See Instructions on back of Copy C)	Copy A File with Form 1120S

Shareholder's name, identifying number, and address (including ZIP code)	Corporation's name, identifying number, and address (including ZIP code)
P. P. Pamida 609 Canine Way Lexington, Kentucky 40500 462-08-0402	The Pamida Corporation 101 University Avenue Lexington, Kentucky 40500 98-7654321

Part I Income	(a) Amount	(b) Form 1040 filers enter col. (a) amount as indicated below. Form 1041 filers enter col. (a) amount in corresponding line of that form.
1 Undistributed taxable income—ordinary income or (loss)............	15,237.83	Sch. E, Part III
2 Undistributed taxable income—long-term capital gain after tax	6,540.00	Sch. D, Part II
Part II Interest on Investment Indebtedness		Form 4952 line reference
1 Interest expense on investment indebtedness..................		Line 3, col. b
2 Net investment income or (loss)		Line 11, col. a
3 Excess expenses over rental income attributable to net lease property		Line 11, col. b
4 Excess net long-term capital gains over net short-term capital losses attributable to investment property................................		Line 11, col. c
Part III Items of Tax Preference		Form 4625 line reference
1 Accelerated depreciation of:		
(a) Low-income rental housing.........................		Line 1(a)(1)
(b) Other real property............................		Line 1(a)(2)
(c) Personal property subject to a net lease		Line 1(b)
2 Amortization of:		
(a) Certified pollution control facilities......................		Line 1(c)
(b) Railroad rolling stock		Line 1(d)
(c) On-the-job training facilities		Line 1(e)
(d) Child care facilities		Line 1(f)
3 Reserves for losses on bad debts of financial institutions.............		Line 1(h)
4 Excess percentage depletion.........................		Line 1(i)
5 Net long-term capital gain after tax	6,540.00	Line 1(j)
Part IV Property Eligible for Investment Credit		Form 3468 line reference
Basis of new investment property	(a) 3 or more but less than 5 years	....	Line 1(a), col. (2)
	(b) 5 or more but less than 7 years	....	Line 1(b), col. (2)
	(c) 7 or more years	....	Line 1(c), col. (2)
Cost of used investment property	(d) 3 or more but less than 5 years	....	Line 1(d), col. (2)
	(e) 5 or more but less than 7 years	....	Line 1(e), col. (2)
	(f) 7 or more years	....	Line 1(f), col. (2)

Part V Property Used in Recomputing a Prior Year Investment Credit

	(1) Description of property (State whether new or used)	(2) Date placed in service	(3) Cost or basis	Column numbers and headings correspond to those on Form 4255
A				
B				
C				
D				
E				

(4) Estimated useful life	(5) Applicable percentage	(6) Original qualified investment (Col. 3 x col. 5)	(8) Date item ceased to be investment credit property	(9) Actual useful life	(10) Applicable percentage	(11) Recomputed qualified investment (Col. 3 x col. 10)	

EXHIBIT 9-4 (Continued)

<table>
<tr>
<td>
SCHEDULE K–1
(Form 1120S)
Department of the Treasury
Internal Revenue Service
</td>
<td>
Shareholder's Share of Undistributed Taxable Income, etc.—1973
For the calendar year 1973, or other taxable year
beginning _ _ _ _ _ _ _ _ _ _ _ _ _, 1973, ending _ _ _ _ _ _ _ _ _ _ _ _ _, 19_ _ _
(Complete a separate Schedule K–1 for each shareholder—See instructions on back of Copy C)
</td>
<td>
Copy A
File with
Form 1120S
</td>
</tr>
</table>

Shareholder's name, identifying number, and address (including ZIP code)	Corporation's name, identifying number, and address (including ZIP code)
W.Y. Pamida 609 Canine Way Lexington, Kentucky 40500 302-80-2040	The Pamida Corporation 101 University Avenue Lexington, Kentucky 40500 98-7654321

	(a) Amount	(b) Form 1040 filers enter col. (a) amount as indicated below. Form 1041 filers enter col. (a) amount in corresponding line of that form.
Part I Income		
1 Undistributed taxable income—ordinary income or (loss).	10,158.56	Sch. E, Part III
2 Undistributed taxable income—long-term capital gain after tax	4,360.00	Sch. D, Part II
Part II Interest on Investment Indebtedness		Form 4952 line reference
1 Interest expense on investment indebtedness.		Line 3, col. b
2 Net investment income or (loss)		Line 11, col. a
3 Excess expenses over rental income attributable to net lease property		Line 11, col. b
4 Excess net long-term capital gains over net short-term capital losses attributable to investment property		Line 11, col. c
Part III Items of Tax Preference		Form 4625 line reference
1 Accelerated depreciation of:		
(a) Low-income rental housing.		Line 1(a)(1)
(b) Other real property.		Line 1(a)(2)
(c) Personal property subject to a net lease		Line 1(b)
2 Amortization of:		
(a) Certified pollution control facilities.		Line 1(c)
(b) Railroad rolling stock		Line 1(d)
(c) On-the-job training facilities		Line 1(e)
(d) Child care facilities		Line 1(f)
3 Reserves for losses on bad debts of financial institutions.		Line 1(h)
4 Excess percentage depletion.		Line 1(i)
5 Net long-term capital gain after tax	4,360.00	Line 1(j)

Part IV Property Eligible for Investment Credit			Form 3468 line reference
Basis of new investment property	(a) 3 or more but less than 5 years	. . . .	Line 1(a), col. (2)
	(b) 5 or more but less than 7 years	. . . .	Line 1(b), col. (2)
	(c) 7 or more years	. . . .	Line 1(c), col. (2)
Cost of used investment property	(d) 3 or more but less than 5 years	. . . .	Line 1(d), col. (2)
	(e) 5 or more but less than 7 years	. . . .	Line 1(e), col. (2)
	(f) 7 or more years	. . . .	Line 1(f), col. (2)

Part V   Property Used in Recomputing a Prior Year Investment Credit

	(1) Description of property (State whether new or used)	(2) Date placed in service	(3) Cost or basis	Column numbers and headings correspond to those on Form 4255
A				
B				
C				
D				
E				

(4) Estimated useful life	(5) Applicable percentage	(6) Original qualified investment (Col. 3 x col. 5)	(8) Date item ceased to be investment credit property	(9) Actual useful life	(10) Applicable percentage	(11) Recomputed qualified investment (Col. 3 x col. 10)	

EXHIBIT 9-5

98-7654321

Statement for Recipients of
Dividends and Distributions 1973

The Pamida Corporation
101 University Avenue
Lexington, Kentucky 40500

Type or print PAYER'S Federal identifying number, name, address and ZIP code above.

Copy A For Internal
Revenue Service Center

1 Gross dividends and other distributions on stock (Total of columns 2, 3, 4, and 5)	2 Dividends qualifying for exclusion	3 Dividends not qualifying for exclusion	4 Capital gain distributions	5 Nontaxable distributions (If determinable)	6 Foreign tax paid (Applicable only to taxes eligible for foreign tax credit)
		12,000			

RECIPIENT'S identifying number ▶ 462-08-0402

P. P. Pamida
609 Canine Way
Lexington, Kentucky 40500

If this is a corrected form, put an "X" to the right of the
number in the upper left corner.

Type or print RECIPIENT'S name, address and ZIP code above.

Form **1099–DIV** ☆ GPO:1972—O-458-090 EI-36-2441915 Department of the Treasury—Internal Revenue Service

---

98-7654321

Statement for Recipients of
Dividends and Distributions 1973

The Pamida Corporation
101 University Avenue
Lexington, Kentucky 40500

Type or print PAYER'S Federal identifying number, name, address and ZIP code above.

Copy A For Internal
Revenue Service Center

1 Gross dividends and other distributions on stock (Total of columns 2, 3, 4, and 5)	2 Dividends qualifying for exclusion	3 Dividends not qualifying for exclusion	4 Capital gain distributions	5 Nontaxable distributions (If determinable)	6 Foreign tax paid (Applicable only to taxes eligible for foreign tax credit)
		8,000			

RECIPIENT'S identifying number ▶ 302-80-2040

W. Y. Pamida
609 Canine Way
Lexington, Kentucky 40500

If this is a corrected form, put an "X" to the right of the
number in the upper left corner.

Type or print RECIPIENT'S name, address and ZIP code above.

Form **1099–DIV** ☆ GPO:1972—O-458-090 EI-36-2441915 Department of the Treasury—Internal Revenue Service

Part I, while ordinary income is transferred to Part II. Other transactions which would not be subject to recapture provisions are also entered in Part I. An example of a transaction not subject to recapture would be the sale of property used in trade or business at a loss, or an involuntary conversion transaction. The total of Part I is transferred to Schedule D to be taxed as capital gain income.

Part II is for ordinary gains and losses. Income recaptured as ordinary income is transferred from Part III to Part II. If Part I results in a net loss, this net loss is transferred to Part II. Under Section 1231 of the *Code,* net 1231 gains are treated as capital gains while net 1231 losses are treated as ordinary losses. Gains and losses on property held for six months or less are also entered in Part II. The final amount in Part II is transferred to line 9c on page 1 of Form 1120-S.

Capital Gains and Losses

Capital gains and losses are entered on Schedule D. (See Exhibit 9-8). This schedule is for capital assets as defined in Section 1221 of the *Code.* Trading in corporate securities creates this type of transaction. Short-term transactions are entered in Part I. Long-term transactions are entered in Part II. Section 1231 gain from Form 4797 is also entered in Part II. If the net short-term capital gain exceeds the net long-term capital loss, the excess is entered on line 7 of Part III. If the net long-term capital gain exceeds the net short-term capital loss, the excess is entered on line 8 of Part III. Note that the amounts can appear on both lines 7 and 8. Such amounts are transferred to lines 9a and 9b on page 1 of Form 1120-S.

Tax Calculation

Under certain circumstances, a Subchapter S corporation may be subject to a tax on its capital gains. Applicability of this tax is discussed in Chapter 6. Exhibit 9-9 illustrates the calculation of this tax, based upon a revised example taken from Regulation 1.1375-1 (e)(2)(ii). The corporate records support the following facts: (1) The taxable income for the year is $100,000. (2) There is a net long-term capital gain of $100,000, which is taxable under Section 1378 of the *Code.* Lines 1 and 2 reflect the application of an upper limit, in that the tax under Section 1378 can be no more than the amount that would result from applying standard corporation rates to total taxable income (22 percent of the first $25,000; 48 percent of any amount over $25,000). Thus, the tax can be no more than $41,500. At this point, the alternative tax is applied to the net long-term capital gain reduced by the net short-term capital loss. The $25,000 statutory exemption is also substituted (lines 3-5). The tax at 30 percent of line 5 is entered on line 6. Line 7 is the actual tax, which is the lesser of regular corporate rates applied to total taxable income or the alternative tax applied to the capital gain less the statutory exemption. As a practical matter, the tax will usually be the alternative tax. It is not likely that a lower tax will be produced by the regular method. The actual tax is also entered on line 29, page 1 of Form 1120-S.

Automatic Extension

A timely tax return cannot always be filed. The typical management of a Subchapter S corporation is probably not adequately concerned with routine matters of tax compliance. Moreover, the tax adviser may be unable to prepare the return within the statutory period. Section 6081 makes provision for late filing of corporate tax returns.

The Subchapter S return must be filed within two and one-half months of the close of the corporate tax year. This is March 15 for a calendar-year corporation. If the return cannot be filed on or before this date, an automatic extension should be requested from the Internal Revenue Service Center where the return is to be filed.

This extension procedure is automatic. Form 7004 (Exhibit 9-10) is completed in duplicate. One copy is submitted before the due date of the return. The other copy is attached to the return. The automatic extension period is three months. The return should be filed within this period. A copy of Form 7004 should be retained by the tax adviser for his files.

Additional Extension

If the corporation is still unable to file its return when the automatic extension period comes to an end, an additional extension may be requested. This extra extension is accomplished by filing Form 7005 (Exhibit 9-11) with the Internal Revenue Service Center where the return is to be filed. Two copies of Form 7005 should be submitted. Approval of the extension is indicated on the form, and a copy is returned to the taxpayer or his adviser. This procedure is not automatic. Some reasons for the extension should be provided, and these reasons must be persuasive. A copy of Form 7005 should be retained by the tax adviser for his files.

Section 6081 provides for a six-month extension. Since the automatic extension period is for three months, the additional extension

EXHIBIT 9-6

Calculation for Fiscal-Year Corporation

Dividend Allocation

Capital Gain

$$\frac{\$10,900.00 \ (capital \ gain)}{\$56,296.39 \ (taxable \ income - capital \ gains \ tax)} \times \$20,000 \ (dividends) = \$3,872.36 \ allocation \ of \ dividends \ to \ capital \ gain$$

Ordinary Income

$$\frac{\$45,396.39 \ (taxable \ income - capital \ gains)}{\$56,296.39 \ (taxable \ income - capital \ gains \ tax)} \times \$20,000 \ (dividends) = \$16,127.64 \ allocation \ of \ dividends \ to \ ordinary \ income$$

Undistributed Taxable Income Allocation

Capital Gain

$$\frac{\$10,900.00 \ (capital \ gain)}{\$56,296.39 \ (taxable \ income - capital \ gains \ tax)} \times \$36,296.39 \ (UTI) = \$7,027.63 \ allocation \ of \ UTI \ to \ capital \ gain$$

Ordinary Income

$$\frac{\$45,396.39 \ (taxable \ income - capital \ gains)}{\$56,296.39 \ (taxable \ income - capital \ gains \ tax)} \times \$36,296.39 \ (UTI) = \$29,268.76 \ allocation \ of \ UTI \ to \ capital \ gain$$

EXHIBIT 9-7

Form **4797**	**Supplemental Schedule of Gains and Losses**	**1973**
Department of the Treasury Internal Revenue Service	Sales, Exchanges and Involuntary Conversions under Sections 1231, 1245, 1250, etc. **To be filed with Form 1040, 1041, 1065, 1120, etc.—See Instruction A**	

Name	Identifying number as shown on page 1 of your return
The Pamida Corporation	98-7654321

Part I   Sales or Exchanges of Property Used in Trade or Business and/or Involuntary Conversions (Section 1231)

SECTION A.—Involuntary Conversions Due to Casualty and Theft (See Instruction D)

a. Kind of property (if necessary, attach statement of descriptive details not shown below)	b. Date acquired (mo., day, yr.)	c. Date sold (mo., day, yr.)	d. Gross sales price	e. Depreciation allowed (or allowable) since acquisition	f. Cost or other basis, cost of subsequent improvements (if not purchased, attach explanation) and expense of sale	g. Gain or (loss) (d plus e less f)
1						

2 Combine the amounts on line 1, enter here and also on the appropriate line as follows . . . . . .
  (a) For all returns, except partnership returns:
    (1) If line 2 is zero or a gain, enter such amount in column g, line 3.
    (2) If line 2 is a loss, enter the loss on line 5.
  (b) For partnership returns: Enter the amount shown on line 2, on line 6, Schedule K (Form 1065).

SECTION B.—Sales or Exchanges of Property Used in Trade or Business and Certain Involuntary Conversions (Not Reportable in Section A) (See Instruction D)

a.	b.	c.	d.	e.	f.	g.
3 Gain from Line 22, Part III						10,400.00

4 Combine the amounts on line 3, enter here and also on the appropriate line as follows 10,400.00
  (a) For all returns, except partnership returns:
    (1) If line 4 is a gain, enter such gain as a long-term capital gain on the Schedule D (Form 1040, 1120, etc.) that is being filed—see instruction D.
    (2) If line 4 is zero or a loss, enter such amount on line 6.
  (b) For partnership returns: Enter the amount shown on line 4, on line 7, Schedule K (Form 1065).

Part II   Ordinary Gains and Losses

a. Kind of property and how acquired (If necessary, attach statement of descriptive details not shown below)	b. Date acquired (mo., day, yr.)	c. Date sold (mo., day, yr.)	d. Gross sales price	e. Depreciation allowed (or allowable) since acquisition	f. Cost or other basis, cost of subsequent improvements and expense of sale	g. Gain or (loss) (d plus e less f)
5 Amount, if any, from line 2(a)(2)						
6 Amount, if any, from line 4(a)(2)						
7 Gain, if any, from line 21						1,900.00
8						

9 Combine lines 5 through 8, enter here and also on the appropriate line as follows 1,900.00

  (a) For all returns, except individual returns: Enter the gain or (loss) shown on line 9, on the line provided for on the return (Form 1120, etc.) being filed—see instruction E, for specific line reference.

  (b) For individual returns:

    (1) If the gain or (loss) on line 9, includes losses which are to be treated as an itemized deduction on Schedule A (Form 1040) (see instruction E), enter the total of such loss(es) here and include on line 29, Schedule A (Form 1040)—identify as loss from line 9(b)(1), Form 4797 . . . . .

    (2) Redetermine the gain or (loss) on line 9, excluding the loss (if any) entered on line 9(b)(1). Enter here and on line 30, Form 1040 . . . .

EXHIBIT 9-7 (Continued)

Part III　Gain From Disposition of Property Under Sections 1245, 1250,
1251, 1252—Assets Held More than Six Months (See Instruction F)

Lines 18 and 19 should be omitted if there are no dispositions of farm property or farmland; or, if this form is filed by a partnership.

10 Description of sections 1245, 1250, 1251, and 1252 property:	Date acquired (mo., day, yr.)	Date sold (mo., day, yr.)
(A) Truck	6-1-70	10-1-73
(B) Warehouse	1-1-65	12-31-73
(C)		
(D)		
(E)		

Correlate lines 10(A) through 10(E) with these columns ▶ ▶ ▶ ▶	Property (A)	Property (B)	Property (C)	Property (D)	Property (E)
11 Gross sales price	3,000.00	20,000.00			
12 Cost or other basis and expense of sale	5,000.00	15,000.00			
13 Depreciation allowed (or allowable)	3,900.00	5,400.00			
14 Adjusted basis, line 12 less line 13	1,100.00	9,600.00			
15 Total gain, subtract line 14 from line 11	1,900.00	10,400.00			
16 If section 1245 property:					
(a) Depreciation allowed (or allowable) after applicable date (see instructions)	3,900.00				
(b) Line 15 or line 16(a), whichever is smaller	1,900.00				
17 If section 1250 property:					
(a) Enter additional depreciation after 12/31/63 and before 1/1/70		-0-			
(b) Enter additional depreciation after 12/31/69		-0-			
(c) Enter line 15 or line 17(b), whichever is smaller		-0-			
(d) Line 17(c) times applicable percentage (see instruction F.4)		-0-			
(e) Enter excess, if any, of line 15 over line 17(b)		-0-			
(f) Enter line 17(a) or line 17(e), whichever is smaller		-0-			
(g) Line 17(f) times applicable percentage (see instruction F.4)		-0-			
(h) Add line 17(d) and line 17(g)		-0-			
18 If section 1251 property:					
(a) If farmland, enter soil, water, and land clearing expenses for current year and the four preceding years					
(b) If farm property, other than land, subtract line 16(b) from line 15; OR, if farmland, enter line 15 or line 18(a), whichever is smaller (see instruction F.5)					
(c) Excess deductions account (see instruction F.5)					
(d) Enter line 18(b) or line 18(c), whichever is smaller					
19 If section 1252 property:					
(a) Enter soil, water, and land clearing expenses made after 12/31/69					
(b) Enter amount from line 18(d), if any; otherwise, enter a zero					
(c) Enter excess, if any, of line 19(a) over line 19(b)					
(d) Line 19(c) times applicable percentage (see instruction F.5)					
(e) Line 15 less line 19(b)					
(f) Enter smaller of line 19(d) or line 19(e)					

Summary of Part III Gains (Complete Property columns (A) through (E) up to line 19(f), before going to line 20)

20 Total of Property columns (A) through (E), line 15	12,300.00
21 Total of Property columns (A) through (E), lines 16(b), 17(h), 18(d), and 19(f). Enter here and on line 7	1,900.00
22 Subtract line 21 from line 20. Enter here and in appropriate Section in Part I (see instructions D and F.2)	10,400.00

may be for only three additional months and may not be renewed. To be effective, Form 7005 should be filed before the close of the automatic extension period. This form may be used if an automatic extension has previously been obtained by filing Form 7004. If tax is due, both Forms 7004 and 7005 provide for payment of the tax before the return is filed. Payment of tax in this manner will prevent interest from accruing. However, most Subchapter S corporations are not liable for any tax. Nevertheless, these extension procedures should still be followed.

The Amending Process

If an error is made in the original return, an amended return must be filed. No special form is provided for this process, as is the case of individuals and regular corporations (Forms 1040X and 1120X). Form 1120-S is merely completed, and the fact that it is an amended return should be conspicuously noted on the face of the return. Needless to say, the original return should be prepared correctly, because an incorrect return is likely to force shareholders to amend their personal tax returns.

Additional Information to be Filed

The following information returns may also be required:

Forms 1096 and 1099 — These are information returns to be filed concerning certain dividends, earnings, interest, rents, royalties, annuities, pensions, foreign items; and prizes, awards, and commissions to nonemployees. For purposes of information returns, the term "dividend" does not include any amount which is treated under Section 1373 (relating to undistributed taxable income of electing small business corporations) as an amount distributed as a constructive dividend. Actual dividend distributions, nondividend distributions, and dividends entitled to exclusion should be reported on Form 1099-DIV.

Forms 966 and 1099L — These are information returns regarding dissolution or liquidation, and distributions in liquidation.

Form 2553 — A copy of the election form should be filed with the tax return for the corporation's first year. Moreover, as new shareholders are added, a copy of their consent should be attached to the tax return, in addition to filing within the statutory period.

EXHIBIT 9-8

| SCHEDULE D (Form 1120S) Department of the Treasury Internal Revenue Service | **Capital Gains and Losses** For the calendar year 1973, or other taxable year beginning ...., 1973, and ending ...., 19....... | **1973** |

| Name   The Pamida Corporation | Employer Identification Number   98-7654321 |

Part I — Short-term Capital Gains and Losses—Assets Held 6 Months or Less

a. Kind of property and description. (Example, 100 shares of "Z" Co.)	b. Date acquired (mo., day, yr.)	c. Date sold (mo., day, yr.)	d. Gross sales price	e. Cost or other basis and expense of sale	f. Gain or (loss) (d less e)
1					

2 Unused capital loss carryover (attach computation) . . . .
3 Net short-term capital gain or (loss) (total of column f) . . . .

Part II — Long-term Capital Gains and Losses—Assets Held More Than 6 Months

4 Enter Section 1231 gain from line 4(a)(1), Form 4797					10,400.00
5 200 Sh. P. C. Stock	1-15-70	4-1-73	4,500.00	4,000.00	500.00
6 Net long-term capital gain or (loss) (total of column f)					10,900.00

Part III — Summary of Schedule D Gains and Losses

7 Excess net short-term capital gain (line 3) over net long-term capital loss (line 6). Enter here and on line 9(a), page 1, Form 1120S . . . .   -0-

8 Excess net long-term capital gain (line 6) over net short-term capital loss (line 3). Enter here and on line 9(b), page 1, Form 1120S 10,900.00

Instructions
(References are to the Internal Revenue Code)

This schedule provides for the reporting of sales or exchanges of capital assets. Every sale or exchange of property must be reported even though no gain or loss is indicated.

For reporting sales or exchanges of property other than capital assets including the sale or exchange of property used in the trade or business and involuntary conversions (section 1231), see Form 4797 and related instructions.

Capital Assets.—Each item of property held by the corporation (whether or not connected with its trade or business) is a capital asset except: (1) inventoriable assets or property held primarily for sale to customers; (2) depreciable or real property used in the trade or business; (3) certain copyrights, literary, musical, or artistic compositions, letters or memorandums, or similar property; (4) accounts or notes receivable acquired in the ordinary course of trade or business for services rendered or from the sale of property described in (1) above; and (5) certain short-term Federal, State, and municipal obligations issued on or after March 1, 1941, on a discount basis.

For special rules applicable to capital gains of Small Business Corporations, see section 1.1375–1 of the regulations.

Capital Losses.—Capital losses are allowed only to the extent of capital gains. A net capital loss, however, may be carried forward as a short-term capital loss for 5 years (10 years to the extent the loss is attributable to a foreign expropriation loss) or until exhausted, whichever comes first.

Short Sales of Capital Assets.—For rules relating to certain short sales of stock or other securities and transactions in commodity futures, see section 1233.

Worthless Securities.—Except for banks, if securities which are capital assets become wholly worthless during the taxable year, the loss is to be treated as a capital loss as of the last day of the taxable year.

Losses Not Allowable.—No loss is allowed for wash sales of stock or securities. (See section 1091.) No loss is allowed (distributions in liquidation excepted) on transactions between related persons. (See section 267.)

Basis.—In determining gain or loss, the basis of property will generally be its cost. If property was acquired by bequest, gift, tax-free exchange, involuntary conversion, or wash sale of stock, see sections 1014, 1015, 1031, 1033, and 1091, respectively. Attach an explanation if the basis used is other than actual cash cost of the property.

If a charitable contribution deduction is allowed by reason of a sale of property to a charitable organization, the adjusted basis for determining gain from the sale is an amount which is in the same ratio to the adjusted basis as the amount realized is to the fair market value of the property.

Minimum Tax on Tax Preference Items.— If the net long-term capital gain exceeds the net short-term capital loss, you may be liable for minimum tax. See Form 4626.

Installment Sales

If you sold personal property for more than $1,000 or real property regardless of amount, you may be eligible to report any gain under the installment method if (1) there are no payments in the year of sale or (2) the payments in the year of sale do not exceed 30% of the selling price. (See section 453.) Such sales must provide for two or more payments, such payments resulting in at least one payment being made in each of two taxable years.

For treatment of a portion of payments as "unstated interest" on deferred payment sales, see section 483.

☆ U.S. GOVERNMENT PRINTING OFFICE: 1973—O–500–117 36-2603-697

227

EXHIBIT 9-9

Schedule J	TAX COMPUTATION (See instructions)		
1 Taxable income (line 28, page 1)			100,000.00
2 (a) Enter 48% of line 1 (members of controlled groups, see instructions)	48,000.00		
(b) Subtract $6,500 and enter difference	6,500.00		41,500.00
3 Net long-term capital gain reduced by net short-term capital loss (from line 9(b), page 1)			100,000.00
4 Subtract $25,000. (Statutory minimum.)			25,000.00
5 Balance (line 3 less line 4) (see instructions)			75,000.00
6 Enter 30% of line 5 (see instructions)			22,500.00
7 Income tax (line 2 or line 6, whichever is lesser). Enter here and on line 29, page 1.			22,500.00

EXHIBIT 9-10

Form **7004**	**Application for Automatic Extension of Time**
(Rev. Oct. 1973) Department of the Treasury Internal Revenue Service	**to File Corporation Income Tax Return** (Under section 6081(b) of the Internal Revenue Code)

Note: Prepare this form in duplicate. File the original with the Internal Revenue Service Center where you are required to file your income tax return. Attach the duplicate to your income tax return.
A penalty for failure to pay tax will generally be imposed upon any corporation which files Form 7004 and **underestimates by more than 10%** its tentative amount of income tax for the taxable year. See instruction 6.

Name of corporation The Pamida Corporation	Employer Identification Number 98-7654321
Number and street 101 University Avenue	Check type of return to be filed: ☐ Form 1120 ☒ Form 1120S ☐ Form 1120L ☐ Form 990-C ☐ Form 1120M ☐ Form 990-T
City or town, State, and ZIP code Lexington, Kentucky 40500	☐ Form 1120F--Check here ☐ if you do not have an office or place of business in the U.S.

An automatic 3-month extension of time until ....June..15......,19..74., is hereby requested in which to file the income tax return of the corporation named above for the taxable year beginning ...January...1....., 19..73, and ending December...31 19..73.

1. If the taxable year above is for a period of less than 12 months, check here if the short period is due to
   - ☐ change in accounting period
   - ☐ filing of initial tax return
   - ☐ filing of final tax return

2. Does this application also cover subsidiaries to be included in a consolidated return? . . . . Yes ☐ No ☒
   If "Yes," complete the following:

Name and Address of Each Member of the Affiliated Group	Employer Identification No.

3. At least 50% of the tax tentatively determined to be due (line 3(c)) must be deposited on or before the original due date of the corporation's income tax return. See instructions for depositary method of payment.
   A penalty for failure to pay tax will generally be imposed upon any corporation which files Form 7004 and underestimates by more than 10% its tentative amount of income tax for the taxable year. See instruction 6.

   (a) Tentative amount of income tax for the taxable year including any—
   Minimum tax on tax preference items
   Personal holding company tax
   Tax from recomputing a prior year investment credit . . . . **None**
   Tax from recomputing a prior year work incentive (WIN) credit
   Foreign tax credit
   Investment credit
   Work incentive (WIN) credit

   (b) Less: (i) Overpayment from prior year allowed as a credit . . . .
       (ii) Estimated tax payments (deposits) for the taxable year . . . . .
       (iii) Less refund of estimated tax for the taxable year applied for on Form 4466 ( )
       (iv) Credit from regulated investment companies . . . .
       (v) Credit for U.S. tax on special fuels, nonhighway gas and lubricating oil. .

   (c) Balance due . . . .

   (d) Amount required to be deposited—at least 50% of line 3(c) . . . . **None**

SIGNATURE (See instruction 9)

Under penalties of perjury, I declare that I have been authorized by the above-named corporation to make this application, that to the best of my knowledge and belief the statements made herein are true, correct, and complete, and that I am: ☐ an officer of the corporation; ☐ a duly authorized agent holding a power of attorney; ☐ an agent enrolled to practice before the Internal Revenue Service; ☐ an attorney in good standing of the bar of the highest court of ....;

(Specify jurisdiction)

or ☒ a certified public accountant duly qualified to practice in .....Florida................

(Specify jurisdiction)

P. Michael Davis	CPA	3-15-74
(Signature of officer or agent)	(Title)	(Date)

A Copy of This Application Must Be Attached to the Corporation's Income Tax Return

EXHIBIT 9-11

Form **7005** (Rev. Nov. 1973) Department of the Treasury Internal Revenue Service	**Application for Additional Extension** **of Time to File Corporation Income Tax Return** (To be used only by corporations and certain exempt organizations that have previously been granted an automatic 3-month extension on Form 7004 and are now requesting an additional extension.)

Note: File two copies of this form with the Internal Revenue Service Center where the return will be filed. Internal Revenue Service will indicate on one of the copies whether the additional extension is granted or denied and return it to the person who filed this form. Attach the copy IRS returns to you to your income tax return when it is filed.
The additional extension of time to file your income tax return does not extend the time to pay the tax.

Name of organization

The Pamida Corporation

Number and street

101 University Avenue

City or town, State, and ZIP code

Lexington, Kentucky   40500

Employer identification number
98-7654321

Check type of return to be filed:

☐ Form 1120   ☒ Form 1120S
☐ Form 1120L   ☐ Form 990-C
☐ Form 1120M   ☐ Form 990-T
☐ Form 1120F—Check here ☐
if you do not have an office or
place of business in the U.S.

An additional extension of time until ....September 15................, 19 74.., is hereby requested to file the return of the organization named above for the taxable year beginning ...January 1..............., 19 73., and ending ...December 31..............., 19 73...

1 If the taxable period above is less than 12 months, is the short period attributable to a change in accounting period? . . ☐ Yes ☐ No

2 Indicate the date of extension previously granted due to the filing of Form 7004 ▶   March 15, 1974

3 Does this application also cover subsidiaries to be included in a consolidated return of a corporation? . . . . . . ☐ Yes ☒ No
If "Yes," please list the subsidiaries on the reverse side.

4 State in detail the reason the additional extension of time to file is needed (see instruction 4) Needed records were
........destroyed by fire on January 10, 1974. Additional time is needed to reconstruct....
........these records from original documents.

5 Tax information:
  (a) Expected income tax liability for the taxable period, reduced by any applicable credits . . . .   None
  (b) Less payments made prior to this application:
    (i) With Form 7004 application for automatic extension of time to file . . . . . . |
    (ii) Other payments . . . . |
  (c) Amount to be deposited (5(a) less 5(b)). This amount must be deposited on or before the date indicated on
line 2 above. See Form 7004 regarding instructions for depositary method of payment . . . .   None

Signature

Under penalties of perjury, I declare that I am authorized to make this application for the above-named organization, that to the best of my knowledge and belief the statements made herein are true and correct, and that I am: ☐ an officer of the organization; ☐ an agent enrolled to practice before the Internal Revenue Service; ☐ a duly authorized agent holding a power of attorney; ☐ an attorney in good standing of the bar of the highest court of ....; or ☒ a certified public accountant duly qualified to practice in ...Florida................
       (Specify jurisdiction)   (Specify jurisdiction)

P. Michael Davis   CPA   6-15-74
    (Signature)   (Title)   (Date)

Notice to Applicant—To be Completed by Internal Revenue Service

☐ Your application for additional extension of time to file is granted to ...., 19...... This form must be attached to the return when filed as evidence that the extension was granted. Interest generally accrues on unpaid tax at the rate of 6 percent a year during the period of any extension. However, if the taxpayer has properly elected to pay the tax in installments, interest on a late installment payment runs only from the due date of the installment.

☐ Your application cannot be considered since it was received in this office after the expiration of a previous extension of time to file the return. The return should be filed without further delay. Please attach this form to the return to explain the delay in filing.

☐ It is the opinion of this office that the reasons given in the application do not warrant an extension. The return should be filed within the extension of time previously allowed or within 10 days of the date of signature of this notice, whichever is later. The 10-day period granted will constitute a valid extension of time for purposes of elections otherwise required to be made on timely filed returns. To avoid penalties, please attach to the return, this form and any additional explanation for the delay in filing the return.

....
     Date   Director

Chapter 10

The Termination Process

When a Subchapter S election becomes effective, it remains operational until some overt act renders it ineffective. Shareholders may conclude for various reasons that the Subchapter S concept of taxation no longer suits their purposes. Under this circumstance, the corporation should remove itself from Subchapter S status with the fewest possible adverse consequences. Moreover, the corporation may undertake a course of action which renders it ineligible for status under Subchapter S. Each of these acts produces specific consequences which should be considered in the corporation's decision-making process.

This chapter discusses the way in which an election may be voluntarily revoked by a corporation by the unanimous consent of all persons who are stockholders on the date of the revocation. Voluntary revocation is compared with involuntary termination. The numerous types of involuntary terminations that may disrupt an electing corporation are covered. Further, mention is made of how to re-elect Subchapter S status after revocation or termination.

Voluntary Revocation

As noted above, Subchapter S status may no longer be acceptable to the corporation and its shareholders. Various reasons can be advanced for this change of position. For example, the corporation may be so successful that it creates too much additional taxable income for shareholders who already face high marginal rates. Second, the advantages of another organizational form may clearly offset any advantages of the Subchapter S election as considered in Chapter 12. A third reason for desiring to revert to regular corporate status may be the fact that the corporation is becoming profitable after a series of loss years. There are tax advisors who honestly believe that the only benefit to be derived from Subchapter S is the ability to pass losses through to shareholders. Once this feature is no longer needed, the election can be terminated. As a practical matter, profitable corporations have obtained a form of Subchapter S taxation through manipulation of salary levels. However, such practices may raise the issue of excessive compensation.

A corporation may revoke its election with the unanimous consent of the current shareholders. Once the election is effective, it must remain active for one tax year. To be effective for the current tax year, the revocation must be made during the first month of that year. If made subsequent to that date, the revocation becomes effective for the next as well as all following tax years.[1] The purpose of the first-month restriction is to prevent an electing corporation from assessing the results of a significant portion of the tax year before deciding to revoke the election. Unfortunately, the typical Subchapter S corporation is not current enough in its affairs to intelligently make this revocation decision within the one-month period. This failure may cause the corporation to consider an "involuntary termination," which removes the corporation from Subchapter S status under more favorable terms. Involuntary termination is discussed later in this chapter.

An election is revoked by filing a statement of revocation with the District Director with whom the election was filed. There is no official revocation form, but Exhibit 10-1 provides the requisite information. The statement should be signed by the officers of the corporation and should indicate the first tax year for which the revocation is to be effective. Each shareholder must consent to revocation of the election. No official form has been provided for this consent, but Exhibit 10-2 suggests the information which must be submitted. Consent forms should be filed with the statement of revocation.

EXHIBIT 10-1

Corporation Revoking Election under Subchapter S

(No Official Form)

As stipulated in Regulation 1.1372-4(b)(2), The Crumb Corporation, 210 Long Avenue, Baton Rouge, Louisiana, hereby revokes the election under I.R.C. Section 1372(a) as to its tax status as a Small Business Corporation. Form 2553 and the appropriate statement of stockholders' consent were filed with the District Director of Internal Revenue, New Orleans, Louisiana, on January 18, 1972. The revocation shall be effective for the tax year beginning on January 1, 1975, and for subsequent years. The statement of shareholders' consent to revocation accompanies this Form.

Under penalties of perjury, I declare that this revocation is duly authorized, and that statements made herein are to the best of my knowledge and belief true, correct, and complete statements.

1-14-75	TONY LAMER	PRESIDENT
(Date)	(Signature of Officer)	(Title)

---

[1]Regulation 1.1372-4(c).

232

EXHIBIT 10-2

Shareholders' Consent to Revocation

(No Official Form)

The undersigned hereby consent to revocation by the corporation of the election under I.R.C. Section 1372(a) to be treated as a Small Business Corporation, made on the Statement of Revocation to which this Form is attached.

As stipulated in Regulation 1.1372-4(b)(2), the following information is submitted:

Name and Address of Corporation
    The Crumb Corporation, 72-8246890
    210 Long Avenue
    Baton Rouge, Louisiana 70803

Name and address of each stockholder	Number of Shares	Signature
Tony Lamer 506 Wright Drive Baton Rouge, Louisiana 70803	410	Tony Lamer
Darlene Lamer 2283 Uniformity Drive Pierre Part, Louisiana 70801	25	Darlene Lamer
John Hill 210 North Avenue Baker, Louisiana 70804	100	John Hill
Total Shares Outstanding	535	

7-14-74
(Date)

The issue of revocation has not been the subject of significant litigation. In *Hoffman*,[2] the procedures outlined in the regulations for revoking an election were not followed. The corporation had made a valid election to be treated as a Subchapter S corporation for the year 1959. For some reason Mr. Hoffman, the sole shareholder, changed his mind about the Subchapter S election. Before April 15, 1960, he filed a standard corporate return (Form 1120) and attached a statement to the effect that the Subchapter S election was in error. The statement was not labeled as a statement of revocation, nor did Mr. Hoffman consent to it as sole shareholder. The government took exception to this procedure.

The Tax Court held that a statement filed with the regular corporate return was in "substantial compliance" with the regulation

---

[2] 47 T.C. 218 (1966), *aff'd.* 21 A.F.T.R. 2d 957 (5th Cir. 1968).

since no special form of revocation is required. However, the effective date of the revocation remained an issue. In accordance with Regulation 1.1372-4(c), the revocation could not be effective for 1959, since that year was already past; neither could it be effective for 1960, since it was filed after January 31. The Court allowed the revocation to be effective for 1961. This position is consistent with the regulation.

A revocation applies to all subsequent tax years. Once an election is revoked, the corporation cannot make a new election until the fifth year following the tax year for which the revocation is effective.[3] It is noted later in this chapter that the Commissioner may consent to an earlier election. However, a voluntary revocation may be an adverse factor in obtaining the Commissioner's consent to a re-election before the statutory five-year period has elapsed.

Revoking a Subchapter S election is a tax event which should be subjected to extensive planning by the corporation and its shareholders. It has been noted that undistributed taxable income is taxed to the shareholders who own stock on the last day of the corporation's tax year. If not distributed, undistributed taxable income becomes previously taxed income two and one-half months after the close of the tax year. Although the shareholder is partially protected from double taxation by adjusting the basis for his stock upward when he is taxed on the income passed through to him, the procedure for withdrawing previously taxed income is complicated when Subchapter S status is lost. Accordingly, many problems are avoided if the corporation distributes all previously taxed income before a revocation is undertaken. Even though the corporation's cash position may make this goal difficult to accomplish, the corporation should still make the effort. As a practical matter, a corporation should never allow undistributed taxable income to become previously taxed income.

Involuntary Termination

A Subchapter S election is terminated whenever the corporation ceases to qualify for the election. Let us briefly review the requirements for electing Subchapter S status that are discussed in Chapter 3. Five requirements deal with eligible shareholders and prohibited income:

1. The corporation must have ten or fewer shareholders.

---

[3]I.R.C. Section 1372(f).

2. All shareholders must be either individuals or decedent's estates. Trusts, partnerships, or corporations cannot be shareholders.
3. Nonresident aliens may not be shareholders.
4. No more than 80 percent of the corporation's gross receipts may be from sources outside of the United States.
5. No more than 20 percent of the corporation's gross receipts may be from sources defined as passive investment income.

Moreover, the corporation must meet the following three requirements:

1. The corporation must be a domestic corporation organized for purposes of making a profit.
2. The corporation may not be a member of an affiliated group.
3. The corporation may have only one class of stock issued or outstanding.

These requirements are considered in Chapters 4, 5, and 8 of this book. On the surface, compliance should not appear difficult. However, it should be noted that the average shareholder/officer in a Subchapter S corporation probably does not have a sophisticated understanding of this tax entity. Clients have a way of not communicating with their advisors until the transaction has become irrevocable through the passage of time. This aspect of operating as a Subchapter S corporation may cause professional tax advisors to avoid the entity whenever possible.

Almost any of the above requirements are subject to breach. For example, a shareholder may inadvertently transfer shares of stock to an eleventh shareholder, to a nonresident alien, or to a trust, partnership or corporation. An otherwise eligible shareholder may simply fail to execute the appropriate consent.[4] Testamentary plans that utilize trusts are especially dangerous in that the death of the settlor makes the trust irrevocable. Unfortunately, such plans are often not known until it is too late. Moreover, the corporation's business may abruptly change to the extent that more than 80 percent of its gross receipts comes from foreign sources or more than 20 percent of

---

[4]There is a remedy for this failure. Regulation 1.1372-3(c) allows a District Director to extend the time for filing shareholder consents if it can be demonstrated that the failure to file a timely consent was for reasonable cause and that the government's interests will not be jeopardized by granting the extension. The courts will police the application of the District Director's discretion. See *Kean* vs. *Commissioner,* 31 A.F.T.R. 2d 73-344 (9th Cir. 1972), *aff'g.* 51 T.C. 337 (1968).

gross receipts comes from passive income sources. Also, the corporation may alter its capital structure to include a second class of stock, or the government may view debt as a second class of stock under the thin capitalization doctrine.

Any of the above disqualifying events may happen to the client corporation without the knowledge of the corporation's tax adviser. When the Subchapter S election is involuntarily terminated, Regulation 1.1372-4(b)(3) requires the corporation to notify the District Director. No official form is provided for notification of termination. However, Exhibit 10-3 provides an acceptable form by which to submit this information to the District Director. That regulation requires information about the cause of the termination and the date that the event occurred. If the termination was caused by transfer of stock to an ineligible stockholder, the statement should set forth the names of the transferor and transferee as well as the number of shares involved. If the termination was caused by the creation of a second class of stock, the statement must specify differences between the classes of stock as well as the number of shares created. Presumably such information will allow the District Director to assess the validity of the involuntary termination.

EXHIBIT 10-3

Notification of Involuntary Termination

(No Official Form)

As stipulated in Regulation 1.1372-4(b)(3), the Crumb Corporation, 210 Long Avenue, Baton Rouge, Louisiana, 70821, hereby notifies you of the termination of the Subchapter S election under I.R.C. Section 1372(a) as a result of an issuance of a second class of stock on June 12, 1974.

Such 1,000 shares of preferred stock were issued in order to obtain additional capital. These shares are nonvoting, cumulative preferred stock.

Under penalties of perjury, I declare that these statements made herein are to the best of my knowledge and belief true, correct, and complete statements.

July 10, 1974	TONY LAMER	PRESIDENT
(Date)	(Signature of Officer)	(Title)

The effective date for an involuntary termination is different than the effective date for a voluntary revocation. Recall that a voluntary revocation is effective for subsequent tax years and, accordingly, has no effect upon the current tax year. However, a termination is effective for the tax year in which the disqualifying event takes place. Once a corporation decides that the benefits of Subchapter S are no longer desired, it is likely that it will not want to wait until the end of the current tax year. Thus, the termination route may offer significant advantages.

Involuntary Termination vs. Voluntary Revocation

If the effective date of the return to standard corporation status is significant, what prevents the corporation from purposely disqualifying itself in order to achieve the desired results? It probably is too difficult to purposely violate the requirements as to the character of the corporation's income. However, a transfer of shares to an ineligible shareholder or the creation of a second class of stock present no permanent disruptive effects for the corporation. Perhaps the simplest step may be to transfer shares of stock to an individual who refuses to consent to the election as required by statute. The following steps would appear to cause a termination:

1. Increase the number of stockholders to eleven or more.
2. Issue a second class of stock.
3. Transfer shares to a nonqualifying shareholder such as a corporation, trust, or partnership.
4. Transfer shares to a nonconsenting individual or estate.
5. Transfer shares to a nonresident alien or have a resident alien shareholder establish residence outside the United States.

Some of these devices, such as disposing of a share of stock or creating a trust, should have no significant economic or control effects upon either the shareholder or the corporation. If the IRS continues to take the position that a second class of stock is created when "any other type of voting control device or arrangement" is entered into by shareholders,[5] a simple way to terminate an election may be provided. If a short-term agreement can create a second class of stock, a thirty-day agreement may have no real economic effect other than to allow a few stockholders to cause an electing corporation to lose its qualification. If two stockholders agree to vote together and achieve effective control of the corporation, or through cumulative voting gain a position on the board of directors, apparently the Commissioner would classify such agreements as a second class of stock. An agreement between all the stockholders may provide a method for revoking an election during the first year in which it

---

[5]Rev. Rul. 63-226, 1963-2 C.B. 341.

was to be effective and thus cause the electing corporation to be taxed as a regular corporation from the beginning of the year.[6] However, under Regulation 1.1371-1(g), artificial classes of stock established in order to elect directors "in a number proportionate to the number of shares in each group" will not terminate the election. But the lack of proportionality will terminate the election.[7] At least one court has held Regulation 1.1371-1(g) and Revenue Ruling 63-226 to be "invalid to the extent that they hold a second class of stock is created unless all of the shares outstanding are identical as to all voting rights."[8] The litigant in this case, Parker Oil Company, in order to resolve discord which had developed within a closely-held corporation, issued irrevocable voting proxies to certain shareholders. This act separated control from ownership, and the Commissioner argued that a second class of stock had been created. The Court drew upon the legislative history of Subchapter S and noted that this arrangement would not complicate the capital structure, which the one-class-of-stock rule was designed to prevent. There were dissents to this opinion. While the government is likely to attack this type of voting arrangement, it remains unlikely that a corporation can remove itself from Subchapter S in this manner.

The stockholders of a Subchapter S corporation will have to be careful when an act is deliberately undertaken to obtain a retroactive termination. The Regulations state that "a donee or purchaser of stock in the corporation is not considered a shareholder unless such stock is acquired in a bona fide transaction and the donee or purchaser is the real owner of such stock. The circumstances, not only as of the time of the purported transfer but also during the periods preceding and following it, will be taken into consideration in determining the bona fides of the transfer."[9] Further, transactions between family members are scrutinized closely by IRS Agents. This principle may be invoked to prevent a desired retroactive termination. For example, in *Clarence Hook*, the principal stockholder transferred a small amount of stock to his attorney in order to terminate the Sub-

---

[6]This could be a valuable device if an electing corporation begins to realize an unexpectedly large amount of income and the shareholders want to terminate the election retroactively.

[7]*Pollack* vs. *Commissioner*, 21 A.F.T.R. 2d 1056 (5th Cir. 1968), *aff'g.* 47 T.C. 92 (1966).

[8]*Parker Oil Co.*, 58 T.C. 985 (1972), *appeal not authorized* (5th Cir. 1973).

[9]Regulation 1.1373-1(a)(2). The Commissioner may try to use the following authorities to attack deliberate terminations: *Commissioner* vs. *Court Holding Co.*, 324 U.S. 331 (1945), or *Higgins* vs. *Smith*, 308 U.S. 473 (1940).

chapter S election. The attorney paid no money and performed no services for the stock, and, upon request, returned it to the stockholder without receiving any consideration therefor. The attorney received the stock as a retainer in order to insure his performance of certain future legal services. The Tax Court held that the election was not terminated since the transfer of stock was not bona fide and had no economic reality. "Moreover, beneficial ownership, as opposed to technical legal title, is determinative as to who is a shareholder for the purposes of Section 1372." The Court refused to answer the question as to whether a transfer of such stock, which had economic reality but was solely for the purpose of terminating the election, would have been effective.[10] The stock transactions of a Subchapter S corporation must have economic reality.[11] *Hook* has been cited for the proposition that "the courts have often recharacterized purported sales by looking to the realities of the situation."[12]

Earlier in this chapter, Exhibit 10-3 provided an example of how to notify the Commissioner that the election has been involuntarily terminated. It appears that this information is also needed to enable the Commissioner to assess the validity of the termination.

The Commissioner may attempt to challenge a deliberate termination of an election in a situation where a gift of a nominal amount of stock is transferred near the end of the tax year to a close relative. In *Henry Duarte,*[13] a so-called gift of Subchapter S stock by a father to his minor son was not recognized because it lacked substance. The Commissioner may have a difficult time in successfully challenging termination from a transfer of even one share to a new unrelated stockholder if the transfer is *bona fide*. But as was noted earlier, this aspect has yet to be litigated.

Re-election after Revocation or Termination

A Subchapter S election is intended to be reasonably permanent; a corporation or its shareholders are not permitted to change this status too often. Termination or revocation should not be taken too lightly, because neither a corporation or any successor to that corporation may make a new election until the fifth tax year following the

---

[10]*Clarence Hook,* 58 T.C. 267 (1972), *appeal dismissed* (9th Cir. 1973).

[11]See *Michael F. Bierne,* 52 T.C. 210 (1969); *Henry D. Duarte,* 44 T.C. 193 (1965).

[12]*Hans P. Kraus,* 59 T.C. 681 (1973); See also *Higgins* vs. *Smith,* 23 A.F.T.R. 800 (1939); *Atkins* vs. *Commissioner,* 15 A.F.T.R. 1127 (5th Cir. 1935).

[13]*Henry D. Duarte,* 44 T.C. 193 (1965); See also *Michael F. Bierne,* 52 T.C. 210 (1969).

first tax year to which the termination or revocation applied.[14] A successor corporation is: (1) one in which at least 50 percent of the stock ownership is the same as that of the predecessor corporation in the year of the termination or revocation, and (2) one which acquires a substantial part of the assets of the predecessor, or in which a substantial part of the assets of a new corporation were formerly assets of the predecessor.[15] The provisions relative to successor corporations are designed to prevent avoidance of the five-year delay by liquidating and re-incorporating the enterprise.

Under appropriate circumstances, the Commissioner may consent to a new election prior to the fifth year.[16] Consent may be obtained through application to the National Office of the IRS in Washington, D.C., setting forth all relevant facts and attaching the election and consent statements. The Regulations state that the following factors will induce the Commissioner to consent to a new election prior to the expiration of the five-year period: (1) a 50 percent change in the stock ownership from the year of termination, or (2) the events causing the termination were not reasonably within the control of the corporation or shareholders having a substantial interest in the corporation.[17] Presumably, if a corporation accidentally loses its elective status, it stands a good chance of regaining it the next year. The burden is on the corporation to prove that the Commissioner should consent to a new election. No official form is provided for re-election after revocation or termination. However, Exhibit 10-4 provides an unofficial form which may be used for this procedure.

Circumstances beyond reasonable control are illustrated in Rev. Rul. 67-382.[18] In the Treasury's example, a Subchapter S corporation owned certain securities and its stockholders operated a partnership. The electing corporation was allowed to become inactive in order to avoid confusion between the corporation and partnership. While inactive, the investment income of the corporation was greater than 20 percent of its gross receipts; thus, the election was automatically terminated. The Ruling stipulated that the event causing this termination was within the reasonable control of the cor-

---

[14]I.R.C. Section 1372(f).
[15]Regulation 1.1372-5(b).
[16]I.R.C. Section 1372(f).
[17]Regulation 1.1372-5(a).
[18]1967-2 C.B. 298.

EXHIBIT 10-4

Election by Small Business Corporation
after Termination or Revocation
(No Official Form)

The Crumb Corporation, 210 Long Avenue, Baton Rouge, Louisiana, hereby consents to the election under I.R.C. Section 1372(a) as to its tax status as a Small Business Corporation. The same corporation involuntarily lost its tax status under Subchapter S in April, 1973, that was effective for the taxable year beginning January, 1973.

As stipulated in Regulation 1.1372-5, the following information is submitted:

1. Approximately 62 percent of the stock in the corporation is owned by Tony Lamer, 506 Wright Drive, Baton Rouge, Louisiana, who did not own any stock in the corporation during the first tax year for which the termination was applicable.

2. The termination was not within the control of the majority, but was caused by a minority. King Neal, 1410 Oakwood Drive, Baton Rouge, Louisiana, stated to the electing corporation that his salary would be doubled or he would set up one share of stock under a short-term trust. The stockholder under consideration did not receive the excessive salary raise and the election was terminated by his unwarranted action.

3. The corporation is a domestic corporation which meets all five of the requirements stated on Form 2553. Form 2553, as well as the Statement of Shareholders' Consent to Election accompany this statement. The election will be effective for the taxable year beginning January, 1974.

Under penalties of perjury, I declare that this election is duly authorized, and that the statements made herein are to the best of my knowledge and belief true, correct, and complete statements.

1-6-74	TONY LAMER	PRESIDENT
(Date)	(Signature of Officer)	(Title)

poration or its stockholders. That is, maintaining an active corporation or selling the securities could have continued the Subchapter S election. This corporation would not be granted an early re-election by the Commissioner.

If a termination occurs within the first month of a tax year, the corporation may be able to make a new election within that month. If the Commissioner consents to a new election, it will be effective that tax year. However, the power of the Commissioner to permit an early re-election does not mean that he can waive the effect of a termination after the first month (except to permit a new shareholder to file a late consent). After the first month, the termination will be effective for that tax year.

Must the corporation wait for five years before re-electing Subchapter S status when that status is "terminated" because the original election was defective? Revenue Ruling 71-549[19] states that when a Subchapter S election is not effective there is no status to terminate. Accordingly, termination concepts do not apply. The corporation merely starts over and complies with provisions of the electing process, which are discussed in Chapter 3.

It appears that the Commissioner will not allow a re-election if the termination resulted from a voluntary revocation. There would have to be at least a 50 percent change in the stock ownership before the Commissioner would consider a consent to a re-election.

---

[19]1971-2 C.B. 319.

Chapter 11

Redemptions and Liquidations

Many instances may arise in the life of a Subchapter S corporation in which it is desirable to redeem shares of stock of certain stockholders.* Regardless of the reason for a stock redemption, the emphasis in this chapter is on obtaining the most advantageous tax treatment of the redemption for both the corporation and the shareholders. A Subchapter S corporation may also have the need for the partial or complete liquidation provisions of Subchapter C. Although the same liquidation rules apply to Subchapter S as with any other corporation, the Subchapter S provisions may override the various liquidation rules. This chapter discusses partial as well as complete liquidations of Subchapter S corporations in detail. Finally, the chapter covers the impact that the collapsible corporation provisions have upon Subchapter S.

Redemptions Under Section 302

Circumstances may arise in the life of a Subchapter S corporation in which it is desirable to redeem shares of stock from certain shareholders. This need may be particularly critical in order to maintain a Subchapter S election should a dissident shareholder consider selling his stock to a nonqualified shareholder (which, of course, would terminate the election). Redemption of stock may also be necessary at the death of a shareholder. Or it may be useful in a "boot strap" acquisition of control of a corporation. Regardless of the reason for stock redemption, the emphasis in this section is on obtaining the most advantageous tax treatment of the redemption for both the electing corporation and the shareholders.

Section 302 governs the tax treatment of redemptions.[1] From the standpoint of taxation, a redemption may be treated either as an exchange of stock for part or full payment or as a dividend. Since, if all conditions are met, an exchange of stock for payment would result in capital gain treatment of any gain realized, it is clearly to the

---

*The authors appreciate the assistance of Russell H. Taylor (affiliated with the Arthur Young & Company office in Tampa, Florida) in the preparation of this chapter.

[1]Redemption is defined by Section 317(b) as the acquisition by a corporation of its own stock in exchange for property without regard to whether the redeemed stock is cancelled, retired, or held as treasury stock.

243

taxpayer's advantage to have the redemption treated as an exchange. In order to qualify as an exchange under Section 302, any one of the following conditions must be met:

1. The redemption must not be essentially equivalent to a dividend. (Section 302(b)(1))
2. The redemption must be substantially disproportionate with respect to the shareholder. (Section 302(b)(2))
3. The redemption must be in complete termination of the shareholder's interest in the corporation. (Section 302(b)(4))
4. The redemption is of certain railroad corporation stock pursuant to a plan of reorganization. (Section 302(b)(4))

If any one of these conditions is met, then the redemption escapes the ordinary income treatment of dividends. Since the fourth test of Section 302(b)(4) is of limited interest, it is not discussed.

Not Essentially Equivalent to Dividends

The first test, provided by Section 302(b)(1), that the redemption not be essentially equivalent to a dividend, is a very unclear test and has produced substantial litigation. Thus, this section is seldom used as a planning tool, and its application is generally limited to a situation where the taxpayer is forced to use it due to the lack of another alternative. The Regulations state that whether or not a redemption is essentially equivalent to a dividend depends upon the facts and circumstances of each case.[2] This flexibility appears to be quite true in light of the many criteria applied by the courts and the wide variance of decisions based upon similar fact situations. Ample case authority can be cited in defense of practically any redemption that even appears to qualify under Section 302(b)(1). For instance, the business purpose test has been relied on to varying degrees by the Tax Court,[3] while some courts of appeal have specifically rejected this test.[4] In *Levin* the Tax Court did mention some of the criteria when it stated:

> The more important of these tests are whether there was a significant shift of ownership and control; whether there was an accumulation of earnings and profits sufficient to make the distributions; whether there was a history of significant divi-

[2]Regulation 1.302-2(b).
[3]See, for example, *Beatrice Levin,* 47 T.C. 258 (1966).
[4]See *McGinty* vs. *Commissioner,* 325 F. 2d 820 (2d Cir. 1964).

dend distributions; and whether the redemption was motivated by a substantial business purpose.[5]

All the tests mentioned above have been used by various courts in arriving at decisions on both sides of the question and may be used as guidelines down the somewhat foggy path of Section 302(b)(1). Several points are clear, however, and should be kept in mind when attempting to qualify redemptions under Section 302(b)(1). If the redemption is pro rata, or fairly close to pro rata redemption, it will be considered to be a dividend under Section 301. The definition of pro rata is not itself completely clear. In Rev. Rul. 57-353 the IRS gives some guidelines for judging pro rata redemptions.[6] Shareholder A owned one hundred shares and B, C, and D each owned fifty shares of stock in the corporation. B and D bought all of A's shares, and, since they were having difficulty making payments to A, B and C, had the corporation redeem the shares. In ruling on the redemption, the IRS stated:

> . . . although the distribution by the corporation to B and C in redemption of the 100 shares of their stock was not precisely pro rata to all the shareholders of the corporation, it was, nevertheless, proportionate as to those persons owning 80 percent of the stock of the corporation and did not substantially change their relative control of the corporation.[7]

Clearly, the attribution rules of Section 318 apply in judging whether a redemption is essentially equivalent to a dividend.[8] Under Section 318, a shareholder may be considered to be the "owner" of stock held by members of his family or held by estates, trusts, partnerships, or corporations of which the shareholder is a beneficiary. These constructive ownership rules materially reduce the usefulness of such redemptions for Subchapter S corporations. There has existed some confusion as to the extent to which the attribution rules applied to Section 302(b)(1) prior to 1970. The Supreme Court recognized the diverse treatment of the attribution rules in the lower courts and granted certiorari in the *Davis* case.[9] In *Davis*, the shareholder owned 250 shares of common stock and 1,000 shares of preferred stock of the corporation, which had a total of 1,000 shares of common outstanding. The other 750 shares of common outstanding were owned

---

[5]*Levin, supra,* note 3, p. 263.
[6]Rev. Rul. 57-353, 1957-2 C.B. 223.
[7]*Ibid.*
[8]I.R.C. Section 302(c)(1).
[9]*United States* vs. *Davis,* 397 U.S. 301 (1970).

by the shareholder's wife and two children equally. When the corporation redeemed the 1,000 shares of preferred stock, the taxpayer did not report any income, since he received $25,000 which was equal to his basis in the stock. The IRS asserted that the redemption was essentially equivalent to a dividend. The District Court and the Court of Appeals ruled in favor of the taxpayer, saying that the redemption qualified under Section 302(b)(1).[10] However, the Supreme Court applied the attribution rules of Section 318, and the shareholder was thereby the "owner" of all 1,000 shares of outstanding common. Since the redemption to him was therefore pro rata, the redemption was held taxable as a dividend.

Another potential problem that can easily be avoided is a procedural problem that has arisen in several cases in which one shareholder purchases all or most of the other outstanding shares and then has the corporation redeem the purchased shares.[11] The redemption would then be pro rata with respect to the redeeming shareholder, and thus taxable as a dividend. If the shareholder wanting a larger interest in the corporation would have the corporation redeem the shares of the other shareholders, the shareholders would receive capital gain treatment under Section 302(b)(3), and the controlling shareholder would not be taxed on the redemption as a dividend.

Substantially Disproportionate

The test applied to redemptions by Section 302(b)(2) is that the redemption be substantially disproportionate with respect to the shareholder. The test is fairly clean and easy to apply. Basically, two percentage guidelines must be met in order for the redemption to qualify for capital gain treatment:

1. After the redemption the shareholder must own less than 50 percent of the outstanding voting stock.
2. The shareholder's proportionate interest after the redemption must be less than 80 percent of what it was prior to the redemption.[12]

Since the Subchapter S corporation has only one class of stock and few shareholders, the test of Section 302(b)(2) should be quite easy

---

[10]*United States* vs. *Davis,* 274 F. Supp. 466 (M.D. Tenn. 1967), 408 F. 2d 1139 (6th Cir. 1969).

[11]See *Edwin J. O'Reilly,* T.C.M. 1968-291 or *McGinty* vs. *Commissioner,* 325 F. 2d 820 (2d Cir. 1964), also Rev. Rul. 57-353, 1957-2 C.B. 223.

[12]Regulation 1.302-3.

to apply. However, keep in mind that the attribution rules of Section 318 also are applicable to Section 302(b)(2) and could easily cause dividend treatment of a redemption otherwise qualified as substantially disproportionate. If the test of Section 302(b)(2) can be met, the redemption will be treated as an exchange and, hence, eligible for capital gain treatment without the uncertainty and potential problems of Section 302(b)(1).

Complete Redemption

Another "safe harbor" is Section 302(b)(3), which is applicable in cases of complete redemption of all of the stock of the corporation owned by the shareholder. In the case where all the shareholders are unrelated, the application of this provision is quite straightforward. However, the real value in this provision is that the family attribution rules of Section 318 are waived if the redemption otherwise qualifies under Section 302(b)(3), where the following conditions are met:

1. No interest is held in the corporation after the redemption either as shareholder, officer, or employee. (One may, however, be a creditor.)
2. One does not acquire any interest in the corporation for ten years except by bequest or inheritance.
3. One agrees to notify the IRS if any interest is obtained in the corporation for ten years.[13]

Shareholder Treatment

In general, when a shareholder's stock is redeemed under Section 302(a), he receives capital gain or loss treatment, depending upon the amount he receives and the basis of the stock which he gives up. Undistributed taxable income (UTI) is defined as taxable income *minus* the amount of money distributed as dividends during the tax year.[14] A distribution in redemption of stock under Section 302(a) is not considered to be a distribution of dividends and therefore does *not* reduce UTI.[15] Only those persons who are stockholders of the electing corporation on the last day of the tax year are required to include UTI in their income.[16] If a stockholder sells his stock before

---

[13]I.R.C. Section 302(c)(2)(A).

[14]I.R.C. Section 1373(c).

[15]Regulation 1.1373-1(d); Regulation 1.1373-1(g), ex. 5.

[16]I.R.C. Section 1373(b); Regulation 1.1373-1(a)(2).

the end of the tax year, he is taxed on no part of its UTI for that year, and his purchaser (or remaining shareholders in the case of a redemption) is taxed on all of it.[17] If the redemption is treated as a distribution under Section 301 (a dividend), UTI could be reduced (assuming it is a cash redemption).

Where there is PTI in the corporation which is personal to the redeemed shareholder, it will be tax-free only to the extent of the shareholder's basis in his stock. It is, of course, possible that the PTI will be subject to a capital gain tax rather than being tax-free, as is usually the case. Capital gain rates, however, may be the best alternative where PTI has become "locked-in" and the corporation is unable to distribute a non-pro rata dividend to the redeemed stockholder before the redemption (due to related shareholders).

In *Erickson*,[18] a corporation redeemed the shares of a major stockholder; the purchase price included his share of profit up to the point of the redemption plus an adjustment for work in process. The Tax Court upheld the seller's position that the entire payment was for the redemption of his stock and therefore to be treated as capital gain. The remaining stockholders had to include all of the profits realized during the year (undiminished by the nondividend redemption) in their taxable income.

This tax trap can be quite painful to the remaining shareholders. It is even more painful if the corporation distributes installment obligations, property subject to a liability in excess of the corporate basis, appreciated LIFO inventory, and depreciable property subject to Sections 1245, 1250, 1251, or 1252. These items are "recaptured," and UTI is increased even more (to the detriment of the remaining shareholders). Only in the case of the investment credit is the selling shareholder caught. When a stockholder disposes of a substantial portion of his stock, he is considered to be disposing of a portion of the property with respect to which he has obtained the benefit of an investment credit.[19] A "substantial portion" is considered to be one-third of the stock owned,[20] and the transfer of such an amount will subject the selling shareholder to an investment credit recapture in

---

[17]Regulation 1.1373-1(g), ex. 5.

[18]56 T.C. 1112 (1971).

[19]Regulation 1.47-4(a)(1).

[20]Regulation 1.47-4(b)(ii).

direct proportion to the disposed stock. These recapture regulations have been upheld.[21]

The Tax Court took a slightly different position in *Henry H. Renard*.[22] Here an executed buy-sell agreement called for the purchase price of the stock to be book value plus 10 percent of the net profits of the three succeeding years. The corporation did in fact redeem some stock, paying book value, plus a pro rata portion of the UTI during the redeeming year, along with the 10 percent contingent payment. Although a literal interpretation of the buy-sell agreement would indicate that *all* of these payments should be for the redemption of stock and not a payment of UTI since the redeeming stockholder was *not* a stockholder on the last day of the corporate year, the Tax Court used the "substance over form" doctrine to "save" the redeeming corporation in this instance. The Court felt that "all parties concerned intended and contemplated the individual shareholder to be responsible for the taxes on the corporation's . . . earnings,"[23] even though the redeeming shareholder would not be a shareholder at the end of the year.

The corporation had recorded the UTI payments as a charge to the surplus account rather than to a treasury stock account. The Tax Court held that the payments of the UTI to the redeeming stockholder was a taxable dividend (not a capital gain) and the corporation received a corresponding reduction in their UTI account. The Tax Court felt it was unfair to tax the remaining shareholder on ordinary income which he never received and double-tax the same amount to the redeeming shareholder (as a capital gain). Taxpayers should probably not rely heavily on the generosity of this Tax Court decision and should set up a tax reserve for the taxes required on the UTI already paid to a redeemed shareholder in the form of payments for his stock.

If Section 302(a) applies to a redemption, then a stockholder's basis in his remaining shares remain the same as before the redemption. For example, if he had a $10 per share basis in 200 shares before a 100-share redemption (total of $2,000), he would have a $10 per share basis in 100 shares after the redemption (total of $1,000). Where a shareholder receives property in a Section 302(a) redemption, the

<hr />

[21]*Charbonnet* vs. *U.S.*, 320 F. Supp. 874 (D.C. La. 1971); *Purvis* vs. *U.S.*, 31 A.F.T.R. 2d 73-428 (D.C. Ga. 1972).

[22]T.C.M. 1972-244.

[23]*Ibid.*

Code does not state how to determine his basis in such property. But fair market value is probably appropriate.

If a redemption is treated as a dividend distribution under Section 301, then a stockholder is allowed to adjust his basis in his remaining shares. For example, if a shareholder's basis in his stock is $100,000 before a one-half redemption, which is treated as a dividend, the basis of his remaining one-half stock is $100,000.[24] Where a shareholder receives property in a dividend redemption, the basis of the property is its fair market value.[25]

Corporate Treatment

From the standpoint of the corporation, a redemption of stock presents different problems. The Regulations state that a Subchapter S election is not terminated by the redemption and the holding of its own shares.[26] There appears to be no authority on whether or not the corporation must file a consent with respect to the treasury shares. However, since no income or tax is attributed to the treasury shares, the filing of a consent would seem to be illogical. As long as the shares are held as treasury shares, the cost of the shares serves as a reduction of owner's equity. Under some state law a restriction must be placed on retained earnings for the cost of the treasury stock held. Since a Subchapter S corporation has different levels of retained earnings, the problem arises as to which level of retained earnings should be restricted. It would seem that a restriction on pre-Subchapter S accumulations or PTI would suffice. However, it would be difficult to generalize in this area due to the variance in state requirements.

Section 312(e) indicates how a redemption is chargeable to earnings and profits and the capital accounts. The amount distributed in a redemption (as well as in a partial liquidation) that is properly chargeable to a capital account shall *not* be treated as a distribution of earnings and profits. The term "capital account" refers to the par value of stock, any paid-in surplus, and other similar items, such as unrealized appreciation or depreciation surplus.[27]

Until Rev. Rul. 70-531, the courts as well as the IRS have followed the practice of first applying the redemption price against the

---

[24]Regulation 1.302-(2)(c).

[25]I.R.C. Section 301(d).

[26]Regulation 1.1371-1(g).

[27]Regulations 1.562-1(b)(1)(i) and (ii); Rev. Rul. 70-531, 1970-2 C.B. 76.

redeemed shares' pro rata part of any capital accounts and then applying any balance of the redemption price to decrease earnings and profits.[28] In an arbitrary attempt to produce the "proper" effect on earnings and profits, Rev. Rul. 70-531 introduces a ratable share limitation on the charge to the earnings and profits account. In effect, the ruling requires that the portion of the redemption price chargeable to earnings and profits be calculated first, and then any balance is chargeable to the capital accounts. Thus, the charge against the earnings and profits account is limited to the redeemed stockholder's ratable share of earnings and profits. Where the redemption price exceeds the redeemed shares' pro rata portion of both earnings and profits and the capital account, such excess is classified as "unrealized appreciation" and reduces the capital accounts. If the redemption price is less than the portion of paid-in capital and earnings and profits ratable attributable to the redeemed shares, earnings and profits are reduced by a portion corresponding to the portion of the stock involved in the redemption. In effect, the "unrealized appreciation" account is a "plug" account.

Rev. Rul. 70-531 adopts a "ratable share" approach in determining the appropriate charge to earnings and profits account. In effect, the charges against the earnings and profits accounts are limited to the redeeming stockholder's ratable share of earnings and profits. An example based upon Rev. Rul. 70-531 can illustrate the calculations necessary in a Subchapter S corporation.

Assume the following facts about Cal, Inc., a Subchapter S corporation for December 31, 1974:

Cash	$270	Liabilities	$270
Fixed Assets	200	Capital Stock (10 shares)	50
	———	Paid-in Surplus	30
	$470	Pre-election E&P (or	
		E&P in excess of UTI)	30
		PTI	60
		UTI	30
			———
			$470

Both X and Y owned five shares each at the beginning of 1974. All five shares of Y's stock are redeemed under Section 302(a) during 1974 for cash of $225. What amount of the $225 distribution is prop-

---

[28]*Helvering* vs. *Jarvis,* 123 F. 2d 742 (4th Cir. 1941), *acq. revoked;* G.C.M. 23460, 1942-2 C.B. 190.

erly chargeable to the capital accounts and to the various earnings and profits accounts?

Method of Allocation

1. $\dfrac{\text{Chargeable to "Regular"}}{\text{Capital Accounts}} = \dfrac{\text{Total in}}{\text{Capital Account}} \times \dfrac{\text{Redeemed Shares}}{\text{Total Shares}}$

2. $\dfrac{\text{Chargeable to}}{\text{Earnings and Profits}} = \dfrac{\text{Earnings and Profits}}{\text{Less UTI}^{29}} \times \dfrac{\text{Redeemed Shares}}{\text{Total Shares}}$
   Accounts

3. $\dfrac{\text{Chargeable to}}{\text{Unrealized Appreciation}} =$ Total Distributions less
   (or Depreciation)   Amount chargeable to Regular
   Capital Account less Amount
   chargeable to E&P Accounts

Answers

Chargeable to:

1. Capital stock . . . . $50 $\times$ 5/10 = $25
   Paid-in surplus . . . . 30 $\times$ 5/10 = __15__ $40

2. E&P less UTI. . . . . $90 $\times$ 5/10 = __$45__
   $85

3. Unrealized Appreciation. . . . . $225 — $85 = __$140__[30]

Equity would suggest that an amount would be chargeable to the PTI ($30 in the previous example) account to the full extent of the PTI even though it is not "personal" to the redeeming shareholder. For example, if there is only $15 in Y's personal PTI account, a total of $30 should be chargeable to the PTI account. PTI is a privileged form of capital since earnings and profits were reduced when UTI "turned" into PTI.[31] A distribution of PTI should never be a dividend even if the Subchapter S election is terminated. While the election is intact, a distribution of money from PTI is considered to be a distribution from sources "other than earnings and profits," as outlined in Regulation 1.316-2(a). Once an election is terminated, PTI is similar to ordinary capital, and if distributed (after all current and accumulated earnings and profits), it is a return of capital under Section 1016.

---

[29] I.R.C. Section 1373(c); only cash dividends can reduce UTI.

[30] To be chargeable to the capital accounts according to Rev. Rul, 70-531, 1970-2 C.B. 76. G.C.M. 23460, 1942-2 C.B. 190.

[31] I.R.C. Section 1377(a).

Of course, there is some authority that the "ratable share" limitation in Rev. Rul. 70-531 is not necessarily valid.[32]

Partial Liquidations

In general, a Subchapter S corporation may have less need for the partial liquidation provisions than a comparable nonelecting corporation. A nonelecting corporation desiring to contract its business activities by selling certain assets and distributing the proceeds to the shareholders faces a capital gain tax at the corporate level and, at the best, another capital gain tax at the shareholder level. On the other hand, the Subchapter S corporation can simply sell the assets and pass the capital gain through to the shareholders subject to the provisions of Section 1375(a) and to the limited possibility of a capital gain tax under Section 1378(a). Notwithstanding the normal advantages of the Subchapter S corporation in these situations, there are several circumstances where the partial liquidation could prove useful, particularly in an extended liquidation, or possibly as an alternative to a Section 302 redemption qualifying as a sale or exchange and not as a dividend. Also, the use of a partial liquidation so as to avoid a corporate tax on distribution of appreciated property to redeem stock can be quite beneficial to a Subchapter S corporation.

Types of Partial Liquidations

Section 331(a)(2) provides that amounts distributed in partial liquidation of a corporation will be treated as in-part or full payment in exchange for the stock. The key point in this seemingly straightforward provision is the definition of partial liquidation found in Section 346. A redemption may qualify under Section 346 as a partial liquidation if one of the following conditions are met:

1. The redemption is one of a series of redemptions leading to complete liquidation pursuant to a plan of liquidation. [Section 346(a)(1).]
2. The distribution in redemption is not essentially equivalent to a dividend. (Section 346(a)(2))
3. The distribution terminates one of two or more active businesses carried on by the corporations. (Section 346(b))

---

[32]*Helvering* vs. *Jarvis,* 123 F. 2d 742 (4th Cir. 1941), *acq. revoked; Woodward Investment Co.,* 46 B.T.A. 648 (1942), *acq. revoked.* See *Herbert Enoch,* 57 T.C. 781 (1972), for a current decision upholding the *Jarvis* rule.

If the redemption satisfies the requirements of Section 346, the redemption will qualify as an exchange of stock for partial or full payment without regard to whether or not the redemption qualifies under Section 302.[33] That is, the redemption can be pro rata and still not be treated as a dividend under Section 301. Perhaps equally important may be the fact that the attribution rules of Section 318 do not apply to redemptions under Section 346, as in the case of Section 302.

There are no precise guidelines that can be set out to qualify a redemption under Section 346(a)(1) as one of a series of redemptions pursuant to a plan of liquidation. However, one of the first steps should be the adoption of a plan. There is no statutory definition of a plan, but, at the least, the board of directors should adopt and record the intended actions of the corporation. Also, Section 6043(a) requires that within thirty days after the adoption of a plan of partial or complete liquidation, the corporation must file Form 966 with the IRS giving the details of the plan.[34] These actions should establish *prima facie* evidence as to an electing corporation's intentions.[35]

Once the plan of liquidation has been adopted and the series of redemptions begin, there is no set time limit as to when the corporation must be completely liquidated. Obviously, a regular series of redemptions over quite a few years would appear to be more like dividends of a going concern than liquidating redemptions. Although the IRS has not set a time limit, it may be significant that it will not ordinarily issue advance rulings on the eligibility of redemptions under Section 346 if the redemptions extend over three years beyond the date the plan is adopted.[36] In some cases the courts have held that redemptions were made in partial liquidation even though the redemptions were made over an extended period of time beyond three years.[37]

The question of whether or not the redemptions qualify under Section 346(a)(1) is a question of fact. If an electing corporation is

---

[33]I.R.C. Section 346(c).

[34]Regulation 1.6043-1.

[35]See *Blaschka* vs. *U.S.*, 393 F. 2d 983 (1968), where claim under Section 346(a) rejected on insufficient evidence of a plan. But in *Fowler Hosiery Co., Inc.*, 36 T.C. 201 (1961), the Tax Court said that a formal plan was not required if, in fact, the shareholders have adopted a plan which shows itself to be a plan of complete liquidation.

[36]Rev. Proc. 69-6, 1969-1 C.B. 396.

[37]See *Estate of Charles Fearon*, 16 T.C. 385 (1951) — an unusual case where the liquidation took 23 years, yet it was still held that the redemptions were in partial liquidation. But see *Old Virginia Brick, Inc.*, 367 F. 2d 276 (4th Cir. 1966), where an estate was held to have become a trust because it was kept open for an unreasonably long time.

indeed selling its assets, paying off its debts, and, in general, winding up its business affairs, it is likely that they can show that any redemptions are in liquidation. Also, the adoption and filing of a plan with the IRS is an important factor in establishing that indeed the corporation is in the process of liquidation. Any expansion of business activity or purchase of new assets would certainly be detrimental to the argument that the corporation was in the process of liquidation pursuant to a plan. In general, if the corporation intends to liquidate by a series of stock redemptions and conducts its activities toward that end, then qualifying under Section 346(a)(1) should present few real difficulties.

The basic test in qualifying a redemption under Section 346(a)(2) as "not essentially equivalent to a dividend" is that there must exist an actual contraction of the electing corporation's business. Note that the dividend equivalency is the same requirement as contained in Section 302 (b)(1). However, the important distinction is that Section 302 views the transaction at the shareholder level, while Section 346 makes the dividend equivalency test at the corporate level. Whether a genuine contraction of corporate business did in fact occur can be a very difficult question and depends upon the circumstances surrounding and leading up to the redemption.

Most of the guidelines for establishing a contraction of a corporate business are found in the case law. One of the leading cases concerned the distribution in redemption of stock of insurance proceeds received by a corporation after a portion of its business facilities had been destroyed by fire.[38] In ruling that the redemptions were in partial liquidation, the court gave some of the criteria which are considered pivotal in determining whether or not a partial liquidation has taken place. The court stated that the question was one of fact depending upon the circumstances in each case and that there was no universal test that could be laid down in defining partial liquidation. Several factors which the court mentioned as being important were:

1. The presence or absence of a real business purpose.
2. The motives of the corporation.
3. The size of the corporate surplus.
4. The past dividend policy.
5. The presence of any special circumstances relating to the redemption.[39]

---

[38]*Joseph W. Imler,* 11 T.C. 836 (1948).
[39]*Ibid.,* p. 840.

A reasonably clear case under the criteria mentioned would be the sale of a factory which completely eliminates the production in one line of business by a corporation which had regularly paid dividends, did not have a large surplus of retained earnings, and clearly intended to eliminate the one line of business. However, even under these circumstances there could be difficulties if the portion of the business sold represented only a small portion of the corporation's total business. An important point in this respect is the comparison of the Subchapter S corporation's activities *before* the distribution in redemption of stock and the activities of the corporation *after* the redemption. If there has indeed been a contraction of the business there should be some distinct differences in the level or type of corporate business after the distribution.[40] For example, a corporation which owned three television stations sold one of the stations and distributed the proceeds pro rata in redemption of some of its stock. The IRS ruled that this was a genuine contraction of the business and the redemption was held to be in partial liquidation.[41] The ruling noted that the funds from the sale were kept segregated and were not used for other business activities during the eight months between the sale and the redemption of stock. The fact that the funds were kept segregated while the corporation decided on the best alternative for them could have been detrimental to qualification under Section 346. If the funds had been either designated by the corporation as (or held by the IRS to be) a reserve for future expansion, Section 346 treatment would not be available.[42]

There are two additional requirements which must also be met under Section 346(a)(2) in order to qualify a redemption in partial liquidation as not equivalent to a dividend. These requirements are that the redemption (1) is pursuant to a plan, and (2) occurs within the tax year in which the plan was adopted or within the succeeding tax year. The first requirement can be met [as discussed under Section 346(a)(1) redemptions] by the adoption of a plan by the board of directors and the subsequent filing of Form 966 with the IRS. Although some courts have held that a formal plan is not a strict requirement, from the standpoint of tax planning a formal plan would be advisable.[43] The third requirement sets the time limit during which

---

[40]Regulation 1.346-1(a).

[41]Rev. Rul. 71-250, 1971-1 C.B. 112.

[42]Regulation 1.346-1(b).

[43]See *Fowler Hosiery Co., Inc., supra,* note 35.

the redemptions must be consumated. The maximum time period is two years; however, the proceeds should be distributed as soon as possible, since the use of the proceeds in other operations of the business would then require the use of Section 346(a)(2) on redemption of the stock. If there is an extended time between the contraction of the business and the redemption of some of the stock, it becomes difficult to demonstrate a casual relationship between the two events.

The third possible route to partial liquidation and the attendant tax treatment under Section 331 is to be found in provisions under Section 346(b). These provisions state that a distribution attributable to a corporation which ceases to conduct one or two or more trades or businesses shall be treated as partial liquidation if the following conditions are met:

1. The terminated trade or business must have been actively conducted for five years prior to the distribution.
2. The terminated trade or business must not have been acquired by the corporation within five years in a transaction in which a gain or loss was recognized.
3. After the distribution the corporation must be actively engaged in a trade or business.

In addition to these requirements, the adoption of a plan and a distribution soon after the termination would be advisable to assure qualification under Section 346(b).

The problems in applying the requirements of Section 346(b) in a given situation are the definitions given to terms such as "active trade or business." In this case the regulations state that the definition of active trade or business is the same as that given under Section 355(b).[44] The active business criteria given by the regulations are primarily negative in that they describe what is not an active business. Some of the activities given as not being an active business are as follows:

1. The holding of securities, land, and other property for investment purposes.
2. The ownership and operation of land or buildings all of which are used by the owner in a trade or business.
3. Activities that are part of a business operated for profit but, in and of themselves, do not produce a profit independently.

---

[44]Regulation 1.346-1(c) referring to Regulation 1.355-1(c), which defines an active business and gives fifteen examples.

Of course, these prohibitions in general might not be applicable to a Subchapter S corporation due to the limitations on passive income. However, in some cases they could have application, for there is not always a clean-cut distinction between an operation which is an active trade or business and one which is not under the tax law.[45] Also, only gains from sale of securities and rental income is considered passive.

The five-year requirement is imposed primarily to prevent tax avoidance by nonelecting corporations. Without the five-year rule, a corporation could purchase assets constituting an active trade or business and immediately distribute them to the stockholders in partial liquidation, thus removing earnings from the corporation without dividend treatment. Of course, the Subchapter S corporation can dispose of the assets and pass any capital gain through to the shareholder without regard to Section 346. However, the capital gain is not likely to be large in relation to the basis, which would not be distributed without dividend treatment unless qualified under Sections 302 or 331, assuming that all earnings and profits had not been distributed and distributions out of PTI are not possible.

Overlapping with Stock Redemptions

In any tax-planning situation involving the redemption of stock, it would certainly be advisable to consider the relative advantages and interrelationship between Section 346 and Section 302.[46] Many instances arise where either may be applicable, so it may be quite important to consider the effects of qualifying the transaction under one section or the other. The following outline gives some of the important distinctions between Sections 346 and 302 which should be considered.

Section 346	Section 302
Effect of transaction viewed at corporate level.	Effect of transaction viewed at the shareholder level.
Distribution may be pro rata.	Distribution may not be pro rata.
The attribution of ownership rules do not apply.	The attribution of ownership rules apply.
The ten-year interest rule of Section 302(b)(3) does not apply.	Redeeming shareholder may not hold an interest in the corporation for ten years under Section 302(b)(3).
The disallowance of losses between related taxpayers (Section 267) does not apply.	Section 267 applicable if individual owns more than 50 percent of stock.

---

[45]See *Howell,* 57 T.C. 546 (1972).

[46]Section 337 is not available in a partial liquidation.

In addition to considering the qualification under either Section 346 or Section 302, it is also possible to consider the application of both sections to one distribution. The Regulations provide an example of such a situation:*

> Corporation X has $50,000 attributable to the sale of one or more of its businesses which, if distributed, would qualify under Section 346(b). The corporation distributes $60,000 in redemption of stock, $20,000 of which is in redemption of all the stock of shareholder A within the terms of Section 301(b)(3). The $20,000 will be treated as a redemption under Section 302 and the remaining $40,000 would be treated as in partial liquidation under Section 346.[47]

The fact that the distribution was first allocated to the Section 302 redemption might be particularly important if a loss to the shareholder resulted from the redemption and the redeeming shareholder owned more than 50 percent of the stock. In any given situation each of the interrelationships between Sections 302 and 346 may have more or less importance. However, in tax-planning redemptions for the Subchapter S corporation, it is not only necessary to look to the interrelationships between Subchapter S and Subchapter C, but also to the planning possibilities among the various provisions of Subchapter C.

Mechanics of a Partial Liquidation

Section 336 indicates that no gain or loss is recognized to both an electing and nonelecting corporation on the distribution of property in a partial or complete liquidation, except as provided in Section 543(d) (involving installment obligations). Other exceptions to nonrecognition treatment in Section 336 include Sections 1245, 1250, 1251, and 1252 recapture and the investment credit recapture. There is, of course, more statutory amnesty under Section 336 than under Section 311 (dealing with corporate redemptions and distributions). Of course, an electing corporation may have to recognize income under the assignment-of-income doctrine and other related doctrines.[48] An electing corporation should have less of a problem with the assignment-of-income doctrine since there is only one tax, except for a possible Section 1378 tax. But an acceleration of income can cause a bunching of income at the stockholder level.

---

[47]Regulation 1.302-1(b).

[48]*Lucas* vs. *Earl,* 281 U.S. 111 (1930); *Jerome Roubik,* 53 T.C. 365 (1969); *Williamson* vs. *U.S.,* 292 F. 2d 524 (Ct. Cl. 1961).

As for the stockholders, gain or loss is computed just as if they were selling their stock. If the stockholders have purchased stock at different times, they may select the particular shares to be surrendered to the electing corporation. In order to determine the gain or loss, the number of shares deemed to have been surrendered must be calculated by the following formula:

$$\begin{array}{ll} \text{\# of Shares} & \text{Total Shares Outstanding} \\ \text{Considered} = \text{Prior to Partial} \\ \text{Redeemed} & \text{Liquidation} \end{array} \times \begin{array}{l} \underline{\text{FMV of Distribution}} \\ \text{Total FMV of Net} \\ \text{Assets on date of} \\ \text{Distribution} \end{array}$$

If the shareholders give up too few shares in relationship to the amounts distributed to them, part of the sale may be subject to dividend treatment under Section 301.[49] Conversely, if the shareholders receive *less* than the adjusted basis of the shares redeemed, there may be a deductible loss.[50]

When a gain or loss is recognized by the stockholders on the receipt of property in a partial liquidation, the property's basis is its fair market value at the time of distribution.[51] If the distribution is treated as a dividend, the usual rules under Section 301(d) are applicable. That is, since an electing corporation cannot have a corporation as a shareholder, the basis will be the fair market value on the date of distribution.

New Section 311(d)

A planning technique used by some Subchapter S corporations is to distribute appreciated property to stockholders in complete redemption of their stock. The Tax Reform Act of 1969 modified this area by requiring a Subchapter S corporation to recognize taxable income on the distribution of appreciated property if it is a redemption of less than a 10 percent stockholder.[52] The corporate gain is capital or ordinary depending upon the type of asset distributed and the period for which it was held. If there is a loss, however, it is not recognized; but the nonrecognition of a loss can be avoided if the corporation first sells the assets and then distributes the proceeds.

A Subchapter S corporation generally does not pay a tax on any

---

[49]Rev. Rul. 54-408, 1954-2 C.B. 165.

[50]But see *Higgins* vs. *Smith,* 308 U.S. 473 (1940), in the case of a one-man corporation.

[51]I.R.C. Section 334(a).

[52]I.R.C. Sections 311(d)(1) and (2)(A).

gain recognized under Section 311(d), unless a capital gain is taxed under Section 1378. Whether taxed or not, any income increases corporate taxable income that is taxed to the stockholders (whether distributed or not) or decreases any net operating loss which can be passed through. Further, there can be two taxes at the shareholder level. For example, an electing corporation has two equal stockholders, X and Y, and redeems one-half of X's stock with securities that are worth $8,000 but have a cost basis of only $2,000. Shareholder X would not only have a potential taxable gain on the redemption of his stock, but also would be taxable on one-third of the corporation's $8,000 gain (as a shareholder of record at year-end). Of course, accumulated earnings and profits are reduced at the close of the tax year to the extent that the gain is included in the gross income of the shareholders[53] (the gain previously increased earnings and profits by a like amount).

A partial liquidation can be used to avoid one of the taxes where appreciated property is used in the nonpro rata redemption of shareholders. Where a redemption qualifies as a partial liquidation, Section 336 is controlling, rather than Section 311(d). Of course, Section 336 provides that gain or loss shall not be recognized to a corporation on the distribution of property in partial or complete liquidation. Thus, since taxable income of an electing corporation would not be increased, there would be no corresponding tax to the shareholders. With the use of Section 346 it should be possible to redeem less than 10 percent of the stockholders with appreciated property without incurring a double tax. But an electing corporation should request a ruling before consumating such a transaction.

Liquidations

For any number of reasons the stockholders of a Subchapter S corporation may wish to discontinue the corporation. If such a desire occurs, the shareholders may simply surrender all of their stock shares in the corporation and receive, after all creditors are paid, their pro rata share of any remaining assets and accumulated earnings and profits. Regulations indicate that liquidation exists when a "corporation ceases to be a going concern and its activities are merely for the purpose of winding up its affairs, paying its debts, and distributing any remaining balance to its shareholders."[54] The liquidation

---

[53]I.R.C. Section 1377(a).
[54]Regulation 1.322-2(c).

rules apply to Subchapter S just as with any other corporation,[55] but the Subchapter S provisions may override the various liquidation rules.

There may be some advantages in liquidating an electing corporation. Amounts distributed in complete liquidation of a corporation are treated as full payments in exchange for the stock.[56] Thus, liquidating distributions are subject to the capital gain and loss provisions rather than ordinary income or loss. Such capital treatment applies to the entire liquidating distribution (with certain exceptions), even though part of the distributions consist of accumulated earnings and profits and "locked-in" PTI as a result of changes in the shareholders (PTI is a personal right). If these former amounts had been distributed in other than liquidation, they would be taxed as ordinary income dividends.

Where an electing corporation has allowed a large amount of PTI to accumulate within the corporation and cannot get such amounts out tax-free because of an anemic cash position, a liquidation may be the last resort. There is no reason to distribute these PTI amounts out prior to the liquidation distributions. Such PTI has already increased the stockholder's stock basis while it was UTI.[57] Any prior distribution of PTI reduces the stock basis in the hands of the shareholder,[58] and, in effect, creates an offsetting transaction. Keep in mind that, in essence, the PTI is distributed tax-free in the liquidating distribution because of the higher shareholder stock basis. In fact, a prior distribution of PTI can be harmful if there have been any changes in the stockholders, such as a result of sale, exchange, death, or gift. Since PTI is a personal right, any premature distribution of PTI would be taxable to these new shareholders; whereas the same items could have been tax-free under a liquidating distribution.

Another benefit of a liquidation is that depreciable assets may obtain a stepped-up-in-tax basis for future depreciation and sales purposes (e.g., larger depreciation deductions and smaller gain or larger loss in case of future sale or exchange). This benefit is reduced somewhat by the recapture provisions in Sections 1245, 1250, 1251, 1252, and 47. Some other benefits upon liquidation may be summarized as follows:

---

[55]Regulation 1.1372-1(c).
[56]I.R.C. Section 331(a)(1).
[57]I.R.C. Section 1376(a).
[58]Regulation 1.1375-4(a).

1. Any new corporation has the opportunity to issue preferred stock without the taint of Section 306.[59]
2. The shareholders may obtain a capital loss (ordinary loss if Section 1244 is applicable) if the basis of their stock is greater than the fair market value of all assets distributed.
3. If the Subchapter S corporation is having passive income problems and would be a personal holding company if it reverts back to regular corporate form, liquidation may be a viable route.

Section 331 Liquidation

The rules covering a straight liquidation are found in Section 331; they apply automatically if none of the other liquidation provisions are controlling. There is no disqualification of a Subchapter S election when the corporation is in the process of liquidation.[60] Of course, the Subchapter S rules are superimposed upon the liquidation provisions. In general, no gain or loss is normally recognized by the Subchapter S corporation under Section 336 upon the distribution of property to its shareholders in a complete liquidation (certain exceptions will be noted later). Instead, there is only one recognition at the stockholder level. As to the mechanics, the shareholder's gain or loss is determined by deducting the adjusted basis of this stock from the fair market value of the liquidating distributions. A capital gain or loss[61] is recognized immediately, unless Section 332 or 333 is effective.[62] The shareholders would pick up a fair market value basis in any property distributed.[63]

Of course, the regular Subchapter S rules are applicable to the corporation during the period of liquidation. Thus, any UTI will flow through and be taxed to the shareholder. For example, any operating income would flow through as ordinary income, capital gains will flow through as capital gains, etc. Furthermore, the liquidation process will accelerate certain income items which will flow through as income *and not liquidation distributions.* If UTI is distributed during the year, or as Section 1375(f) distributions, such distributions will be dividend distributions rather than liquidation distributions.

---

[59]I.R.C. Section 306(c)(2); The IRS does have weapons to fight the reincorporation bailout — D, E, and F reorganizations.

[60]*Hauptman* vs. *Commissioner,* 309 F. 2d 62 (2d Cir. 1962).

[61]Ordinary income if the collapsible provisions are applicable under Section 341.

[62]A Subchapter S corporation can make a Section 332 election.

[63]I.R.C. Section 334(a).

For example, assume a Subchapter S corporation has a single shareholder. During the year of liquidation the UTI is $4,000, and $2,000 of income items are accelerated (e.g., 1245 recapture, 453 obligations, etc.). The $6,000 is included in the shareholder's taxable income no matter what liquidating distributions are made during the year.[64] Of course, his stock basis would be increased by $6,000.[65] Only the amount distributed in excess of $6,000 would be liquidating distributions which could take advantage of the capital gain rates.

Certain items are accelerated or otherwise result in ordinary income treatment during a liquidation. These are:

1. Installment sales obligations.[66]
2. Depreciation recapture under Sections 1245 and 1250, 1251, and 1252.
3. Assignment of income doctrine (e.g., earned accounts receivable).[67]
4. Method of accounting change may be required to "clearly reflect income" under Section 446(b).
5. Investment credit recapture.[68]
6. Tax benefit rule may be applied to previously-expensed items.[69]
7. Restoration of bad debt reserves.

Under a complete liquidation, the assets are distributed to the stockholders, and they may sell these assets. Before 1954 under the so-called *Court Holding Company* doctrine,[70] the corporation itself could not plan, negotiate, or sell the assets. It is cumbersome for shareholders to have to sell the assets individually. It is obviously best for the corporation to sell them, but before 1954 this would result in a corporate tax on any gain on the sale. Further, the stockholders would have to pay a second capital gain tax on the distribution. Thus, Congress passed in 1954 Section 337 to alleviate this situation.

---

[64]I.R.C. Section 1373(a).

[65]I.R.C. Section 1376(a).

[66]I.R.C. Sections 453(d)(1) and 336.

[67]*Williamson* vs. *U.S.*, 292 F. 2d 524 (Ct. Cl. 1961).

[68]I.R.C. Section 47(a)(1); *Franklin Clayton*, 52 T.C. 911 (1969).

[69]For example, *Spitalney* vs. *U.S.*, 430 F. 2d 195 (9th Cir. 1970).

[70]*Commissioner* vs. *Court Holding Co.*, 324 U.S. 331 (1945).

Section 337 Liquidation

If a regular corporation adopts a plan of complete liquidation and, within twelve months following the adoption of the plan, distributes all assets of the corporation to the stockholders, then the corporation will not recognize any gain or loss on sales of its property during the twelve-month period. It might appear at first that a Subchapter S corporation would have no need for this liquidation provision, since the corporation generally does not recognize gains or losses at the corporate level. However, there are several circumstances where Section 337 can be a valuable tax-planning tool in the liquidation of a Subchapter S corporation. This gives the tax planner a four-way option to choose either: (1) the normal liquidation procedures without the Subchapter S election; (2) the Section 337 liquidation without Subchapter S status; (3) Subchapter S with a 331 liquidation; or (4) a combination of Subchapter S election combined with a Section 337 liquidation. Before considering the special circumstances under which each liquidation method might be selected, it is desirable to consider some of the technical aspects of qualifying under Section 337.

Section 337 is a nonelective provision; that is, if its terms are met the tax treatment is prescribed, notwithstanding the actions or intentions of the stockholders. Also, Section 337 only applies to the nonrecognition of gains or losses *at the corporate level.* If Section 337 treatment is desired for a liquidation, certain actions are required by the corporation and its shareholders to insure qualification under Section 337. The first required step is the adoption of a plan of complete liquidation. The Regulations do not prescribe what form the plan should take or what provisions it should contain. Regulation 1.337-1 only states that the plan should be "a resolution authorizing the distribution of all the assets of the corporation (other than those retained to meet claims) in redemption of all stock." As a practical matter, it would probably be advisable, in addition to the shareholders resolution, to be specific in reference to the fact that the adopted plan is intended to qualify under Section 337. The date of adoption of the plan is quite critical in that it sets the beginning of the twelve-month liquidation period and the date after which the corporation may not recognize gains or losses on sales of certain property.

A second requirement for qualification under Section 337 is that all the assets (except those held to meet known or contingent claims) must be distributed to the shareholders within twelve months of the date the plan is adopted. Regulation 1.337-2(b) states that the asset distribution requirement is deemed to be met if the only assets left in the corporation at the end of twelve months are:

1. cash equal to known liabilities and liquidating expenses, and
2. a reasonable amount of cash to meet contingent liabilities and expenses.

No other assets may be held by the corporation, and this prohibition includes amounts held to redeem any stockholder's shares in the corporation. In one court case, the court did apply a *de minimis* rule where the corporation still had five of its 3,622 shares outstanding at the end of twelve months.[71] The court ruled that Section 337 applied to the liquidation in spite of the five shares still unredeemed. The corporation had some reasonable explanation for the outstanding shares; however, the risk, in terms of the potential tax cost to a non-Subchapter S corporation, makes the holding of any extra assets a dangerous position. It would certainly be advisable to transfer any assets held to redeem stock still outstanding near the end of the twelfth month to a trustee who could handle the remaining distribution. The IRS has approved the use of a trustee in the case of an asset that was difficult to distribute; so, there is some basis for believing that the use of a trustee to hold assets for shares which might be difficult to redeem due to missing shareholders would be allowable.[72]

Certain property held by the corporation is not eligible for the nonrecognition of gain or loss provisions of Section 337. In general the term "property" in a Section 337 liquidation *does not* include the following:

1. Installment obligations acquired from the sale of inventory made either before *or* after the adoption of the plan of liquidation.
2. Installment obligations acquired from the sale of other than inventory property sold or exchanged *before* the date of adoption of the plan.
3. Inventory (other than a bulk sale to one buyer).

These exclusions are to prevent capital gain treatment to certain ordinary income items, even though other ordinary income items are accorded capital gain treatment if the provisions of Section 337 are met.

---

[71]*Mountain Water Co. of LaCrescenta,* 35 T.C. 418 (1960).
[72]Rev. Rul. 63-245, 1963-2 C.B. 144.

Having outlined some of the requirements necessary for qualification under Section 337, the next step is to consider some of the applications of Section 337 to the liquidation of a Subchapter S corporation. One of the primary instances where a Section 337 liquidation would benefit a Subchapter S corporation is a situation where the corporation may face the capital gain tax imposed by Section 1378(a). In this case a Section 337 liquidation avoids this tax at the corporate level. Retaining the Subchapter S election while qualifying a liquidation under Section 337 can also be beneficial when the corporation has a net operating loss in the year of liquidation. Maintaining the Subchapter S election allows the pass-through of the net operating loss to the shareholders, while the qualification under Section 337 will not result in any dilution of the loss due to gains on the sale of assets.

Also, where a corporation has a large amount of ordinary income assets (e.g., bulk sale of inventory),[73] a Section 337 liquidation would eliminate the tax on a sale of such assets at the corporate level and apply a capital gain tax at the shareholder level; whereas the same sale of bulk inventory would result in ordinary income treatment at the shareholder level through an increase in UTI. Of course, the Subchapter S corporation could elect Section 337 to avoid this ordinary income treatment, assuming the corporation is not collapsible.[74]

Two rules of thumb may prove helpful:

1. Where a corporation's adjusted basis for its assets is equal to or larger than its stockholder's stock basis, a Subchapter S election is more beneficial.
2. Where the stockholder's stock basis is larger than the corporation's adjusted basis of its assets, a Section 337 liquidation is more beneficial.

If the corporation liquidates under both situations, the net result will be the same. Two examples should indicate the validity of these two rules:

> Assume a corporation has assets with an adjusted basis of $1,000 and FMV of $3,000. The shareholder's adjusted basis in his stock is $1,000. If the assets are sold in a Subchapter S corporation, there would be $2,000 UTI and the shareholder would

---

[73]I.R.C. Section 337(b)(2); if the inventory is not sold in a package to one buyer, there would be an ordinary income at the Subchapter S level.

[74]Regulation 1.1372-1(c).

recognize a $2,000 capital gain. Important, however, is that the corporation retains all of the previously-mentioned advantages of being Subchapter S (e.g., does not have to liquidate, does not have a twelve-month clock, etc.). Under a regular corporate status with a valid Section 337 liquidation, there would be no tax at the corporate level and a $2,000 gain at the shareholder level.

Assume, however, that in the previous example the shareholder's adjusted basis in the corporate stock is $2,000. If the assets are sold in a Subchapter S organization, there would be $2,000 UTI taxable to the shareholder. Whereas, under a regular corporate form and a Section 337 liquidation, there would be only a $1,000 taxable gain. Keep in mind that a Section 337 liquidation is not elective; if the conditions of Section 337 are met, its application is automatic.

There are several advantages of liquidating the Subchapter S corporation without the use of Section 337. One of the most important of these advantages is that the installment method of Section 453 may be used with respect to asset sales on liquidation. To gain the benefits of installment reporting it will be necessary to keep the Subchapter S corporation in existence until all proceeds have been received. The only danger in this technique is that the interest income received on the installment obligations could possibly terminate the Subchapter S election if the total interest exceeded 20 percent of the total payments during the year. Another advantage of the Subchapter S election without the use of Section 337 in liquidation is that there is no time limit imposed on a normal Subchapter S liquidation. The absence of a time limit could be quite beneficial with respect to assets which may be difficult to sell at an expected price.

Section 333 Liquidation

Section 333 is an elective liquidation procedure which, under certain circumstances, will allow the shareholders to defer recognition of any gain (but not loss) realized on liquidation. As might be expected, the terms of the nonrecognition provisions of Section 333 are rather specialized. Basically the requirements under Section 333 are as follows:

1. That shareholders totaling at least 80 percent of the voting power elect Section 333.
2. A plan of liquidation must be adopted.
3. All of the stock must be redeemed and cancelled.
4. The complete liquidation must be completed within one calendar month.

Section 333 applies to the postponement of gains only, not to losses. Further, in certain circumstances a shareholder may have to recognize a gain. Taxable gain is the *lesser* of (a) the actual gain, or (b) the *greater* of:

1. The stockholder's share of post-February 28, 1913, accumulated earnings and profits,[75] or
2. The sum of the cash, stock, or securities (acquired by the corporation after December 31, 1953) received in the liquidation.

The gain may be taxable as dividend income *or* as capital gain. A shareholder must recognize dividend income to the extent of his share of accumulated earnings and profits (after February 28, 1913), and short-term capital gain or long-term capital gain on any balance.[76] Thus, UTI and PTI are not considered to be earnings and profits for this purpose.

This election is usually advantageous in a situation where an electing corporation holds some appreciated property and has little or no cash or earnings and profits. Where a corporation has always operated as a Subchapter S corporation, there should be little accumulated earnings and profits since they are passed to the stockholders at the end of each year (except where current earnings and profits exceed UTI). If the shareholder is required to recognize any gain on liquidation, his basis in the assets received will be increased by the amount of gain recognized.

The most unusual requirement under Section 333 is that all property (except for amounts held to meet known and contingent liabilities) must be distributed within one calendar month. Fortunately, the date the plan of liquidation is adopted does not start the one-month period running.[77] This allows the corporation time to arrange for the distribution in any calendar month it chooses. Also, the corporation may retain its charter after the complete liquidation[78] and is not required to effect a complete dissolution under state law.[79]

Except to the extent that the sale of installment obligations under Section 453(d) or provisions of Sections 1245 and 1250 apply, the corporation will not recognize any gain on the assets distributed

---

[75]This refers to earnings accumulated prior to the Subchapter S election (and not UTI or PTI) and earnings and profits in excess of UTI.

[76]I.R.C. Section 333(e).

[77]Regulation 1.333-1(b)(1).

[78]Rev. Rul. 54-518, 1954-2 C.B. 142 allows retention of a charter to protect a corporate name.

[79]Regulation 1.333-1(b)(2).

in complete liquidation under Section 333.[80] Any gain on unrecognized appreciation will be recognized by the shareholders in the event they sell the assets, since the shareholders' basis in the assets will be the same as his stock basis. The basis of the assets to the shareholders will be decreased to the extent of cash received and increased by any gain recognized at liquidation.[81]

The general rules of Section 333 are applicable to a liquidating Subchapter S corporation, except that the Subchapter S provisions take precedence over the rules of Section 333. (See these exceptions in the previous discussion on Section 331 liquidation.) However, a regular corporation anticipating a liquidation should strongly consider a Subchapter S election for several reasons. First, Section 337 cannot be used in conjunction with Section 333. Thus, a Subchapter S election can provide the corporation with Section 337-like treatment (e.g., no gain at the corporate level on the sale of assets), and the shareholders are free to elect Section 333 treatment.

Second, the *Court Holding Company* doctrine can cause a double tax in a Section 333 liquidation of a regular corporation, followed by a sale of the assets.[82] Under the *Court Holding Company* doctrine in which a regular corporation sells the corporate assets or negotiates the sale, there will be corporate taxable income unless there is Section 337 treatment. This doctrine is still applicable to liquidations under Section 331, 332, or 333, a liquidation of a collapsible electing corporation, installment obligations, and sale of inventory property. A Subchapter S election can alleviate the adverse effects of this doctrine by eliminating the corporate tax, except to the extent of Section 1378. For example, if the doctrine was applicable to an electing corporation, corporate taxable income would be increased but with no corporate tax (except under Section 1378). Even though earnings and profits are critical in a Section 333 liquidation, the imposition of this doctrine would not increase earnings and profits, since the accumulated earnings and profits as of the close of the tax year are reduced by the UTI included in the gross income of the stockholders at the end of the tax year.[83]

One final comment is appropriate. A Section 333 election is not available in a situation where the Subchapter S corporation is deemed

---

[80]I.R.C. Section 336.

[81]I.R.C. Section 334(c).

[82]*Commissioner* vs. *Court Holding Co.*, 324 U.S. 331 (1945).

[83]I.R.C. Section 1373(b).

"collapsible" under Section 341(a), unless the Section 341(e)(3) or Section 341(d)(3) exceptions are applicable.[84]

Section 332 Liquidation

The tax-free liquidation of subsidiaries under Section 332 should have little applicability to Subchapter S corporations. A requirement in Section 332(b)(1) makes this liquidation applicable to a parent corporation which owns 80 percent or more of a subsidiary. A Subchapter S election, of course, terminates under Section 1371(a) if it is a member of an affiliated group. Thus, only where a Subchapter S corporation owned 80 percent or more of one of the seven nonincludible corporations listed in Section 1504(b) would this provision be useful (e.g., DISC, etc.).

Collapsible Electing Corporations

In a normal situation, a shareholder who sells his stock in a corporation realizes a capital gain or loss measured by the difference between his basis in the stock and the price received for the stock. The same result is equally true when the stock is surrendered to the corporation in complete liquidation. It was this capital gains treatment on sale of stock or liquidation that led certain taxpayers to develop what became known as a "collapsible corporation." In a typical case, a builder might form a corporation to build an apartment complex. After the complex was completed, the corporation would be liquidated, and the builder (and possible other shareholders) would receive the apartment complex in exchange for their stock in the corporation. The shareholders would recognize a capital gain to the extent of the difference between their stock basis and the fair market value of the apartment complex, and their basis in the apartments would then be the fair market value at the date the corporation was liquidated. Thus, if the apartments were sold, little or no taxable gain would be recognized. The same tax result could have been obtained for the shareholders by simply selling their stock in the corporation. Either way, only one tax was paid, and that at capital gain rates.

Recognizing this potential for converting what would have been ordinary income into capital gain, Congress enacted what is now Section 341. The effect of Section 341 is to tax gain that is realized from the sale or exchange of stock in a collapsible corporation as

---

[84]See Rev. Rul. 63-114, 1963-1 C.B. 74; Rev. Rul. 57-491, 1957-2 C.B. 232.

ordinary income rather than as a capital gain. This ordinary income treatment of gain will apply if the corporation is deemed collapsible when:

1. The stock is sold or exchanged.
2. The stock is redeemed by the corporation.
3. There is a corporate distribution of property without sur render of stock under Section 302(c)(3)(A).[85]

Section 341(a) states that any gain realized in these transactions, to the extent that the gain would have been long-term capital gain, will be treated as a gain from the sale of a noncapital asset (ordinary income). Notice that if the disposition of stock results in a long-term capital loss, a short-term capital gain or loss, or ordinary gain or loss, Section 341 would not apply to the transaction.

Basically, a collapsible corporation is any corporation formed or availed of principally for the manufacture, production, or purchase of property with a view toward a liquidation, sale, or distribution before the corporation has realized a substantial portion of the taxable income to be derived from the property.[86] The definition is quite comprehensive and can easily be a trap for the unwary, for the meanings applied to the terms within the definition are rather broad. An examination of the meanings attached by the IRS is therefore necessary in order to understand the full impact of Section 341.

The first part of the definition would cover most electing corporations. That is, most corporations are "formed or availed of principally for the manufacture, production, or purchase of property." However, Section 341 gives these terms their strictest meanings.[87] For example, an electing corporation that owned some unimproved land contracted to have improvements made and deposited funds in escrow to insure completion of the improvements. These acts were held to be construction under Section 341.[88] The meaning attached to the completion of manufacture, production, or purchase is equally broad and extends as long as any activity continues which might increase the value of the property. The ending date of manufacture, production, or purchase is quite important, since an exception is provided under Section 341 that the property is no longer considered

---

[85]Since a partial liquidation does not include a distribution in redemption, such a transaction apparently escapes collapsible treatment.

[86]I.R.C. Section 341(b)(1).

[87]I.R.C. Section 341(b)(2)(A) provides that engaging in these activities "to any extent" is sufficient.

[88]*Abbott,* 2 A.F.T.R. 2d 5232 (1961), *aff'g.,* 28 T.C. 795 (1957).

collapsible property three years beyond the completion of manufacture, of production, or of the purchase of the property.[89]

The next important aspect is the "view toward liquidation." The view is usually the most critical issue in determining whether a corporation is or is not collapsible. The Regulations provide an equally comprehensive meaning for the view, in that this view may exist if sale or liquidation before most of the income is realized "was contemplated, unconditionally, conditionally, or as a recognized possibility."[90] Potentially, this definition could apply to most stockholders, since most of them know that they might sell their stock or liquidate the corporation for some price. In actual practice, the definition of the view as a "recognized possibility" is not so broad, unless the stockholders make a practice of using a corporation as a tax-avoidance scheme.

Another difficult aspect of the definition of a collapsible corporation is the meaning of "substantial." An electing corporation is not considered collapsible if it has realized a substantial amount of the income to be derived from the property.[91] The first problem presented is the difficulty of measuring the total expected income to be derived from the property, and the second problem is the determination of what constitutes a substantial amount of that total income. Normally, the total income figure has to be an estimate, which is subject to question or compromise. Some courts have held that the realization of one-third of the potential income is substantial.[92] But, other courts have held that the corporation is still collapsible if there remains a substantial portion of unrealized income attributable to the property.[93] The IRS recently accepted the more favorable one-third formula in the *Kelly* decision.[94] The Tax Court had previously held that realization of 23 percent of taxable income by a corporation was substantial.[95] Since the IRS has announced its acquiescence to this decision, 33-1/3 percent may not be the lowest point at which the Service would concede that there has been a substantial realization.

---

[89]I.R.C. Section 341(d)(3).

[90]Regulation 1.341-2(a)(2).

[91]I.R.C. Section 341(b)(1)(A).

[92]*Commissioner* vs. *Kelly,* 8 A.F.T.R. 2d 5232 (1961).

[93]*Abbott* vs. *Commissioner,* 2 A.F.T.R. 2d 5479 (1958), *aff'g.* 28 T.C. 795 (1957).

[94]Rev. Rul. 72-48, 1972-1 C.B. 102.

[95]*E. J. Zongker,* 39 T.C. 1046 (1963), *acq.* 1972-1 C.B. 2.

In addition to defining a collapsible corporation and the attendant tax consequences, Section 341(c) contains a clause giving percentage tests that can be used to support a presumption of collapsibility. The criteria are:

1. Is the fair market value of the Section 341 (collapsible assets) 50 percent or more of the fair market value of the total assets?
2. Is the fair market value of the Section 341 assets 120 percent or more of the adjusted basis of those Section 341 assets?

This presumption of collapsibility is rebuttable, but the burden is initially on the taxpayer to prove that the corporation is not collapsible by showing that the definition under Section 341(a) does not apply or that one of the exceptions of Sections 341(d), (e), or (f) does apply. These exceptions will be discussed in terms of how they might apply to a Subchapter S corporation in a tax-planning situation.

There is no doubt that the collapsible corporation provisions of Section 341 do apply to the Subchapter S corporation, since the Regulations specifically point out that fact:

Section 341, relating to collapsible corporations may apply to gain on the sale or exchange of, or a distribution which is in exchange for, stock in an electing small business corporation.[96]

However, even though Section 341 does apply to the Subchapter S corporation, the tax effects of collapsible status are much less severe for the Subchapter S corporation than for the regular corporation. Unless the particular Subchapter S corporation is subject to a capital gain tax at the corporate level under Section 1378(a), the only real effect collapsible status will have is to restrict certain options on sale of stock, redemptions, or liquidations otherwise available to the corporation and shareholders.

Normally the character of the gain is determined by reference to the nature of the asset at the corporate level. However, the Regulations contain an exception to cases where a "substantial" shareholder is a dealer in the property held by the corporation.[97] In this event, the gain at the corporate level will be of the same character as it would have been in the hands of the "substantial" shareholder. Of course, it is possible for a dealer in real estate to also be an investor in real estate, but, in a collapsible corporation situation, a holding that the dealer is an investor would be rather unlikely.

---

[96]Regulation 1.1372-1(c)(8).
[97]Regulation 1.1375-1(d).

The fact that a Subchapter S corporation is deemed to be collapsible does drastically reduce the options available to the shareholders as to sale or redemption of their stock, distributions, or liquidation of the corporation without adverse tax consequences (i.e., ordinary income treatment). Under Section 341(a) any of these transactions result in ordinary income treatment of any gain, unless one of the exceptions under Section 341(d), (e), or (f) apply. Additionally, the corporation may not normally be eligible for a liquidation under Section 337[98] or elect a liquidation under Section 333 for nonrecognition of the shareholder's gain.[99] Although the nonavailability of Sections 337 and 333 would not, in the usual case, be a serious concern to the Subchapter S corporation, there might be some cases where their use would be desirable.

Section 341(e)(4) provides some limited relief to the use of Section 337 for the liquidation of a collapsible corporation. Section 337 may be used if:

1. At all times following the adoption of the plan of complete liquidation, the net unrealized appreciation of the "subsection e" (ordinary income) assets does not exceed 15 percent of the total net worth.
2. Substantially all of the corporation's property is sold within twelve months.
3. The corporation does not distribute any depreciable property.

If the corporation can meet the first test (less than 15 percent appreciation in "subsection e" assets), it may qualify to have its shareholders elect a Section 333 liquidation. The other requirement to qualification under Section 333 is a rather strict shareholder reference test.[100] This test expands the classification of "subsection e" assets to include assets held by the corporation that would be ordinary income assets in the hands of a more-than-5-percent stockholder of the corporation.

Another potential escape route for the shareholders of a collapsible Subchapter S corporation lies in Section 341(f). Basically, this provision allows the shareholder to sell his stock and realize a capital gain if the corporation signs a consent to be taxed on any gain which would otherwise be nontaxable if the property were sold or exchanged. The property to which the consent applied (called subsec-

---

[98]I.R.C. Section 337(c)(1)(A).

[99]I.R.C. Section 333(a).

[100]Regulation 1.341-6(f).

tion f assets) generally covers real estate and noncapital assets. In the event a Subchapter S corporation signed such a consent, the recognition of gain would still apply at the shareholder level, rather than at the corporate level, in keeping with the normal Subchapter S procedure. The consent under Section 341(f) might be a viable solution if the corporation were subject to the capital gain tax under Section 1378(a). However, the development of such a situation would be unusual.

If the Subchapter S corporation can maintain its election and avoid the capital gain tax of Section 1378(a), the collapsible corporation situation does not, as a practical matter, present a major tax problem. However, a tax advisor should not underestimate the seriousness of the tax consequences of an electing corporation also being a collapsible corporation. For example, a shareholder who sells his stock in a collapsible Subchapter S corporation may be surprised to discover that he has ordinary income upon a subsequent audit where the corporation failed to file a consent under Section 341(f). Also, there may be an impact on subsequent shareholders. For example, if a consent is filed at the time shareholder A sells his stock to shareholder B, then shareholder B may be subsequently affected by the requirement that the corporation take into taxable income any gain on the later sale of the property (which would otherwise have been a nontaxable gain).

Summary

A summarization of the liquidation and collapsible sections should be helpful:

1. Elective Section 332 liquidation has little applicability to electing corporations.

2. An elective Section 333 liquidation (one-month) applies only to nonrecognition of gain at the stockholder level.

3. A collapsible electing corporation cannot elect Section 333 unless the exceptions in Section 341(e)(3) or Section 341(d)(3) are applicable.

4. A regular liquidation under Section 331 is applicable to an electing corporation.

5. There is no exception in Section 341(e) for a regular liquidation under Section 331 in case of a collapsible electing corporation. Thus, capital gain could be converted into ordinary income.

6. Nonelecting Section 337 liquidation (twelve-month) applies to the nonrecognition of either gain or loss at the corporation level.

7. The installment method cannot be used with the Section 337 liquidation.

8. Sections 333 and 337 cannot be used together.[101]

9. A collapsible electing corporation cannot use Section 337 unless the exception in Section 341(e)(4) is applicable.

10. The *Court Holding Company* doctrine may still be applicable to a regular liquidation under Section 331, a Section 332 or 333 liquidation, liquidation of collapsible electing corporation, installment obligations, and sale of inventory property. But a Subchapter S election can be used to avoid the corporate tax on any gain.

11. Section 337 cannot be used where there is a Section 332 liquidation plus a Section 334(b)(1) basis.[102]

---

[101]Rev. Rul. 69-172, 1969-1 C.B. 99.
[102]*Ibid.*

Chapter 12

A Comparison of Organizational Forms

One of the first major problems of a business organization is the choosing of a legal form under which it shall operate. There are three major possibilities: sole proprietorship, partnership, or corporation. Further, the tax laws permit certain corporations to operate as a hybrid, having characteristics of both the corporation and partnership. This chapter points out the differences and similarities among these four operational forms. Emphasis is placed upon what organizational form is best under various circumstances. This chapter concludes with a checklist of the advantages and disadvantages of the Subchapter S corporation.

Preview

Before comparing these various organizational alternatives, a short preview of each alternative is desirable.

Sole Proprietorship

A sole proprietorship is an unincorporated organization owned by a single individual. Relative to absolute number, the proprietorship is the most popular form, but, in terms of total assets or net income, the corporation is more significant. The proprietorship is not a tax-paying entity. Any income of the business is reported by the proprietor on his personal tax return (Form 1040). The proprietorship is a conduit through which income or losses flow directly to the owner. Thus, the income of a proprietorship is subject to the progressive personal tax rates. (Rates have generally ranged from 14 to 70 percent since 1965; there was a maximum tax of 60 percent in 1971 and 50 percent in years thereafter on certain earned income.)

Partnership

A partnership is an association of two or more competent parties which operate as co-owners in a business for the ultimate realization of a profit. The partnership form is often employed by smaller businesses and by those in the medical, legal, and accounting professions. A partnership is also not a tax-paying entity. Its income is reported by the partners on their personal tax returns, whether or not the income is actually distributed. Under the "conduit principle," income or losses flow directly to the partners' personal tax returns and are subject to progressive tax rates.

Corporation

As has been mentioned, a corporation is conveniently defined as "an artificial being, invisible, intangible and existing only in contemplation of law."[1] This definition emphasizes the concept that the legal entity has an independent existence, distinct and separate from its officers and shareholders. However, a second concept often expressed is that the corporate entity is merely an association of parties united for a mutual purpose and allowed by law to use a common name. This latter concept is evidenced by such phrases as "disregarding the corporate entity" or "piercing the corporate veil" in the legal literature as well as in judicial decisions.

A regular corporation is subject to a normal tax of 22 percent on all taxable income and a surtax of 26 percent on taxable income over $25,000. Taxable income of a corporation is computed in much the same manner as is normal accounting income. When the after-tax income is passed to the stockholders as dividend distributions, it is taxed again at the individual's personal tax rate. There is an 85 percent dividend exclusion available to stockholders who are corporations.

Subchapter S Corporation

Suffice it to say that this special creature is still in many respects a corporation; the major exception being that the earnings of the entity are passed through the corporate form in a way similar to the conduit nature of a partnership.

Choice of Operating Entity

One important decision of an enterprise is the choice of the form of organization under which it plans to operate. The following broad generalization is a helpful starting point: Tax considerations aside, a corporation is probably the best organizational form. With this in mind, the proprietorship and partnership are compared with the corporation and Subchapter S corporation in the next two sections.

Non-Tax Advantages of Incorporation

A list of the non-tax advantages of the corporation or the Sub-

---

[1] *Dartmouth College* vs. *Woodward*, 17 U.S. (4 Wheat), 518 5 L.Ed. 629 (1819).

chapter S corporation over the partnership and sole proprietorship appears below:

1. Creditors can get to personal property of partners and proprietors whereas a corporate stockholder's liability is normally limited to the par value of the stocks issued to him.
2. Shares of stock are normally easier to sell or transfer than interest in a partnership or proprietorship.
3. The existence of a corporate-type organization is not interrupted by the death or withdrawal of an owner.
4. The possible number of shareholders is generally unlimited;[2] whereas there is a practical ceiling on the number of partners. However, there are some fairly large partnerships (i.e., certain accounting firms).
5. Major employees may own stock in their corporation, but there may be good reasons for not admitting these same individuals as partners.
6. Corporations may issue different classes of stock (voting, nonvoting, etc.).[3]

Unfortunately, there are some disadvantages in the corporate form, such as state supervision, extra organization costs, and lack of ease of formation. For purpose of comparison, Exhibit 12-1 summarizes these nontax attributes. Note that these statements are generalities and not absolutes.

Tax Advantages of Incorporation

Although the major disadvantage of the corporation is the double taxation of profits, there are some tax advantages of the corporate-type organization over the unincorporated enterprise. Some major advantages are summarized as follows:

1. When the shareholders liquidate a corporation, they obtain capital gains treatment (if the corporation is not a collapsible corporation). However, any gains in inventory assets, or unrealized receivables are ordinary income to partners and proprietors.
2. Fringe benefits (such as qualified pension plans, profit-sharing plans, or stock bonus benefits) are a major tax advantage of

---

[2]Subchapter S corporations are limited to ten stockholders.

[3]Subchapter S corporations are limited to one class of outstanding stock.

EXHIBIT 12-1

Nontax Attributes of Business Organization

	Proprietorship	Partnership	Subchapter S Corporation	Corporation
1. Ease of formation	simple	simple	complicated	complicated
2. Cost of formation	inexpensive	inexpensive	expensive	expensive
3. Owners' liability to creditors	unlimited	unlimited	limited (usually)	limited
4. Ease of acquisition of capital	difficult	less difficult	less difficult	least difficult
5. Ease of transferability of ownership of interest	awkward	awkward	less awkward	easy
6. Amount of governmental supervision	nominal	nominal	great deal	great deal
7. Longevity	limited life	limited life	uncertain life	indefinite life

shareholder-employee relationships. If a person is an owner in a partnership, then he can no longer be classified as an employee and draw a deductible salary (except certain guaranteed payments). Further, a partner's contributions to qualified pension and profit-sharing plans are limited.

3. It is easier to split income among the members of a family (with gifts of stock) when operating as an incorporated business.

4. If a stockholder is in a high tax bracket, he may wish to accumulate the profits in the corporation (to a certain extent).[4] When he dies, his heirs will obtain a "stepped-up" basis, and any accumulated earnings escape the income tax.

5. There is a 48 percent ceiling on the regular corporate tax rate versus the higher ceiling for unincorporated businesses as well as for Subchapter S corporations (not considering any surcharge or minimum tax on certain preference items).

For comparison purposes, the above tax attributes (as well as others) are summarized in Exhibit 12-2.

Advantages and Disadvantages of Subchapter S

A Subchapter S election generally offers overall tax savings in many situations, but along with the election come numerous dangers and disadvantages that must not be overlooked. The election is not a step to be undertaken haphazardly, and the taxpayer that contemplates the election must realize that the return to the corporate form of taxation may well be impossible without substantial tax cost. However, the election is too useful a tool to discard because of the complications that may arise, for the dangers may be reduced by a proper understanding of the numerous pitfalls.

There is no general formula or rule that can be used to decide when a Subchapter S election should be utilized. Each business must be given individual attention, and this special election should be made only after giving judicious consideration to the advantages and disadvantages viewed from the perspective of the circumstances surrounding the particular business and its owners. There are, however, some common situations where the election may be advisable.

---

[4]Unlimited accumulations are penalized either by the accumulated earnings tax or by the personal holding company tax.

EXHIBIT 12-2

Major Tax Attributes of Business Organizations

	Proprietorship	Partnership	Subchapter S Corporation	Corporation
1. Incident of tax	progressive rate, single tax	progressive rate, single tax	progressive rate, single tax	double taxation progressive rate, flat rate
2. Liquidation	ordinary income for inventory and receivables	ordinary income for inventory and receivables	same as partnership	capital gains for inventory and receivables[4]
3. Fringe benefits	not deductible[1]	not deductible[1]	deductible	deductible
4. Maximum tax rate	70 percent[2]	70 percent[2]	70 percent[2]	48 percent + individual rate
5. Splitting of income among family members	difficult	difficult	easy[3]	easy
6. Accumulation of earnings in entity	impossible	impossible	possible, but dangerous	allowable to a certain extent
7. Gross income	Computed the same as per individual. Retains source characteristics		lose all source characteristics except for certain capital gains and net operating losses	lose all source characteristics
8. Dividend received exclusion	allowable	allowable	not allowed	allowable

EXHIBIT 12-2 (Continued)

	Proprietorship	Partnership	Subchapter S Corporation	Corporation
9. Capital gains	passes through to proprietor, and taxable at close of year	passed through to partner, and taxable at close of year	passed through to shareholder and taxable at close of year (unless allocable to a dividend distribution)[5]	taxed at corporate level and again when distributed[6]
10. Capital losses	passes through to proprietor	passes through to partner — unlimited carryover.	deductible only to the extent of capital gains — 5 years carryforward	same as Subchapter S; but also a 3 years carryback
11. Net Section 1231 gain	passed through to proprietor and taxable at close of year	passed through to partner	treated as a long-term capital gain at corporate level	treated as a long-term capital gain at corporate level
12. Net Section 1231 loss	passed through to proprietor, and deductible at the close of the year	passed through to partner	treated as an ordinary loss at the corporate level	treated as ordinary loss at corporate level
13. Charitable contributions	passed through to proprietor 20 percent — 30 percent — 50 percent limit	passed through to partner 20 percent — 30 percent — 50 percent limit	deductible, subject to 5 percent limit / 5 percent limit	same as Subchapter S
14. Bonus depreciation	passed through to proprietor and subject to his limitation	passed through to partner and subject to his limitation — apply to each partner separately	deductible, but subject to corporate limitation	same as Subchapter S
15. Soil and water conservation expenses	passed through to proprietor	passed through to partner	deduction taken at corporate level — no pass through	Same as Subchapter S

EXHIBIT 12-2 (Continued)

	Proprietorship	Partnership	Subchapter S Corporation	Corporation
16. Exploration expenses	passed through and subject to $100,000 annual and $400,000 overall limitation[6]	passed through and each partner has a $100,000 annual and $400,000 overall limitation[6]	No pass through and $100,000 annual and $400,000 overall limitation apply at corporate level, regardless of number of shareholders[6]	same as Sub-chapter S
17. Organization costs	cannot amortize	cannot amortize	may elect to amortize	same as Sub-chapter S
18. Recaptured depreciation	passed through	computed at partner-ship level — increases ordinary income	computed at corporate level — increases ordinary income	same as Sub-chapter S
19. Net operating loss	passed through — offset against other income	passed through — offset against other income	passed through to persons who were shareholders at any time during the year — limited to shareholder's basis	not passed through — carried back 3 years or forward 5 years
20. Choice of fiscal year	may make selection of year (at time of first return) without re-striction	free selection not allowed — fiscal year of partnership must coin-cide with principal partners' year	free selection allowed at time first return filed without restriction	same as Sub-chapter S
21. Timing of taxation	all earnings taxed at close of year	all earnings (including salary, interest, etc.) taxed at close of year	salary, dividends, and interest taxed at time paid — UTI taxed at close of year	corporate tax at end of year — sec-ond tax in year, dividends, interest, etc., paid to owners

EXHIBIT 12-2 (Continued)

	Proprietorship	Partnership	Subchapter S Corporation	Corporation
22. Foreign tax credit	passed through	passed through	lost	available at corporate level
23. Investment credit	passed through	passed through	passed through to shareholders on last day of the year	available at corporate level

---

[1] Partners and proprietors may qualify as self-employed individuals under Section 404(a)(8), in order to participate in an H.R. 10 plan. However, proprietors and partners may never be employees of their business. But guaranteed payments to a partner for services performed may be deductible by a partnership.

[2] A proprietor or partner (of a business where capital is a material factor) is allowed to include a reasonable salary (not to exceed 30 percent of his share of the profits) in earned income, which is subject to a 60 percent maximum tax in 1971 and 50 percent in years thereafter. However, a stockholder's share of Subchapter S income is not earned for purposes of the maximum tax rate.

[3] But see *Bierne*, 52 T.C. 210 (1969).

[4] This assumes no special provisions apply, such as Sections 333 or 337.

[5] Capital gains may be taxed under Section 1378 at both the corporate and individual levels. Further, such a gain may be considered a preference item under Section 58(d) at both the corporate and shareholder levels.

[6] These limitations are *not* applicable in years after 1969. Now all such expenses are subject to recapture.

Advantages

The average small businessman and the family business may find it beneficial to make a Subchapter S election. Up until 1958 these small businesses had to choose between limited liability and limited taxation. Now, an election can protect a family, as well as the businessman, from creditors, and they will still remain subject to just a single tax at the stockholder's level. Thus, corporations owned by a small group of shareholders whose tax brackets are lower than that of the corporation and who desire the distribution of all available income may benefit from a Subchapter S election. Even shareholders with higher tax brackets can obtain advantages from the election, since there is only one tax involved in getting earnings to the owners. Further, the stockholders may average their income in order to spread a high income year over a longer period of time. Likewise, as discussed in Chapter 4, professional persons may wish to incorporate and make the Subchapter S election.

Infancy Period

Frequently a newly formed corporation has net operating losses during its early life. If some of the stockholders have substantial outside income, they may wish to make an election and reduce their personal income tax by using any net operating losses to offset their outside income. Such an election should attract equity capital to a new corporation anticipating start-up losses, for an investor in a high tax bracket may recoup much of his investment in the form of tax deductions. However, net operating losses can be deducted only to the extent of the shareholder's stock and debt bases.

Conversely, a business that survives its infancy period may need additional capital in high-risk situations. Such an election provides an attractive opportunity for investors to obtain ordinary losses in the event of an unsuccessful corporation. Prior to 1958 there was little incentive to invest in a new corporation because if the business was not successful, the investor was usually permitted only a capital loss. Now, however, if an electing corporation has a net operating loss for a tax year, the loss is deductible by the stockholders in the same year that it is incurred at the corporate level and in proportion to their shareholdings.[5] Again, NOLs are deductible only to the extent of an amount equal to the cost basis of each shareholder's stock plus loans or advances by him to the corporation.[6]

---

[5]I.R.C. Section 1374(b).

[6]I.R.C. Section 1374(c)(2).

Avoidance of Penalty Taxes

The Subchapter S election is a useful tool to mitigate the impact of the extra tax on an unreasonable accumulation of earnings. This penalty tax is applied if a corporation is formed or availed of for the purpose of preventing the imposition of the income tax upon its shareholders or the shareholders of any other corporation, through the medium of permitting earnings or profits to accumulate instead of being divided or distributed.[7] If a corporation is forced to make substantial distributions to the stockholders to avoid this penalty tax, the Subchapter S election may be an advisable refuge.

Similarly, a corporation can avoid the onerous 70 percent personal holding company tax by electing Subchapter S status, but only if the election is made before the corporation is classified as a PHC. The purpose of the PHC tax is to prevent high tax bracket individuals from sheltering certain passive types of income in corporations they own and control. A Subchapter S election may provide a relief valve from this punitive tax, even though Subchapter S also has a passive income limitation. For example, income from rents where substantial services are rendered or income from personal service contracts may be PHC income but is not passive income for the purpose of terminating a Subchapter S election. Refer to Chapter 8 for a discussion of the differences between the two passive income limitations.

Where a regular corporation has been taxed by the accumulated earnings or personal holding company penalty taxes and switches to Subchapter S status, there may be an overlapping of distributions. For example, assume Dlar, Inc. was a regular corporation for 1973 and prior years. In 1974 the corporation elects Subchapter S status and makes a $10,000 dividend distribution on March 5, 1974. During 1973, Dlar was subject to the accumulated earnings tax. May the March 5, 1974, distribution of $10,000 be used both in determining accumulated taxable income for 1973 (under Section 535) and in determining UTI for 1974 (under Section 1373(c))? Revenue Ruling 72-152[8] answers this question in the affirmative. This above position is also applicable if the corporation was a personal holding company in 1973.

Unsubstantiated Expenses and Unreasonable Compensation

Some commentators initially felt that an election would avoid

---

[7] I.R.C. Section 532(a).

[8] Rev. Rul. 72-152, 1972-1 C.B. 272.

the penalty aspects of unsubstantiated expenses, since the disallowance of expense deductions would not result in a double tax but only a single tax on the shareholder receiving the distribution. However, several court cases now indicate that a corporation must prove both that expenditures are made and they are proximately related to the business.

In one case the Tax Court partially disallowed travel, entertainment, boat maintenance, automobile depreciation, office, and other miscellaneous expenses since the taxpayer failed to carry his burden of proof. The stockholders realized additional income from the electing corporation because of the disallowed corporate deductions.[9] In another case, the Tax Court disallowed claimed deductions under I.R.C. Section 404(a)(5) for payments to a widow of a deceased employee of the Subchapter S corporation. "Payments made under such an agreement are clearly not ordinary and necessary expenses of the corporation, and are not deductible as such."[10] The disallowed deductions increased the UTI of the corporation and the shareholders' individual incomes were correspondingly increased by the amount of the disallowed deductions.[11]

Similarly, a Subchapter S election may permit a corporation to lessen the penalty aspects of salaries classified as unreasonable compensation. In one early case, a court asserted that the reasonableness of salaries is not a problem of Subchapter S corporation. "This subchapter permits small business corporations, who qualify, to elect to be taxed, in effect, as partnerships. Under such an election the reasonableness of salaries paid to stockholders is not an issue."[12] However, the area of reasonableness of compensation has not been settled.

If the normal rule for disallowed excessive compensation (as well as disallowed expenses) is followed by the courts, there will be no problems. Under Regulation 1.162-7(b)(1), a disallowed deduction for unreasonable compensation is treated as a dividend distribution from current earnings and profits. Thus, the disallowed deductions

---

[9] *Theodore T. Benson,* T.C.M. 1967-74; See also *William duPont, Jr.,* 234 F. Supp. 681 (D.C. Del. 1964); *Jack Haber,* 52 T.C. 255 (1969); *August F. Nielsen Co.,* T.C.M. 1968-11.

[10] *Donald J. Wallace,* T.C.M. 1967-11.

[11] *Ibid.* The IRS did not bring up the possible issue that a gift had been made from the stockholders to the widow. See Regulation 25.2511-1(h), example 1.

[12] *Weaver Airline Personnel School, Inc.* vs. *Bookwalter,* 218 F. Supp. 599 (W.D. Mo. 1963); but see *Jack Haber, supra,* note 9.

would not increase the final amount of UTI, since UTI is defined as taxable income minus the sum of (1) the amount of money distributed as dividends, and (2) the capital gains penalty tax.[13] The Tax Court has on at least two occasions held that excessive compensation to stockholders of nonelecting corporations should be treated as a dividend.[14]

However, if the unreasonable compensation (or disallowed expenses) is not treated as a cash dividend, any disallowed amounts would not reduce the UTI. The net effect would be a double tax. The disallowed salary would be taxed once as income to the recipient and a second time as a constructive dividend of UTI to all of the stockholders.

Section 1377(b) states that "the earnings and profits of an electing small business corporation for any taxable year . . . shall not be reduced by any amount which is not allowable as a deduction in computing its taxable income . . ." Further, the Senate Finance Committee Report notes that Section 1377(b) is "necessary in order that a corporation may not decrease its current earnings and profits by expenditures and losses which do not qualify as deductions for federal tax purposes and, thereby, defeat the general purpose of taxing the corporation's taxable income as dividends to the shareholders."[15] Therefore, practitioners should keep a watchful eye on this particular area to see how the courts will react to this question. Readers should refer to the section on "Employee Relationship" in this Chapter.

Before the passage of the 50 percent maximum tax in the Tax Reform Act of 1969, it was immaterial whether payments made to stockholder-employees were labeled "dividend" or "salary." Now, with the 50 percent ceiling rate on earned income, it may be beneficial that the largest possible salary be paid to the stockholder where such salary falls into brackets above 50 percent. Such a procedure will permit the greatest benefit from the maximum tax, since UTI, dividend, and PTI distributions do not qualify as earned income. Thus, with the caveat in the previous paragraph in mind, Subchapter S corporations in many situations should try to maximize their salary payments.

---

[13]I.R.C. Section 1373(c).

[14]*Challenge Manufacturing Co.,* 37 T.C. 650 (1962); *W. T. Wilson,* 10 T.C. 251 (1948).

[15]*Report of the Committee on Finance,* Senate Report No. 1983, 85th Congress, 2d Session (Washington: United States Government Printing Office, 1958).

Salary payments should be clearly documented, for any post mortem attempt to classify previously unidentified distributions as salary may fail. For example, one electing corporation paid out all income as dividends even though its shareholder-employees rendered valuable services to the corporation. When the corporation later discovered that the election had terminated several years earlier, it was unsuccessful in claiming that part of the distributions were, in fact, compensation.[16] This area is an example of how, as statutes and case law develop and change, the pendulum (representing the litigation position of the taxpayer and the IRS) swings in one direction and then in the reverse direction. The pendulum may now be reversing its direction.

Differing Taxable Years

An election gives a business an opportunity to choose a tax year that is different from those of its shareholders. The taxpayer can choose a tax year that conforms more closely to the needs of the corporation, or one which produces tax holidays and tax deferment to the owners. This differing tax year is advantageous in that it may allow deferment of income taxes and more control over income between years. The UTI of an electing corporation is included in the stockholder's personal return for his tax year in which, or with which, the tax year of the corporation ends.[17] Therefore, the shareholders may defer the tax on eleven months of income for as long as twelve months; they will have an interest-free loan from the Treasury. For example, if the corporation's tax year ends on January 31, 1975, and the stockholder's year ends on December 31, 1974, the stockholder would not report his share of the corporation's undistributed taxable income for the year ending January 31, 1975, until he filed his personal return in 1976 for the calendar year of 1975.

Revenue Procedure 72-51, 1972-2 C.B. 832 indicates the procedure for a requested change in accounting period by an electing corporation. An existing Subchapter S corporation may not change its taxable year without securing *prior* approval from the Commissioner, unless all of its principal shareholders have the same taxable year to which the corporation changes, or unless all of its principal stockholders concurrently change to such tax year. In order to secure prior approval, the electing corporation must establish a business purpose to the satisfaction of the Commissioner. The

---

[16]*Paula Construction Co.,* 58 T.C. 102 (1972).

[17]Regulation 1.1373-1(a)(1).

IRS will generally approve a change if the deferral of income to the stockholders is three months or less. Even when such a change is allowed, the electing corporation must agree to the adjustments as described in this Revenue Procedure.

Section 337 Liquidation

As stated in Chapter 2, the Treasury had to retract the Proposed Regulations that would have disqualified a corporation in the process of liquidation from electing to be taxed under Subchapter S. Hence, the Subchapter S corporation may circumvent the stringent qualifying rules for I.R.C. Section 337 and allow a single capital gain to its stockholders. The IRS may attack such a move, but presumably, there are no statutory provisions that will disqualify a liquidating corporation from making a Subchapter S election.[18]

In fact, it may be well advised for a corporation to elect to be treated as a Subchapter S corporation and then to liquidate. A closely-held corporation which sells its assets and liquidates will generally rely on I.R.C. Section 337 (under which corporate assets can be sold without recognition of gains if the corporation has adopted a plan of complete liquidation). An important point, however, is that under I.R.C. Section 337 all assets except those reserved to meet claims must be distributed within twelve months after adopting the plan. Should the liquidation take more than a year, a Subchapter S election will eliminate the tax on the capital gains at the corporate level and impute the gains to the shareholders. Also, these exceptions to the I.R.C. Section 337 liquidation make it unattractive:

1. Investment credit recapture.
2. Depreciation recapture under I.R.C. Sections 1245 and 1250.
3. Cash basis receivables must be included in income.
4. Recapture of bad debt reserve.
5. Assignment of income concept.[19]

Even if the liquidation can be completed within twelve months, it may be advantageous to forego I.R.C. Section 337 if an election can be made. If a liquidating corporation sells its assets under I.R.C. Section 337 on the installment sale basis, the fair market value of the installment notes received and distributed less the basis of the

---

[18]See *Hauptman* vs. *Commissioner,* 309 F. 2d 62 (2d Cir. 1962). *cert. denied,* 372 U.S. 909 (1963); *Nova-Plas Mfg. Co., Inc.,* 8 A.F.T.R. 2d 5188 (D.C. N.Y. 1961).

[19]*Commissioner* vs. *Kuckenberg,* 309 F. 2d 202 (9th Cir. 1962).

stock received in exchange will be taxed to the shareholders in the year of liquidation. A sale could be made by an electing corporation, and the installment payments received and passed through to the shareholders as a capital gain could be spread over several years instead of pushed into one year because the unrecognized corporate gain will not be taxable to the stockholders until the liquidation distributions are made.[20] Furthermore, under a single year election of Subchapter S, a corporation can get most of the advantages of Section 337, and the corporation does not have to liquidate.

There are, of course, some situations where the Section 337 liquidation may be preferable to a Subchapter S election. For example, when a corporation has a large amount of ordinary income assets (e.g., bulk sale of inventory),[21] a Section 337 liquidation would eliminate the tax on a sale of such assets at the corporate level with a capital gain tax at the shareholder level. Whereas the same sale of bulk inventory would result in ordinary treatment at the shareholder level through an increase in UTI. Of course, the Subchapter S corporation could elect Section 337 to avoid this ordinary income treatment, assuming the corporation is not collapsible.[22]

Two rules of thumb may be helpful:

1. Where a corporation's adjusted basis for its assets is equal to or larger than its stockholder's stock basis, a Subchapter S election is more beneficial.
2. Where the stockholder's stock basis is larger than the corporation's adjusted basis of its assets, a Section 337 liquidation is more beneficial.

If the corporation liquidates under both situations, the net result will be the same. Two examples should indicate the validity of these two rules.

Assume a corporation has assets with an adjusted basis of $1,000 and FMV of $3,000. The shareholder's adjusted basis in his stock is $1,000. If the assets are sold in a Subchapter S corporation, there would be $2,000 UTI, and the shareholder would recognize a $2,000 capital gain. Important, however, is that the corporation retains all

---

[20]George P. Brickford, "Special Liquidations Other Than Under Section 337," *Western Reserve Law Review,* Vol. 13 (March, 1962), p. 270; Robert C. Odmark, "A Practitioner's Guide to Subchapter S Planning Opportunities and Pitfalls," *Journal of Taxation,* Vol. 30 (June, 1969), p. 364.

[21]I.R.C. Section 337(b)(2); If the inventory is not sold in a package to one buyer, there would be an ordinary income at the Subchapter S level.

[22]Regulation 1.1372-1(c).

of the previously mentioned advantages of being Subchapter S (e.g., does not have to liquidate, does not have a twelve-month clock, etc.). Under a regular corporate status with a valid Section 337 liquidation, there would be no tax at the corporate level and a $2,000 gain at the shareholder level.

Assume, however, that the shareholder's adjusted basis in the corporate stock is $2,000 in the previous example. If the assets are sold in a Subchapter S organization, there would be $2,000 UTI taxable to the shareholder. Whereas, under a regular corporate form and a Section 337 liquidation, there would be only a $1,000 taxable gain. Keep in mind that a Section 337 liquidation is not elective; if the conditions of Section 337 are met, its application is automatic.

In situations where there is a net operating loss during the year of the contemplated liquidation and the corporation has meager profits in the prior years, it may be better to make an optional election and maintain the election until the losses have been imputed to the shareholders.[23] But the corporation must be very careful not to receive more than 20 percent of gross receipts from passive income, which would terminate the election.

A liquidation and flow-through of capital gains is more advantageous where the Subchapter S election has been in effect for three or more years, or since incorporation if shorter. However, the 1966 amendment imposing a tax at the corporate level on capital gains may only be a minor encumbrance, since the first $25,000 of capital gains in each year is exempted from this special tax. Especially in smaller companies, the installment payments can be arranged so that no more than $25,000 of the gain is recognized in any tax year (or the gain does not exceed 50 percent of taxable income).[24]

Finally, the sale of I.R.C. Section 1231 assets incidental to a liquidation will often result in a loss. If the corporation has elected to be taxed as a Subchapter S corporation, the loss can be passed through to the shareholders either as a capital loss or as an ordinary loss. This is an advantage over an ordinary liquidation where such a loss to the corporation might be wasted, for the corporation may have no gain or earnings from which such a loss can be deducted.[25]

---

[23]Brickford, *op. cit.*

[24]Rev. Rul. 65-292, 1965-2 C.B. 319.

[25]Richard H. Valentine, "Taxation of Shareholders of Subchapter S Corporations During the Election Period," *The New York University Eighteenth Annual Institute on Federal Taxation,* Vol. 18 (1960), p. 703.

Employee Relationship

The resulting fringe benefits of an employee relationship are often significant and may justify incorporating a sole proprietorship or partnership and electing to be taxed as a Subchapter S corporation. Reasonable salaries paid to employees (even to stockholder-employee) are deductible. Further, stockholder-employees of an electing corporation are eligible for such benefits as participation in profit-sharing plans, stock bonus plans, qualified pension plans, group life insurance plans, accident and health insurance plans,[26] death benefits,[27] medical reimbursement plans,[28] a sick pay exclusion up to $100 per week,[29] various deferred compensation arrangements,[30] exclusion for value of meals and lodging furnished by employer,[31] and moving expenses.

The Supplement S provision in 1940 barred personal service corporations from establishing pensions or profit-sharing plans. Subsequently, the original tax option proposal as embodied in H.R. 8300 in 1954 disallowed electing corporations from establishing profit-sharing and pension plans. Also, the Subchapter R tax option, which allowed sole proprietorships and partnerships to be taxed as a corporation, contained the same prohibitive clause. (This special election is no longer available.) However, the IRS has ruled that nothing prevents a Subchapter S corporation from adopting qualified profit-sharing plans which benefit the employee-stockholders.[32]

Effective after December 31, 1970, Congress has placed a restriction on some fringe benefits. Under this restriction, contributions to qualified pension and profit-sharing plans for 5 percent shareholders which exceed the limitations under H.R. 10 for partners or proprietors (15 percent of earned or accrued compensation, or $7,500, whichever is less) will be treated as if paid to such stock-

---

[26]Rev. Rul. 58-90, 1958-1 C.B. 88.

[27]Death benefits paid to a deceased's widow were disallowed for lack of a corporate business purpose, *Donald J. Wallace, supra,* note 10.

[28]A medical reimbursement arrangement cannot discriminate in favor of employee-stockholders; *Larkin,* 48 T.C. 629 (1967); but see *Bogene, Inc.,* T.C.M. 1968-147.

[29]The $100 sick pay exclusion does not continue indefinitely; *Samuel Levine,* 50 T.C. 422 (1968).

[30]See Thomas P. Sweeney, "Deferred Compensation Plans for the Close Corporation and Subchapter S Corporation," *New York University Twenty-Sixth Annual Institute on Federal Taxation,* Vol. 26 (1968), pp. 1103-1119, for an excellent discussion of deferred compensation plans.

[31]*Wilhelm* vs. *U.S.,* 257 F. Supp. 16 (D.C. Wyo. 1966).

[32]Rev. Rul. 66-218, 1966-2 C.B. 120.

holder and will be taxable to him. Only the family attribution rules of Section 318 apply in determining stock ownership for purposes of the 5 percent test.[33] Where an individual is a stockholder in more than one Subchapter S corporation, he may exclude no more than $7,500 in any one year.[34]

Although these *Keogh*-like dollar limitations will apply to contributions to qualified pension and profit-sharing plans for stockholder-employees of electing corporations, any excess amounts are treated as voluntary contributions by the shareholder to the trust. Thus, the excess amounts do not have to be returned to the shareholder-employees (as is required under retirement plans for the self-employed), and income of the trust is exempt from tax. Where the latter total payout to the shareholder-employee (or his beneficiary) is less than the total amount included in his gross income, the taxpayer (or beneficiary) is allowed to deduct such excess in the tax year the rights terminate (I.R.C. Section 1379(b)(3)).[35]

However, under I.R.C. Section 1379(a), forfeitures may not be allocated to the remaining participants (as is allowed under a regular qualified corporate plan). If the electing corporation contributes less than the allowable maximum amount, such difference can be contributed in a succeeding Subchapter S year. But an under-contribution may not be carried forward from a Subchapter S year to a non-Subchapter S year under I.R.C. Section 1379(c).[36] An under-contribution may be carried forward from a regular corporate year to a Subchapter S year. Where a Subchapter S corporation makes contributions to a qualified plan during a loss year, such contributions are deductible, as long as the deduction and the loss do not exceed accumulated and previously taxed income.[37] Thus, corporations may deduct contributions from previously taxed income, which may be one way of reducing locked-in PTI.

Thus, although pension and profit-sharing plans for Subchapter S corporations may be better than retirement plans for the self-employed under H.R. 10, the greatest tax benefits and flexibility may be obtained under the regular corporate qualified plans or professional corporation plans. A comparison of some of the more importan aspects of these three alternatives is summarized in Exhibit 12-3.

---

[33]Prop. Reg. 1.1379-4.

[34]Prop. Reg. 1.1379-2(e)(1).

[35]Prop. Reg. 1.1379-2(e)(1).

[36]Prop. Reg. 1.1379-3.

[37]Rev. Rul. 71-257, 1971-1 C.B. 131.

EXHIBIT 12-3

Comparison of Retirement Plans

	H.R. 10 Plans	Subchapter S Plans	Regular Corporation or Professional Corporation
1. Eligibility requirement	all employees must be included (except those employed less than 3 years)	more discrimination is permitted (i.e., age and 5-year waiting period)	same as Subchapter S
2. Vesting	contributions vest immediately	contributions need not vest immediately (may be based upon years of service)	same as Subchapter S
3. Maximum deductible contribution per year	lesser of $7,500 or 15 percent of earned income	lesser of $7,500 or 15 percent of earned compensation	Pension: greater of (1) 5 percent of total compensation + actuarial amount needed to fund the plan, (2) normal cost + 10 percent of total cost of past service benefits.* Profit-sharing plan: 15 percent of total compensation paid + up to 15 percent more if available carry-forward amounts

EXHIBIT 12-3 (Continued)

	H.R. 10 Plans	Subchapter S Plans	Regular Corporation or Professional Corporation
4. Excess contributions	must be given back to participant	may be retained in the retirement plan	same as Subchapter S
5. Under-contributions	may not be made up in later years	may be made up only in Subchapter S years	may be made up in later years
6. Definition of an owner-employee	owns more than 10 percent of partnership or sole proprietor	owns more than 5 percent of corporation	N.A.
7. Integration with Social Security	Yes, if no more than 66-2/3 percent of deductible contributions made on behalf of owner-employees	Yes	Yes
8. Limitation on distributions	not prior to age 59½ and must begin before age 70½	distribution may be made before retirement	same as Subchapter S
9. Federal income tax treatment of distributions	ordinary income	some capital gain treatment available; special averaging rule applies to ordinary income	same as Subchapter S
10. Federal estate tax treatment of death benefits	includible in participant's gross estate	employer's contributions payable to a beneficiary are not included in participant's gross estate	same as Subchapter S
11. $5,000 death benefits exclusion	not available	available	available

*Probably cannot exceed 25 percent of compensation.

The IRS has tried to prevent Subchapter S stockholders from taking advantage of corporate fringe benefits. In *Wilhelm*,[38] the IRS tried to disallow the exclusion from gross income for meals and lodging furnished for the convenience of the employer. The court rejected the Commissioner's contention that Subchapter S tax treatment is similar to the tax treatment of partnerships and proprietorships. The deductions for food and lodging were allowed, and the employees were allowed an exclusion under Section 119.

This election is especially helpful where a shareholder is not active or where an employee-shareholder contributes less time or service. Further, if the other shareholders cooperate, he may still receive a salary (within limits) from the company even though he voluntarily or involuntarily retires. But, as we will see next, there are limits to successful income splitting.

Income Splitting

A Subchapter S election may be a useful tool for family income-splitting. A family can obtain the benefits of the corporate form and still arrange the shareholdings so that the income can be divided among the family members in order to minimize the overall tax. The corporate income is taxed from the first dollar, but each family member has various exemptions that afford some tax savings. Further, income can be removed from high income taxpayers to lower income taxpayers who may use the income for support purposes.

If there is a gift of stock involved, the gift should be bona fide, and the donor should retain no interest in the transferred shares.[39] *Duarte*[40] dramatizes the point that a transfer of stock must have economic reality. In this case, the father owned all of the stock in the Graham Corporation, but gave 25 percent each to his two minor sons. The taxpayer filed a gift tax return although there was no gift tax liability. Not until a year later was their mother's name typed in as custodian. The taxpayer's salary was reduced from $30,000 to $15,000. Subchapter S tax returns were filed showing substantial dividend distributions to the sons, but they did not receive such distributions. Custodian bank accounts were not opened for the children until several years later.

---

[38]257 F. Supp. 16 (D.C. Wyo. 1966).

[39]Regulation 1.1373-1(a)(2); For a complete discussion, see Crumbley, *A Practical Guide to the Preparation of a Federal Gift Tax Return* (Tucson: Lawyers and Judges Publishing Co., 1972).

[40]44 T.C. 193 (1965).

The father prepared and signed tax returns for the children and paid the appropriate tax liabilities from his own funds. However, the court held that the stock transfers to the sons had "no economic reality" and were therefore not bona fide [citing I.R.C. Section 1375(c) and Regulation 1.1373-1(a)]. The court also applied the doctrine of "substance over form"[41] to reallocate to the father all of the corporate income.

Likewise, in *Michael F. Bierne,*[42] a father transferred 90 percent of the stock of a Subchapter S corporation to his minor children. The Tax Court held that the transfer was not bona fide for tax purposes since the father retained control of the securities. Thus, the father was taxed on all of the income of the Subchapter S corporation.

In two other cases the Commissioner used I.R.C. Section 1375(c) to frustrate the use of Subchapter S as an income-splitting device. Under this section ". . . any dividends received by a shareholder from an electing small business corporation (including any amount treated as a dividend under Section 1373(b)) may be apportioned or allocated by the Secretary or his delegate between or among shareholders of such corporation who are members of such shareholder's family . . . if . . . allocation is necessary in order to reflect the value of services rendered to the corporation by such shareholders." Shades of reasonableness of compensation!

In *Pat Krahenbuhl,* T.C.M. 1968-34, the Commissioner tried to allocate the UTI to the father as reasonable compensation for his services. The converse of the usual I.R.C. Section 162(a) situation, the court allowed the Commissioner to raise the major shareholder's salary to a reasonable amount under I.R.C. Section 1375(c).

Similarly, in *Walter J. Roob,*[43] the Tax Court asserted that the same criteria used under I.R.C. Section 162(a) applied in this situation:

> Thus, the nature of the services performed, the responsibilities involved, the time spent, the size and complexity of the business, prevailing economic conditions, compensation paid by comparable firms for comparable services, and salary paid to company officers in prior years are all relevant in determining whether the salary . . . was reasonable.

This case involved a photography business operated by a husband (a skilled photographer) and his wife. Ownership of stock was

---

[41]*Gregory* vs. *Helvering,* 293 U.S. 465 (1935); *Knetsch* vs. *U.S.,* 364 U.S. 361 (1960).
[42]52 T.C. 210 (1969).
[43]*Walter J. Roob,* 50 T.C. 891 (1968).

divided equally nine ways among them and seven children. The Commissioner claimed that the father's salary should have been larger to reflect the high value of the father's services to the operation of the business. The Tax Court agreed with the IRS and thereby increased the father's salary for each of the years involved.

However, in another case, the Tax Court held in favor of the controlling shareholders. In *Carletta*,[44] the court felt that the stated salaries were fair compensation for the performed services. Further, in *Rocco*,[45] the Tax Court again would not reallocate salary and distributions without some justification. Here the major stockholder's salary was comparable to the salary he received from his former employer and his services were no greater for the new corporation.

Thus, the Commissioner does have a number of weapons in his arsenal to stop flagrant acts of income-splitting. I.R.C. Section 1375(c) may be used to reallocate income among the stockholders, and Regulation 1.1373-1(1)(a)(2) may be used where there is not a bona fide gift. Further, the general taxation principles of *Gregory* and *Knetsch* may be used where "economic reality" is missing from a transaction.[46]

Miscellaneous Advantages

Various other advantages are summarized below:

1. The corporate form has attractive features that may tempt a sole proprietorship or a partnership to contemplate incorporation and then elect to be taxed as a Subchapter S corporation. Transferability of interests, longevity, limited liability, centralization of control, inclusion in qualified deferred compensation plans, and availability of various other fringe benefits are all advantages of the corporate form of organization.

2. Even though a net operating loss is treated as a trade or business deduction,[47] a "gentleman" farmer may have better success under Subchapter S showing a sound business purpose. (See Chapter 4.)

---

[44]*Carletta,* 57 T.C. 826 (1972), *acq.* 1972-2 C.B. 1.

[45]*Rocco,* 57 T.C. 826 (1972), *acq.* 1972-2 C.B. 1.

[46]See J. J. McCoy, "Assignment of Income: Possibilities Under Subchapter S," *Tax Law Review,* Vol. 23 (January, 1968), pp. 213-226.

[47]I.R.C. Section 1374-2; thereby, the NOL is subject to the hobby loss limitation. I.R.C. Section 183(a).

3. Where a corporation wants to sell a capital asset and distribute the proceeds and cannot meet the liquidation provisions, a one-shot election may still result in less tax than the non-electing corporation (under certain circumstances). Further, with careful tax planning, the installment tax method may be used to avoid the capital gains penalty tax.

4. The electing corporation may adopt a method of accounting different from the unincorporated business without obtaining the Commissioner's consent or incurring penalties. A regular corporation cannot make the election and then change the method of accounting without the Commissioner's consent.

5. Stockholders may avoid self-employment tax or restrictions on social security benefits while continuing to work by simply not paying themselves a salary and withdrawing the profits as dividend distributions. But see prior discussion on income-splitting, and *Jack Haber,* 52 T.C. 255 (1969).

6. Under the current basis rules, ordinary income can be converted into capital gains by holding a portion of the Subchapter S interest in the form of debt, reducing such debt by losses, and after the election is terminated, the debt can be redeemed at a time when a partial stock redemption is treated as a dividend.

7. A Subchapter S election can be used at the time of incorporation to pass through immediately bonus depreciation deductions and investment credits on equipment purchases. For example, a corporation immediately after incorporation on August 20 may purchase equipment qualifying for the investment credit and bonus depreciation. If the electing corporation selects a September 1 to August 31 fiscal year, then a short return will have to be filed for the period between August 20 and August 31. The election can be revoked for the next full corporate year, but the bonus depreciation and/or investment credit would have been passed through immediately.

8. This election during the construction or development period of a real estate company allows an immediate pass-through of losses to the stockholders. Under the completed-contract method, expenses are accumulated until a construction project is completed or accepted. The difference between the contract price and the accumulated expenses (i.e., income or

loss) is reported in the year of completion or acceptance. This method produces maximum deferral of taxes due on the income of the project — an interest-free "loan" from the government from the taxes deferred into the future.

General expenses not directly related to a particular long-term contract (i.e., office salaries, taxes, or rent) do not have to be deferred but are deductible as incurred. Thus, a Subchapter S election will allow these losses in the early life of the contract to be passed through immediately to the stockholders. If the company is going to rent the project, then the Subchapter S election will, of course, terminate later because of the failure to meet the gross receipts test.

A caveat is appropriate. Passive types of income cannot exceed 20 percent of gross receipts. In *Temple N. Joyce,* 42 T.C. 628 (1964), the company had losses of $211,000 which would have flowed through, except for the fact that the election was terminated because there was a $10,000 gain on the sale of stock. This unfortunate termination cost the company approximately $46,000 in additional taxes. Watch those passive income items and arrange to have some non-passive income to avoid terminating the election. For example, cattle may be bought near the end of the year and sold at the beginning of the next year. Or depreciable assets could be sold and leased back to the company.

9. I.R.C. Section 1231 gains and losses may be passed through to the shareholder as capital gains and losses without having to be offset against I.R.C. Section 1231 gains and losses of the stockholders.[48] These must be offset against each other if the organization is operating as a partnership.

10. There is no stock attribution between stockholders under the rules of constructive ownership of I.R.C. Section 267, whereas, the stock owned by a partner is attributed to the other partners.

11. Under I.R.C. Section 1373(d)(2), organization expenses are deductible by Subchapter S corporations, whereas, a partnership must capitalize such expenses indefinitely.[49]

12. Under the farm loss recapture rules, an electing corporation is allowed the $25,000 exemption if none of its shareholders have personal net farm losses and none of its shareholders is a stockholder in another Subchapter S corporation which has

---

[48]I.R.C. Section 1375(a)(1).

[49]*Meldrum & Fewsmith,* 21 T.C. 790 (1953), *aff'd.* 230 F. 2d 283 (6th Cir. 1956).

a net farm loss. Obviously, a Subchapter S corporation should rid itself of such shareholders whenever possible. A regular corporation must add all of its regular farm losses to its EDA, so there is normally a larger recapture under a regular corporation than under Subchapter S status.

Disadvantages and Hazards

As with most tax-planning tools, there are disadvantages or potential hazards to a Subchapter S election. The IRS can be quite hostile in this area by making compliance with technicalities difficult. In fact, it appears that the IRS is trying to limit this optional election to a few small businesses. However, the courts have been somewhat more liberal than the IRS in many areas.[50] Therefore, instead of being less concerned with taxation, a Subchapter S corporation must be constantly aware of the tax traps in order to avoid the ever-present danger of unintentional termination and the resulting "locked-in" earnings.

Some more cogent disadvantages or potential hazards are summarized below:

1. A foreign tax credit is not allowed,[51] so the electing corporation has to deduct any taxes paid to foreign countries.

2. The 85 percent dividends received deduction is not available.

3. A net operating loss from nonelecting years cannot be utilized at the corporate level, and the running of the carryback and carryforward period continues.

4. PTI is a personal right that cannot be transferred. Thus, a donee, a purchaser, or estate cannot receive any PTI tax-free; it must report the income and again pay taxes on the distributions.[52]

5. There is the ever-present danger of unintentional termination and the resulting "locked-in" earnings. See Chapter 7 for tax-planning suggestions to mitigate this hazard.

6. Incorporation may subject the enterprise to unemployment and increased F.I.C.A. taxes.

---

[50]See Albert C. O'Neill, Jr., "Literal Compliance: The IRS Weapon That Blunts Subchapter S Benefits," *Journal of Taxation,* Vol. 30 (February, 1969), pp. 90-93.

[51]Rev. Rul. 68-128, 1968-1 C.B. 381.

[52]Rev. Rul. 66-172, 1966-1 C.B. 198.

7. All tax-exempt incomes lose their identities as they pass through and are taxed as ordinary dividends at the shareholder level. Thus, the shareholders should hold any tax-exempt securities personally rather than having the securities in the name of the Subchapter S corporation. Further, an electing corporation should avoid receiving PTI from a DISC.

8. Blackmail by shareholders can occur because of the numerous easy ways of terminating an election. For example, it is entirely possible for a stockholder-employee who owns only a minimal amount of stock to ask for a larger salary, a new yacht, etc., or he will transfer his stock to a trust (thus terminating the election).

9. Corporate capital losses in excess of capital gains do not pass through to the shareholders.

10. Since stockholders are taxed on income when it is distributed, then two years' income can be bunched into one year. For example, assume a Subchapter S corporation had $10,000 of earnings for both the tax year ended June, 1973, and the year ended June, 1974. The electing corporation distributed $10,000 in 1973, but the 1973 earnings were not distributed and will be taxed as a dividend on June 30, 1973. The $10,000 distribution in November, 1973 (although considered a distribution of earnings for the year ended June, 1974) is taxable when distributed in 1973. Thus, the stockholders would have to include $20,000 in their taxable income for 1973. Even with the two and one-half-month grace period, doubling up still occurs in this case since the November distribution was made after the grace period ended.

11. Incorporation may result in state and local incorporated business taxes. Partnerships and proprietorships are often exempt from such taxes.

12. The $100 dividend exclusion is not allowed on a Subchapter S corporation's dividends from current years' earnings and profits.[53]

13. Distributions in kind (i.e., property distributions) are not deductible in computing UTI. Thus, if there are any accumulated earnings and profits, the stockholders are taxed on the amount in excess of taxable income.

---

[53]Regulation 1.1375-2.

14. The sale of Subchapter S stock before the end of the fiscal year will result in an extra tax on earnings accumulated during the tax year — once to the seller as capital gains on the increase in value of the stock and again to the buyer on distributions from the taxable income or from UTI. Hint: Pay cash dividends immediately before the sale of the securities.

15. The maximum limit for the first year's bonus depreciation deduction is applied at the corporate level; whereas, in a partnership, the maximum limitations apply to each partner separately.[54]

16. A Subchapter S stockholder's basis for the limitation on the deduction of losses is limited to his equity and debt investments. Conversely, a partner's basis includes his proportionate share of the partnership liabilities.[55]

17. A net capital loss is not deductible by the electing corporation, but it may be carried over to the next five years as a short-term capital loss (a regular corporation has a three-year carryback also). Thereby, they are deductible only to the extent of capital gains, Whereas, in a partnership, capital loss deduction limitations apply to each individual partner.

18. There is a possibility of a double state income tax in certain states (once at the corporate level and again when dividends are distributed).[56] Further, some states permit a deduction for federal income taxes, so a Subchapter S election will result in higher state taxes.

19. An unused investment credit arising in a nonelecting year and which is a carryback or carryover to a tax year for which the corporation is a Subchapter S corporation cannot be taken as a credit by the Subchapter S corporation. However, the Subchapter S years count as years to which the tax credit may be carried back and then carried over (Regulation 1.46-2(h)). For example, a regular corporation is unable to take an investment credit in 1973 as a result of a net operating loss. If the

---

[54]Regulation 1.179-2(d)(1).

[55]See I.R.C. Sections 704(d) and 752(a).

[56]"Double Tax on Subchapter S Income in One State," *Journal of Taxation,* Vol. 27 (December, 1967), p. 381; but see Florida Income Tax Code Ch. 220.13(2)(i), which does not impose a state income tax on Subchapter S corporations.

corporation elects Subchapter S status in 1974, the carryover credit may not be passed through to the stockholders. If the Subchapter S election continues for seven years, the carryover investment credit would be lost forever, even if the election is later terminated.[57]

20. Percentage depletion in excess of cost depletion does not decrease earnings and profits (although allowable in computing taxable income).[58] If such amounts are distributed to the stockholders, they are required to report such distributions as ordinary income. This disadvantage may reduce the importance of this election for corporations in the natural resources field, since, in effect, the corporation is denied a deduction for the excess of percentage depletion over cost depletion. In 1969 Congress decreased the oil depletion percentage to 22 percent, which may tend to reduce this disadvantage somewhat. However, this same adverse situation occurs whenever earnings and profits exceed taxable income.

21. Where more than 20 percent interest in a Subchapter S corporation is given to a stockholder in exchange for future services, the appreciation on property transferred by other stockholders is taxable, since transferors are not in "control" after the exchange.[59]

22. A trust is not a permissible shareholder. Thus, many of the common estate-planning tools are not available to Subchapter S shareholders.

23. Although an estate is a permissible stockholder, if the estate is held open too long, it may be considered a trust, and the election will be terminated.

24. A stockholder's portion of UTI is not considered a "dividend" for purposes of determining the maximum allowable retirement income credit.[60]

25. Charitable contributions are subject to the 5 percent of taxable income limitation in I.R.C. Section 170(b)(2) and the five-year carryforward provision. Whereas, a partner is subject to the more liberal 20-30-50 percent of adjusted taxable income limitation and the five-year carryover period.

---

[57]Regulation 1.46-2(n).

[58]Regulation 1.1373-1(g), example 2.

[59]I.R.C. Section 351.

[60]I.R.C. Section 1375(b).

26. Since Subchapter S income loses its character as it passes through the entity, only the salaries of the employee-stockholders qualify as "earned taxable income" for purposes of the 50 percent maximum tax. Whereas, "earned taxable income" of a partnership is considered to be the same in the hands of the partners.

27. Under I.R.C. Section 1212(a)(3), a Subchapter S corporation is not allowed a capital loss carryback, and a regular corpora tion cannot carryback its capital losses to a Subchapter S year.

28. Under I.R.C. Section 163 certain interest paid or incurred to purchase or carry investments is disallowed in years after 1971. This disallowance applies to noncorporate taxpayers (including Subchapter S corporations) but does not apply to regular corporations (except personal holding companies) In years before 1972 the excess of interest to carry such in vestments over net investment income is considered a prefer ence item for the 10 percent minimum tax [I.R.C. Section 58(d)].

29. The retirement income credit provisions of Section 37 are not applicable.

30. An electing corporation is not allowed a special deduction for the western hemisphere trade corporation and cannot be a domestic international sales corporation.

31. One major disadvantage of the Subchapter S election is that the combination of Sections 1377 and 312(m) neutralizes the advantage of using an accelerated depreciation method. Section 312(m) indicates that, for purposes of computing earnings and profits for an electing corporation for any tax year beginning after June 30, 1972, the straight-line method of depreciation is deemed to be used. Where an accelerated method is used in the early life of an asset, the "current earnings and profits" of the Subchapter S corporation is greater than its "taxable income." Under the tier structure of Section 1377, any amount distributed during the year up to "taxable income" is treated as a taxable dividend to the shareholders who receive the distributions. Any distribution in excess of taxable income is considered to be a dividend distribution *to the extent of earnings or profits.* If the excess earnings and profits is not paid out in the current year, it becomes accumulated

earnings and profits and is subject to dividend treatment when and if paid out. The villain is Section 1377(b), which indicates that earnings and profits of an electing corporation "for any tax year (but not its accumulated earnings and profits) shall not be reduced by any amount which is not allowable as a deduction in computing its taxable income (as provided in Section 1373(d)) for such taxable year." Thus, even though in later years current earnings and profits may be less than taxable income, Section 1377(b) requires current earnings and profits to be equal to taxable income by not allowing the larger depreciation deduction to be used in computing current earnings and profits. Of course, there remains the minor benefit that, if the excess is never distributed and the stock is sold, liquidated, or redeemed, ordinary income may be converted into capital gain. Or if the shareholder holds his stock until death, his heirs receive a stepped-up tax basis for the stock (thereby avoiding any tax).

Chapter 13

Statement Preparation and Recordkeeping

A number of accounting problems are encountered when a company elects to be a Subchapter S corporation. Although this new form of hybrid organization has characteristics of both the partnership and corporation (see Chapter 12), the accounting profession has not formulated guidelines for the proper presentation of the balance sheet and income statement of an electing corporation. This chapter discusses some of the reporting problems of the Subchapter S corporation and offers suggestions for adequate statement presentation. Likewise, this chapter points out some helpful hints for record-keeping purposes.

Is it, or is it not, a Corporation?

Is a Subchapter S corporation another type of business organization having characteristics that are distinct from those of other organizations? The answer to this question can be obtained by examining the opinions found in tax literature and court cases:

It is in fact a corporation with all the corporate attributes with one notable exception — federal income taxation.[1]

A hybrid form of taxation which combines some of the attributes of partnership taxation to corporations in an attempt to allow certain corporations to eliminate a tax at the corporate level.[2]

A Subchapter S election does not have the effect of creating an entirely new tax entity.[3]

Corporation for all purposes under state law. Separate entity for income tax purposes.[4]

It is the Government's position that the effect of an election . . . is to convert a corporation into a partnership and to make the shareholders, in effect, partners. Counsel for the Government have cited no authority for this position and independent re-

---

[1]John N. Kamp, "Application of Subchapter S," *Journal of Accountancy,* Vol. 109 (June, 1960), p. 51.

[2]Henry G. Nagel, "The Tax-Option Corporation," *Taxes — The Tax Magazine,* Vol. 44 (June, 1966), p. 364.

[3]*W. H. Leonhart,* T.C.M. 1968-98, *aff'd. per curiam,* 414 F 2d. (4th Cir. 1969).

[4]Arthur B. Willis, "Incorporate and Elect Subchapter S," *Journal of Taxation,* Vol. 11 (August, 1959), pp. 67-68.

search by this court has not found any to support it. It is a separate and distinct corporate and taxable entity.[5]

Only domestic corporations can make the Subchapter S election.[6]

A Subchapter S corporation is not a pseudo corporation per se; it is a real corporation for all corporate purposes but has elected to be subject to federal income tax in a special way.[7]

The effect of a valid Subchapter S election is merely to subject the stockholders to the taxation of the corporation's income to the stockholders.[8]

The purpose of this election is to eliminate the influence of the Federal income tax in the selection of the form of business organization which may be more desirable under the circumstances.[9]

The validity of a dividend declaration [of a Subchapter S corporation] is governed solely by the applicable corporation law of the state of incorporation.[10]

Section 1371 . . . does not provide . . . that the shareholders should be considered partners. It is logical to conclude, therefore, that Congress repudiated the proposal to convert corporations into partnerships. It is the corporation, not the shareholders that elects not to be subject to the taxing of its income.[11]

The taxation of a Subchapter S corporation differs from that of a partnership in many fundamental respects.[12]

. . . the effect of this new tax legislation is not to convert the corporation into a partnership.[13]

Congress utilized the concept of corporate taxable income in structuring this organization [I.R.C. Section 1373(d)]. The corporation, not the stockholders, makes this special election under Section 1372.

---

[5] *Wilhelm,* 257 Supp. 16 (D.C. Wyo. 1966).

[6] I.R.C. Section 1371(a).

[7] William A. Patty, "Qualifications and Disqualifications Under Subchapter S," *New York University Institute on Federal Taxation,* Vol. 18 (1960), p. 661.

[8] Regulation 1.1372-1(b)(2).

[9] *Report of the Committee on Finance,* Senate Report No. 1622, 83rd Congress, 2nd Session (Washington: United States Government Printing Office, 1954), p. 118.

[10] Bernard Barnett, "Balance Sheet Presentation of a 'Subchapter S' Corporation's Undistributed Earnings," *New York Certified Public Accountant,* Vol. 37 (April, 1965), p. 283.

[11] *Wilhelm, supra,* note 5.

[12] Edwin C. Cohen, "Tax Planning with Subchapter S in 1967: Problems and Prospects," *Tax Counselor's Quarterly,* Vol. 11 (December, 1967), p. 464.

[13] Carman G. Blough, "New Tax Election for Small Business Corporations," *Journal of Accountancy,* Vol. 107 (February, 1959), p. 75.

We agree with the observation of the Tax Court that the statute is designed "to permit a qualified corporation and its shareholders to avoid the double tax normally paid when a corporation distributes its earnings and profits as dividends" and this is accomplished in a specific manner which does not involve ignoring the corporate entity. *Byrne,* 361 F. 2d 939 (7th Cir. 1966).

It should be noted, however, that we have treated this aspect of the case [Section 481] as though the petitioner and the corporation, which elected Subchapter S treatment for the year in issue, were the same taxable entity. [This approach] seems sound in light of the purposes of Subchapter S. *Paul Travis,* 47 T.C. 502 (1967).

. . . the corporation herein is a Subchapter S corporation and its income is attributed directly to its stockholders in the same manner that partnership income is attributed to the partners, with the consequence that the same taxpayers are involved and that the Subchapter S corporation is merely a continuation of the old partnerships for purposes of Section 481 regardless of whether a Subchapter S corporation itself may properly be treated as a taxpayer for other purposes elsewhere in the Code. However, . . . we express no opinion as to its [this argument] merits. *E. Morris Cox,* 43 T.C. 448 (1965).

To the extent that other provisions of . . . the Code are not inconsistent with those of Subchapter S . . . such provisions will apply with respect to both the electing small business corporation and its shareholders in the same manner that they would apply had no election been made. Regulation 1.1372-1(c).

The leading literature, case law, and regulations agree that a Subchapter S election does not convert the entity into a partnership. Instead, for all other purposes, except taxation, a Subchapter S corporation is still a corporation. A review of Exhibit 12-2 in Chapter 12 reveals that the Subchapter S corporation is more closely related to the corporation than the partnership. But the Subchapter S corporation does differ from the regular corporation. Further, the IRS may not abandon the notion that this election converts the entity into a partnership, especially if remedial legislation is not adopted in the area of stockholder-employee fringe benefits.[14]

Since the Subchapter S corporation does differ from the regular corporation in the tax area, there are some differences in financial

---

[14]Note, the Tax Reform Act of 1969 limits the amount excluded from employee-stockholder's gross income under qualified pension and profit-sharing plans; I.R.C. Section 1379(b)(1).

statement preparation. These differences and problem areas are discussed in subsequent sections.

Similarities in the Four Types of Businesses

Asset, liability, income, and expense accounts of proprietorships, partnerships, Subchapter S corporations, and corporations in the same industry are similar (with a few minor exceptions). Obvious exceptions are the Federal income tax expense account and the Federal income tax liability account that appear only in the corporation's accounts. Further, salary accounts and other fringe benefits of the owner-employees may appear only on the tax books of the corporation and Subchapter S corporation. Deductible organizational expenses are uncommon to partnerships and proprietorships. Corporations and Subchapter S corporations may have certain capitalized promotors' fees and other underwriting costs which are often amortized over a period of sixty months or more. Thus, the legal form of organization has minimal effect on the structure of asset, liability, income, and expense accounts.

Differences in Owner's Equity

Some important differences do occur in the owner's equity sections of the four forms of organization. Equity accounts of the proprietorship and partnership are classified by owners' categories. Each owner has his personal equity account, and any income or losses are distributed to the various owners according to the appropriate profit-and-loss ratios. But, within each capital account, the contributed capital and any subsequent earnings are merely combined.

Owner's equity accounts of corporations and Subchapter S corporations are classified according to the sources of the contribution. Original investments or additional investments are recorded in a Capital Stock account or Additional Paid-In Capital account. Income and losses are accumulated in a Retained Earnings account. In situations where any assets are written-up, another account, Appraisal Capital, is maintained for such mark-up of assets. However, the contributed capital, earned capital, or appraisal capital are not mingled (as occurs in partnerships and proprietorships).

Equity Accounts of a Corporation

Since the stockholders of a corporation have limited liability, the laws of most states require that their investment in the corporation be clearly stated and not subject to shrinkage by withdrawals.

Such a limitation that asset distributions can be made only to the extent that the enterprise has a credit balance in the Retained Earnings accounts, provides a cushion of protection for the creditors of the corporation.

Initial contributions of the owners or future additional investments are recorded in the proprietary account, Capital Stock. There are two principal classes of Capital Stock: common and preferred. Further, many varieties exist within these two classes, providing for varying rights relating to income distribution, control, and treatment in case of liquidation. Each variety of stock has its own proprietary account, and any premium contribution above par value (or a designated portion of shares without a par value) is maintained in an Additional Paid-In Capital account.

Profits and losses of a corporation are accumulated in the Retained Earnings Account. A corporation's revenue and expense accounts for an accounting period are summarized in the Revenue and Expense Summary account, and the net profit or loss is transferred to the Retained Earnings account. Since the payment of a dividend is a proportional distribution of earnings, the Dividends account is closed to Retained Earnings. If there are restrictions on portions of the Retained Earnings account, then part of the account is appropriated (e.g., set aside) with the remainder classified as Unappropriated Retained Earnings.

Dividends normally cannot be paid in excess of Retained Earnings, unless (1) the enterprise is going out of business, or (2) the company distributes part of the contributed capital recovered from the sales of wasting assets. Capital stock of a corporation can shrink, however, through the acquisition of the corporation's own stock, called treasury stock. Methods of accounting for this reacquired stock vary.

Aside from the paid-in capital and retained earnings classifications, corporate capital may originate from two other sources. First, a stockholder or some other party may make a donation to a corporation. To compliment the asset placed on the books, a similar amount is credited to a Donated Capital Account. Second, charges to asset accounts for increases in value established by independent appraisal are accompanied by corresponding credits to appraisal capital accounts. Such appraisal capital is disclosed separately in the capital section of the balance sheet.

The stockholders' equity section may be conveniently presented in the manner illustrated by Exhibit 13-1. Separate schedules may be prepared to show the changes that occur in the paid-in capital section and the retained earnings section.

EXHIBIT 13-1

Stockholders' Equity

Paid-in Capital:		
Common Stock, $20 par, 100,000 shares	$2,000,000	
Premium on Common Stock	300,000	
		$2,300,000
Preferred Stock, $10 par, 20,000 shares		200,000
		$2,500,000
Donated Capital		350,000
Appraisal Capital		420,000
Retained Earnings:		
Appropriated for Bond Redemption	$ 170,000	
Unappropriated	650,000	
Total Retained Earnings		820,000
Total Stockholders' Equity		$4,090,000

Equity Accounts of a Subchapter S Corporation[15]

The paid-in capital, appraisal capital, and donated capital sections of a Subchapter S corporation are similar to a regular corporation, except that the former can have only one class of stock issued and outstanding. Differences do occur in the retained earnings (earned surplus) account.

Retained earnings of a Subchapter S corporation may be separated into at least the three following categories:

1. Pre-election accumulations (PEA).*
2. UTI accumulations.**
3. PTI accumulations.

Any earnings accumulated before this special election (PEA) are separated, since not only are they taxable if distributed but they are, in effect, "frozen-in" until all UTI and PTI accumulations are dis-

---

[15]The reader may wish to review the sequence of distributions by Subchapter S corporations in Chapter 7 before reading this section.

*This account may also include earnings and profits in excess of UTI during the election years.

**This account could be divided into "Current UTI" and "UTI during the Grace Period."

tributed. Undistributed taxable income (UTI) is the earnings that are not distributed during the taxable year or during a two-and-one-half-month grace period after the close of the tax year. Shareholders must pay taxes on this undistributed amount. If UTI is not distributed, then it should be transferred to the Previously Taxed Income (PTI) account. PTI is personal and is tax-free only to the shareholder who actually included the UTI in his income tax return. Also, PTI can be distributed only after all UTI has been distributed to the stockholders.

One might feel that undistributed taxable income (UTI) should be classified as a current liability payable to the stockholders (see Example 4 ahead). Under I.R.C. Section 1371(a), a Subchapter S corporation is considered to have paid a dividend to the stockholders in the amount of the undistributed taxable income as of the last day of the tax year. However, whether or not a dividend has been declared rests solely on the applicable state corporate law. A liability does not exist until a dividend is properly declared by the board of directors.[16] Thus, a liability should not be recorded at year end for UTI; segregation of the retained earnings account is sufficient.

At year end, the income and expense accounts of an electing corporation are closed to the Revenue and Expense Summary and the net profit or loss is transferred to the UTI Accumulations Account. The Dividends account is also closed to this account. If there is an amount in the UTI Accumulations account two months and fifteen days after the close of the year, this remainder is closed to the PTI Accumulations account. If the Dividends account is greater than the UTI account, then the excess is debited to the Pre-election Accumulations account, if any. Further, if the dividend is greater than all of the accumulations mentioned previously, any excess is applied as a reduction of the taxpayer's basis in the capital stock at no tax consequence to the shareholder. Finally, if the payment is greater than the shareholder's basis, the remaining amount would be taxable as a capital gain.

A stockholders' equity section of a Subchapter S corporation can be conveniently presented as shown in Exhibit 13-2.

Before proceeding to some examples of current accounting practices of Subchapter S corporations, it is beneficial to summarize the differences in the accounting structure of the four organizational forms. Exhibit 13-3 illustrates that the major accounting differences occur in the equity and expense accounts of the organization.

---

[16]Barnett, *op. cit.,* p. 283.

EXHIBIT 13-2

Stockholders' Equity

Paid-in Capital:

Common Stock, $10 par, 6,000 shares	$60,000	
Premium on Common Stock	3,000	
		$63,000
Donated Capital		10,000
Retained Earnings:		
Pre-election Accumulations (PEA)	$31,000	
UTI Accumulations	7,000	
PTI Accumulations	12,000	50,000
Total Stockholders' Equity		$123,000

Examples of Current Practice

In actual practice the retained earnings account is often not segregated. This is probably due to an early article stipulating that no separation on the balance sheet was necessary; instead, a footnote was considered sufficient for full disclosure of this special election.[17] However, where financial statements are to be circulated to outsiders (i.e., banks, Securities and Exchange Commission, creditors, purchase requests, etc.), full and adequate disclosure would suggest that retained earnings should be segregated along with footnote(s) explaining the contingencies involved in a voluntary or involuntary termination of an election.

Due to the danger of involuntary termination and the hostile attitude of the IRS toward Subchapter S corporations, merely including a footnote as to a possible contingent liability may not be sufficient. Besides, with the two and one-half month grace period available to Subchapter S corporations after 1966, financial statements may now be prepared and circulated before this grace period has expired. Adequate disclosure would suggest that UTI accumulations should be separated from PTI accumulations. Remember, if a Subchapter S corporation is involuntarily terminated, the loss of election is retroactive to the beginning of the year. Not only is PTI taxable to the

---

[17]Blough, *op. cit.,* p. 76; but Blough continued: "Records should, however, be maintained which will permit the corporation to indicate to the stockholders whether or not any subsequent dividends are taxable to him . . . if a stockholder sells his shares, any undistributed earnings on which he had paid the tax may become taxable again when distributed to the new stockholder."

EXHIBIT 3-3

Comparison of Accounting Structures for Major Organizational Forms

	Proprietorship	Partnership	Subchapter S Corporation	Corporation
Assets	No	Substantial	Differences	
Liabilities	No	Substantial	Differences	
Owners' equity	One account	One account each partner	Earned and contributed. Appropriation of retained earnings	earned and contributed
Income	No	Substantial	Differences	
Expenses	No Substantial Differences		Deductible compensation; organization expenses amortized	Income tax exp.; deductible compensation; organization expenses amortized

stockholder, but also a corporate tax must be paid on all earnings during the year. Quite frequently a corporation will not know that the election is terminated until one or two years later. Statements should be prepared which will be as meaningful as possible to prospective users.

Some examples of footnotes often found on Subchapter S financial statements giving various degrees of information are presented below. These examples are subsequently discussed in detail.

EXAMPLE 1

Retained Earnings (including $174,600 which has
    been taxed to the shareholders)
See Note A $605,857

Note A — Income Tax Status

Since 1958 the Company has elected to be taxed as a Subchapter S corporation under I.R.C. Section 1372(a). Under this election, no federal income tax is paid by the Company, inasmuch as all income is reported by the shareholders on their individual income tax returns. For the year ended June 30, 1974, the Company would have been required to pay approximately $8,700 federal income tax if it was not reporting income as a Subchapter S corporation.

EXAMPLE 2

Net income before Income Taxes	$30,000
Provisions for Income Taxes:	
State	(3,000)
Federal (due to the election by the Company	
to include its income in that of its stock-	
holders, the tax of $6,160 otherwise payable	
by the Company on above income was eliminated).	
See Note B.	—0—
Net Income	$27,000

Note B — Status of Income Taxes

In September, 1973, the Company made an election not to be subject to federal income taxes at the corporate level for 1973 and later years. As a result, the income of the Company is includable in the current taxable income of the individual shareholders under I.R.C. Section 1372(a). The federal income taxes to be paid by the shareholders on the income for 1973 is expected to be somewhat less than the $6,160 in taxes which would otherwise have been payable by the Company (on book income).[18] It is anticipated that most of the $27,000 of undistributed taxable income (which can be distributed to the shareholders without being subject to any further federal income tax) will be distributed within the two and one-half month grace period.

EXAMPLE 3

	1974	1973
Net Income before taxes	$11,160	$52,010
Provisions for Income Taxes:		
State	(446)	(2,080)
Federal (by election of the Company to include its 1974 income in that of its stockholders the tax of $2,250 otherwise payable by the Company on this income was eliminated.) See Note C.	—0—	(18,030)
Net income after taxes	$10,714	$31,900

Note C — Status of Income Taxes

For the year ended December 31, 1974, the Company has elected to have its income taxed to the stockholders. Thus, the provision for federal income taxes of $2,250 otherwise payable by the corporation was omitted in the determination of net income for the year then ended. However, provision has been made in the accompanying income statement for anticipated future distributions to stockholders. Since the Company will not pay federal income taxes while the election is effective, the reserve of $21,075 for deferred federal income taxes arising from accelerated depreciation is no longer required and has been transferred to "Income from Extraordinary Items."

EXAMPLE 4

As of December 31, 1974 from Pro Forma Statements

Current Liabilities:	
Amounts distributable to shareholders of Subchapter S corporations	$ 134,000.00
Total current liabilities	$2,950,591.00
Long-term debt:	
Deferred Federal income taxes (Note D)	12,950.00
Total liabilities	$3,267,893.00
Income before federal income taxes	$1,114,788.13

[18]There is an advantage to showing the taxes based upon book income: any difference between book and taxable incomes which would otherwise dictate income tax allocations are automatically recognized.

Provision for federal income taxes (including deferred taxes)	216,057.58
Income before charge equivalent to provision for federal income taxes on Subchapter S corporations	898,730.55
Charge equivalent to provision for federal income taxes on Subchapter S corporations (Note D)	220,650.00
Net income	678,080.55
Earned surplus, beginning of year	795,063.98
Total	1,472,144.53
Amounts distributed and distributable to shareholders of Subchapter S corporations LESS charge equivalent to provision for federal income taxes (Note D)	715,816.29
Earned surplus, end of year	$ 757,328.24

Note D — Federal Income Taxes

The shareholders of A, B, and C corporations have filed elections under Section 1372(a) of the Internal Revenue Code to be treated as small business corporations (Subchapter S corporations) whereby the net profits or losses of such companies (as determined for tax purposes) will be ratably reported by the respective shareholders on their individual income tax returns. Such elections were terminated, effective January 1, 1975. In the accompanying statement of combined income and earned surplus, a charge equivalent to Federal income taxes has been provided for these companies and the amounts shown as distributed and distributable to their shareholders have been reduced accordingly.

EXAMPLE 5

Net loss (The Company elected under I.R.C. Section 1371 to include this loss in the income of the stockholders. Thus, the Company will not obtain the tax benefit of the carryback refund of $30,556 to which would otherwise accrue to the Company.)	($77,200)

Miscellaneous Accounting Problems

When a corporation elects, operates under, or terminates a Subchapter S election, several accounting or auditing problems are encountered.

Provisions for Income Taxes

While operating as a Subchapter S corporation, no Federal income taxes are normally paid at the corporate level. Should the absence of income tax provisions on the balance sheet and income statement be explained? Since this special type of taxation is so precarious (due to the ever-present danger of voluntary or involuntary termination), then at a minimum, a footnote should clearly inform the reader of this contingent liability. The contingent liability is the possibility that the earnings may be taxed at the corporate level if any of the stringent requirements have not been met during the year. The footnote should also inform the user that the right to withdraw PTI tax-free is personal, and, if there is a sale, transfer, or death, the PTI will be taxed again to the recipient.

The first four previous examples demonstrate how the absence of Federal income taxes can be presented on the income statement. Footnote B to Example 2 is fairly complete. The reader is informed that the undistributed taxable income is to be distributed within the two and one-half month grace period. However, the reader is not informed that any PTI is a personal right and can be withdrawn tax-free only by the original stockholder who included it in his individual income tax return.

Conversely, an electing corporation may have a net operating loss during an election year[19] which is included in the shareholder's taxable income. Thus, there is no corporate carryback or carryforward of such operating losses that occur in an election year. The company will not receive the tax benefit of the carryback refund or the right to carry the loss to future years in order to offset taxable income. The loss of this tax benefit should be adequately disclosed on the financial statements. Example 5 suggests the wording of a footnote that can be attached to the income statement to inform readers that the operating loss was used at the stockholder level and is not available for future years.

Comparative Financial Statements

Especially during the first year of an election or the year after termination, there is a problem in making financial statements comparable. Several alternatives may be suggested to minimize misinterpretation by users of financial statements:

1. Explain the effects of this special election in a footnote.[20]

---

[19]Net operating losses occurring before an election year are not necessarily lost since they can be carried forward to nonelection years. However, the five-year carryover period continues to run while the Subchapter S election is in effect.

[20]Blough, *op. cit.*, p. 76.

2. The complete income statements can be presented together, but for the periods in which there is no election, the amount of net income before deducting federal income taxes can be shown.[21]

3. The amount of federal income taxes which the company would have to pay if there were no election can be presented in a footnote or indicated parenthetically.[22]

4. The complete income statements can be presented together, and, for the periods in which there is no election, net income can be shown after deducting federal income taxes. But, in a footnote or parenthetically, the amount of federal income taxes which the company would have to pay if it had not made the election can be indicated. Example 3 illustrates this approach.

This last approach is probably more informative, especially where comparative earnings or earnings per share figures are presented to the public in connection with a sale of securities or purchase request. Effective for annual reports commencing January 1, 1969, at least one presentation of earnings per share is required to be shown on the face of the income statement in order to conform with generally accepted accounting principles (APB Opinion No. 15, "Earnings Per Share"). This requirement applies to Subchapter S corporations.

Pro Forma Statements

Frequently pro forma financial statements are prepared for Subchapter S corporations. For example, assume that such statements are prepared for use in a possible merger or sale. To be meaningful to a prospective purchaser, the statements should probably contain a charge equivalent to federal income taxes, since the Subchapter S election will usually be terminated. The preceding Example 4 reflects the federal income taxes which would otherwise be payable by the companies and the resultant net income computed without the benefit of the Subchapter S election. The reader should note the current liability "Amount distributable to shareholders of Subchapter S corporations" of $134,000.00. We have discussed previously that a liability for dividends does not exist until properly declared by the

---

[21] *Ibid.*
[22] *Ibid.*

board of directors. Thus, if these dividends have not been declared, a liability should not be recorded.

Disposition of Deferred Income Tax Accounts

Deferred or prepaid income tax accounts are often provided to record the difference between book and tax incomes. Often, where either accelerated depreciation or installment tax method has been used only for income tax purposes, these income tax allocation amounts can be substantial. What should be done with deferred or prepaid income tax amounts made in periods prior to the Subchapter S election?

Since the Subchapter S corporation does not have to pay a federal income tax while the election is effective, then any deferred or prepaid income tax accounts should be eliminated and any items shown "net of taxes" should be increased to their full value.[23] See Example 3. Such amounts should not be carried directly to retained earnings but should be transferred to "income or loss from extraordinary items."[24] If and when the Subchapter S election is terminated, the appropriate income tax allocation amounts should be reinstated. Due to the precarious duration of this special tax election, the financial statements should inform the reader of any material differences between financial and tax accounting. Omission of material differences may be misleading to users considering the probable reinstatement of such amounts when the election is terminated.

Auditor's Opinion

Independent public accountants often audit the financial records of Subchapter S corporations. In many cases the auditor will issue an unqualified, qualified, or adverse opinion, or he will disclaim an opinion. A Subchapter S election should not require the auditor to change the format of his audit opinion. Additional steps should be added to his audit program in order to satisfy himself that the proper shareholders' consents have been filed and the requirements for a valid election have been satisfied. See annual checklist at the end of Chapter 3. Otherwise, there may be an inadvertent termination of this special election with the resulting harsh tax consequences.

---

[23]*Ibid.* Blough mentioned (but did not recommend) that "the adjustments of items shown 'net of taxes' [could] work themselves out in subsequent periods as the deferred charges are amortized or the estimated liabilities are liquidated."

[24]APB Opinion No. 9, "Reporting the Results of Operations," pp. 114-115.

Application of generally accepted accounting principles should be consistent from year to year. Where a change has been made from one acceptable practice to another, the user may make wrong decisions if he is not informed of such change. Although a Subchapter S election will cause a change in conditions, it does not cause a change in the application of generally accepted accounting principles. Thus, the auditor does not have to state a consistency exception in his audit opinion.

Recordkeeping

Owners of closely-held corporations frequently fail to appreciate the importance of maintaining and retaining adequate records. Simply because the Subchapter S corporation does not pay a corporate tax, the business is not relieved of its obligation to maintain adequate documentations. Besides, the Subchapter S corporation does have to file an informational return, Form 1120S, which contains, in effect, both an income statement and balance sheet. Further, the stockholders must maintain adequate records for filing their own tax returns.

Readers may wish to refer to M. D. James, editor, *Portfolio of Accounting Systems for Small and Medium-Sized Businesses* (Englewood Cliffs: Prentice-Hall, Inc., 1968). These two volumes by the National Public Accountants contain seventy different accounting systems for small businesses, ranging from advertising agencies to veterinarians.

I.R.C. Sections 6001 and 6011(a) require all taxpayers to file a tax return each year and to keep such records as the Commissioner may prescribe. The willful failure to comply therewith constitutes a misdemeanor. The penalty is a fine of not more than $10,000 or imprisonment for not more than one year, or both, together with the costs of prosecution.[25] Regulation 1.6001(a) requires all taxpayers (except certain farmers and wage-earners) to "keep such permanent books of account or records, including inventories, as are sufficient to establish the amount of gross income, deductions, credits, or other matters . . ." A civil penalty is imposed upon a taxpayer who fails to file a return unless it is shown that such failure is due to reasonable cause and not due to willful neglect. An amount of 5 percent of the deficiency is added to the tax liability per month up to a maximum of 25 percent of the deficiency in the aggregate.[26]

---

[25]I.R.C. Section 7203.
[26]I.R.C. Section 6651(a).

Along this same line, Regulation 1.446-1(a)(4) requires each taxpayer to maintain such accounting records as will enable him to file a correct return. To clearly reflect income, the income must be indicated with as much accuracy as standard methods of accounting permit.[27] In fact, cases are legion in which the decision went against a taxpayer because his records were inadequate, since in most situations the burden of proof is upon him to show that any alleged deficiency is incorrect. Thus, as a practical matter, supporting records may be needed at the corporate as well as at the shareholder level in order to prove the correctness of items of income or deductions when challenged by the Commissioner. *William H. Leonhart*[28] may be recommended for constructive nighttime reading. The shareholders of this Subchapter S corporation attempted to deduct everything except the kitchen sink without adequate documentation.

Aside from the criminal penalties mentioned above, the failure to maintain proper records may subject taxpayers to a 5 percent negligence penalty.[29] In *William H. Leonhart,*[30] a 5 percent negligence penalty was imposed upon the shareholders of the electing corporation because of their "negligence or intentional disregard of rules and regulations . . ." The Tax Court said that the Commissioner is presumed to be correct, and the taxpayer must convince the court that such a determination is erroneous. However, in *Golden Nugget, Inc.,* T.C.M. 1969-149, the court refused to uphold the negligence penalty since the shareholders had only high school educations, were inexperienced in bookkeeping and accounting, had engaged the services of a qualified public accountant, and had followed his advice.

Where the failure to file a return is with an intent to evade or defeat a tax, a fraud penalty of 50 percent of the underpayment is added to the tax liability.[31]

Method of Accounting

The financial books of the Subchapter S corporation should be set up to coincide with its method of accounting and its tax year. In fact, Regulation 1.446-1(a) provides that taxable income must be

---

[27]*Caldwell* vs. *Commissioner,* 202 F. 2d 112 (2d Cir. 1953).

[28]T.C.M. 1968-98, *aff'd. per curiam,* 414 F. 2d 749 (4th Cir. 1969).

[29]I.R.C. Section 6653(a).

[30]*Supra,* note 28; See similar decision involving negligence penalty in *Robert L. Bunnel,* 50 T.C. 837 (1968).

[31]I.R.C. Section 6653(b).

computed under the method of accounting on the basis of which a taxpayer regularly computes his income in keeping his books. However, stockholders of the electing corporation do not have to adopt the tax year of the corporation. Chapter 12 discusses the opportunity of deferring income taxes of stockholders by adopting a corporate tax year that is different from those of its stockholders. The electing corporation may adopt either a fiscal year or a calendar year, but if no books are kept, it has no choice and must use a calendar year.[32]

A taxpayer is free to adopt almost any method of accounting he chooses, as long as the method meets certain requirements, namely:

1. The method clearly reflects income for a twelve-month period.
2. It is based upon adequate records.
3. It is consistently used without distorting annual income.
4. It cannot cause excessive administrative inconveniences or result in undue loss of revenue.[33]

The permissible methods are:

1. Cash receipts and disbursements method.
2. Accrual method.
3. Special methods, such as installment tax method.
4. Combination of the above methods which clearly reflect income.[34]

If books are not maintained, the proper accounting method is determined by the Commissioner.[35] The accrual method must be used to report sales and purchases in all cases where the Subchapter S corporation has an inventory (Regulations 1.446-1(c)(i) and 1.471-1).

The Commissioner May Be Arbitrary

If the Commissioner determines that a taxpayer has no regular accounting method or that his books and records do not clearly reflect income, he may impose certain changes. The taxpayer's accounting period may be shifted from a fiscal to a calendar year basis, or vice versa. Or, the taxpayer's accounting method may be converted from an accrual basis to the cash basis or any combination thereof.[36]

The Commissioner may use several indirect methods to ascertain

---

[32]I.R.C. Section 441(g)(1)

[33]*Harden* vs. *Commissioner,* 202 F. 2d 418 (10th Cir. 1955).

[34]I.R.C. Section 446(c).

[35]Regulation 1.446-1(b)(1); *James W. England, Jr.,* 34 T.C. 617 (1960).

[36]I.R.C. Section 446(b).

income when records do not adequately reflect true income. In the "percentage markup" method, the income from a business is compared with the income from similar businesses. In another approach the taxpayer's gross income may be approximated by substituting the aggregate amount of bank deposits during the tax year for the amount shown on the tax return. This is designed to shift to the taxpayer the burden of proving which, if any, of these bank deposits should not be taxed as income.

Probably the method used most often by IRS agents is the "net worth" test. By this procedure the taxpayer's beginning and ending net worths are compared to arrive at the increase for the year. By adding nondeductible expenditures for personal and living expenses and subtracting nontaxable receipts, taxable income is thereby reconstructed.[37] But nontaxable income (such as gifts or the repayment of a loan) will be deemed fully taxable if the taxpayer cannot by adequate records show its true source.

The reader is reminded that the Commissioner's power to redetermine taxable income is based upon the absence of adequate records. Thus, a taxpayer would be safe from challenge if his tax returns substantially conformed with his books, and the latter clearly reflected income in a consistent manner.[38]

Though the weight to be given bookkeeping entries and other accounting records must be strong when it comes to supporting a deduction or determining income, this evidence is by no means conclusive.[39] At best one can say that these records shift to the Government the burden of proving otherwise. Of course, in most situations where acceptable accounting practices exist, the taxpayer may be considered to have placed himself in a safe tax position.[40]

Cohan Rule

Brief mention should be made of the Cohan decision that gave a break to a taxpayer who had claimed tax deductions supported by nothing but his general statements.[41] The absence of records was not deemed fatal, and the taxpayer, none other than George M. Cohan,

[37]The Supreme Court has approved the "net worth" method; *Holland* vs. *United States,* 348 U.S. 121 (1954).

[28]*Bent Co.,* 26 B.T.A. 1369 (1932).

[39]*Northwestern States Portland Cement Co.* vs. *Huston,* 126 F. 2d 196 (8th Cir. 1942).

[40]*Lime Cola Co.,* 22 T.C. 593 (1954); *Beacon Auto Stores, Inc.,* 42 B.T.A. 703 (1940); *Chicago, Rock Island and Pacific Railways, Co.,* 47 F. 2d 990 (7th Cir. 1931).

[41]*Cohan* vs. *Commissioner,* 39 F. 2d 540 (2d Cir. 1930).

was allowed a reasonable estimate as deduction for travel and entertainment expenditures. The Court emphasized, however, that any doubtful and uncertain items must be resolved against the taxpayer. Thus, even here there was a price to pay for lack of records.

It has generally been held that the Cohan case can be applied to support the deduction of other expenses besides travel and entertainment. In *Golden Nugget, Inc.,*[42] a Subchapter S corporation operated a bingo parlor, paid all jackpots in cash, but then destroyed the duplicate tickets showing the number of bingo cards sold after the net amounts were recorded on daily report sheets. The Commissioner disallowed all the amounts shown as daily net losses, but the Tax Court used the Cohan rule to estimate the losses. Likewise, in *William H. Leonhart,* T.C.M. 1968-98, the court used the Cohan rule to estimate charitable contributions. But in *Theodore T. Benson,*[43] the court did not use the Cohan rule to estimate deductions for travel, entertainment, office, and miscellaneous expenses.

The Cohan rule is still applicable in certain areas. Even for travel and entertainment expenses, it can be used to estimate unsubstantiated elements in limited situations.[44] Charitable contributions, gambling losses, deductible taxes, casualty losses, medical expenses, interest, and child care expenses are a few areas where approximation may be applicable.[45] However, in the last several years taxpayers have had less and less success with the Cohan rule.[46]

Adequate Books and Records

There are two reasons for the Subchapter S corporation and its shareholders to maintain adequate records. First, the corporation and shareholders need to adopt accounting methods based on their records that will reflect their true income when they prepare their various income tax returns and the informational Form 1120S. Second, if the

---

[42]T.C.M. 1969-149; See also *William duPont, Jr.,* 234 F. Supp. 681 (D.C. Del. 1964); *August F. Nielsen,* T.C.M. 1968-11.

[43]T.C.M. 1967-74.

[44]Cohan rule may be used if the taxpayer loses his records and to aggregate certain incidental items, such as tips, cab fare, and so forth; Regulation 1.274-5(c)(5) and (6). See *Louis,* T.C.M. 1966-204; *Loos,* T.C.M. 1967-37; *Hayes,* T.C.M. 1967-80; *Thompson,* T.C.M. 1967-252.

[45]See, for example, *Thompson, supra,* note 44; *Larsen,* T.C.M. 1950-268; *Lambert,* T.C.M. 1949-160; *Bonus,* T.C.M. 1948-234.

[46]See, for example, *Bennett,* T.C.M. 1968-71; *Dick,* T.C.M. 1968-32; *Greenfeld,* T.C.M. 1966-83; *Mears* vs. *Commissioner,* 386 F. 2d 450 (5th Cir. 1968); *Cox,* T.C.M. 1968-9.

Commissioner audits the taxpayers' returns, they will be able to determine whether the taxpayers' accounting methods and the supporting records do reflect true income. Although the Cohan rule may allow a taxpayer some deduction in certain cases, it cannot be considered anything but a desperate approach to the problem. Not only is the full applicability of this rule none too certain, but it has never proved popular with the IRS. All this means, of course, is that the shareholders may have to resort to costly court action to secure support for their position. From a practical tax-planning standpoint, one must assume that the matter of record keeping goes beyond a judicially determined minimum and involves, instead, that which may be necessary to satisfy the IRS at an administrative level.

The kind of records that should be maintained is not specified in the law. A formal set of books in addition to supporting documents, should be maintained at the corporate level. As previously mentioned, the retained earnings account should be maintained in such a manner as to be able to easily compute UTI, PTI, and earnings from non-Subchapter S years. Likewise, each stockholder must keep a record of his own share of UTI and PTI. [See Regulations 1.1375-4(f) and 1.1375-6(a)(5).] Aside from the above requirements, the shareholders' records need not be elaborate or formal. The simplicity of the records should encourage the stockholders to make the entries promptly as income items and cash distributions are received and payments for any deductible expenses are made. The Form W-2 received by an employee-stockholder is an adequate record of the salary received from the corporation. Sales slips, bills, invoices, receipts, canceled checks, and other documents are sufficient evidence to support deductions or credits claimed on his individual tax return. It is imperative that the stockholder maintain sufficient records to verify his basis in the Subchapter S corporation. Dates of cash distributions are very important due to the technicalities involved with PTI and UTI.

Copies of old income tax returns (both corporate and individual) should be retained to facilitate the filing of amended returns, the calculation of income-averaging and the shareholder's tax basis, and the preservation of certain elections. Even though copies of these returns can be obtained from the IRS at nominal charges, this procedure can be costly in terms of time and interest charges. Further, supporting documents which substantiate entries in a taxpayer's records should be filed in an orderly manner and stored in a safe place.

Many businessmen fail to appreciate the value of a contemporaneously recorded diary which contains pertinent financial data. This record, regardless of the form which is utilized, possesses a high probative value even in the complete absence of supporting receipts. Its value turns upon the fact that the individual made the entry on or about the time of the expenditure at a point when the factual situation was still fresh in his mind. *Calwell* vs. *Coard*[47] demonstrates the value of a detailed diary. The taxpayer, a truck driver, kept a detailed log of all stops made and also maintained a diary where he recorded the cost of his meals, the place, and date. A district court allowed him to deduct $2,173 for meals and $326 for tips (almost $11 per day for 220 days on the road).

Employee-Stockholder Problems

Gross income of a shareholder-employee does not include (within prescribed limits) wage contribution payments made to him as a result of an absence from work on account of personal injuries or sickness.[48] A taxpayer-claimant should attach a statement to his return showing the nature of the injury or illness, the date of absence, and the computation of the exclusion. Furthermore, he should obtain a doctor's explanation of any illness and attach a photostatic copy of the same to the tax return (especially if a pregnancy is involved). In the event of hospitalization this fact should be noted (including dates of admission and discharge) since it is pertinent to the computation. Form 2440 ("Statement to Support Exclusion of Sick Pay") may be used if all the sick pay received has been included in total wages as reported on Form W-2.

In certain instances the employee's burden of substantiation may be absolved by substituting a statement issued by the Subchapter S corporation. Such a statement which, in essence, eliminates the need of filing Form 2440, can only originate from employers that carry out the following procedures:

1. Maintain the records specified by Regulation 31.3401(a)-1(b)(8).
2. Assume full responsibility for the accuracy of the sick pay figures furnished to its employees.
3. List excludable sick pay in a separate block on Form W-2.[49]

Brief mention should be made of the substantiation requirements for travel and entertainment expenses. The ominous I.R.C. Section 274(d) provides that there will be no deduction for these expenses, unless the taxpayer substantiates by "adequate records" or by "suf-

---

[47]19 A.F.T.R. 2d 1697 (D.C. N.M. 1967).

[48]I.R.C. Section 105(d).

[49]Rev. Proc. 57-1, 1957-1 C.B. 721.

ficient evidence corroborating: (1) the amount, (2) the time and place, (3) the business purpose, and (4) the business relationship."

The amount for each separate expenditure for travel must be established (i.e., cost of transportation, cost of lodging, etc.). The daily cost of meals and other expenditures may be aggregated if set out in reasonable categories, such as meals, gasoline, and taxi fares. The dates of departure and return and the number of days away from home spent on business must be proven.

As for entertainment expenses, each separate expenditure must be established. Again, incidental items such as taxi fares and telephone calls may be aggregated. The taxpayer should be able to substantiate the date, name or location, and the type of entertainment. The occupation or other information relating to the persons entertained, including name, title, or designation sufficient to establish a business relationship, must be maintained.

Documentary evidence, such as receipts, paid bills and similar evidence sufficient to support an expenditure shall be required for lodging and any other item of $25 or more (except transportation charges).[50] Otherwise, documentary evidence is not necessary and a contemporaneously recorded diary may suffice.

Although employee-shareholders fall into one of the two classifications normally exempt from having to maintain permanent books or other formal records (Regulation 1.6001-1(b)), occasions may arise where such records may be necessary. Probably most important would be those employees who wish to deduct unreimbursed business expenses such as, for example, travel and local transportation. Regulation 1.162-17(d) requires independent substantiation by the employee who attempts to claim a deduction for unreimbursed expenses or who does not adequately account to the Subchapter S corporation. Accumulating and computing the cost of using one's personal automobile on behalf of the business has been somewhat simplified by the new 15¢ per mile allowance for the first 15,000 business miles (10¢ per mile over 15,000), but the number of business miles traveled still poses a threat.[51] The employee should maintain an accurate log of business miles driven, for the time when rough approximations of business mileage would suffice appears to be about over.[52] Since parking and

---

[50]Regulation 1.274-5(c)(2)(iii).

[51]Rev. Proc. 70-25, 1970-2 C.B. 506.

[52]See, for example, *Theodore T. Benson,* T.C.M. 1967-74; *William H. Leonhart,* T.C.M. 1968-98.

toll charges are deductible in addition to the standard rate, these items should also be recorded.

Note, if the employee-stockholder has income from nonwage sources (such as from the sale of real estate) more formal records are required.[53] The possibility that claiming a sick-pay exclusion could add to an employee's record-keeping burden has already been mentioned in a previous paragraph.

Statute of Limitations

The period for assessment of income taxes from the stockholders of a Subchapter S corporation is normally three years per I.R.C. Section 6501(a). However, if more than 25 percent is omitted from gross income, I.R.C. Section 6501(e) extends the period of limitation to six years. Of course, if the shareholder files no return, attempts to evade taxes, or files a fraudulent return, the period for assessment remains open without limitation (I.R.C. Section 6501(c)).

In *Benderoft* vs. *U.S.*, 398 F. 2d 132 (8th Cir. 1968), the taxpayer omitted cash distributions that amounted to more than 25 percent of gross income. When the IRS issued a deficiency notice, the taxpayer argued that the assessment was barred by the three-year statute of limitations. The IRS asserted that the six-year statute of limitations was applicable. Taxpayer's Form 1040 specifically referred to the income from the Subchapter S corporation, stating the name of the electing corporation and the amount of the taxpayer's share of the corporation's undistributed taxable income. The Eighth Circuit felt that the taxpayer's return, coupled with informational Form 1120S, adequately disclosed to the IRS the distribution of undistributed taxable income. The taxpayer won the battle.

Similarly, in *Elliott J. Roschuni,* 44 T.C. 80 (1965), an electing corporation sold a hotel and realized approximately a $71,000 long-term capital gain. The sole shareholder mistakedly reported only $34,000 of this gain on his individual tax return under the installment tax method, but he referred to Form 1120-S which included the pertinent information about the sale. The Tax Court would not extend the statute of limitations to six years under the 25 percent understatement of income rule. The court reasoned that disclosure "was made in a manner adequate to apprise the IRS of the so-called omitted amount of gross income."

The outcome was different in *Taylor* vs. *U.S.,* 24 A.F.T.R. 2d

---

[53]*Fellows,* T.C.M. 1950-14.

69-5747 (5th Cir. 1969). In this case, the taxpayer received cash distributions from a Subchapter S corporation totaling more than 25 percent of her gross income, but she failed to report the distributions on her personal tax return. The Fifth Circuit held that the six-year limitation was applicable since the taxpayer's personal tax return made no reference to her ownership of 25 percent of the Subchapter S corporation. The informational Form 1120-S alone was insufficient to fulfill the "adequate disclosure" clause in I.R.C. Section 6501(e)(1)(A)(ii). The taxpayer lost the battle.

Where there is a valid Subchapter S election, the three- and six-year limitation periods begin to run from the date of filing of the shareholder's personal tax return *or* from the due date of such return, if later. (See *William H. Leonhart,* T.C.M. 1968-98.) Where a Subchapter S election is invalid, the period of limitation on assessment runs from the date of filing of the Form 1120-S instead of the shareholder's personal tax return (I.R.C. Section 6037). However, in the case of assessment of taxes as a result of I.R.C. Section 481 adjustments, such assessments are not barred by the three-year statute of limitations merely because these adjustments indirectly relate to years beyond the statute of limitations. (*Weiss* vs. *Commissioner,* 395 F. 2d 500 (10th Cir. 1968), *aff'g* T.C.M. 1967-125.)

Record Retention

A warning is appropriate at the beginning of this section: retention periods of records vary with the various state and federal statutes and the company's future business needs. Tax practitioners should consult some of the better articles[54] and books[55] dealing with retention periods in order to develop a formal retention program for Subchapter S clients. Many companies will provide records-management specialists to advise a business. Remember: although records are important, it is foolish to retain all records permanently. A legal advisor should be consulted so that a small business does not overlook any of the applicable state or federal laws and regulations.

---

[54]See Brian A. Wyles, "Records Retention — Some Guides for the Smaller Company," *N.A.A. Bulletin* (now *Management Accounting*), November, 1962, pp. 21-28; Robert A. Shiff, "Can Your Records Go to Washington?" *The Controller,* November, 1962, pp. 552-559. Readers may wish to peruse *Records Management Quarterly,* a magazine published by American Records Management Association.

[55]Theodore Cohn, editor, *A Fast Guide to Record Retention* Newark: New Jersey Certified Public Accountants, 1967); William E. Mitchell, *Record Retention: A Practical Guide* (Evansville: Ellsworth Publishing Co., 1959); Robert B. Wheelan, *Corporate Records Retention* (New York: Controllership Foundation, Inc., 1958).

As a broad generalization, if a Subchapter S corporation and its shareholders comply with the federal statutes, they will usually be complying with most other requirements. However, there is nothing in the *Code* specifically dealing with the retention period for books and records. The "Guide to Record Retention Requirements" published by the Federal Government contains record requirements for many departments and agencies. This guide indicates what records must be kept, who must keep them, and how long they must be kept. However, many of the examples merely conclude that records should be retained so long as the contents thereof may become material in the administration of any Internal Revenue Law.[56] Regulations stipulate that all records "shall at all times be available for inspection by [Internal Revenue officers]."[57]

The minimum retention period is as long as the statute of limitations for further assessment is open for the particular taxpayer. As previously discussed, the normal statute of limitations for a Federal income tax return expires three years after the return is due to be filed or two years from the time the tax was paid, whichever expires later.[58] Incomplete returns will keep the tax year open beyond the three-year minimum period. The normal period is extended to six years by I.R.C. Section 6501(e)(1)(A) where a taxpayer omits from his return an amount of gross income properly includable therein, if the amount omitted exceeds 25 percent of the amount reported. In instances of a false return, a willful attempt to evade a tax, or the absence of a filed return, a tax can be assessed or a proceeding in court for the collection of the tax may be begun at any time.[59] Regulation 31.6001-1(e)(2) does stipulate that records are generally to be maintained for at least four years after the due date of the tax return or the date the tax is paid, whichever is the later.

There are certain cases, however, where the shareholders and corporation should definitely keep their records longer than the normal four-year period. Only a few of the most common instances are listed below:

1. Corporate records such as certificate of incorporation, constitution and by-laws, charter, minutes and resolutions of board of directors, stock ledgers, stock transfer registers,

---

[56]*Federal Register,* "Guide to Record Retention Requirements."

[57]Regulation 31.6001-1(e)(1).

[58]Regulation 301.6501(a)-1(a).

[59]Regulation 301.6501(c)-1.

trademarks and registrations, and so forth should be retained permanently.

2. Such accounting records as the following should be kept permanently: general ledgers, most subledgers and journals, annual reports, etc.

3. Records should be kept indefinitely when there are changes in the method of accounting or the "Lifo" method of inventory valuation is adopted.

4. Claims for refunds from bad debts or worthless securities require that records be retained for at least seven years.

5. Substantiation for transactions affecting the basis of an asset should be retained until the expiration of the statute of limitations from the tax year in which the asset is disposed of.

6. Under certain circumstances a stockholder can increase the basis of any stock received by gift if he can substantiate, by records and appraisals, the donor's basis, the fair market value of the stock at the date of the gift, and the gift tax paid. If the donee later sells the stock for a gain, his basis will be the donor's basis increased by any gift tax paid by donor on the gift (but not to exceed the fair market value of the stock on the date of the gift).

Changes in Accounting Method

Once an accounting method is adopted, a Subchapter S corporation is required to obtain a consent from the Commissioner before changing its method of accounting for tax purposes, except for a change by a dealer from the accrual to the installment method, a change from the FIFO to the LIFO inventory method, or a change from DDB to SYD or SYD to SL method of depreciation. Such a consent must be obtained whether or not the corporation regards the method from which it desires to change to be proper.[60]

A change in the method of accounting includes a change in the overall method of accounting for gross income or deductions or a change in the treatment of a material item. Regulation 1.446-1(e)(2)(ii) gives examples of changes which require a consent from the Commissioner: a change from the cash receipts and disbursements method to an accrual method or vice versa, a change involving the method or basis used in the valuation of inventories, a change from

---

[60]I.R.C. Section 446(e); Regulation 1.446-1(e)(2).

the cash or accrual method to a long-term contract method or vice versa, and a change involving the adoption, use, or discontinuance of any other specialized method (i.e., crop method). However, effective for tax years beginning after 1966, an electing corporation may automatically switch from an overall cash receipts and disbursements method of accounting to an accrual method, subject to the several conditions outlined in Rev. Proc. 67-10, 1967-1 C.B. 585.

In the case of a change in the accounting method, an electing corporation must agree to take into account all adjustments necessary to prevent duplication or omission of income or deductions.[61] These adjustments are made with respect to the taxable income of the electing corporation in the year of the change (Regulation 1.481-2 (c)(2)(ii)). Such adjustments must consider inventories, accounts receivable, accounts payable, and any other item necessary to prevent amounts from being duplicated or omitted.[62]

In order to prevent bunching of income into one tax year, I.R.C. Section 481(b) allows the shareholders of the electing corporation to prorate such income under either of two elective methods. Under the first method, when adjustments increase the taxable income of a shareholder in the year of change by more than $3,000 and the old accounting method has been used for the two preceding years, each stockholder is subject to the increase in the tax liability in the year of change only to the extent of the increase which would result if the adjustments were included ratably in the year of change and the two preceding tax years. It is not necessary for the stockholder to have been a member of the electing corporation for the two tax years immediately preceding the year of change in order for this relief method to apply.[63]

If a stockholder can reconstruct his taxable income using the new method for one or more years preceding the year of change, his additional tax is limited to the amount of tax that would have been paid for these years if the new method had been used. Adjustments not allocated to these prior years are included in the income in the year of change.[64] A shareholder may apply this relief clause even though he was not a stockholder, or the corporation was not an

---

[61]I.R.C. Section 481(a); Regulation 1.446-1(a)(3).

[62]Regulation 1.481-1(b).

[63]Regulation 1.481-2(c)(5)(ii).

[64]I.R.C. Section 481(b)(2).

electing corporation, for all of the tax years affected by the allocations.[65]

If a Subchapter S corporation elects to change from the accrual method to the installment method of reporting income from installment sales, it must follow a specified procedure to avoid having the same income taxed twice. The accrual basis taxpayer is taxed on the total profit when the installment obligation is created. However, when the installment method is used, the collection of each installment creates taxable income. Section 453(c) requires that such installments be included in taxable income but also makes provision for adjustment of the tax resulting from inclusion of the already taxed income in the current taxable income. The adjustment is described in Regulation 1.453-7.

Since the adjustment is made to tax liability rather than to taxable income, it is clear that such an adjustment would provide no relief in a Subchapter S context unless it can be passed through to shareholders. Revenue Ruling 72-33[66] makes the adjustment procedure available at the shareholder level. This relief is accomplished in the following manner. The Subchapter S corporation prepares a schedule which indicates the collection of installment sales and allocates the profit to shareholders on the basis of stock ownership. Each shareholder then adjusts his present tax liability in the manner provided by Regulation 1.453-7(b). The procedure also requires that the shareholder adjust the basis of his stock downward because, in the absence of any such adjustment, that basis has been increased both when the sale was made as well as when the installment was collected.

This relief procedure is not available when the Subchapter S election and the change from the accrual method to the installment method are both made in the same year.[67] Revenue Ruling 72-33 appears to be applicable to those situations where the installment obligations were created during years for which a Subchapter S election is in effect. However, the procedure outlined in Revenue Ruling 72 33 does not appear to be workable in a situation where the corporation is taxed under the accrual method (pre-Subchapter S years) and the shareholders incur the additional tax because the

---

[65]Regulation 1.481-2(c)(5)(ii).

[66]1972-1 C.B. 130; For a more complete discussion of the installment method, see Crumbley and Crews, "Use of Installment Tax Method for Revolving Accounts," *Journal of Accountancy,* Vol. 128 (July, 1969), pp. 33-40.

[67]Rev. Rul. 73-144, 1973-1 C.B. 614.

collection of the installment obligation creates additional taxable income.

Nevertheless, the same income is still being taxed twice, and it can be argued that some relief is still in order. In the absence of this relief, Subchapter S corporations should consider postponing changes from accrual to installment method until all obligations of pre-Subchapter S years have been collected in full.

The waters in several areas are quite muddy for Subchapter S corporations. Judicial treatment for these troublesome areas may be conveniently divided into the following categories:

1. A proprietorship or partnership incorporates and makes a Subchapter S election.

2. An existing corporation elects Subchapter S status.

Unincorporated Business Becomes Subchapter S Corporation

In one court case,[68] an accrual basis partnership became an accrual basis Subchapter S corporation. The Tax Court felt that I.R.C. Section 481 adjustments were inapplicable since there was no change in the accounting method. Relying on a previous case involving the transfer of a partnership into a non-electing corporation,[69] the court stipulated that since the Subchapter S corporation did not have a previous tax year, there could be no change in the electing corporation's method of accounting.

In a later case [*Paul H. Travis,* 47 T.C. 502 (1967)], a sole proprietorship was transferred to a corporation that immediately filed a Subchapter S election. Both the proprietorship and the electing corporation reported their receipts on the cash basis but deducted expenses on the accrual basis. The Tax Court upheld the Commissioner's contention that the accounting method of the Subchapter S corporation did not clearly reflect income. However, the court did not accept the Commissioner's position that the *Birren* rule[70] requires full inclusion of the accounts receivable since they have a zero basis to the Subchapter S corporation. The *Birren* rule was not applicable since the proprietorship and the electing corporation "were the same

---

[68]*E. Morris Cox,* 43 T.C. 448 (1965).

[69]*Ezo Products Co.,* 37 T.C. 385 (1961).

[70]*P. A. Birren & Son, Inc.* vs. *Commissioner,* 116 F. 2d 718 (7th Cir. 1940); the courts have accepted the position that an individual transferor is not taxed, but the transferee corporation must report the income when collected (where a cash basis proprietorship is transferred to a controlled corporation in a tax-free I.R.C. Section 351 exchange).

taxable entity . . . which seems sound in light of the purpose of Subchapter S."[71] In noting the inconsistency of this decision, one commentator stated that if *Travis* is taken literally, a cash-basis proprietor who decides to incorporate and to operate as a Subchapter S corporation on the accrual basis of accounting has changed his accounting method, which requires the consent of the Commissioner.[72] The Tax Court did not rule on whether or not I.R.C. Section 481 applied to the Subchapter S corporation.

Existing Corporation Elects Subchapter S

At least two court cases have held that a Subchapter S corporation may not adopt a method of accounting different from the method it used as a regular corporation without obtaining the Commissioner's consent. In *Weiss* vs. *Commissioner*,[73] a regular corporation elected to be taxed under Subchapter S status but changed its method of valuing inventory from the nominal to the actual value. The Tenth Circuit affirmed the Tax Court's determination that the increase in income resulting from the IRS's adjustments under I.R.C. Section 481 was includable in the taxable income of the stockholders. "Section 481 does not expressly state, of course, that it applies to Subchapter S shareholders but there is no doubt that it does."[74]

In a related case with a similar conclusion,[75] a corporation switched from the accrual basis to the cash basis in reporting commission income in the same year that it elected Subchapter S status. The taxpayer argued that a Subchapter S election creates a new tax entity and such entity is free to elect its own accounting methods. The Tax Court stated that "we are not aware of any provision of the Internal Revenue Code which would entitle an existing corporation which elects to be taxed as a small business corporation under Subchapter S to change its accounting methods without the consent of the Commissioner solely on account of such election . . ."[76]

---

[71]*Paul H. Travis,* 47 T.C. 502 (1967).

[72]Thomas R. White, 3rd, "Recurring and New Problems Under Subchapter S," *New York University Twenty-Seventh Annual Institute on Federal Taxation,* (New York: Matthew Bender, 1969), p. 759.

[73]395 F. 2d 500 (10th Cir. 1968), *aff'g.* T.C.M. 1967-125.

[74]*Ibid.*

[75]*William H. Leonhart,* T.C.M. 1968-98.

[76]*Ibid.*

Chapter 14

Subchapter S Tax Planning

Small businesses are often burdened with double taxation but do not derive much economic or legal advantage from operating as a corporation. Small corporations and their advisors must develop new techniques and concepts to cope with the proliferation of more complex tax laws. Tax education is a vital factor in the continuance of small businesses. A lack of general tax knowledge probably accounts for the larger share of the federal and local taxes being borne by the small corporation when compared to its larger corporate counterpart. The Subchapter S election is one tax-planning tool which can be used most effectively by small businesses.

Tax Planning Concepts

Steps can be undertaken to get the earnings of a close corporation into the pockets of the shareholders at a minimum loss of profits to taxes. A comprehensive tax plan which considers all tax and non-tax issues has a greater chance of being successful, of course, than a superficial plan. The following is a brief review of the more significant Subchapter S tax-planning concepts developed in this treatise.

•The Subchapter S corporation is a highly useful tax-planning device which allows the taxpayer the benefits of the corporate form of doing business yet allows him to escape corporate taxation. Subchapter S is not without its dangers. In order to avoid problems, the taxpayer and his advisers must have a firm understanding of the advantages and limitations of electing to be taxed as a Subchapter S corporation.

•Not every corporation can qualify for Subchapter S. In order to be eligible for Subchapter S status, a corporation must be able to meet stringent requirements with respect to the ownership of its stock and the character of its income. These requirements must be met on a continuing basis in order to maintain the corporation's status under Subchapter S. It may not always be advisable for an eligible corporation to make this election.

•The corporation must file an election in order to receive Subchapter S treatment. All shareholders must file their consent to the election. This applies to future as well as present shareholders.

•A Subchapter S corporation is a tax-reporting entity but not a tax-paying entity. In accordance with the conduit principle, the income is passed to the shareholders for inclusion in their gross incomes. The rate of taxation is based upon the individual's income position. If the Subchapter S net income pushes the individual into a high personal tax bracket, he may find that the standard corporation is a more appropriate form.

•Profits are allocated among shareholders for tax purposes in accordance with their proportionate holdings at the end of the tax year. A shareholder who owns 25 percent of the stock on the last day of the tax year will have 25 percent of the corporation's income allocated to him. Changes of ownership during the year are irrelevant.

•Losses are allocated among shareholders on a daily basis and do take into consideration changes of stock ownership during the tax year. This causes the purchase of Subchapter S stock during the tax year to be dangerous because the purchaser of the stock will have to share some of his loss with the former shareholder.

•Most income items lose their special character as they are passed through the Subchapter S corporation to the shareholders. Of particular significance is the fact that tax-exempt interest becomes taxable to shareholders. Accordingly, it is bad tax planning to allow a Subchapter S corporation to hold tax-exempt municipal securities.

•The character of long-term capital gain is not lost as it passes through to the shareholders. Each shareholder treats his share of the Subchapter S long-term capital gain just as he would any other long-term capital gain.

•A corporation with a long-term capital gain in excess of $25,000 may find that it is subject to taxation at the corporate level. Use of the installment method may soften the impact of this tax.

•In order to be able to deduct his share of the Subchapter S net operating loss, the loss must be less than the shareholder's adjusted basis for his stock, plus the adjusted basis of any indebtdness of the corporation to the shareholder. If it appears that the corporation is to sustain losses, each shareholder should insure that his basis is sufficient to absorb his share of the loss. If necessary, the shareholder may increase his loss-absorbing capacity by making loans to the corporation.

•A Subchapter S corporation should plan to distribute its earnings on a current basis. Any earnings which are not distributed on a current basis become previously taxed income and, as such, cannot be distributed in a subsequent period until all of that year's current earnings are distributed.

• The corporation has two and one-half months after the close of the tax year to measure its income and distribute it to the shareholders. Any income not distributed by the end of the two and one-half month period becomes previously taxed income.

• The corporation should strive to measure its book income in accordance with tax concepts. If book income is greater than taxable income, a distribution of this excess will constitute a taxable dividend when received by the shareholders.

• A corporation that measures its income for book purposes in accordance with tax concepts and distributes its income on a current basis avoids the problems inherent in previously taxed income.

• Previously taxed income is personal to the shareholder who included it in his gross income and cannot be received tax-free by any other individual. The possibility that the income may be taxed twice provides still another reason why income should be distributed on a current basis.

• Shareholders can provide the corporation with a good source of short-term working capital. In order to avoid creating a fatal second class of stock, the loans should be evidenced by a note which contains a maturity date and bears a reasonable rate of interest. Periodically, the interest should be paid. When the notes mature, they should be paid, if this is possible. Otherwise, a new note should be prepared, and its face value should include any unpaid interest. The rate of interest should approximate the rate which would be paid in an arm's-length transaction.

• Since a trust is not a permissible shareholder, that device is not available for estate-planning purposes. However, there are alternatives which can be used for disposing of the stock upon the death of the shareholder. The stock may be transferred by specific bequest, or it may be held jointly with the person who is to receive the stock at the shareholder's death. A legal life estate can also be used as an estate-planning device.

• A preincorporation agreement between the shareholders can be a useful part of a plan for protecting the Subchapter S election. It should state the intent of the parties to maintain a valid Subchapter S election. The agreement should place restrictions on the sale of the stock, but must not be so restrictive that the individual has no means of disposing of his stock. The orderly disposal of the stock upon the death of the shareholder may be accomplished by a buy-sell agreement. The two most common buy-sell agreements are the stock-redemption plan and the cross-purchase plan.

•A stock-redemption plan provides a vehicle whereby the stock of the deceased is bought by the corporation and cancelled. The estate is thus removed from the picture. Since cash will be necessary to effect this plan, the corporation should insure the lives of the shareholders. A shareholder's death generates the cash to enable the corporation to purchase the stock.

•A cross-purchase plan establishes a procedure whereby the shares of the deceased are purchased by the surviving shareholders. However, each shareholder must be able to pay the estate; life insurance can provide the needed funds.

•Each plan has its own advantages and limitations. The cross-purchase plan tends to become complicated as the number of shareholders increases. Therefore, the stock redemption plan may be superior for corporations with nine or ten shareholders.

•Stockholder agreements probably cannot bind the successor for specific performance. However, the shareholders may deposit their endorsed shares of stock in escrow. The power of the escrow holder must be limited in order that the holder will not be classified as a trustee, which would terminate the election.

•Valuation of the stock of a closely-held corporation is always a real problem. A fair-market-value approach may provide the best measure, and this should be subject to periodic revision. The method of valuation selected should be made a part of any shareholder agreements.

•A Subchapter S corporation can have only one class of stock issued and outstanding. Loans by shareholders to the corporation in proportion to their stock holdings do not constitute a second class of stock.

•A Subchapter S election offers many corporate advantages to the small business. Among these are employee benefits for owners. The Subchapter S corporation, however, can avoid corporate taxation.

•There are advantages to establishing the corporation with a high debt-to-equity ratio. However, the thin capitalization doctrine may be applied, and this will cause the debt capital to be treated as equity capital.

•Although property distributions cannot be used to reduce undistributed taxable income, they can be used to liquidate shareholder loans to the corporation.

•Loans may be obtained from outsiders and may be guaranteed by shareholders. However, transactions of this nature do not increase the shareholder's basis for net operating loss purposes.

•The limitations on foreign income and passive-investment income are based upon gross receipts rather than gross income.

•Passive-investment income includes royalties, rents, interest, dividends, annuities, and sales or exchanges of stock or securities.

•Rents are not considered to be passive income for Subchapter S purposes if the lessor also provides the lessee with significant services.

•A Subchapter S election will allow net operating losses to be passed to shareholders on an annual basis. This is not possible with the standard corporation.

•The penalty for unreasonable accumulation of earnings does not apply to Subchapter S corporations. However, a corporation that distributes its earnings on a current basis should not be concerned with this penalty tax.

•Because the Subchapter S election is always in danger of being lost, the taxpayer and his advisers must constantly be aware of tax traps in order to protect the election. Although the notion of avoiding corporate taxation may appear to simplify matters, the Subchapter S procedure is by no means simple.

•A Subchapter S corporation should have an accounting system that will reflect the status of undistributed taxable income, previously taxed income, pre-election accumulations, and dividends. The undistributed taxable income account remains open for two and one-half months after the close of the tax year to indicate the amount which must be distributed in order to avoid previously taxed income. Any amount not distributed by that time is closed to the previously taxed income account. This procedure will help management to keep appraised of its situation and to avoid costly errors.

•A corporation may not wish to remain a Subchapter S corporation forever. However, a voluntary revocation may not be advantageous since the election is not terminated until the next year. All undistributed taxable income and previously taxed income should be distributed before the revocation is effective. A re-election cannot be made within the next five years unless there is at least a 50 percent change in stock ownership.

●Involuntary disqualifications terminate an election retroactively. The transfer of some shares of stock to a nonconsenting individual or the creation of a second class of stock by a short-term stockholders' agreement may be simple ways to terminate an election. Any action must be a *bona fide* transaction.

●Income may be shifted by *bona fide* gifts of stock. However, where shares are transferred and the donor is named the custodian, the courts may not recognize the gift even though the transaction is valid under the state's Uniform Gifts to Minors Act.

The Future of Subchapter S

There is nothing unreasonable about the notion that a small, closely-held corporation is no different than a proprietorship or partnership and should receive similar tax treatment. Although Subchapter S is by no means perfect, it is being adopted by an increasing number of small businesses, and this trend will probably continue. In spite of the fact that the Treasury often acts as if it does not like Subchapter S and would like it to be repealed, there is no evidence that this will ever happen. Nevertheless, no one believes that Subchapter S is perfect in its present form.

As a practical matter, we may hopefully expect Subchapter S to become more workable in the future. As is true in the case of any new tax legislation, the authors of Subchapter S could not be expected to write a perfect law. Nevertheless, the experiences of the last one and a half decades have indicated certain areas where Subchapter S can stand improvement. Improvements have been made during this period. The addition of the grace period provisions is an outstanding example.

Unfortunately, all suggestions for Subchapter S reform have not been positive in nature. For example, Congress, in 1969, brought some of the Subchapter S employee fringe benefits in line with partnerships. Legislation of this nature can only serve to diminish the usefulness of Subchapter S.

We may expect meaningful reforms to be made in the future. A prime area for reform is the treatment of rental income as passive investment income. This is a glaring defect in the Subchapter S package. Without arguing the merits of personal holding company treatment of rental income, it is unthinkable to deny Subchapter S treatment to owner-operators of rental property on grounds that they have earned that income passively.

The requirement that all earnings be distributed on a current basis or become "locked in" creates a highly artificial situation for a small business. If a small business is to grow, its capital structure must also grow. It is unreasonable to force the small business to distribute its earnings and then have the shareholders loan them back to the corporation in order to provide it with working capital. Further, a trust should be allowed as an eligible stockholder; and a "consent" from a new shareholder should be required only if he does not want to continue the Subchapter S status.

The Subchapter S provisions will probably not be repealed. The complexity of Subchapter S requires that all who transact business in this form have a working knowledge of its provisions. Accountants and attorneys have great responsibilities in this area. However, it is also incumbent upon the taxpayer to have a working knowledge of Subchapter S. As a practical matter, even the best advised taxpayer will make improper decisions without consulting his adviser in advance. An accounting system which provides the taxpayer and his advisers with information pertinent to Subchapter S decisions is also an important factor.

In the final analysis, success with Subchapter S depends upon the willingness of the taxpayer and his advisers to remain alert to the hazards of all transactions. The authors hope that this treatise will be helpful in achieving these ends.

Table of Cases

A & N Furniture and Appliance Company
271 F. Supp. 40 (D.C. Ohio 1967)........................ 27, 65, 113, 131, 132

Abbott
2 A.F.T.R. 2d 5232 (1961), *aff'g,*
28 T.C. 795 (1957).. 272, 273

Adkins-Phelps, Inc., vs. U.S.
400 F. 2d 737 (8th Cir. 1968)................................. 46

Allison, Estate of
57 T.C. 174 (1971), *appeal dismissed per stipulation,*
(9th Cir. 1973).. 121

Amory Cotton Oil Co. vs. U.S.
27 A.F.T.R. 2d 71-567 (N.D. Miss 1970)
aff'd, 30 A.F.T.R. 2d 72-5665 (5th Cir. 1972)................. 123

Atkins vs. Commissioner
15 A.F.T.R. 1127 (5th Cir. 1935)............................. 239

Attebury et al. vs. U.S.
26 A.F.T.R. 2d 70-5317 (5th Cir. 1970), *rev'g,*
23 A.F.T.R. 2d 69-912 (N.D. Tex. 1969)...................... 176

Barnes Motor & Parts Co. vs. U.S.
25 A.F.T.R. 2d 70-1241 (D.C. N.C. 1970)................... 106, 130

Barney vs. First National Bank
90 P. 2d 584 (Cal. App. 1939)................................. 65

Beacon Auto Stores, Inc.
42 B.T.A. 703 (1940).. 329

Benderoft vs. U.S.
398 F. 2d 132 (8th Cir. 1968)................................ 334

Bennett, Harry
T.C.M. 1968-71... 330

Benson, Theodore T.
T.C.M. 1967-74.................................... 137, 290, 330, 333

Bent Company
26 B.T.A. 1369 (1932)....................................... 329

Bierne, Michael F.
52 T.C. 210 (1969)...................................... 239, 301

P.A.Birren & Son, Inc. vs. Commissioner
116 F. 2d 718 (7th Cir. 1940)............................... 340

Blaschka vs. U.S.
393 F. 2d 983 (1968).. 254

Blum, Peter E.
59 T.C. 436 (1973)...................................... 126 151

Bogene, Inc.
T.C.M. 1968-147. 296

Bone, Thomas E.
52 T.C. 913 (1969). 29

Bonus, Lawrence M.
T.C.M. 1948-234. 330

Borg, Joe E.
50 T.C. 257 (1968). 126, 153

Bramlette Building Corporation
52 T.C. 200 (1969), aff'd, 25 A.F.T.R.,
2d 70-1061 (5th Cir. 1974). 199

Branch vs. U.S.
20 A.F.T.R. 2d 5302, 67-2 U.S.T.C.
¶9396 (D.C. Ga. 1967). 203

Brennan vs. O'Donnell
21 A.F.T.R. 2d 1028 (N.D. Ala. 1968). 119

Brennan vs. O'Donnell
25 A.F.T.R. 2d 70-1250 (5th Cir. 1970), rem'g
21 A.F.T.R. 2d 1028 (N.D. Ala. 1968). 120

Brennan vs. O'Donnell
27 A.F.T.R. 2d 71-1560 (N.D. Ala. 1971). 120

Britt vs. U.S.
22 A.F.T.R. 2d 5571 (D.C. Fla. 1968). 47

Buhler Mortgage Company, Inc. vs. Commissioner
51 T.C. 971 (1969), aff'd per curiam,
28 A.F.T.R. 2d 71-5252 (6th Cir. 1971). 202

Bunnel, Robert L.
50 T.C. 837 (1968). 327

Byrne vs. Commissioner
361 F. 2d 939 (7th Cir. 1966), aff'g
45 T.C. 151 (1965). 136, 142, 153, 186, 187, 313

Caldwell vs. Commissioner
202 F. 2d 112 (2d Cir. 1953). 327

Calwell vs. Coard
19 A.F.T.R. 2d 1967 (D.C. N.M. 1967). 332

Carletta, Ralph
57 T.C. 826 (1972), acq. 1972-2 C.B. 1. 302

Carzis, John G.
T.C.M. 1971-73. 142

Catalina Homes, Inc.
T.C.M. 1964-225. . . . . 23, 64, 112, 131

Challenge Manufacturing Company
37 T.C. 650 (1962). 291

Charbonnet vs. U.S.
27 A.F.T.R. 2d 71-751 (D.C. La. 1971), *aff'd,*
29 A.F.T.R. 2d 72-633 (5th Cir. 1972)...............................158, 249

Chicago, Rock Island and Pacific Railways Company vs. Commissioner
47 F. 2d 990 (7th Cir. 1931)..329

City Markets, Inc.
T.C.M. 1969-202, *aff'd,*
26 A.F.T.R. 2d 70-5760 (6th Cir. 1970)....................................199

Clark, Randall N.
58 T.C. 94 (1972) 176, 180

Clayton, Franklin
52 T.C. 911 (1969)..264

Clemens, Arthur B.
T.C.M. 1969-235, *aff'd,*
29 A.F.T.R. 2d 72-390 (9th Cir. 1972)...................................32, 63

Coca-Cola Bottling Company of Gallup
69-2 U.S.T.C. ¶9465 (D.C. N.M. 1969), *aff'd,*
443, F. 2d 1253 (10th Cir. 1971)..106

Cohan vs. Commissioner
39 F. 540 (2d Cir. 1930)..329

Commissioner vs. Kelly
8 A.F.T.R. 2d 5232 (1961)...273

Cornelius, Paul G.
58 T.C. 421 (1972)..153

Court Holding Company
324 U.S. 331 (1945)..............................238, 264, 270, 277

Cox, E. Morris
43 T.C. 448 (1965)..............................136, 313, 340

Cox, Herman
T.C.M. 1968-9..330

Creston Corporation
40 T.C. 937 (1963)..117

Curran, Joseph W.
T.C.M. 1970-160...98

Darby Investment Corporation vs. Commissioner
37 T.C. 839 (1962), *aff'd,* 315 F. 2d 551 (6th Cir. 1963)....................153

Dartmouth College vs. Woodward
17 U.S. (4 Wheat.) 581, 5 L. Ed. 629 (1819)........................135, 280

David's Specialty Shops, Inc. vs. Johnson
131 F. Supp. 458 (D.C. N.Y. 1955)...96

Davis vs. Jacoby
1 Cal. 2d 370, 24 P. 2d 1026 (1934).......................................72

United States vs. Davis
397 U.S. 301 (1970), *rev'g,* 408 F. 2d 1139 (6th Cir. 1969)............245, 246

de Bonchamps, Dale K.
278 F. 2d 127 (9th Cir. 1960). 74

Demler, Norman C.
T.C.M. 1966-117. . . . . 27, 98

DeTreville vs. U.S.
312 F. Supp. 362 (D.S.C. 1970), *rev'g,*
445 F. 2d 1306 (4th Cir. 1971). 179

Dick, Ronald
T.C.M. 1968-32. 330

Duarte, Henry
44 T.C. 193 (1965). 239, 300

Ducros vs. Commissioner
272 F. 2d 49 (6th Cir. 1959). 76

du Pont vs. U.S.
234 F. Supp. 681 (D.C. Del. 1964). 27, 96, 290, 330

Easson vs. U.S.
294 F. 2d 653 (9th Cir. 1961), *rev'g,*
33 T.C. 963 (1960). 127

England, Jr., James W.
34 T.C. 617 (1960). 328

Enoch, Herbert
57 T.C. 781 (1972). 253

Erickson, Gordon A.
56 T.C. 1112 (1971), *appeal dismissed,* (8th Cir. 1972). 84, 198, 248

EZO Products Company
37 T.C. 385 (1961). 340

Fearon, Estate of
16 T.C. 385 (1951). 254

Feingold, Max
49 T.C. 461 (1968). 196, 199

Feldman, Joseph W.
47 T.C. 329 (1966). 29

Fellinger vs. U.S.
363 F. 2d 826 (6th Cir. 1966). 117

Fellows, Roy A.
T.C.M. 1950-14. 334

525 Company vs. Commissioner
342 F. 2d 759 (5th Cir. 1965). 195

Forrester, Homer W.
49 T.C. 499 (1968). 32

Fountain, C. D. et al.
59 T.C. 696 (1973), *acquiesced in,* I.R.B. 1973-47, p. 6. 180

Fowler Hosiery Co., Inc.
36 T.C. 201 (1961). 254, 256

Frederick Steel Co. vs. Commissioner
375 F. 2d 351 (6th Cir. 1967), *cert. denied,* 389 U.S. 901 (1967). 46

Frentz, J. William
44 T.C. 485 (1965), *aff'd,* 375 F. 2d 662 (6th Cir. 1967). 29

Friend's Wine Cellars, Inc.
T.C.M. 1972-149. 63

Fulk & Needham, Inc.
288 F. Supp. 39 (D.C. N.C. 1968), *aff'd,*
411 F. 2d 1403 (4th Cir. 1969). 64, 73, 131

Gamman, W.C.
46 T.C. 1 (1966), *appeal dismissed,* (9th Cir. 1967). 23, 112, 117, 119

Glenn, Thomas K.
3 T.C. 328 (1944). 96

Gloucester Ice and Cold Storage Company
298 F. 2d 183 (1st Cir. 1962). 117

Golden Nugget, Inc.
T.C.M. 1969-149. 330

Gooding Amusement Co., Inc. vs. Commissioner
236 F. 2d 159 (6th Cir. 1956), *cert. denied,*
352 U.S. 1031 (1957). 117, 125

Greenfeld, Aaron
T.C.M. 1966-83. 330

Gregory vs. Helvering
293 U.S. 465 (1935). 301

Guzowski, Ray
T.C.M. 1967-145. . . . . 65, 66

Haber, Jack
52 T.C. 255 (1969). 126, 179, 186, 290, 303

Hagerty Oil Co.
30 A.F.T.R. 2d 72-5288 (D.C. Mont. 1972). 30, 71

Hanover Bank vs. Commissioner
369 U.S. 672, 82 S. Ct. 1080,
9 A.F.T.R. 2d 1492 (1962). 203

Harden vs. Commissioner
202 F. 2d 418 (10th Cir. 1955). 328

Hauptman vs. Commissioner
309 F. 2d 62 (2d Cir. 1962), *cert. denied,*
372 U.S. 909 (1963). 263, 293

Hayes, John M.
T.C.N. 1967-80. 330

Hellis vs. Usry
30 A.F.T.R. 2d 72-5107 (5th Cir. 1972), *aff'g,*
27 A.F.T.R. 2d 71-1266 (E.D. La. 1971)................................. 205

Helvering vs. Jarvis
123 F. 2d 742 (4th Cir. 1941), *acq. revoked,*
G.C.M. 23460, 1942-2 C.B. 190.................................... 251, 253

Henderson vs. U.S.
16 A.F.T.R. 2d 5512 (M.D. Ala. 1965), *appeal dismissed,*
(5th Cir. 1966).. 23

Herbert vs. Riddell
103 F. Supp. 369 (D.C. Cal. 1952)...................................... 96

Higgins vs. Smith
308 U.S. 473 (1940)... 238, 239, 260

Hill, Raymond G.
51 T.C. 621 (1969)... 38

Hodge, Leroy
T.C.M. 1970-280... 39

Hoffman, Alfred N.
47 T.C. 218 (1966), *aff'd,*
391 F. 2d 930 (5th Cir. 1968)................... 67, 117, 119, 126, 233

Hoffman, Claire G.
2 T.C. 1160 (1943)... 83

Hoffman, Gerald
T.C.M. 1970-16... 38, 81

Holland vs. U.S.
348 U.S. 121 (1954)... 329

Holstein, George M.
23 T.C. 923 (1955)... 39

Hook, Clarence
58 T.C. 267 (1972), *appeal dismissed,* (9th Cir. 1973)......... 238, 239

House, Joseph L., Jr.
T.C.M. 1970-125, *rev'd. on other grounds,*
29 A.F.T.R. 2d 72-360 (4th Cir. 1972)........................... 200, 202

Howell, William B.
57 T.C. 546 (1972).. 141, 258

Howes, Ernest G.
30 T.C. 909 (1958)... 127

Hulsey vs. Campbell
13 A.F.T.R. 2d 466 (D.C. Tex. 1963)............................... 32, 63

International Trading Co. vs. Commissioner
32 A.F.T.R. 2d 73-5500 (7th Cir. 1973), *rev'g,*
57 T.C. 455 (1972).. 142

Jennings vs. U.S.
272 F. 2d 842 (7th Cir. 1959)....................................... 126

Joyce, Temple N.
42 T.C. 628 (1964)..201, 304

Kates, Morris
T.C.M. 1968-264..33, 65, 66

Kean, H. C. vs. Commissioner
51 T.C. 337 (1968), *aff'd,*
31 A.F.T.R. 2d 73-344 (9th Cir. 1972).....................33, 63, 65, 66, 68, 235

Kelly, Commissioner vs.
8 A.F.T.R. 2d 5232 (1961).......................................273

Knetsch vs. U.S.
364 U.S. 361 (1960)..301

Kobacker, Arthur J.
37 T.C. 882 (1962), *acquiesced in,* 1964-2 C.B. 6.............127

Krahenbuhl, Pat
T.C.M. 1968-34..301

Kraus, Hans P.
59 T.C. 681 (1973)..239

Kuakenberg, Commissioner vs.
30d F. 202 (9th Cir. 1962)......................................293

Lake vs. U.S.
406 F. 2d 941 (5th Cir. 1969)....................................87

Lambert, Justine L.
T.C.M. 1949-160...330

Land vs. Commissioner
303 F. 2d 170 (5th Cir. 1962).....................................83

Lansing Broadcasting Company vs. Commissioner
52 T.C. 299 (1969), *aff'd,*
25 A.F.T.R. 2d 70-1398 (6th Cir. 1970)...........................202

Larkin, Alan B.
48 T.C. 629 (1967)...296

Larsen, James M.
T.C.M. 1950-268..330

Leonhart, W. H.
T.C.M. 1968-98, *aff'd per curiam,*
414 F. 2d 749 (4th Cir. 1969)..........136, 311, 327, 330, 333, 335, 341

Levin, Beatrice
47 T.C. 258 (1966)...244, 245

Levine, Samuel
50 T.C. 422 (1968)...296

Levy, Herbert
46 T.C. 531 (1966).......................................28, 153, 187

Lewis Building and Supplies, Inc.
T.C.M. 1966-159, *appeal dismissed,*
(5th Cir. 1967)...........................23, 33, 70, 112, 117, 126

357

Libson Shops, Inc. vs. Koehler
353 U.S. 382 (1957)... 46

Lime Cola Company
22 T.C. 593 (1954)... 329

Littick, Estate of
31 T.C. 181 (1958)... 83

Loos, Theodore
T.C.M. 1967-37.. 330

Louis, Francois
T.C.M. 1966-204... 330

Lucas vs. Earl
281 U.S. 111 (1930)... 259

Lyle, William C.
T.C.M. 1971-324... 29

Marsan Realty Corporation
T.C.M. 1963-297... 127

Marshall, I. J.
60 T.C. 242 (1973)... 200, 202

Maxwell Hardware Co. vs. Commissioner
343 F. 2d 713 (9th Cir. 1965)... 46

Mazo, *et al.*
T.C.M. 1973-125.. 63

McDonnell, M. H.
T.C.M. 1965-125... 29

McGinty vs. Commissioner
12 A.F.T.R. 2d 6139, 325 F. 2d 820 (2d Cir. 1964)............... 244, 246

McIntosh, Sam F.
T.C.M. 1967-230.................. .... 83, 186

McSorley's Inc.
323 F. 2d 900 (10th Cir. 1963)....................................... 117

Mears vs. Commissioner
386 F. 2d 450 (5th Cir. 1968)... 330

Meldrum vs. Fewsmith
21 T.C. 790 (1953), *aff'd,*
230 F. 2d 283 (6th Cir. 1956)... 304

Merlo Builders, Inc.
T.C.M. 1964-34, *appeal dismissed,* (7th Cir. 1964, 1965)..................... 127

Miles Production Co.
T.C.M. 1969-274, *aff'd,* 29 A.F.T.R. 2d 72-855 (5th Cir. 1972)................. 152

Mitchell Offset Plate Service, Inc.
53 T.C. 235 (1969), *acquiesced in,* 1970-1 C.B. xvi........................... 30

Modern Home Fire and Casualty Insurance Co.
54 T.C. 839 (1970), *acquiesced in,* 1970-2 C.B. xx..........................28, 45

Moline Properties, Inc. vs. Commissioner
319 U.S. 436 (1943)..102

Mora, Ray
T.C.M. 1972-123..29

Morgan, Wesley H.
46 T.C. 878 (1966)...38

Mountain Water Co. of La Crescenta
35 T.C. 418 (1960)..266

Murphy Logging Company vs. U.S.
339 F. Supp. 794 (D.C. Ore. 1965),
rev'd, 378 F. 2d 222 (9th Cir. 1967)............................127

Nassau Lens Company vs. Commissioner
308 F. 2d 39 (2d Cir. 1962).......................................125

National Bellas Hess, Inc. vs. Commissioner
220 F. 2d 415 (8th Cir. 1955).....................................64

Neal vs. U.S.
25 A.F.T.R. 2d 70-896 (D.C. Cal. 1971)...........................126

Nielsen, August F., Inc.
T.C.M. 1968-11.....................23, 117, 119, 125, 126, 290, 330

Northwestern State Portland Cement Company vs. Houston
126 F. 2d 196 (8th Cir. 1942)....................................329

Nova-Plas Manufacturing Company, Inc.
8 A.F.T.R. 2d 5188 (D.C. N.Y. 1961)..............................293

Novell, Sam
T.C.M. 1969-255..117, 119, 187

Novell, Sam
T.C.M. 1970-31..153

Old Virginia Brick Company
44 T.C. 724 (1965), *aff'd,*
367 F. 2d 276 (4th Cir. 1966)..................65, 72, 87, 88, 254

O'Neill vs. Commissioner
170 F. 2d 596 (2d Cir. 1948)......................................96

O'Reilly, Edwin J.
T.C.M. 1968-291...246

Ortmayer vs. Commissioner
265 F. 2d 848 (7th Cir. 1959).....................................125

Osborne, Weldon F.
55 T.C. 329 (1970)..194

P. M. Finance Corporation
302 F. 2d 786 (3rd Cir. 1962).....................................116

Pacific Coast Music Jobbers, Inc. vs. Commissioner
55 T.C. 866 (1971), *aff'd,*
29 A.F.T.R. 2d 72-816 (5th Cir. 1972)....................................33, 66

Parker Oil Co.
58 T.C. 985 (1972)..131, 238

Paula Construction Co.
58 T.C. 102 (1972)...292

Perry vs. Commissioner
392 F. 2d 458 (8th Cir. 1968)..153, 187

Perry, Donald M.
49 T.C. 508 (1968)..153, 187

Perry, William H.
47 T.C. 159 (1966), *aff'd,* 392 F. 2d 458 (8th Cir. 1968)......................126

Perry, William H.
54 T.C. 1293 (1970), *aff'd,*
27 A.F.T.R. 2d 71-1464 (8th Cir. 1971)..152

Pestcoe, William
40 T.C. 195 (1963)..29

Peterson, Albert W.
T.C.M. 1965-145..126

Peterson, Donald J.
T.C.M. 1965-151...117, 126

Pinellas Ice & Cold Storage Co. vs. Commissioner
287 U.S. 462 (1933)...40

Plowden, Richard L.
48 T.C. 666 (1967), *aff'd per curiam,* 398 F. 2d 340
(4th Cir. 1968), *cert. denied,* 393 U.S. 936 (1968).....................153, 186, 187

Pollack, Samuel vs. Commissioner
392 F. 2d 409 (5th Cir. 1968), *aff'g,* 47 T.C. 92 (1966).................65, 132, 238

Portage Plastics Co., Inc.
24 A.F.T.R. 2d 69-5301 (W.D. Wisc. 1969)......................23, 114, 117, 122

Portage Plastics Co., Inc. vs. U.S.
27 A.F.T.R. 2d 71-1038 (W.D. Wisc. 1971)......................................122

Portage Plastics Co., Inc. vs. U.S.
30 A.F.T.R. 2d 72-5229 (7th Cir. 1972)...122

Portage Plastics Co., Inc. vs. U.S.
31 A.F.T.R. 2d 73-864 (7th Cir. 1973)..124

Portland Oil Co. vs. Commissioner
109 F. 2d 479 (1st Cir. 1940)...39

Poulter, Frank E.
T.C.M. 1967-220, *aff'd per curiam,*
397 F. 2d 415 (4th Cir. 1968)...29

Prashker, Ruth M.
59 T.C. 172 (1972)..151

360

Purvis vs. U.S.
31 A.F.T.R. 2d 73-428 (D.C. Ga. 1972). 249

Putnam vs. Commissioner
352 U.S. 82 (1959). 127

Ray vs. U.S.
409 F. 2d 1322 (6th Cir. 1969). 117

Raynor, Milton T.
50 T.C. 762 (1968). 23, 117, 119, 126, 152

Renard, Henry H.
T.C.M. 1972-224. . . . . 85, 249

Richardson Foundation vs. Commissioner
306 F. Supp. 755 (D.C. Tex. 1969), aff'd,
430 F. 2d 710 (5th Cir. 1970), cert. denied, 4/5/71. 68

Richardson Foundation vs. U.S.
26 A.F.T.R. 2d 5144 (5th Cir. 1970). 142, 166

Roberts vs. Commissioner
398 F. 2d 340 (4th Cir. 1968), aff'g, 48 T.C. 666 (1967),
cert. denied, 393 U.S. 936 (1968). 153, 187

Robertson vs. U.S.
32 A.F.T.R. 2d 73-5556 (D.C. Nev. 1973). 152

Rocco, Charles
57 T.C. 826 (1972), acquiesced in, 1972-2 C.B. 1. . . . . 47, 302

Roesel, George A.
56 T.C. 14 (1971), appeal dismissed, (5th Cir. 1971). 180

Roob, Walter J.
50 T.C. 891 (1968). 301

Roschuni, Elliot J.
44 T.C. 80 (1965). 334

Roubik, Jermone J.
53 T.C. 365 (1969). 103, 259

Roughan vs. Commissioner
198 F. 2d 253 (4th Cir. 1952). 102

In re Roundtable, Inc.
17 A.F.T.R. 2d 299 (S.D. N.Y. 1965). 29

Rowland vs. Commissioner
315 F. Supp. 596 (D.C. Ark. 1970). 29

Sauvigne, Donald J.
T.C.M. 1971-30. 151

Seven Sixty Ranch Company vs. Kennedy
17 A.F.T.R. 2d 587 (D.C. Wyo. 1966). 97, 112

Shores Realty Co., Inc. vs. U.S.
27 A.F.T.R. 2d 71-681 (S.D. Fla. 1971), aff'd,
30 A.F.T.R. 2d 72-5672 (5th Cir. 1972). 124

Sieh, Alfred M.
56 T.C. 1386 (1971), *aff'd,*
31 A.F.T.R. 2d 73-419 (8th Cir. 1973). 200

Silverstein vs. U.S.
31 A.F.T.R. 2d 73-902 (E.D. La. 1973). 152

Simons vs. U.S.
208 F. Supp. 744 (D.C. Conn. 1962). 29

Smith, Joe E.
48 T.C. 872 (1967), *aff'd,*
424 F. 2d 219 (9th Cir. 1970). 154

Smoot Sand and Gravel Corp. vs. Commissioner
241 F. 2d 197 (4th Cir. 1957). 102

Spinner, H.R., Corp.
T.C.M. 1970-99, *appeal dismissed,* (9th Cir. 1973). 121

Spitalney vs. U.S.
430 F. 2d 195 (9th Cir. 1970). 264

Stinnet, James L., Jr.
54 T.C. 221 (1970), *appeal dismissed without opinion,* (9th Cir. 1973). 23, 120

Swank & Son, Inc. vs. U.S.
32 A.F.T.R. 2d 73-5781 (D.C. Mont, 1973). 195

Taylor vs. U.S.
24 A.F.T.R. 2d 69-5747 (5th Cir. 1969). 334

Thompson, J. Riley
T.C.M. 1967-252. 330

Travis, Paul H.
47 T.C. 502 (1967). 136, 137, 313, 340, 341

Truschel, W. H.
29 T.C. 433 (1957). 127

Valley Loan Assn. vs. U.S.
18 A.F.T.R. 2d 5793 (S.D. Colo. 1966). 200

Wallace, Donald J.
T.C.M. 1967-11. . . . . 290, 296

Weaver Airline Personnel School, Inc. vs. Bookwalter
218 F. Supp. 599 (W.D. Mo. 1963). 290

Weiss vs. Commissioner
395 F. 2d 500 (10th Cir. 1968), *aff'g,*
T.C.M. 1967-125. . . . . 335, 341

Wheat vs. U.S.
31 A.F.T.R. 2d 73-808 (S.D. Tex. 1973). 126

White vs. Ryan
15 Pa. County Ct. 170 (1894). 78

Whitfield, Estate of
14 T.C. 766 (1950). 102

Wiebusch, G. W.
59 T.C. 777 (1973).. 40

Wilhelm vs. Commissioner
257 F. Supp. 16 (D.C. Wyo. 1966)........................... 136, 296, 300, 312

Williamson vs. U.S.
292 F. 2d 524 (Ct. Cl. 1961)...................................... 259, 264

Wilson, W. T.
10 T.C. 251 (1948).. 291

Wise, George W.
T.C.M. 1971-38... 151

Wood Preserving Corp. vs. U.S.
347 F. 2d 111 (4th Cir. 1965).. 125

Woodward Investment Co.
46 B.T.A. 648 (1942), *acq. revoked*................................. 253

Zaretsky, Samuel
T.C.M. 1967-247.. 29

Ziegelheim, Jack
T.C.M. 1967-87.. 186

Zychinski, Joseph B.
60 T.C. No. 100 (1973).. 202

Revenue Rulings

Revenue Ruling 54-408
1954-2 C.B. 165. 260

Revenue Ruling 54-518
1954-2 C.B. 142. 269

Revenue Ruling 57-353
1957-2 C.B. 223. 245

Revenue Ruling 57-491
1957-2 C.B. 232. 271

Revenue Ruling 58-90
1958-1 C.B. 88. 296

Revenue Ruling 59-60
1959-1 C.B. 237. 82

Revenue Ruling 59-286
1959-2 C.B. 103. 76

Revenue Ruling 60-183
1960-1 C.B. 625. 34

Revenue Ruling 61-112
1961-1 C.B. 399. 196

Revenue Ruling 61-120
1961-1 C.B. 245. 74

Revenue Ruling 61-134
1961-2 C.B. 250. 76

Revenue Ruling 62-116
1962-2 C.B. 207. . . . . 33, 70

Revenue Ruling 63-114
1963-1 C.B. 74. 271

Revenue Ruling 63-226
1963-2 C.B. 341. . . . . 65, 128, 237

Revenue Ruling 63-245
1963-2 C.B. 144. 266

Revenue Ruling 64-94
1964-1 C.B. 317. 106

Revenue Ruling 64-162
1964-1 C.B. 304. 153

Revenue Ruling 64-232
1964-1 C.B. 34. 196

Revenue Ruling 64-249
1964-2 C.B. 332. 74

Revenue Ruling 64-250
1964-2 C.B. 333. 109

Revenue Ruling 64-308
1964-2 C.B. 176. . . . . 82, 138

Revenue Ruling 64-309
1964-2 C.B. 333. 111

Revenue Ruling 65-40
1965-1 C.B. 429. 196

Revenue Ruling 65-83
1965-1 C.B. 430. 197

Revenue Ruling 65-91
1965-1 C.B. 431. 197

Revenue Ruling 65-192
1965-2 C.B. 259. 82

Revenue Ruling 65-193
1965-2 C.B. 370. 82

Revenue Ruling 65-292
1965-2 C.B. 319. . . . . 140, 295

Revenue Ruling 66-116
1966-1 C.B. 198. 67

Revenue Ruling 66-172
1966-1 C.B. 198. . . . . 118, 183, 305

Revenue Ruling 66-218
1966-2 C.B. 120. 296

Revenue Ruling 66-266
1966-2 C.B. 356. 69

Revenue Ruling 66-327
1966-2 C.B. 357. 140

Revenue Ruling 67-269
1967-2 C.B. 298. 111

Revenue Ruling 67-382
1967-2 C.B. 298. 240

Revenue Ruling 68-128
1968-1 C.B. 381. . . . . 157, 205, 305

Revenue Ruling 68-227
1968-1 C.B. 381. . . . . 33, 67

Revenue Ruling 68-537
1968-2 C.B. 372. 154

Revenue Ruling 69-47
1969-1 C.B. 94. 86

Revenue Ruling 69-168
1969-1 C.B. 24. 159

Revenue Ruling 69-172
1969-1 C.B. 99. 277

Revenue Ruling 69-192
1969 1 C.B. 207. 203

Revenue Ruling 69-357
1969-1 C.B. 101... 39

Revenue Ruling 69-566
1969-2 C.B. 165.. 106

Revenue Ruling 70-110
1970-1 C.B. 176.. 203

Revenue Ruling 70-206
1970-1 C.B. 177.. 197

Revenue Ruling 70-232
1970-1 C.B. 177.. 107

Revenue Ruling 70-306
1970-1 C.B. 179.. 137

Revenue Ruling 70-458
1970-2 C.B. 3.. 35

Revenue Ruling 70-531
1970-2 C.B. 76... 250, 253

Revenue Ruling 70-615
1970-2 C.B. 169... 33, 62

Revenue Ruling 71-102
1971-1 C.B. 263... 174

Revenue Ruling 71-250
1971-1 C.B. 112... 256

Revenue Ruling 71-257
1971-1 C.B. 131.. 189, 297

Revenue Ruling 71-266
1971-1 C.B. 262... 108

Revenue Ruling 71-287
1971-2 C.B. 317... 33

Revenue Ruling 71-288
1971-2 C.B. 319... 152

Revenue Ruling 71-407
1971-2 C.B. 318... 203

Revenue Ruling 71-455
1971-2 C.B. 318... 203

Revenue Ruling 71-549
1971-2 C.B. 319.. 29, 242

Revenue Ruling 71-552
1971-2 C.B. 316... 111

Revenue Ruling 72-33
1972-1 C.B. 130... 339

Revenue Ruling 72-48
1972-1 C.B. 102... 273

Revenue Ruling 72-152
1972-1 C.B. 272. 289

Revenue Ruling 72-188
1972-1 C.B. 383. 88

Revenue Ruling 72-201
1972-1 C.B. 271. 107

Revenue Ruling 72-257
1972-1 C.B. 270. 28

Revenue Ruling 72-320
1972-1 C.B. 270. 108

Revenue Ruling 72-457
1972-2 C.B. 510. 203

Revenue Ruling 73-144
1973-1 C.B. 614. 339

Revenue Procedures

Revenue Procedure 57-1
1957-1 C.B. 721. 332

Revenue Procedure 61-30
1961-2 C.B. 568. 34

Revenue Procedure 67-5
1967-1 C.B. 575. 156

Revenue Procedure 67-10
1967-1 C.B. 585. 338

Revenue Procedure 69-6
1969-1 C.B. 396. 254

Revenue Procedure 70-25
1970-2 C.B. 506. 333

Revenue Procedure 72-51
1972-2 C.B. 832. 292

Index

A

Accelerated depreciation. 161

Accounting for Subchapter S Corporations. 314-41
    Adequate books and records. 330-32
    Auditor's opinion. 325-26
    Changes in method. 337-41
    Comparative financial statements. 323-24
    Disposition of deferred tax accounts. 325
    Equity accounts. 314-18
    Financial reporting. 323-24
    Methods in general. 327-28
    Net worth test. 329
    Pro forma statements. 324-25
    Provision for federal income taxes. 322-23
    Recordkeeping. 326-27
    Record retention. 335-37

Accounting methods. 314-41

Adjusted basis. 186-87
    Initial basis. 186
    Net operating loss deduction, effect upon. 126, 307, 344
    Stepped-up basis. 93, 283

Affiliated group. 104-09

Agreement, recapture of investment credit. 36

Alien, non-resident, as shareholder. 27, 66

Annual checklist. 59

Annuities, as passive income. 201

Asset Depreciation Range System (ADR). 48-57
    Annual election. 48
    Eligible assets. 49-50
    First-year conventions. 50
    Repairs and maintenance. 53-54
    Retirements. 54-56
    Salvage value. 51-53
    Vintage account. 50-55

Auditor's opinion. 325-26

B

Bankruptcy. 69

Basis (See Adjusted basis)

Beneficial ownership. 62, 66

Blackmail, by stockholders. 306

Book value. 79, 83

Books and records. 337

Business purpose test. 27, 78, 81, 95-103, 302

Buy-sell agreements. 75-77, 346
    Checklist of tax and non-tax consequences. 90-93
    Comparison of. 76-77
    Cross-purchase plan. 76
    Stock redemption. 75-76, 90
    Valuation of stock. 82

C

Capital gains. 140, 221
    Limitation on. 140
    "One-shot election. 21-22, 145, 303
    Pass-through to shareholders. 138-40, 285, 304
    Taxed at corporate level. 21-22, 144-46

Capital gains tax. 22, 144-46, 344
    Avoidance of. 146, 295
    Exceptions to. 145
    Installment tax method. 146, 344
    10% minimum tax. 161

Capital losses. 142, 161, 221, 285, 344

Cash distributions. 167-71, 344-45
    After close of taxable year. 168
    Order. 168-70, 173-76
    Timing. 172
    2½-month rule. 167

Chartered partnership. 2, 10

Class Life System (See ADR System)

Class of Stock. 23, 109-14, 182, 281, 346

Cohan rule. 329-30

Collapsible corporation. 18, 271-76, 281

Comparative financial statements. 323-24

Conduit principle. 2, 13, 135-62, 279, 344

Consents. 67-69, 344, 349
    Extension of time to file. 67
    New shareholders. 67, 344, 349
    Requirements of,. 67
    Transactions between shareholders. 68

Controlled corporation. 162

Convertible debentures. 111

Corporate tax on capital gains. 22, 144-46, 344

Corporations. 1, 5, 135, 280-83
   Advantages of. 280-83
   Compared with. 2, 5, 311-14
   Described. 135, 280
   Equity accounts. 314-16
   Pension plans. 296-300

Court Holding Co. doctrine. 264, 270, 277

Credits. 156-60
   Commercial depository. 156
   Foreign tax. 157
   Gasoline excise tax. 156-57
   Investment tax. 156-60

Cross-purchase plan. 76, 92-93, 346

D

Death of a shareholder. 19-20, 155-56
   Agreement to sell stock. 155-56, 345
   Special problems created by. 155-56

Debt. 113-26, 344-46
   As a second class of stock. 112, 345
   From outsiders. 112
   In relation to equity. 113-14, 346
   Repayment of. 154
   Safety zones. 113
   Shareholder's. 117-25, 344
   Subchapter S stock as security for. 66
   Thin capitalization. 22-24, 114-17

Deferred income tax accounts. 325

Depletion. 308

Depreciation recapture. 160-61

Disqualification. 20, 348

Distributable taxable income. 165-67

Distributions. 163-84
   Cash. 167-71, 344
   Non-prorata. 188, 189, 258
   Planning for. 180-84
   Previously taxed income and 2½-month rule. 167

Property. 176-80, 306, 344, 348
Reallocation. 300-02
Sources. 163-67
Timing of. 172, 343

Dividends. 27, 200, 205-06, 284, 305-06, 347
As Passive investment income. 27, 200, 205-06, 347
85% received deductions. 305
Exclusion. 284, 306

Domestic corporation. 27, 62, 95-104

Domestic International Sales Corporation. 41-44

E

Earnings and profits. 58, 84, 164, 344-45
Accumulated. 58, 164
Capitalization of. 84
Current. 58, 164, 344-45
Per share. 324

Elections. 95-133
After prior terminations. 234-39, 242
Consent to early new. 234-45
Extension of time to file. 28, 29, 34-35
Five-year waiting period. 234
Investment tax credit. 34-35
Postmark. 30
Registered mail. 30
Revocation. 231-34
Timely filing requirement. 28-32
When to file. 28
Where to file. 28

Election and consents. 28-32

Election of Subchapter S. 340-41
Existing corporations. 341
Unincorporated businesses. 340-41

Eligible shareholders. 12, 27, 61-93, 343-44

Employee relationships. 296-300, 332-34

Employee stockholder problems. 332-34

Entity concept. 135, 280

Equity accounts. 314-18
Corporation. 314-18
Subchapter S Corporation. 315

Escrow of stock. 81, 346
Agent not as shareholder. 81
To protect Subchapter S election. 81

Estate.. 62-65, 69-77, 81-90, 345-46
   As shareholder... 62-63, 70
   Buy-sell agreements for.................................. 75-77, 82, 346
   Compelling filing of consent by.. 72
   Consents by.. 70
   For life.. 74, 345
   Installment payments on... 88-90
   Problems caused by consent for...................................... 72
   Prolonged as a trust................................... 65, 72-73, 308
   Redemption of.. 84-88
   Trusts, use of.................................... 63-65, 72-73, 345
   Valuation problems in............................... 81-84, 346
   Voting trust in... 64-65
   Widow-shareholder also executrix.................................... 71

Excess deduction accounts.. 99

Extensions.................................... 29, 34-45, 222-26
   Additional.................................. 29, 34-35, 222-26
   Automatic... 34, 222

F

Failure to consent to election....................................... 67-69

Farm Loss deduction.......................... 96, 99, 147-48, 302-05

Federal Housing Administration........... 111

Fiscal-year corporations.. 184-86

Five-year waiting period... 234

Foreign income.................................... 203-05, 345
   As prohibited... 203, 205
   80% rule... 203-04
   Tax credit on.. 157, 205

Forms, tax.................................. 214-19, 224-25
   966... 226
   1040X... 226
   1096... 226
   1099... 226
   1099-DIV.. 210, 220
   1099-L... 226
   1120... 209
   1120S.................. 209-211, 214-19, 221-22, 226-28
   1120X... 226
   2553... 226
   4797.. 211, 224-25
   7004.. 222, 226, 229
   7005.. 222, 226, 230

Forms of ownership............................... 1, 62, 279-87

Fringe benefits................... 24, 281-84, 296, 299, 345, 348

G

Gift of stock to minors. 66-67, 348

Grace periods. 21-22, 58, 116, 167, 318, 321, 345

Gross receipts 27, 191-94, 200-04, 207, 304
    Contrasted with gross income. 191, 200, 203, 347
    80% receipts rule. 203-04
    Expanding receipts. 207
    Limitations on source and type. 27
    20% receipts rule. 27, 191-92, 202, 304

H

Hidden shareholder. 33, 66

Hobby losses. 97, 99, 304

I

Inactive subsidiary. 105

Income splitting. 281, 300-02

Incorporation. 280-83
    Non-tax advantages of. 280-81
    Tax advantages of. 281-83

Indebtedness (See Loans and Class of Stock)

Ineligible shareholders. 27, 62-63, 66, 72-73, 131-32, 308, 345

Installment tax method. 146, 293

Interest. 114, 125, 200-01, 347
    As passive investment income. 200-01
    Exceptions to 20% rule. 202
    Reasonable rate of. 125, 347
    Shareholder's loans, rates of. 114, 125, 347

Interest Deduction Limitation. 162, 309

Investment credit. 156-60
    Agreement with respect to election of Subchapter S. 36
    Carryover. 307
    $50,000 limitation on used § 38 property. 159
    Passed through. 287
    Recapture of. 34-38, 159

J

Joint tenants, as shareholders. 62-63

K

Kintner regulations. 103

L

Libson Shops doctrine..44-46

Life estates..74

Life insurance..75-77, 91-93
    Buy-sell agreement...75-77, 90-93
    Transfer for value rule...91, 93

Liquidations...261-71, 293-95
    Advantages of..262-63
    Recaptured items...262
    Regular (Section 331)..263-64
    Section 332 election...271
    Section 333 election...268-71
    Section 337...265-68, 293-95

Loans...23, 66, 109-14, 344-46
    As a second class of stock....,....................23, 109-14, 182, 281, 346
    From outsiders...112
    Repayment of..154
    Safety Zones...113
    Shareholders'...117-25, 344
    Subchapter S stock as security for..66
    Tax planning for..125-26

Loss (See Net Operating Losses)

M

Making the election...28-32

Marital deduction trust..69

Maximum tax on Earned income...279, 287, 309

Mergers (See Reorganization)

Minimum Tax (See Tax preference items)

Minors..33, 66-67, 300, 348
    Election on behalf of...33
    Uniform Gifts Act...66-67, 300, 348

N

Net operating losses...........19-20, 97-99, 126, 139-48, 151-54, 261-71, 304, 323-25
    Adjusted tax basis..126, 307, 344
    Allocation to shareholders...148
    Attributable to trade or business......................................139, 147
    Computed...148
    Death of a shareholder caused by......................................19-20
    Hobby loss rule..97, 99, 304

Liquidation. 261-71
Offset against income. 97, 288
Statement presentation of. 323-25
Wasted. 126, 151-54

Net worth test. 329

New shareholder. 62-63
Avoidance of termination by. 77-81
Consent to Subchapter S election by. 67-69
Failure to consent by. 67-69
Non-consenting notification to IRS by. 68-69

Non-resident alien as shareholder. 27, 62, 65-67

Number of returns. 3-5, 9-10
Comparison. 5
Growth of. 3-5
Industry groups 5-9
Relation to net income and assets. 10

O

One Class of stock (See Class of stock)

One-shot election. 21-22, 145, 303

Options, as second class of stock. 111

Order of Distribution. 163-67
Cash. 167-71, 344
Property. 176-80, 306, 343-44

Organization costs 186, 281, 304

Ownership of stock 33, 62-63

P

Partial liquidations. 253-61
Advantages of. 262-63
Comparison, Section 302. 243-44
Comparison, Section 311(d). 260-61
Mechanics of. 259-60

Partnership. 65, 279-80
As shareholder 65
Comparisons with. 14-15, 282-87

Pass-through. 138-62
Corporate income. 138-40, 308-09
Interest deduction limitations. 162
Investment tax credit 156-60
Long-term capital gains. 140-44, 304

Losses.. ..19-20, 146-54, 304, 306
  Recapture of depreciation.................................... 160-61
  § 1231 gains.. 140
  Tax preferences... 161-62
  Undistributed taxable income....................... 138

Passive investment income....................................... 192-205
  Annuities as... 201
  Dividends as... 27, 200, 205-06
  Exceptions on 20% rule.................................... 22, 201
  Expanding gross receipts as................................ 207
  Gains from stock... 201, 303
  Interest as.. 200-01
  Rents as.. 195-200, 206, 347, 349
  Royalties as... 194-95
  Tax planning for.. 205-07
  20% rule.................................. 27, 191-92, 202, 207, 304

Penalty taxes.. 146, 289

Percentage markup method... 329

Personal holding company.. 192-93
  Avoidance of tax on income................................ 200, 289
  Penalty tax.. 193

Personal service corporations................................. 13-14, 129-30

Planning for Subchapter S distributions............................ 180-84

Pre-incorporation agreements............................... 78-80, 345-46

Present value theory... 84

Previously taxed income... 57, 166
  Distribution.. 57
  Personal to shareholder......................... 52, 182, 316-17, 344
  Records.. 166-67, 330-31, 348
  Statement presentation of............................ 323-25, 330-31
  2½-month related to...................................... 57, 167

Professional corporations.. 103-04

Pro forma statements... 324-25

Prohibited income.. 191-207
  Foreign income as..................................... 203-05, 344
  Passive investment income as................ 192-203, 205, 303, 344-46
  Tax planning for.. 205-07

Property distribution.............................. 176-80, 306, 344, 346

Proprietary concept.. 279-80

Proxies.. 65-66, 128

R

Re-election. 234-35, 239-42

Real estate operations. 303-04

Recapture of depreciation. 160-61

Recapture of investment credit. 34-38, 160-61

Record retention. 335-37

Redemption. 84-88, 243-77
    Appreciated property with. 272-73
    Complete. 247
    Corporate treatment of. 250-53
    Dividends not equivalent to. 244-46
    Section 302. 243-44
    Section 303. 85-88
    Shareholder treatment of. 247-50
    Substantially disproportionate. 246-47

Rents. 195-200, 206, 344, 346

Reorganization. 106-07

Repayment of loans (See Loans)

Retirement plans. 296-300

Return of capital. 167

Revocation. 231-42
    Consents of shareholders to. 233
    Effective date. 233
    Practical effects of. 234
    Re-election after. 233, 239-42
    Voluntary. 231-34
    Voluntary vs. involuntary termination. 237-39

Royalties. 194-95

S

Second class of stock (See Class of stock)

Section 351 transfer. 39

Significant services. 195-200, 344

Shareholders. 12, 27, 61-93, 343-44
    Agreements. 128-33
    As a second class of stock. 128, 237
    Death of. 155-56, 343
    Escrow of stock. 81, 343
    Illustrated agreements. 78-80

New. 32-34, 67, 344, 346
Notice of restrictions for. 81
Pre-existing. 32
Pre-incorporation agreements of. 78-81, 345
Protecting the Subchapter S election for. 78
Restrictions in transfers of stock for 78-79
Stock redemption vs. cross-purchase plan among. 76

Shareholder consents (See Consents)

Shareholder reference test. 18, 143

Sick Pay. 296, 332, 334

Small business. 10, 15-16

Small business corporation stock. 35-38

Statute of limitations. 334-35

Stock, One class of (See Class of stock)

Stock bonus plan (See Fringe benefits)

Subchapter R. 15-19, 296

Subchapter S eligibility checklist. 27-28, 61

Subchapter S tax return. 209-29

Successor corporation. 234-35

Supplement S. 13-14, 130, 296

Supplement, 1975. 385

T

Taxable income. 136-40, 163-64

Tax-exempt securities. 200, 205-06, 305-06, 344

Tax-free transfer. 91-93

Tax planning. 343-49
As a result of differing taxable years. 292-93
By liquidating corporation. 294
For a business purpose. 101-03
For income splitting. 300-02
For passive investment income. 205-07
For shareholder loans. 125-26
For Subchapter S distribution. 180-84
To avoid thin capitalization. 114-17

Tax preference items. 161-62

Tax Reform Act of 1969. . . . . 25, 97-103, 114, 127, 148, 161-62, 205, 297

Technical Amendments Act of 1958. 16-18

Tenants by the entirety, as shareholders. 63

Tenants in common, as shareholders. 63

Termination. 231-42
    By new shareholders. 77-81
    Effective date. 233
    Involuntary. 234-37
    Methods of. 237
    New shareholders' failure to consent. 77-81, 238
    Re-election after prior. 237-39
    Voluntary vs. involuntary. 237-39
    Voluntary revocation and. 231-34

Thin capitalization. 22-24, 114-17, 346
    Advantages of. 116
    Debt. 113, 346
    Justification for. 114
    Outsiders' loans. 126-28, 348
    Stockholders' loans. 117-25, 348

Timing of cash distributions. 172

Transfer for value rule. 91, 93

Travel and entertainment expenses. 289, 330, 332-34

Treasury stock. 14-15

Trusts. 63-65, 72-75
    Alternatives to use of. 73-75
    Estate planning consequences of. 344
    Ineligible stockholder's use of. 63-64, 344
    Prolonged estates as. 65, 72-73
    Voting. 64-65, 131-33

Twelve-month liquidation. 293

U

Undistributed taxable income. 57, 165
    Included in shareholder's income. 138
    Records of. 330-31, 348
    Statement presentation. 323-25

Uniform Gifts to Minors Act. 33, 66-67, 300, 348

Unreasonable Accumulation of earnings. 288

Unreasonable compensation. 289-92, 301

Unsubstantiated expenses. 289-92

Usufructuary, as a shareholder. 74

V

Valuation. 81-84, 346
    Appraisal. 83
    Book value. 79, 83
    Capitalization. 83-84
    Specific formula. 83

Vintage account (See ADR system)

Voting trust. 64-65, 131-33
    As shareholder. 64
    Beneficial ownership governs. 65
    Creates a second class of stock. 27, 128, 131-33

W

Warrants. 112, 133

Wasted net operating losses. 151-54

Western Hemisphere Trade Corporation. 41

1975 Supplement

The Tax Reduction Act of 1975 (Public Law 94-12, 94th Congress 1st Session 1975) has little effect upon the Subchapter S corporation. Relevant portions of that act are noted here and the reader is urged to consider these topics as he reads the text. It should be noted that the changes have greater impact upon the discussion of peripheral matters, rather than upon those which are central to the law of Subchapter S corporations.

Earned Income Credit

This part of the new law is applicable to 1975 only. It provides a 10 percent credit up to a maximum of $400. The credit is phased out for incomes above $4,000 and is completely eliminated once earned income reaches $8,000. Since profit from a Subchapter S corporation is not considered earned income, the corporation should consider salary payments if this aspect of the law would otherwise be applicable.

Investment Tax Credit (pp. 156-160 of 1974 edition)

The investment tax credit is increased to 10 percent for qualifying property placed in service after January 21, 1975 and before January 1, 1977. Moreover, the dollar limitation for used equipment has been increased to $100,000. For married persons who file separate returns, the amount is raised to $50,000.

Corporate Surtax Exemption

For 1975 only, the regular corporation will be a less costly alternative. For that year only, tax rates are as follows: 20 percent on first $25,000; 22 percent on income exceeding $25,000; 48 percent on income exceeding $50,000. This results in a $7,000 extra saving for regular corporations with taxable incomes in excess of $50,000.

Accumulated Earnings Tax

The credit for accumulated earnings has been increased to $150,000. This change is permanent. It affects regular corporations' decisions only.

The Employment Retirement Income Security Act of 1974 (Public Law 93-406, 93d Congress 2d Session 1974) was enacted after the

1974 edition had already gone to press. Nevertheless, it does reflect the increase in limits to the lesser of $7,500 or 15 percent of compensation (p. 296 of 1974 edition).

Earned Income Limitation
In order to enhance its anti-discrimination provisions, the act allows only the first $100,000 of compensation to be considered for purposes of computing contributions to self-employed retirement plans.

Defined Benefit Plans
The act makes a defined benefit plan available to shareholder-employees of Subchapter S corporations.

Time for Making Contributions
The act allows cash basis taxpayers to make contributions for previous tax years before the due date of the tax return. Thus, contributions can now be based upon operating results rather than upon estimates. While the act made this provision effective for 1976 and later years, the Tax Reduction Act of 1975 makes it applicable to the 1975 tax year.

The reader is urged to consult a modern treatise on pension plans for additional information. Exhaustive treatment of this highly technical topic is beyond the scope of this supplement.

OTHER PUBLICATIONS CURRENTLY AVAILABLE

Catalog No.

500-G

A PRACTICAL GUIDE TO PREPARING A FEDERAL ESTATE TAX RETURN. Dennis A. Brown. $6.95

507-K

ORGANIZING, OPERATING AND TERMINATING SUB-CHAPTER S CORPORATIONS. D. Larry Crumbley and P. Michael Davis. Hard cover, 400 pp. $22

508-U

A PRACTICAL GUIDE TO PREPARING A FEDERAL GIFT TAX RETURN. D. Larry Crumbley. $6.95

510-S

A PRACTICAL GUIDE TO PREPARING A FIDUCIARY IN-COME TAX RETURN. P. M. Davis and Frederick W. Whiteside. $6.95

509-N

WHAT EVERY EXECUTOR SHOULD KNOW. Daniel R. Fritz. Written for the layman, to be given by the attorney to his exec-utor-client. 75¢ ea. (10 copies minimum order)

511-Q

AN ESTATE PLANNING QUESTIONNAIRE. Stanley G. King. An inventory to be prepared by the client for the estate plan-ner's use in planning the estate, and for a permanent record. Keyed to the Schedules of the Estate Tax Return for easy computation of potential tax liability. 95¢ ea. (10 copies min-imum order)

73-3

TAX CALCULATOR. Neal Kurn. Federal Gift, Estate and In-come Taxes. A sturdy slide computer. $5.95 ea., 3 for $15

104-7

FUTURE DAMAGE CALCULATOR. Richard M. Markus. Life expectancy, work expectancy and present value tables. A sturdy slide computer. $5.95